SOCIAL WORK
WITH FAMILIES

Also available from Lyceum Books, Inc.

ENDINGS IN CLINICAL PRACTICE: EFFECTIVE CLOSURE IN DIVERSE SETTINGS, by Joseph Walsh

CLINICAL ASSESSMENT FOR SOCIAL WORKERS: QUALITATIVE AND QUANTITATIVE METHODS, 2E, edited by Catheleen Jordan and Cynthia Franklin

CASE MANAGEMENT: AN INTRODUCTION TO CONCEPTS AND SKILLS, 2E, by Arthur Frankel and Sheldon Gelman

"RAISE UP A CHILD," Human Development in an African-American Family, by Edith Hudley, Wendy Haight, and Margaret Miller

WORKING WITH CHILDREN, ADOLESCENTS, AND THEIR FAMILIES, 3E, by Martin Herbert and Karen Harper-Dorton

SOCIAL WORK PRACTICE: TREATING COMMON CLIENT PROBLEMS, edited by Harold Briggs and Kevin Corcoran

SCHOOL SOCIAL WORK: PRACTICE, POLICY, AND RESEARCH PERSPECTIVES, 5E, edited by Robert Constable, Shirley McDonald, and John Flynn

NAVIGATING HUMAN SERVICE ORGANIZATIONS, by Margaret Gibelman

TEAMWORK IN MULTIPROFESSIONAL CARE, by Malcolm Payne, foreword by Thomas M. Meenaghan

GENERALIST PRACTICE IN LARGER SETTINGS: KNOWLEDGE AND SKILL CONCEPTS, by Thomas Meenaghan and W. Eugene Gibbons

INTRODUCTION TO SOCIAL WORK: THE PEOPLE'S PROFESSION, 2E, by Ira Colby and Sophia Dziegielewski

MODERN SOCIAL WORK THEORY: A CRITICAL INTRODUCTION, 2E, by Malcolm Payne, foreword by Stephen C. Anderson

SOCIAL POLICY ANALYSIS, by Thomas Meenaghan, Keith Kilty, and John McNutt

SOCIAL WORK WITH FAMILIES

Content and Process

Robert Constable
Loyola University, Chicago

Daniel B. Lee
Loyola University, Chicago

LYCEUM
BOOKS, INC.
Chicago, Illinois

MT

Published by

LYCEUM BOOKS, INC.
5758 S. Blackstone Ave.
Chicago, Illinois 60637
773+643-1903 (Fax)
773+643-1902 (Phone)
lyceum@lyceumbooks.com
http://www.lyceumbooks.com

10 9 8 7 6 5 4 3 2 1

ISBN 0-925065-77-3

Library of Congress Cataloging-in-Publication Data

Printed in Canada

Constable, Robert T.
  Social work with families : content and process / Robert
Constable. Daniel B. Lee.
    p. cm.
  ISBN 0-925065-77-3 (paperback : alk. paper)
  1. Family social work. I. Lee, Daniel B., 1939– II. Title.
  HV697.C665 2004
  362.82′53—dc21
                                        2003011687

12/17/04

Dedication

To our many mentors
whose ideas and friendship have become parts of us,
whom we acknowledge
with profound gratitude
and to those
where space prevents recognition
we ask forgiveness
for debts unpaid.

Harriett Bartlett

Felix Biestek S. J.

Richard Schwartz

Mollie Utkoff

Sarah Austin

Man Keung Ho

David Mace

Virginia Satir

About the Authors

Robert Constable is a social work practitioner working with families in Valparaiso, Indiana and in an inner city parish in Chicago. He has been a practitioner for more than thirty years. He is professor emeritus in the school of social work at Loyola University, Chicago and continues teaching assignments in the United States and overseas. Professor Constable has published extensively in social work, including the widely used *School Social Work: Practice, Policy, and Research Perspectives*, now in its fifth edition.

Daniel B. Lee is professor of social work and family therapy in the school of social work at Loyola University, Chicago. He has been a clinical member of the American Association for Marriage and Family Therapy since 1972. He is also the founder of the Transcultural Family Institute and co-founder and former president of the Global Awareness Society International. Professor Lee was educated in Korea and in the United States. Professor Lee served as an officer and a commissioned social worker, overseas and in the United States, in the U.S. Army. He served as a consultant on cross-cultural family life and family advocacy to several offices in the Department of Defense. Professor Lee is also an ordained minister in the United Methodist Church. He has been in private practice since 1987 and is the author of several books and over 100 journal articles.

Contents

List of Tables and Figures

Preface

The purpose of this book is to elaborate process and content of social work with families. It is meant to assist the reader to use the social work perspective to draw from a rich variety of developing approaches to working with families. Generous numbers of case illustrations help make the connection between theory and practice, family development, emergent family structure, multicultural realities, institutional and environmental realities, and the work of the social worker, engaging: family members to restructure relations through communication and interaction.

The book is meant to help develop the theoretical and practice foundations in social work practice with families. This is an area that has been a primary focus for social workers in most fields of practice for more than a century. Recognizing the value of social work as an organizing framework, the book draws from and integrates theory about family interaction from a wide range of theorists and practitioners, including diverse schools of family therapy. The social work professional orientation, with its focus on family members interacting to define family meanings and achieve basic needs, allows for this integration. The book can be used as an overview of social work practice with families. It is compatible with basic methods texts in social work, whose emphasis are more strongly oriented to individual and group intervention methodologies. It also fits well with basic methods texts in family therapy, providing the social work perspective on a very diverse field. The book brings together themes that connect social work with family intervention as it is practiced today.

The book relies heavily on cases for a number of reasons. First of all, the case is the best individual test of the usefulness of particular theories. The case is the closest metaphor to the phenomenon of actual practice. Family intervention theories are still early in their quest for comprehensiveness. In the absence of a well-developed overall theory, the case provides another way to integrate theory and practice. Our focus is on family members interacting at family life cycle stages, creating relational structure and carrying out relational and institutional tasks with the social worker. This focus is best seen in the case. Cases in this book represent the actual practice of many social workers. They have been individually altered so as to be unrecognizable in an individual sense. On the other hand, these cases reflect the content and process of situations that social workers encounter every day in family work. The reader may recognize the outlines of a wide variety of case situations, since none of the situations are esoteric.

The focus of this volume is on *integration* of all of this content in a model that mirrors practice. In the complexity of practice, the family social worker needs to relate theory to the practice situation. There is a set of family members with a variety of strengths, limitations, cultural beliefs and patterns, needs, and intentions. The family members, not the social worker, need to begin to take charge of their various concerns and construct a more secure relational base. When this does happen, we treat it from an existential perspective as a little miracle. Use of the case as a pedagogical tool allows the reader to follow the threads of this little miracle, and thus understand how content and process are integrated with practice in action. The functional model of content and process (Hofstein, 1964) allows for this much-needed integration. Integration demands we follow without distraction the threads of content and process. Integration can best be seen in basic examples of everyday practice. The focus on theory rests on how it may be used. The focus on content rests on what needs to be done and how people process and employ difference. The focus on practice rests on family members actively constructing a more secure base with the social worker's assistance. Thus we follow the threads of process and content closely so that students can apply these ideas to the tremendous diversity of families constructing their relational networks in a multicultural society. Building on process and content, other sources in the literature of methods become ever more useful for exploring pieces of the process.

Reviews of massive bodies of effectiveness research have put aside as unresolvable the old question of whether there are many discrete theories or one or whether there is an underlying paradigm in the nature of social relations, unifying different approaches (Bergin &Garfield, 1994; Gurman & Jacobson, 2002, p. xv). Both responses to this question are useful, but not in exclusion of each other. From the multitude of competing intervention theories now comes *integration*, a systemic use of concepts and techniques from different approaches (Bergin & Garfield, 1994, p. 821). The larger outcomes of this process in social work are still uncertain (Reid, 2002), particularly when the functional threads of process and content are lost. In any case, practitioners must discover integration, and students develop their own practice models (Mullen, 1983). For the moment, the language of the case, with its focus on process, on persons constructing family relationships within larger cultural, community, and social-institutional contexts, the case itself with its closeness to real practice, provides an excellent overall framework for integrative learning.

The primary paradigm of the book is the same relational paradigm that has governed social work for more than a century. In this context, the actuality of human needs, which only can be fulfilled in family relationships, brings with it the concepts of *relational justice* and *human solidarity*. This solidarity extends from internal family relations to social institutions. Social work is not neutral in relation to human needs and the obligations of all members of society to care for each other, particularly those closest to us. Another important concept is that of *difference*. Family solidarity, paradoxically, is created out of differences. Family members are constantly bringing these differences together into workable units at different life cycle stages. Our emergent multicultural world is also full of differences. These realities affect all relational systems, and families in particular.

A transcultural perspective assumes the multicultural perspective in a diverse society and focuses on the possibilities of developing connections between families and social institutions and among family members of diverse cultural experiences and socioeconomic backgrounds. It assumes an understanding both of what is common to all cultures and what is different, but shifts in focus to persons actively constructing secure bases in a multicultural world. People construct relationships with the hope of securing similar basic needs and relational goods. Yet they may interact with each other in somewhat different ways and may have different understandings of relationships. The key to a transcultural understanding can be found in the helping process itself. The helping process involves a search for the substantive, the ontological meaning of *being with* each other, despite many perceived barriers. This perspective assumes that differences exist and that the transcultural work of the family members is already embedded in their internal and external relational work. The internal work has to do with family developmental tasks; the external work involves complex transactions with social institutions. The social worker assists family members doing this relational work. The rivers of difference flow toward the sea, toward what they discover in common and the relational worlds they construct together.

Part of an introduction to this book is an acknowledgment of credits and debits. In the cover leaf we acknowledged some of our mentors. We have both been very fortunate in our life narratives to have been influenced by a large number of people, and we apologize to those whom space has prevented us from mentioning. Perhaps our greatest teachers and mentors have been our own clients. Their untold stories of resilience, courage, and creativity in the art of living have somehow been blended into every case. These stories, their greatest living lessons, validate the book's perspective and methodology. It is not an accident that in the cases cited, things have turned out not always as the client or family wanted, but not badly, and sometimes much better than expected. This has been our general experience. Rather than any triumph of methodology and perspective, the credit goes to human will and intelligence, galvanized by a helping process. It is our clients' success, not ours, a success best explained by no other expertise than human collaborative process.

Finally, we must credit our own families, those closest to us at our life stage, those who have left us legacies, some going back deep into our family histories, and, looking forward, those coming and still to come. Paul Shao Jung Huang, Robert Constable's grandson, was born as this book was being completed. Paul, with his transcultural heritage, is a metaphor of the human family and the exciting worlds we are entering. We dedicate this book to the students who will use it. You are also part of our family. In particular, we remember our best and closest friends, Pauline Constable and Grace Lee, friends for forty-four and forty-three years, respectively, who have taught us the many meanings of love.

Robert Constable   Daniel Booduck Lee

REFERENCES

Bergin, A. E., & Garfield, S. L. (1994). *Handbook of psychotherapy and behavior change* (4th ed.). New York: Wiley.

Gurman, A. S., & Jacobson, N. S. (2002). *Clinical handbook of couple therapy* (3rd ed.). New York: Guilford.

Hofstein, S. (1964). The nature of process: The implications for social work. In R. Wessel (Ed.), *Journal of social work process,* Vol. 14. Philadelphia: University of Pennsylvania Press.

Mullen, E. J. (1983). Personal practice models. In A. Rosenblatt & D. Waldbogel (Eds.), *Handbook of clinical social work* (pp. 623–649). San Francisco: Jossey-Bass.

Reid, W. J. (2002). Knowledge for direct social work practice: An analysis of trends. *Social Service Review,* 76(1), 6-33.

CHAPTER 1

A Theoretical Framework for Social Work with Families

The fabric of our lives is woven from the people closest to us: our families, our friends, and our memories of both. Family mediates most of our fundamental relations with our environment. We are all part of a family of some sort, and families are a part of us. They may be the families of actual, current experience, or the families of our memories. There can be many ways we establish associations to satisfy our deepest needs for permanency of relationships and for a secure base for action. An understanding of family relationships is essential for understanding every person's relational situation, even persons who are isolated and alone, who live outside of a family framework. Each of us, whether living in a family or not, houses a set of relations, an interior family, perhaps a family of hurt and anger, of regrets, of experiences, perhaps a family of conflicting memories. These are the known patterns with which each day we face the world anew. They become the joys and sorrows of memory and lived experience. They become the models with which we construct and interpret experiences. They become fuel for our reflections. This is the bitter and the sweet poetry of our lives. These are the rivers we all travel toward the sea.

This chapter develops an overview of social work practice with families, the scope of this practice, and its history in brief. Families are primary systems of human well-being. The analysis of social work's historic involvement with families, the relational person in families, the methodological contributions of the family therapy movement, and the resilient family become the bases for the social work frame of reference.

SOCIAL WORK AND FAMILIES

The constant and continuing theme of social work is the relation of persons and their environments. Families are the crucial and continuing participants in social situations. In every society, the family becomes the basic system of personal development and identity, of mutual support and distribution. The family is the basic system of social welfare. Other social welfare systems, external to the family, do their work best when they help the family to function better without taking its place.

There are different ways of understanding family. Family can be seen as something static, a background for what one does as an individual. Family can also be seen as a complex network of persons, held together by empathy and obligations, with different relational structures in different life-cycle phases. Paradoxically, when the family is understood as a background for one's individual activities, it loses its uniqueness, its power, and even its value for individuals. The family, if it is to work, must be seen as this complex network and as a set of commitments beyond individual self-interest.

Social work is rooted in work with families. Social workers assist families to resolve issues of relationship, attachment, and membership, and to solve problems in situations of external and internal stress. Work with individual persons is work with their own patterns of coping, relating, belonging, and valuing, learned through interaction with others in a family of memory. These patterns are experienced, developed, melded, and changed again and again in new relationships and new structures and stages of family life. They are especially relevant when, acting with others, people form new families, bringing together the well-trodden pathways, the places and persons known, with new possibilities. The conversational dance of development, the shifts in current relationships in each person's life, can revise patterns and gradually shift the personal meaning of memories (Lewis, 1999).

Relational Justice

Social work became a profession because serious breakdowns in social life were possible but no longer acceptable. The interaction process between societal expectations of family life and the profession of social work continues today. In the complexity of modern life, things fail (Tillich, 1962) in one way or another. On the inside of the family, the delicate networks of empathy and obligation can fail. On the outside, institutions and communities can fail. In the context of relational justice, these failures are no longer acceptable. There was a conviction on the part of social workers that people could be helped to change their circumstances and their personal situations. Given the cost of these failures to persons, when effective professional intervention is possible, such intervention becomes legitimate and necessary. This becomes a rationale for social work.

Some of the human costs of the failures can be remedied, even prevented. Sometimes this can be done by working singly with the problems, sometimes by developing programs for whole groups of people, by working with institutions, by developing policies, or sometimes by doing all of these.

Such failures and breakdowns (and their remedies) can take place within institutional systems themselves when these systems of work, justice, human welfare, education, and so on fail to accommodate fully the human needs of some of their participants. These institutional systems cease to carry out their own assigned functions of healing, educating, ensuring justice, distributing work, and ensuring human welfare.

In the diversity and complexity of society, where economic and political power privileges certain groups over others, conflicts and discrimination unfortunately take place. In these circumstances, families become less able to operate in the broader society and less able to carry out their very personal function for each of their members. Persons who reflect societal and familial confusion and conflict can experience difficulty developing their own potential as participants in family and in society.

The Transcultural Perspective

The transcultural perspective assumes the need for multicultural understandings in a diverse society. It focuses on the possibilities of developing connections between families and social institutions and among family members of diverse cultural experiences and socioeconomic backgrounds. It assumes an understanding both of what is common to all cultures and what is different, but with a shift in focus to persons actively constructing secure bases in a multicultural world. People construct relationships with the hope of securing similar basic needs and relational goods, yet they may interact with each other in somewhat different ways and may have different understandings of relationships. The key to a transcultural understanding can be found in the helping process itself. The helping process involves a search for the substantive, the ontological meaning of *being with* each other, despite many perceived barriers. This perspective assumes that differences exist and that the transcultural work of the family members is already embedded in their internal and external relational work. The internal work has to do with family developmental tasks; the external work involves complex transactions with social institutions. The social worker assists family members doing this relational work.

The Scope of Social Work

The scope of social work, as it is carried into different practice Education situations, is the enhancement of social functioning ([CSWE, Council on Social Work Education] 1994, p. 135; 1982) within the complex of relationships of persons with each other and with their personal, familial, and institutional environments.

> *The fundamental zone of social work is where people and their environments are in exchange with each other* [italics added]. Social work historically has focused on the transaction zone where the exchange between people and the environment which impinge on them results in changes in both. Social work intervention aims at the coping capabilities of people and the demands and resources of their environment so that the transactions between them are helpful to both. Social work's concern extends to both the dysfunctional and deficient conditions at the juncture between people and their environment, and to the opportunities there for producing growth and improving the environment. It is the duality of focus on people and their environments that distinguishes social work from other professions (Joint NASW-CSWE Task Force, 1979, p. 2).

Throughout the history of social work, its constant and most productive focus has rested on person(s) and environment together and in relation to each other—a simultaneous dual focus on the transactions between person(s) and the environment (Gordon, 1969). At times the predominant focus has rested on persons, at other times on the environment, but at no time was the other fully left out of the equation. Social workers work to promote change in people's relations with themselves, with each other, and with the environment, seen as a network of systems.

The systems perspective permitted social workers to understand relations both within systems and between these systems and other parts of their environment, and to integrate intervention theories at different levels (Hearn, 1969). A *system* can be defined as a holistic, organized unit of interdependent, transacting, and mutually influencing parts within an identifiable environment (Siporin, 1972a, p. 106). This perspective is very important for an understanding of family interaction, and it is developed in greater detail in chapter 2.

Families and Social Institutions

Ernest Burgess (1926; Burgess & Locke,1953) recognized the family as a "unity of interacting personalities," a unit of study and action, and thus a subject, a mediator of relations, an agent of its own development. Family intervention assumes this understanding of family interaction. Research points out the benefits, indeed the necessity, of some type of family membership for any person (Waite & Gallagher, 2001). The family is the fundamental crucible of human identity, attachment, and interaction—the basic membership system for human well-being.

Yet the family is also rooted in social institutional anchors and societal guidance systems. These direct its ability to act effectively and also limit its actions and possibilities. In modern society, families cannot really act effectively without simultaneous interaction with societal institutions of health care, education, work and welfare, law, justice, and religion (especially laws regulating family). Family often mediates its members' access and use of these institutions, and these institutions often mediate the possibilities inherent in family structure. Nor can the institutions be successful without collaboration with families. It is no accident that, working with families, social workers also work with (and often for) each of these social institutions. Without these crucial institutional links, families would quickly experience stress and face breakdown. Often families bear the brunt of institutional failure (Ryan, 1971). Among societal institutions, religion—so personal, so closely linked to culture and belonging, and to a secure base of identity—is also a crucial social institution where social workers work with families. This practice is discussed in greater detail in chapter 9.

Social workers work on both the inside and the outside of families. Their work encompasses family therapy: that is, intervention aimed at restructuring family (and thus personal) patterns from the inside. They work with family members as they struggle with the implications of their membership and attachments, and as they cope with particular developmental tasks, needs or stresses and with the needs, stresses, or tasks of the family itself. They work on the outside in the relations between families and societal institutions. These latter include schools, health care systems, justice systems, welfare systems, and work systems that often regulate and set the parameters of what families are able to do. Working between institutions and family members in relation to each other, the combination of family and institutional intervention comprises an intervention approach of great power to affect people's lives and development.

CONTENT AND PROCESS: TOWARD AN ORGANIZING FRAMEWORK

Social work practitioners have routinely found they had to draw from different bodies of method theory to carry out their mission (Cocozzelli & Constable, 1985; Constable & Cocozzelli, 1989; Jayaratne, 1978). Other family practitioners are generally accustomed to doing this as well (Nichols & Schwartz, 2001, pp. 414–415). With an appropriate organizing framework, the social worker can use a variety of approaches to intervention in different situations and in different institutional and cultural contexts. The personal and family narratives of practice become an entryway for a basic understanding of process and content and the development of personal practice models (Mullen, 1983, p. 623).

To understand the uses of method, one needs to understand content and process. The *purposes* of intervention and the *sequences* of intervention, content and process together govern methods and the means. Methods are orderly and systematic means of proceeding, governed by purposes and processes. Clarifying content, process, and purpose, where things fit, it becomes possible to use a variety of different effective approaches to work with couples and families (Corcoran, 2000).

A Brief History of Social Work with Families

The professional roots of social work provide a rich organizing framework for its practice. The focus on persons interacting with each other and with institutions, rather than a focus on a particular method, allows social workers to adjust their response to the needs and meanings inherent in a situation. From the beginning, social workers served families. The Charity Organization Society (COS) motto, "not alms, but a friend," denoted an early redirection of the helping process from provision of goods alone toward helping persons take action on a problem or situation through the provision of a helping relationship. Implicit in this is a shift in emphasis from a science of giving to a concern for persons organizing their worlds, using assistance to cope with a situation. The shift to persons organizing their worlds would also be a shift to a focus on the helping process. By the 1920s, social work could be conceptualized as the art of helping people out of trouble (De Schweinitz, 1924). The focus of this art would rest on assisting persons coping with situations. Methods of helping, whether with individuals, groups, families, or the institutional environment, would become the resources for a more personalized coping. These methods would become aids for people to recompose their situations, revise their patterns and relationships, find resources, and get out of trouble. The natural basis for social work would be the interactions of people with each other and with institutions, these interactions aiming to meet complex personal needs. In this context the social worker becomes a type of mentor for interaction that takes place in any case, but that is in danger of failing.

Over the past half century, many social work theorists have emphasized what takes place between persons in a helping sequence or *process* (Smalley, 1967; Bartlett, 1972; Lewis, 1982; Siporin, 1972a; Pincus & Minahan, 1974; Schwartz,

1977; Shulman, 1999). Over time, the conceptual shift would eventually signal a move away from deterministic, closed-system explanations for behavior and a positivist focus on method as a measure for process. In a post-positivist world, method, a necessary and systematic way of proceeding, no longer is the criterion for process. An emphasis on process is an emphasis on social workers working with persons, acting with others, and using resources to develop relationships and to cope. The emphasis on process rests on purposes, on strengths, and on open-system explanations and a functional use of different methods, as appropriate, to help get a job done. There is a celebration of particularities and of differences, and an inclusion of spiritual and cultural capacities as resources. The social worker uses a wide range of methods in the process of helping individuals, families, and institutions to achieve purposes and carry out tasks. These tasks are inherent in the human condition and in the dilemmas and strains of social interaction. They are not simply personal tasks. They are relational tasks, the tasks of a whole network in a situation.

Determining Units of Attention Within the Situation

With the focus on persons interacting to secure needs the *case* and later the *situation*, would become the basic units of assessment and intervention. These basic units had to contain the units of attention: the context where the person acted, the context of the problems, and the context of the possible solutions. For Mary Richmond, social work was family service (Richmond 1907, pp. 32–37; 1917). Her basic unit of assessment and intervention, the case, inevitably contained the family. She made it clear that no help could be provided without respecting the family's ways of operating, its decision making, its hierarchy, and its cultural patterns: what would later be called *family structure*. Assistance given without respecting this structure would only undermine the family (1907, p. 36). Reflecting this perspective, the first professional journal in social work was *The Family*.

Ada Sheffield (1937) broadened this focus on the family to include the relations of the family with an institutional environment—the *situation*—as a focus for intervention. In any case, Richmond and Sheffield had used the family and its institutional connections as the basic frame of reference for the case or the situation. Only later did this focus become narrowed to the person with a lessened reference to the person's dynamic context, as Ann Hartman and Joan Laird discuss in their work on social work with families (1983, pp. 3–22). Later, systems theory would allow for a broadening of focus. It would allow for the interaction of persons, family units, institutions, and communities to be better understood and mapped out. Moving from the hegemony of method alone, systems theory would also reintroduce to social workers the complex world of process (Hearn, 1969; Hartman & Laird, 1983).

Fields of Social Work Practice with Families For cases and situations fields of practice were the contexts. Early in the history of social work, the COS model, with its emphasis on persons acting in a broader context, was adopted by other developing areas of practice. Experiments with social work in schools, hospitals, courts, and child welfare agencies became the basis for fields of practice. From the first decades of the twentieth century, school social workers in New York City were working between home and school with immigrant families and their children. In Hartford Connecticut, social workers took part in the first school guidance teams, working with families, pupils, and school (Lide, 1959; Costin, 1969). In Massachusetts, General Hospital physicians and social workers expanded medical intervention to the social and familial world of the patient (Nacman, 1977; Carlton, 1984). The field of child welfare work moved from its early roots in the orphanage to begin to work with children in foster families and in their own families. During the First World War the Red Cross developed counseling for families of servicemen, which included virtually everyone in those days (Watts, 1964). After the War, services for psychiatric patients and their families followed quickly (Southard & Jarrett, 1922). In the analysis of all of this diversity and the integration of multiple theories, a functional model of process gradually emerged. Social work "functions," each different in what they addressed, developed in the interaction between social institutions, families, and individuals (Witmer, 1942). Additionally, many services in the private sector were sponsored by religious organizations and cultural subgroupings. Here the emergent personal focus was adapted not only to a function, but also to the particular needs of a community of membership, as well as to others not of that community.

The Situation It was clear that a term was needed to describe this dynamic geography unique to social work. This term became the *situation*. The basic context of social work and the boundaries for assessment and intervention are contained in the situation. The situation brings together personal, familial, and institutional environments in an interactive context. It is a particular picture of persons, families, and a network of community institutions and resources; it is a form of social system or group focused in action around a problem; a need or a resource (Siporin, 1972a, p. 237; 1972b, pp. 91–109). Situational assessment involves the varied social systems and social situations in which clients are actively functioning participants, where persons have *role, status, identities,* and *responsibilities* (Siporin 1972a, p. 238). The situation contains all the information about persons and their contexts that is necessary to explain behavior and to intervene where it may be most effective. Assessment has as its focus the problems, needs, or relational tasks that need to be dealt with. The social worker's agreement (or contract) with the client system establishes the purpose of this coordinated work.

In a situational assessment, there are three major systems nested within each other:

1. The family members involved as individual persons. This involves their personal systems, developmental struggles, needs, and stuck patterns (depression, chronic worry, acute anxiety, psychotic perceptions and beliefs, and so on), in relation to their needs and/or relational tasks.
2. The couple (the central subsystem of a family), together with children and other family members.
3. The broader resources within the environmental situation, which comprise both formal systems, social institutions such as schools, courts, and health,

welfare, and work systems; and informal systems, such as extended family, friends, neighbors, and co-workers.

Each of the persons involved in the situation may have different perceptions of that situation and of the problems, needs, or tasks to be dealt with. Some parts of the situation, both institutional systems and personal systems, may be particularly slow to respond, if they respond at all. The assessment of a situation, in all of its necessary complexity, and the judgment of where in the situation to intervene demand a high level of professional experience, shared with other key members of the change effort. Key questions are: with what units of attention is change most likely to occur? How should it occur? What roles might the different participants take in this change?

Situational intervention involves a restructuring of relationships, the way persons perceive and relate to personal resources, to each other, and to institutional resources or the network of informal relationships essential to the situation. This restructuring of relationships and resources has a profound influence on persons. It can lead to different consciousness and values, status-role expectations and performances, and social and self identities of the persons involved (Siporin, 1972b, p. 237). For many, this restructuring takes place in families, the crucibles of belonging, attachment, and development. Family mediates the development of two major human capacities: the capacity to act and to cope, which is human *agency*; and the capacity to communicate and develop support, which is *communion*. These capacities can shut down in the face of illness or excessive stress (McDaniel, Hepworth, & Doherty, 1992). For each family member, one's capacity to act, to communicate, and to provide and receive support is in balance with other family members in a delicate relational architecture. Any restructuring has a powerful effect on family members and the family's ability to continue as a family.

The problem for social work theory is how to conceptualize the relational work of the family and the persons in it, and then understand the work of the social worker in helping persons to reconstruct family life. Until there is a frame of reference for social work with families, there will be different theoretical languages for intervention with individuals and with family units. A focus on individual persons tends to place families and broader structures in the background; a focus on structures without persons does the reverse. What is the theoretical balance between a focus on persons and a focus on structures? In physics, the languages of wave and particle theories each can be used to describe similar phenomena, and each has a certain level of accuracy. In social work, too, the languages of different foci each can be used to describe similar behavior, and each has a level of accuracy. There is a need for a unifying theory.

THE PRACTICE OF SOCIAL WORK WITH FAMILIES

Social work with families comprises intervention with persons in families, with couples, and with family units. The social worker works in the midst of complex interaction between persons in families and with social institutions, when these institutions can assist families to carry out relational tasks. The fundamental tasks of the social worker in this process are to assist families to reconstruct their relationships when these are at risk and to work with the broader institutional context, so that the institutions are able to assist family members, particularly the most vulnerable, in carrying out their functions.

Despite all of its diversity of form and meaning, family has always been the basic informal welfare system in any society. In modern society, however, its effectiveness depends on a whole network of community resource systems and social institutions. The implications of this concept provide a starting point for social work. Persons and families, interdependent from the beginning, develop complex relationships with each other. One presupposes the existence of the other, if only in memory and in the fabric of a person's interactive patterns and beliefs.[1] Being human presupposes relational capacities and some sort of family membership. One cannot *not* have a family of some kind. In the absence of actual family, friends become "like family." One's choices and sense of self even become influenced by the family one doesn't have. In the patterns of interaction with each other in the family unit, and with community institutions, the family composes itself to satisfy the needs of its members for belonging and growth, and to resolve potential conflicts between agency and communion. These interactional patterns have their own logic. They form the architecture of relationships and interactions where social workers work.

Working between family members reconstructing relationships with each other and with institutions, there is a natural basis for the work of the social worker in this necessary interaction. Social workers intervene between families and social institutions, with families to help family members do what they must risk doing in any case and with institutions so that they can achieve their societal missions. The social worker becomes a coach or a mentor to help persons to deal with themselves and with each other. In order to assist them in this, social workers may draw from any appropriate method that can be effective and that respects the capacity of the family to do its reconstructive work effectively. These possible methods would include family therapy methods as well as parent training, case management, the use of institutional resources and expectations, group meetings, family day care, and so on (Corcoran, 2000). Methodology validates itself as an instrument when it effectively serves the content and process of the relational work. Relational work is work, tasks that members of families must do for the unit to maintain its internal and external connections and thus its viability. These tasks are clarified in a deeper understanding of family development and family coping with internal and external changes.

THE LANGUAGES OF THEORY IN FAMILY INTERVENTION

As the practice of social work with families and social situations developed early in the twentieth century, social work theory had to clarify its focus and integrate knowl-

---

[1] This concept is developed most clearly by object relations and attachment theorists. See Josselson (1992), Levy (2000), and Clulow (2001).

edge from different areas into a picture of practice (Gordon, 1969; Bartlett, 1972). Theory was built on developing pictures of an architecture of social relations and of persons coping within relational fields. There is need for integration between theories focused on individuals, theories used to understand the family as a unit, and theories related to an institutional and community environment. Although knowledge about families could be found in several disciplines, such as sociology, psychology, and psychiatry, no single discipline could adequately explain practice.

The concept of the *relational* person has long history. This history, essential to social work, is beginning to be reclaimed. Toward the end of the nineteenth century, William James developed a concept of the "social self." A person "has as many social selves as there are individuals who recognize him and carry an image of him in their mind" (James, 1981, pp. 281–282.) Later, his students, John Dewey and George Herbert Mead, developed further the concept of the social nature of mind, the social self, and its relations to society.[2] Jessie Taft 1926, a key figure in the development of functional social work, had George Herbert Mead as her doctoral mentor at the University of Chicago. Mead's (1934) concept of the birth of *mind* in social relationships had considerable impact on Jessie Taft and on the functional school of social work. Otto Rank's related ideas of the birth of the self through differentiation and reconnections with others would have a useful fit with Taft's ideas (Rank, 1947, pp. 195–220). The functional school, and later mainstream social work theory, drew heavily from these concepts without always acknowledging their conceptual roots.

In a parallel process, Mary Richmond (1907; 1917) took up the theme of the centrality of social relations in the beginning of *Social Diagnosis*:

> One of the most striking facts with regard to the consciousness of any human being is that it is interwoven with the lives of others. It is in each man's social relations that his mental history is mainly written, and it is in his social relations likewise that the causes of the disorders that threaten his happiness and his effectiveness, and the means for securing his recovery are mainly sought (1917, p. 4).

At about the same time, Harry Stack Sullivan was developing similar concepts in an interpersonal psychotherapy (Sullivan, 1938–39). In the middle of the twentieth century, despite a renewed focus on treatment methods for individuals, there remained latent a focus on persons interacting with each other. Family therapy developed from this interactive emphasis, often nourished by contact with social workers who had generally retained a family focus. Object relations theory (Greenberg & Mitchell, 1983), attachment theory (Bowlby, 1969; Ainsworth, 1978; 1973) self psychology (Kohut, 1977; Kernberg, 1976), membership (Falck, 1988), and family therapy theories (Nicholas & Schwartz, 2001) would in their own ways develop approaches to what were essentially related concepts.

---

[2]There is a long history of theory dealing with this issue, recently summarized by Christian Beels (2002), a psychiatrist and family therapist.

In developmental theory, the concepts of interdependence and attachment deepened. The recurrent findings of interdependence, inherent to the human condition, dominates the discussion of personal development. Daniel Stern (1985) and others see maturation of the development as greater differentiation throughout the life cycle within the context of interdependence (Fishbane, 2001). With Stern and others, developmental theory shifts from a single focus on the developing individual to a progressive exploration of relational space and the ways that people are connected with each other as they develop.

Persons, Relationships, and Commitments

Understanding and living a balance of personal and environmental needs, rights, and obligations is expected to come with the development and maturity of every person. Family membership involves a balance between human capacities and needs for agency and communion. Agency always is in delicate balance with obligations, relationships, and established commitments. Despite these realities, the *autonomous* person, "self-made," self determined, master of the environment, is very much a construct—indeed, a dominant narrative—of Western mythology. The narratives of autonomy influence the way North Americans think and set Western standards for mental health. These narratives influence approaches to marriage, child-rearing, and educational policy (Fishbane, 2001). Autonomous persons are considered to be progressive and evolutionary, having arrived at "a state of maturity arrived at as the outcome of a developmental process" (Haworth, 1986, p. 8). The autonomous person is minimally bound by obligations, and these only rooted in and limited by individual contract. Social relations are entirely voluntary. They can be dissolved. Nature is to be mastered. These beliefs, if carried to their implicit conclusions, would preclude people from ever effectively living in families.

Sometimes we see families who are a caricature of certain North American beliefs in autonomy. Their example is useful to an understanding of the ordinary process of family interaction. They are cut off from their roots, colonized by the market or the mass media, and have little commitment going beyond the self. The result of their "autonomous" (actually depersonalized) patterns is a lack of construction of human, personal, and relational values. These families and couples often have very little keeping them together. Membership becomes something from which to defend one's self. Communication, often hurtful, becomes talking to the self that one projects into others (or defending one's self from this projection) rather than communicating with the other *as other*. Personal goals and a drive for achievement can overshadow the relational commitments necessary for family life. There can be a consequent inability to agree on and to develop balanced roles or commitments together. Although there may be some of this in every family or couple at certain times, in some families or couples, the patterns become relentless so that nothing else seems remotely possible. The case of John and Eileen Murphy (see chapter 5) is a good example of such patterns. These families don't often come voluntarily for help. When they come, it is often involuntarily, and with great ambivalence about any possibility of change.

Power, Dominance, and Autonomy

The concept of personal autonomy becomes a simple and potentially dysfunctional solution to the much more complex reality that social relations are inherent, indeed essential, to the human condition. Autonomy, when translated by some into relational terms, can very easily become dominance over others. Although the socialization process demands different levels of *authority*, the language of dominance is an impossible language in family relations. During the 1980s, a number of prominent women in the family therapy movement challenged an implicit acceptance of gender dominance in theory development and in practice (McGoldrick, Anderson, & Walsh, 1989; Walters, Papp, & Silverstein, 1988). The concept of dominance needed to be distinguished from functional power, not attached to achieved autonomy but to legitimated role. For example, for the socialization of young children to take place, parents need a certain amount of functional power, a legitimate control over certain contingencies. This is clearly not dominance, the imposition of one's personality, of one's preferences—it is not the personal need to *control* another person.

The societal shifts in gender awareness heightened the feminist critique of unjust interpersonal arrangements. These shifts pushed theory to make distinctions between personal dominance and the functional power parents need if they are to be effective. The shifts pushed social workers working with families to find ways to assist family members to move to more balanced positions, gradually coming to a balance of needs, rights, and obligations. Since not every relational arrangement would be acceptable, the changes in gender awareness paved the way for a reintroduction of the ethical and of relational justice in family practice. These shifts also paved the way for greater development of the implicit balances of relational justice within the actualities of social relations. Depersonalized or skewed family relationships, which sacrifice one person for another, become dysfunctional. There are better solutions as families find balance and persons find *co-responsibility*. The co-responsible person is neither the total master nor the total victim of one's fate; he or she is neither fully responsible for, nor unconcerned about, the other.

THE RELATIONAL PERSON: THE DEMANDS AND DILEMMAS OF FAMILY MEMBERSHIP

Over a century there has been a gradual shift in the West from autonomous pictures of the person to relational ones, but the issue is by no means resolved. In Italy, relational sociology developed as a critique in postmodern society of an over-individualized image of the person, which undermined social institutions including family (Donati, 1991; 2001, pp. 147–177) and made them ineffective. In the United States during the Great Depression and the Second World War, the construct of individual autonomy, with its accompanying societal sentiments, underwent a crisis. A picture of autonomy clashed with the life as it was observed, experienced, and studied. Autonomy tended to override values such as intergenerational loyalty, obligation, or interdependence (Bellah, Madson, Sullivan, et al. 1986) and send them underground. Autonomy clashed with the growing awareness of ethnic subcultures (Carter & McGoldrick, 1999) and of women (Gilligan, 1982; McGoldrick, Anderson, & Walsh, 1989; Walters, Carter, Papp, & Silverstein, 1988). Even the language of autonomy becomes profoundly problematic in worlds where human welfare hangs on a delicate balance. Communitarians (see Etzioni, 1993) began to explore other solutions to this problem in the development of *civility*. In the United States in the final decades of the century, a movement for the invigoration of family values developed and gained considerable strength (Blankenhorn, Bayme, & Elshtain, 1990). The picture of human agency, developing amid systemic/structural constraints, was balanced by communion. The relational person can be concerned for the other without losing the self; indeed, the person becomes more of a person through these concerns and through giving to the other.

In the North American popular culture, the events of September 11, 2001, and following were to signal a return toward relational pictures of self and ethical obligations. The crisis of postmodern society is that the lack of a social fabric of reciprocal obligations and rights may produce a myriad of characters who may use their personal picture of social utility to justify anything in the name of autonomy, religious orientation, or perceived personal injustice. In the heyday of autonomous persons—the self-made men, the Gatsbys of the world—other pictures of life, other languages, more communal, more complex, and more nuanced, went underground. Life could not be lived safely and human agency would be impossible without communion, however. The social fabric was a manifestation of these normative arrangements. The malaise of the autonomous life style of the twentieth century runs headlong into needs for connectedness and the belief in the importance of obligations of the twenty-first century. The collision of these images would give birth to the explicit need for relationality, which is never quite as far from the surface of life as it has to be lived.

The basic concern behind both relational justice and functional family assessment is whether the unit can become *personal*—whether it can support the development and needs of persons. Both demand an understanding of persons as members of families. To the extent that family members aspire to productive interpersonal relations and a sense of a genuine, intertwined interdependent narrative, they become aware that some of their patterns are dysfunctional, unproductive, even hurtful. Overcoming those patterns becomes a task and a challenge for family members.

For the *relational* person, life is and should be experienced with others. As life is experienced, autonomy is useful, but not primary. The older concept of autonomy becomes the concept of responsibility, that is, a "person's ability to be responsible to others, and to take into account relational consequences of one's own actions" (Fishbane, 2001 p. 276). Obligations and legacies are an inherent part of living. The family movement has begun to recognize this as a fact of life that is essential to an understanding of family relations but that is also a tool of intervention. Emergent multiculturalism would inevitably lead in the same direction. The deeper one descends into multicultural experience, the more one finds a nexus of relational meanings and obligations, some voluntary and some involuntary. Overriding values that certain differences need to be protected place obligations on society, on social workers, and on families themselves. Roots become important, and with roots come permanent relationships and family legacies. Contextual family therapy would develop these concepts into a particular model for family practice (Boszormenyi-Nagy & Spark, 1973; Boszormenyi-Nagy & Grunebaum, 1991).

Things fail, however, whether inside or outside the family, and the relational circle can be broken. This fact and a demand for relational justice becomes a most important rationale for social work. People can be treated badly. They may not flourish and they may not achieve all of what they can be. Family members can fail to respond to the needs of others. Children can experience abuse and neglect. Injustice, whether relational or societal, can create further injustice in a never ending spiral. The social worker cannot take up all of this burden, nor remove the responsibility of family members and society itself to be just and fair, to act for the common good of all, especially the most vulnerable. Social workers, however, have a special responsibility to be a conscience where others will listen, to be instruments of relational justice in the situations they encounter. In families, they challenge patterns of exploitation, dominance, and abuse. Issues of injustice are often carried from generation to generation. Debts and legacies, passed across generational lines, can either limit or expand possibilities for family members. Working between generational lines, social workers may help family members rebalance debts and legacies, in themselves and with others in the family. This rebalancing in the interest of development is essentially relational justice. In this sense, justice extends to what is happening in the family's transaction with the broader society, within the family and across generational lines (Ducommon & Nagy, 1999).

The historic reconfiguration of autonomy into relational meanings and obligations does include clarity about one's own needs and desires, so well developed in earlier decades. This clarity is balanced, or even fulfilled, by a "readiness for the relational." Marsha Mirkin describes this relational readiness:

> By readiness for the relational I mean a willingness to be moved by the other, to see and be seen, to stay connected even through conflict, to hear the other's narrative, even while articulating one's own, and to negotiate differences without resorting to "power over" tactics. Readiness for the relational also entails relational accountability to the other, and an openness to being affected by the other's response (Fishbane, 2001, p. 276).

Ruthellen Josselson (1992, pp. 6–8) explores relational space in eight "primary ways in which we overcome the space between us." Thus from the *holding* relationship we move to *attachment* to a particular person. From the earliest forms of libidinal life, *passionate experience*, we move to communication with another through eye contact, *eye-to-eye validation*, and from there to *idealization and iden-tification*, ways of linking to powerful others and striving to become like them. Awareness of others eventually becomes companionship and mutuality in the late primary years. As we move through adolescence we find a place for ourselves, be-longing to one group rather than another, an *embeddedness* in a concrete social re-ality of belonging, in family and ethnic group identity. Finally, the developing per-son has been learning about taking care of others, offering the self to others' needs, bridging the space through *tending and care*. We hold others, cradling them, actu-ally or symbolically in our arms (Josselson, 1992). Within the concept of attach-ment is also contained the idea that relationships are personal, accommodating the unique needs of persons and containing the implicit obligations and value base that must accompany a personal orientation.

Contrary to less complex cultural expectations of individual autonomy, people at most life-cycle stages form interdependent bonds with each other (Cohler & Geyer, 1982; Galatzer-Levy & Cohler, 1993); the maps of our need for each other can be traced and observed in the consciousness and cognitive growth of persons (Mahler, Pine, & Bergman, 1975, Piaget, 1954; Kohlberg,1969). Object relations theorists (Greenberg & Mitchell, 1983; Kernberg, 1976) and attachment theorists (Levy, 2000; Lewis & Gossett, 1999; Atkinson & Zucker, 1997; Bartholomew & Horowitz, 1991; Sperling & Berman, 1994, p. 189) emphasize the empirical and theoretical implications of this interdependence.

Social work, as family-oriented practice, demands an understanding of family interaction and interpersonal relationships. Rather than segmenting a focus on one *or* the other, as social and behavioral sciences tend to do, social workers need to ac-count for persons *and* social structures and for the interaction between them. Ac-counting for social reality by focusing on persons without environments or vice versa is, as Ralph Turner (1970) terms it, a pseudo question because it presumes that the two kinds of explanation are independent. Either kind of explanation, if carried far enough, subsumes the other. When we focus on the family patterns alone, we tend to blur individual differences of the members, the way these differences themselves create the patterns, the way certain members survive and others are vulnerable. When one focuses on individual differences alone, the patterns can be lost. These patterns can be created out of shared relationships and understandings. They are lifeways inherent in nature, which bring some to survive, to adapt, and to differenti-ate themselves, finding solutions to problems and needs, while others become more vulnerable. It is the old problem of creating harmony between human agency and communion in the human condition. The rivers of difference can move toward ac-commodation in common human values.

THE FAMILY THERAPY MOVEMENT

Since the early 1960s, a group of social workers, psychologists, and psychiatrists, whose fundamental frame of reference is the family, have been working to differen-tiate work with families from ways of helping individuals. Because the family therapy model reflected what social workers had been dealing with since the beginnings of their profession, social workers have been a most important part of this interdisciplinary movement. Family therapy theories are most useful and can be drawn upon as approaches to practice as long as there is a broader understanding of 1) family structure and family development—how families compose themselves at different stages of development, and 2) the characteristic focus and tasks of social work practice with families. The methods and theories of family therapy are most useful for social workers when placed within these two contexts. This is the unfolding focus of the next two chapters.

In the relatively short time that family therapy has been developing, much of the initial focus has been on developing approaches to working with families. Throughout the 1970s and 1980s, these methodologies multiplied into competing approaches. Each approach had something to say about how people function in families and how families themselves function. Each tried to balance human agency with communion. Possibly because of this, each had a certain level of effectiveness over interventions that lacked a larger context than individual concerns. However, in the absence of an organizing framework, these methods themselves competed with each other. No one method was a panacea. Each could be more or less appropriate to a particular problem.

The picture of competing approaches to family therapy has gradually changed over the period of the mid-1990s through the present for several reasons. Studies of the effectiveness of differing approaches to family, together with the experience of practitioners dealing with families, created a shift in the field from particular approaches to intervantion to broader organizing frameworks for theory and family intervention (Pinsof & Wynne, 1995). Family therapists had moved from competing approaches to some integration of approaches. Practitioners themselves had been drawing from different schools, rather than limiting themselves to a particular set of interventions. Theorists began to find it more useful and appropriate to integrate these different approaches into an overarching picture of practice (Bruenlin et al. 1992; Pinsof, 1995). Effectiveness research found that utilizing several of these differing approaches to practice with families were at least as effective, if not more, than individual approaches, and often worked more quickly (Pinsof & Wynne, 1995). However, each approach carried with it its own limitations of perspective on the family as a whole. Theorists, researchers, and practitioners began to assume that a broader focus integrating different approaches would be more effective. The key question then became: what then were the common properties and underlying dimensions of these more or less effective approaches? What made them effective at all? Recognizing this field-wide trend as a second stage of theory and practice, Lebow (1997) suggested that integration presumed a more extensive melding of approaches into a meta-level theory.

As a first step in doing this, Bruenlin, Schwartz, and MacKune-Karrer (1992) posited six levels of theory or *metaframeworks* that applied to family therapy. Rather than being opposed to each other, these were simply different levels of the complex realities that families experience, and thus different levels of valid understandings of intervention in families:

1. The mind and the self
2. Sequences of interactional patterns
3. Organization and structure of the relational contexts of our experience
4. Life cycle development
5. Multicultural understandings of experience and interaction
6. Gender issues

William Pinsof (1995) approached the same theoretical issues, but from understanding that the differing family problems demand different responses. For Pinsoff, there are different spheres of problems or *systemic constraints* to functional relations and interaction. These systemic constraints maintain family problems. He posited six spheres of systemic constraints. These could operate at the same time, but on different system levels, to maintain family problems. These were the spheres of:

1. Organizational constraints: how the (client) system organizes and conducts itself in relation to the problem
2. Biological constraints: how the system operates as a biological and physical system in relation to the presenting problem
3. Meanings and attributions: how the system thinks and feels in relation to itself and to the problem
4. Transgenerational constraints: issues and processes that derive from families of origin
5. Object relations constraints: the way in which the psychodynamic parts of members are organized in relation to the problem
6. Self-system constraints: the way in which the collective self system and individual self structures interact with the problem.

These assessment schema of systemic constraints and responses imply a relationship between different theories and approaches to practice. They contribute to the development of some order within the many theories of intervention into the complex and recursive social relationships of families.

A SOCIAL WORK FRAME OF REFERENCE FOR WORKING WITH FAMILIES

We develop our approach based on the constant reality that family members (and families as collective units) interact within recursive and naturally occurring social realities of family interaction and family structure. These interactions take place within historical and developmental processes which are shaped by communication and are essential to the development of persons. Communication shapes the shared meanings of family life and the personal and familial story or narrative that results from the process.

Persons take part in families to realize basic, uniquely personal needs. Among the basic needs and capacities that persons seek to realize in a family are:

- *The Need for Safety.* Where there is safety and discretion, the persons and fragile identities of others in the family are protected and belonging is possible.
- *The Need for Belonging.* Where there is belonging, the family can be a secure base for action and there can be communication.
- *The Capacity for Communication.* Where there is communication, one can respond and value the feelings and thoughts of others in the family, express one's own, and there can be the capacity for appropriate choice.
- *The Capacity to Choose in an Ethical, Relational Framework.* In a relational framework of appropriate concern for the worth and dignity of self and others, one can have the capacity to choose. Where there is the capacity to choose, respecting one's own dignity and that of others, there can be the capacity to grow as a person and to some extent to change patterns, to be an agent of one's own development.
- *The Capacity to Grow, to Interact, to Care, and to Love.* Growth takes place in a context of interaction, communication, care for the needs of the self and others, and role differentiation. Where there is the capacity to grow as a person and to interact with others, there can also be the capacity to care appropriately for the needs of the self and others and ultimately to love.

Family Intervention

Families construct environments to meet these needs and capacities. The experience of various approaches to family therapy has found at least six points of effective intervention with families:

1. Working with individual family members on personal and relational tasks
2. Working to change family communication and meanings
3. Working to reframe the family's interpersonal narratives and stories of their experience
4. Working to assist families with family life cycle developmental tasks where they have gotten "stuck"
5. Working to change the family's relational structure, and from this to change their experience of each other
6. Working to change the family's relationship with environmental systems

From the family's perspective, each of these levels addresses and constructs in different ways the goods that can emerge from family interaction. Recent developments in family therapy theory have sought to combine these approaches and adapt them to the needs of a particular situation (Pinsof, 1995; Bruenlin, et al. 1992).

These levels of functioning and their relation to the human needs they foster are illustrated in Table 1.1

Every one of these human needs—safety, belonging, communication, choice, and so on—can be and are profoundly violated within particular families. The fact

Table 1.1
Levels of Family Functioning and Human Needs

Human Needs and Capacities	Levels of Family Functioning					
	Personal Development & Interpersonal Process	Family Communi- cation and Meanings	Interpersonal & Spiritual Narratives & Stories	Family Developmental Processes	Family Structure	Family Environmental Systems
Safety	X	X	X	X	X	X
Belonging	X	X	X	X	X	X
Capacity for effective communi- cation	X	X	X	X	X	X
Capacity to choose in an ethical, relational framework, to be concerned for self and others	X	X	X	X	X	X
Capacity to grow, to interact and to take care of self and others, to love	X	X	X	X	X	X

of needs violated argues for the interest of the community in protecting family members, and for a professional approach to working with them. When these needs are grossly violated, the surrounding community with its organized social welfare institutions steps in. This often creates greater difficulty, as family members struggle to deal with possible colonization by outside institutional structures, which are often perceived as representing a different culture or class, influences from the market, money, images from the mass media, and so on. Social workers, often working for a social agency, work within this constant field: families, social institutions, agencies, and communities, including the political system.

The delicate and elaborate relational (and intentional) architecture of family interaction cannot easily be described and analyzed. This task demands a systematic way of understanding and dealing with the validity of human subjective experience without reducing it to something else. Social psychology and relational sociology (Cooley, 1922; Mead, 1934; Shibutani, 1962; Blumer, 1969; Turner, 1970; Burr, 1979; Donati, 1989) have made some progress in developing an understanding of mutual communication, intentionality, and mutual action in families. Social relationships are created out of human experience and interaction. There are relations between the way people perceive reality, the way people act, their patterns of action, and the structures of relationships that they create. These structures in turn stabilize personal patterns and perceptions in a dense, complex recursive relationship. The relation between people's patterns of behavior and their constructions of their worlds does not necessarily make behavior predictable in any linear or mechanical way. On the contrary, when we allow for people's differing perceptions, behavior becomes somewhat indeterminate. An intentional social world is an indeterminate social world. It is open to reconstruction through mutual communication, mutual commitments, and mutual action. In the world of practice, therapists intervene in people's interchanges and interactions: in the patterns and sequences, in communication, in the way relations with others are construed, and in what people are accustomed to doing. Through these guided interventions in human interaction, the phenomenal world is altered. The social worker assists family members to communicate appropriately and creatively and to make effective mutual commitments, thus assisting them to preserve relationships and to restructure their patterns of communication and interaction. This body of knowledge about family relationships and interaction becomes a basis for family intervention (Constable, 1984).

Table 1.2 shows a model of the interaction between personal and family needs, the response of the social worker, the response of the family, and principles of practice.[3] The family and each of its members, if they are to be able to act in a fully human way toward themselves and each other, have particular human needs. These needs are prerequisites to personal action and choice in the family. Family members strive to develop common understandings, often reinforced by membership with other families in relational communities of concern.

The priority given to family members interacting and constructing this purposefully human environment, as they must, allows the social worker to use of a variety of intervention methods to help the family do this. The interactions of family members create the context, the goals, and the boundaries of the helping process. The social worker assists family members to construct their relationships with each other, develop personal capacities for membership, and ultimately modify the family structure. The social worker responds to the family members with whom he or she has chosen to work, and simultaneously to the family as a whole. The social worker's choice of where in the family to work is based on an assessment of family function-

---

[3]The table is similar in inspiration to an approach that Felix Biestek took to social work with individual persons (Biestek, 1957).

ing, structure, and tasks in a systems framework. For example, work with the parents may be the most powerful way to affect children. On the other hand, choosing to work with children without some work with the parents would undermine parents.

Ethical Practice Principles

Members of families seek certain goods through family membership and through work with the social worker. These—safety, belonging, communication, the capacity to choose in an ethical, relational framework, the capacity to grow, to interact, and to care—are illustrated in the first column of Table 1.2. These are basic human goods necessary for the development of every person, which each family member must help secure. The work of constructing a family, whether as family member or social worker—coach, is inherently moral. The values do not need to be imposed from the outside. They are already present in what the protagonists are seeking each in their own way from the situation, and in the issues and choices with which the family and the social worker are dealing (Constable, 1983; 1989). Social work practice principles associated with relational needs (illustrated in Column 4 in the table) become both ethical and technical practice principles. The social worker uses methods and techniques to assist family members to realize values, such as human worth and dignity, in their interaction.

Diverse Family Situations

Culture, gender, generational divisions, and simple human differences bring about tremendous diversity of family both in form and interaction (McGoldrick, 1998). Without prescribing how a family ought to be, each family in different ways seeks to construct its own version of safety, belonging, communication, and other values. The job of parenting, for example, may be done in a family, by birth parents, grandparents, siblings, aunts, adoptive parents, single foster parents, and others with a wide variety of beliefs about themselves and the family relations they are constructing together. Some of these forms of family are discussed in chapter 8 and elsewhere throughout the book. However, it is beyond the scope of this book to enter into discussion in any depth of all possible family situations. In some cases, bodies of literature are only beginning to develop. Space has had to limit our discussion to content and process itself, but the concepts apply broadly to many family situations.

Families have conflicting visions and different patterns of seeking the same values. In a diverse society there are inevitable collisions between family members and between families and the larger society. Such collisions can be either destructive or creative. The social worker offers the possibility of an informed helping process, that can assist family members to come to terms with and find some resolution for some of the differences and dilemmas inherent in their situation. An understanding of the many ways families can resolve these dilemmas would need to inform this process. Within the normal constraints and consequences of society, the issues are for the family to resolve.

Table 1.2
Needs of Persons in Families, Response of the Social Worker, and
Ethical-Technical Practice Principles

First Direction	Second Direction	Third Direction	Fourth Direction
Persons interacting at individual and family life-cycle stages establish family structure & satisfy human needs	*The response of the social worker*	*The awareness and response of persons in the family*	*Ethical-technical practice principle (to assist the family unit to. . . .)*
I Safety To maintain safety and discretion, protecting the dignity and fragile identities of others	The social worker responds to these needs, the family's personal and relational tasks, by assisting family members, individually and with each other to communicate, to respond to each other's needs, to accomplish developmental tasks, and to create a network of understandings (Family Structure)	The family members respond to the social worker's sensitivity, understanding, and response to them, and the identification of personal and relational tasks in the sessions; they begin to learn to respond appropriately to each other and develop a climate of understanding and support with each other where these tasks can be accomplished.	*Develop confidentially, discretion and trust*
II Belonging To be treated as a unique person of worth; to respond to others in this way; to withhold negative judgments of worth			*Support the worth, dignity and uniqueness of each person*
III Communication To respond accurately to the feelings and thoughts of others; to express one's own feelings and thoughts			*Develop purposeful, skillful and constructive communication*
IV Capacity to choose, to be concerned for self and others To grow into making choices and decisions in an ethical-relational framework; to respect others' similar freedom			*Support self determination; principled choices; altruistic beliefs*
V Capacity to grow, to interact, and to take care of self and others To carry out developmental tasks with family support: to care appropriately for the needs of self and the others.			*Support differentiation of self and care for others in revised family structure*

Family Resilience

Cultural groups who have experienced extreme stress—such as slavery and subsequent discrimination, the holocaust, deportation to Siberia, or refugee status—may carry with them the pain imposed by oppressive conditions, but also the qualities that have allowed them to survive in inhuman conditions. The concept of family resilience as developed by Froma Walsh (2003, 1999) extends the concept of family activity developed in Table 1.3. In Table 1.3 family members interact to create relational goods necessary for persons to survive and grow as persons. Social workers can help them to achieve these goods. In stressful situations, such activity may be more difficult. Yet resilient families are able to carry on, and thus the concept is of great importance.

Resilience is not a matter of a particular family structure, but of process. The resilient family forges transformation and growth from adverse circumstances (Walsh, 2003). In the midst of difficulty, the resilient family develops its meanings, interacts with its circumstances, and adapts creatively to them, preserving its own values. Paradoxically, the effects of oppressive conditions may act to suppress the very qualities, that could lead to survival. Family members are able to communicate their needs and solve problems. The resilient family is able to:

- Approach adversity as a challenge shared by the whole family
- Normalize and contextualize distress
- Use adversity to gain a sense of its own coherence
- Make sense of how things have happened through causal or explanatory attributions
- Have a hopeful and optimistic bias
- Master the art of the possible
- Draw upon spiritual resources
- Develop flexibility and adaptability
- Develop its internal connections
- Use social and economic resources appropriately
- Communicate clearly and openly with each other
- Solve problems collaboratively

The key processes in family resilience are developed in greater detail Table 1.3.

Social work has been working with families for more than a century. It has learned that, to be effective, its focus needs to be based on what family members actually do when they construct (or reconstruct) relational realities. Since what they do involves persons interacting with each other and with institutional realities, social workers are prepared to act in the same arena. The identity and position of social work permits it to draw more readily from social psychology, family therapy, and other areas without the contradictions that would come if social work was referenced primarily to method or addressed only one level or one approach to human functioning.

In the following chapters we identify a life-cycle history of family development, family structure at points of the life cycle, and family intervention—the content, process, and stories of social work practice at points in the life cycle. We draw freely from larger bodies of family intervention theory, integrating these theories into a picture of social work practice with couples and families. Our brief treatment is necessarily limited to content, process, and integration. We use as examples basic situa-

Table 1.3
Key Processes in Family Resilience

Belief Systems
1. Make Meaning of Adversity
   - View resilience as relationally based vs. "rugged individual"
   - Normalize, contextualize adversity and distress
   - Sense of coherence: crisis as meaningful, comprehensible, manageable challenge
   - Casual/explanatory attributions: How could this happen? What can be done?

2. Positive Outlook
   - Hope, optimistic bias; confidence in overcoming odds
   - Courage and en-*courage*-ment; affirm strengths and focus on potential
   - Active initiative and perseverance (Can-do spirit)
   - Master the possible; accept what can't be changed

3. Transcendence and Spirituality
   - Larger values, purpose
   - Spirituality: Faith, congregational support, healing rituals
   - Inspiration: envision new possibilities; creative expression; social action
   - Transformation: learning, change, and growth from adversity

Organizational Patterns
4. Flexibility
   - Open to change: rebound, reorganize, adapt to fit new challenges
   - Stability through disruption: continuity, dependability, follow-through
   - Strong authoritative leadership: nurturance, protection, guidance
      - Varied family forms: cooperative parenting/caregiving teams
      - Couple/Co-parent relationship: equal partners

5. Connectedness
   - Mutual support, collaboration, and commitment
   - Respect individual needs, differences, and boundaries
   - Seek reconnection, reconciliation of wounded relationships

6. Social and Economic Resources
   - Mobilize kin, social, and community networks; seek models and mentors
   - Build financial security; balance work/family strains

Communication/Problem-solving
7. Clarity
   - Clear, consistent messages (words and actions)
   - Clarify ambiguous information; truth-seeking/truth-speaking

8. Open Emotional Expression
   - Share range of feelings (joy and pain, hopes and fears)
   - Mutual empathy; tolerance for differences
   - Take responsibility for own feelings, behavior; avoid blaming
   - Pleasurable interactions; humor

9. Collaborative Problem-solving
   - Creative brainstorming; resourcefulness; seize opportunities
   - Shared decision-making; conflict resolution: negotiation, fairness, reciprocity
   - Focus on goals; take concrete steps; build on success; learn from failure
   - Proactive stance: prevent problems; avert crises; prepare for future challenges

SOURCE: *Family Process*, Vol. 42, No. 1, 2003 © FPI, Inc., Walsh (2003), with permission.

tions at life-cycle stages, with children and/or vulnerable older generations, that social workers encounter every day and where knowledge and experience has had the most development.

REFERENCES

Ainsworth, M. D. S. (1973). The development of infant-mother attachment. In B. M. Caldwell & H. N. Ricciutti (Eds.), *Review of child development research* Vol. 3 (pp. 1–94). Chicago:

Ainsworth, M. D. S., Bleher, M. C., Waters, E. & Wall, S. (1978). *Patterns of attachment: A psychological study of the strange situation*. Hillsdale, NJ: Lawrence Erlbaum Associates.

Atkinson, L., & Zucker, K. (1997). *Attachment and psychopathology*. New York: Guilford.

Bartholomew, K., & Horowitz, L. (1991). Attachment styles among young adults. *Journal of Personality and Social Psychology, 61*, 226–244.

Bartlett, H. (1972). *The common base of social work practice*. New York: National Association of Social Workers.

Beels, C. 2002. Notes for a cultural history of family therapy. *Family Process, 41*(1), 67–82.

Bellah, R. N., Madson, R., Sullivan, W. M., Swidler, A., & Tipton, S. M. (1986). *Habits of the Heart*. Berkeley, CA: University of California Press.

Biestek, F. J. (1957). *The casework relationship*. Chicago: Loyola University Press.

Blankenhorn, D., Bayme, S., & Elshtain, J. B. (1990). *Rebuilding the nest: A new commitment to the American family*. Milwaukee: Family Service America.

Blumer, H. (1969). Symbolic interactionism. Englewood Cliffs, NJ: Prentice Hall.

Boszormenyi-Nagy, I., & Spark, G. (1973). *Invisible loyalties: Reciprocity in intergenerational family therapy*. New York: Harper & Row.

Boszormenyi-Nagy, I., Grunebaum, A., & Ulrich, D. (1991). Contextual therapy. In A. S. Gurman, & D. P. Kniskern, (Eds.), *Handbook of family therapy II* (pp. 200–238). New York: Brunner-Mazel.

Bowlby, J. (1969). *Attachment and loss, Vol. 1, Attachment*. New York: Basic Books.

Breunlin, D. C., Schwartz, R. C., & MacKune-Karrer, B. (1992). *Metaframeworks: Transcending the models of family therapy*. San Francisco: Jossey-Bass.

Burgess, E. W. (1926). The family as a unity of interacting personalities. *The Family, 7*, 3–9.

Burgess, E. W., & Locke, H. J. (1953). *The family: From institution to companionship*. New York: American Book.

Burr, W., Hill, R., Nye, F. I., & Reiss, I. L. (1979). *Contemporary theories about the family*. New York: Free Press.

Carlton, T. O. (1984). *Clinical social work in health settings: A guide to professional practice with exemplars*. New York: Springer.

Carter, E., & McGoldrick, M. (1999). *The expanded life cycle: A framework for family therapy*. New York: Allyn & Bacon.

Clulow, C. (Ed.). (2001). *Adult attachment and couple psychotherapy*. London: Brunner-Routledge.

Cocozzelli, C., & Constable, R. (1985). An empirical analysis of the relation between theory and practice in clinical social work. *Journal of Social Service Research, 9*(1), 47–63.

Cohler, B., & Geyer, S. (1982). Psychological autonomy and interdependence within the family. In F. Walsh, (Ed.), *Normal family processes*. New York: Guilford.

Constable, R. (1983). Values, religion and social work practice. *Social Thought, 15*(2), 29–40.

Constable, R. (1984). Phenomenological foundations for the understanding of family interaction. *Social Service Review, 58*(1), 117–132.

Constable, R. (1989). Relations and membership: Foundations for ethical thinking in social work. *Social Thought, 15*(3–4), 53–66.

Constable, R., & Cocozzelli, C. (1989). Common themes and polarities in social work practice theory development. *Social Thought, 15*(2), 14–24.

Cooley, C. H. (1922). *Human nature and the social order*. New York: Scribners.

Corcoran, J. (2000). *Evidence-based social work practice with families*. New York: Springer.

Costin, L. B. (1969). A historical review of school social work. *Social Casework 59*, 439–453.

Council on Social Work Education. (1982). *Curriculum policy statement for the bachelors and masters degree levels in social work education*. New York: Author.

Council on Social Work Education. (1994). *Curriculum policy statement for the bachelors and masters degree levels in social work education*. New York: Author.

DeSchweinitz, K. (1924). *The art of helping people out of trouble*. New York: Houghton.

Donati, P. (1989). *La Famiglia come relazione sociale*. [The family as a social-relational set]. Milano: Franco Angeli.

Donati, P. (1991). *Teoria relazionale della societa*. [A relational theory of society]. Milano: Franco Angeli.

Donati, P. (2001). Freedom vs. control in relational society. In L. Tomasi (Ed.), *New horizons in sociological theory and research*. Ashgate: Aldershot.

Ducommon-Nagy, C. (1999). Contextual therapy. In D. Lawson, & F. Prevett, (Eds.), *Casebook in family therapy* (pp. 1–26). Belmont, CA. Wadsworth.

Etzioni, A. (1993). *The spirit of community: Rights, responsibilities and the communitarian agenda*. New York: Crown.

Falck, H. S. (1988). *Social work: The membership perspective*. New York: Springer.

Fishbane, M. D. (2001). Relational narratives of the self. *Family Process, 40*(3), 273–293.

Galatzer-Levy, R. M., & Cohler, B. (1993). *The essential other: A developmental psychology of the self*. NewYork: Basic Books.

Gilligan, C. (1982). *In a different voice: Psychological theory and womens' development*. Cambridge, MA: Harvard University Press.

Gordon, W. E. (1969). Basic concepts for an integrative and generative conception of social work. In G. Hearn (Ed.), *The general systems approach: Contributions toward an holistic conception of social work*. New York: CSWE.

Greenberg, J. R., & Mitchell, S. A. (1983). *Object relations in psychoanalytic theory*. Cambridge, MA: Harvard University Press.

Hartman, A., & Laird, J. (1983). *Family-centered social work practice*. New York: Free Press.

Haworth, L. (1986). *Autonomy*. New Haven: Yale University Press.

Hearn, G. (1969). *The general systems approach: Contributions toward an holistic conception of social work*. New York: CSWE.

James, W. (1981). *The principles of psychology* (Vol. 1). Cambridge, MA: Harvard University Press.

Jayaratne, S. (1978). A study of clinical eclecticism. *Social Service Review, 52*(4), 621–631.

Joint NASW-CSWE Task Force on the Development of Specialization in Social Work. (1979). *Specialization in the social work profession* (NASW Document No. 79-310-08). Washington, DC: NASW.

Josselson, R. (1992). *The space between us: Exploring the dimensions of human relationships*. San Francisco: Jossey Bass.

Kernberg, O. F. (1976). *Object relations theory and clinical psychoanalysis*. New York: Jason Aronson.

Kohlberg, L. (1969). *Stages in the development of moral thought and action*. New York: Holt Rinehart and Winston.

Kohut, H. (1977). *The restoration of the self*. New York: International Universities Press.

Lebow, J. (1997). The integrative revolution in couple and family therapy. *Family Process, 36*(1).

Levy, T. M. (2000). *Handbook of attachment interventions*. New York: Academic Press.

Lewis, H. (1982). *The intellectual base of social work*. New York: Haworth Press.

Lewis, J. M., & Gossett, J. T. (1999). *Disarming the past: How an intimate relationship can heal old wounds*. Phoenix: Zeig & Tucker.

Lide, P. (1959). A study of historical influences of major importance in determining the present function of the school social worker. In G. Lee (Ed.), *Helping the troubled school child*. New York: National Association of Social Workers.

Mahler, M., Pine, F., & Bergman, A. (1975). *The psychological birth of the human infant*. New York: Basic Books.

McDaniel, S. H., Hepworth, J., & Doherty, W. (1992). *Medical family therapy: A biopsychosocial approach to families with health problems*. New York: Basic Books.

McGoldrick, M., & Carter, E. (1999). Self in context: The individual life cycle in systemic perspective. In B. Carter & M. McGoldrick (Eds.), *The expanded family life cycle: Individual, family and social perspectives* (3rd ed., pp. 27–36). Boston: Allyn & Bacon.

McGoldrick, M., Anderson, C., & Walsh, F. (1989). *Women in families: A framework for family therapy*. New York: Norton.

McGoldrick, M. (Ed.). (1998). *Revisioning family therapy: Race, culture and gender*. New York: Guilford Press.

Mead, G. H. (1934). *Mind, self and society*. Chicago: University of Chicago Press.

Mullen, E. (1983). Personal practice models. In A. Rosenblatt, & D. Waldfogel (Eds.), *Handbook of clinical social work*. San Francisco: Jossey-Bass.

Nacman, M. (1977). Social work in health settings: A historical review. *Social Work in Health Care*, 2(4), 407–418.

Nichols, M. P., & Schwartz, R. C. (2001). *Family therapy: Concepts and methods*. Boston: Allyn & Bacon.

Piaget, J. (1954). *The construction of reality in the child*. New York: Basic Books.

Pincus, A., & Minahan, A. (1974). *Social work practice: Model and method*. Itaska, IL: Peacock.

Pinsof, W. M. (1995). *Integrative, problem-centered therapy*. New York: Basic Books.

Pinsof, W. M., & Wynne, L. C. (1995). The effectiveness and efficacy of marital and family therapy: Introduction to the special issue. In W. M. Pinsof, & L. C. Wynne (Ed.), *Journal of Marital and Family Therapy*, special issue, 21(4), 341–343.

Rank, O. (1947). *Will therapy and truth and reality*. New York: Knopf.

Richmond, M. (1907). *The good neighbor*. Philadelphia: Lippincott.

Richmond, M. (1917). *Social diagnosis*. New York: Sage.

Ryan, W. (1971). *Blaming the victim*. New York: Pantheon Books.

Schwartz, W. (1977). The interactionist approach. In *Encyclopedia of social work* (pp. 1328–1338). New York: National Association of Social Workers.

Sheffield, A. (1937). *Social insight in case situations*. New York: Appleton-Century Crofts.

Shibutani, T. (1962). *Society and personality*. Englewood Cliffs, NJ: Prentice-Hall.

Shulman, L. (1999). *The skills of helping* (3rd ed.). Itaska, IL: Peacock.

Siporin, M. (1972a). *Introduction to social work practice*. New York: Macmillan.

Siporin, M. (1972b). Situational assessment and intervention. *Social casework*, 53, 91–109.

Smalley, R. (1967). *Theory for social work practice*. New York: Columbia.

Southard, E. E., & Jarrett, M. C. (1922). *The kingdom of evils: Psychiatric social work presented in 100 case histories*. New York: Macmillan.

Sperling, M. B., & Berman, W. H. (1994). *Attachment in adults*. New York: Guilford.

Stern, D. N. (1985). *The interpersonal world of the infant: A view from psychoanalysis and developmental psychology*. New York: Basic Books.

Sullivan, H. S. (1938–39). A note on formulating the relationship of the individual and the group. *American Journal of Sociology*, 4, 932–937.

Taft, J. (1926). The effect of an unsatisfactory mother-daughter relationship upon the development of a personality. *The Family*, 7, 10.

Tillich, P. (1962). The philosophy of social work. *Social Service Review*, 36, 513–516.

Turner, R. (1970). *Family interaction*. New York: Wiley.

Waite, L., & Gallagher, M. (2001). *The case for marriage: Why married people are healthier, happier and better off financially*. New York: Doubleday.

Walters, M., Carter, E., Papp, P., & Silverstrein, O. (1988). *The invisible web: Gender relations in family relationships*. New York: Guilford.

Walsh, F. (1999). *Strengthening family resilience*. New York: Guilford.

Walsh, F. (2003). Family resilience: A framework for clinical practice. *Family Process*, 42(1), 1–18.

Watts, P. A. (1964). Casework above the poverty line: The influence of home service in World War I on social work. *Social Service Review*, 27(3) 303–315.

Witmer, H. L. (1942). *Social work: An analysis of a social institution*. New York: Farrer & Rinehart.

CHAPTER 2

The Family Life Cycle and Relational Tasks

This chapter develops theories of relational processes in families from a family life-cycle perspective. Case studies illustrate the connections of these concepts with social work assessment and intervention.

RELATIONAL PROCESSES IN FAMILIES

Differing approaches to the helping process with families address different dimensions of family experience. When social workers work with families, they work with all of these dimensions. The problem is to find the relation of these dimensions to an encompassing, social work intervention process. This will be the task of the remainder of the book. Some approaches to family intervention focus on intervening in time and process: that is, in events occurring in sequences and in the way these developmental sequences proceed. Other approaches focus on space: that is, in the organization of experiences through the structure of relationships. Relational space can be integrated with developmental time (Josselson, 1992). Time and space are further integrated for each person in narrative or story: that is, the use of language to shape what has occurred in time and space into structures of meaning. The fourth dimension (or capacity) of human experience is spiritual (Anderson &Worthen, 1997). The capacity of spirit to reshape (rather than to be totally determined by) certain realities is limited by the reality that we are finite beings, living in contingency and continually faced with our own complexities of body and soul. The search for recognition of spiritual realities and on going search is implicit in the human condition.

The first dimension of human experience is time. Time, the measure of change, provides order to a sequence of events. In the context of the perceptions of a person, time allows a particular developmental narrative or story. In this chapter we will examine developmental sequences and relational stories of persons in families. The themes of this chapter are the personal and relational tasks necessary to complete stages of the family life cycle. These personal and relational tasks are implicit in every family life-cycle stage. From the perspective of personal development, the key concepts are *differentiation* and *connectedness* of self in relation to others. A framework of relational tasks is used to clarify differentiation and connectedness at particular stages of family relationships. Time is also part of the helping process—beginnings, middles, and endings. Beginnings, middles, and endings of an intentional helping process intersect with the personal and relational tasks of the family life cycle. There is an unfolding relationship between the intentional time of the helping process and the tasks of each life-cycle period.

Relational space is the second dimension of the family. This is a relational architecture of the family with different structures for different life-cycle periods and different situations. We integrate relational space or family structure with relational time or family development. Relational stories are found throughout the book in the form of case studies. While these case studies are necessarily composites of experiences, they do offer particular glimpses of real life stories in which the social worker has participated through practice.

THE PERSON

The basis of family membership is the person-in-relation seeking to develop as a human being, seeking relational safety, belonging, communication, growth, friendship, and other human goods within the fold of the family. A person-in-relation is different from a statistical "individual." Although the concept of the individual, signifies a separable unit, personhood includes the necessary relations with the outside world that become part of ourselves. Frederick Allen, a pioneer in psychiatry, reflecting his colleague Harry Stack Sullivan, discusses these relations that get to the core of a person's being. These are learned patterns of interaction with others, structures of which we have become part, and processes that place us on a line of development. These give us a past and a future. Persons learn and become unique through their stories: their experiences of present and past relationships with other persons, their relations to larger social units and to institutional structures and through persons who are significant others to them. They learn through the reflected expectations of societal contexts, both those that they have chosen and those that have been thrust upon them. Growing and becoming a person reflect an ever more complex, progressive relation of person with environment. From the sense of oneness with the environment experienced by the infant through a progressive differentiation of self, the relation between individual and environment continues. Growth can bring new levels of consciousness of the relation of self and other, of choice, and of capability for forming new social units in relations with others. Growth is a continuous process of the formation of new wholes from the elements of the preceding ones (Allen, 1942). Persons are capable of growth in a process of progressive differentiation of function that results in a more complex unity.

Persons gradually acquire the ability to distinguish between those parts of their experience that are a part of their own selves and those parts that are not of their own selves. The self-process is ongoing, ever changing, and dynamic, carried out in relation to and in interaction with others. The process of growth moves from the initial differentiation of the parts of one's body from one's surroundings to the discovery and development of inclinations, tendencies, and traits. We each become a self through social interaction, through connections with others at greater levels of maturity, through the progressive awareness of difference, of the "not self," through the taking and making of roles, and through a developed understanding of the role of the other and the other's relations with us. These characteristics are formed in a process of finding similarity and differences from others.

The "I" and the "me"

Each person is a blend of the "I" and the "me," the spontaneous and the patterned (Burr, Hill, Nye, & Reiss, 1979 p. 47–48), the qualities, that reflect human agency and the qualities that reflect communion and connectedness. The "I" is a creative, acting self, the subject, normally the initiating and the mediating part of the person.[1] It takes part in an internal, reflective conversation of consciousness through which the individual can delay responses, see himself or herself from the perspective of the other, review the past, and envision the future (Shibutani, 1961). The "I" can be unpredictable, spontaneous, and unique to a particular person. The "I" need not be reduced to a part of the self. For Ruth Smalley and functional social work, it becomes the will, an essential life force, self organizing, central to growth, and transforming its world (1967, pp. 81 ff). When the "I" is engaged, it becomes central to the helping process. The "I" is present in the language and discourse of compassion. Indeed, the discovery that one can speak of suffering to another, that both can listen and acquire a compassionate language of their own, may be the chief tool of a healing process. It is the "I" who finds words, then a language, for discourse; it is the "I" who can listen and respond. No longer colonized or paralyzed by unspeakable injustices or by suffering, the "I" can discover itself and its newly found ability to respond. It is different from the injustice. It is not encapsulated by the suffering that takes place. It allows us to find a way to transcend the injustice and the suffering (Reich, 1989).

The constellation of patterns, learned through continuous social interaction, is the "me." These parts of the self are learned and repetitious, patterns that denote an actor's response to the expectations of significant others. These are the parts that others learn they can rely on. They are social parts in that they are drawn from the response to these perceived expectations.

There may indeed be many different "me's," many patterns of feeling and behaving, drawn from different experiences and from memories. There is a "me" that becomes anxious and fearful in certain circumstances. There is a "me" that becomes sad. There is a "me" that is confident, and so forth. It is like an internal family, sometimes ordered, sometimes riotous, sometimes confused and conflicted. As with parents in families, in not all cases is the "I" fully in charge, able to help these different parts of the self or use fully their great potential contributions. In different language, Richard Schwartz (1995) points out that the aim of help is for the leadership part of the person to become fully in conversation with the many other parts, the internal family of the person—to become a principle of harmony.

---

[1] The concept of an "I," the leadership part of the person, the subject, is a theme that has been explored throughout the history of philosophy and theology, but particularly in the twentieth century by Martin Buber (1958; 1965), and others (see the discussion in Shivanandan, 2002).

In a somewhat similar vein, although the language is again different, there is a long tradition of ego-oriented casework (Hollis, 1972; Goldstein, E.,1995; Parad, 1958) in social work, essentially engaging the person from the "outside-in" (Simon, 1960, pp. 33–36), from reality tasks to ego functioning, with the goal of improving ego function in certain areas of need (Goldstein, 1995, p. 1950).

CASE STUDY 2.1

Gloria, a single Philippina pediatric nurse in her late thirties, struggled every day with her obsessions about her beloved boss, Dr. Smith, who was married with several children. She remained very productive at work. When she was not focused on her work, her feelings about him filled the empty spaces of her life. She was fearful that that her way of dressing (the colors she chose to wear) and other actions, which others would consider insignificant, would hurt him. She would worry when she didn't say "good morning" to him halfway down the hall or when she spoke to another man in his presence. These obsessions often put her in embarrassing situations. She would want to ask him, "I didn't hurt you, did I?" or do other somewhat unusual things to reassure herself. Her obsessions were torturing her. Dr.Velu, her psychiatrist, considered her "quite fragile." The social worker, working with Velu, took a modified cognitive and problem-solving approach, helping Gloria to identify those parts of herself, left over from childhood experiences, which were making her insecure and pushing her to obsessive behavior. Each week, and the starting point of the helping relationship, the major focus was on her daily activities and perceptions, and on what she could do about the situation in which she found herself. There was support for her strengths; her weaknesses were buttressed (Simon, 1960).

With the help of her social worker Gloria corrected some of her perceptions in the context of her active coping. She began an exercise program and made an effort to broaden her friendships with other women. She began to become reflective, to see her own strengths and to see that she could gently take leadership of her self with her own wisdom and experience. She could reassure the parts that became anxious, even try to lead those parts to a better understanding. She also began to try to see her behavior as her boss might perceive it. This helped her enormously, since she didn't want to displease him. Although many of her difficulties continued, she was gradually learning to reassure herself, to maintain her unimpaired professional competence, and to avoid many of the problems into which she had fallen previously. She received an award for her work. While accepting her fears and obsessions as part of her, she gradually saw herself beginning to transcend the fears and obsessions, that previously had controlled her so completely.

Gloria's concerns will not change quickly. She needs to discover her capacity to sort all this out. She is alone and isolated. She will need to find other friendships and resources. In working with individual clients, such as Gloria, the social worker is helping her to learn, to grow, and to cope. Working with families is somewhat more complex. The social worker will shuttle from personal to relational tasks with different family members within individual sessions and within the overall process, always within the context of family as a network of relations and the relational tasks that flow from this reality.

The Self Is Spiritual

In the "I" there can be a growing inner awareness of its own spirituality, of a certain ability to transcend some of the limitations of other dimensions of experience—space, time, and language—in its search for meaning and its leadership capacity. Ed Canda (1986), a social worker, considers the central dynamic of spirituality to be the person's search for a sense of meaning and purpose through relationships between self, other people, the nonhuman world, and the ground of being. This theme is inherent in human nature: a search for connection with a higher power and, for many, this takes the form of the search for a personal Creator-God. Augustine (1960) summarizes his discovery of who he is in this relationship: "You have made us for yourself alone and our hearts cannot rest until they rest in you." Spirituality is a resource, not only profoundly individual but also profoundly social, a manifestation of community membership. The general contents of religion are the specific, concrete, and necessarily social expressions of spirituality, coalesced into particular forms: rituals, sacred scriptures, doctrines, rules of conduct, and other practices.

Query: # for Augustine?

Empathy

Gloria (case study 2.1) gradually discovered that she could begin to test, even transcend, the limits of her obsessions in the context of an empathic relationship: that she could see others not simply as an extension of herself. The act of empathy involves a spiritual process, that can transcend anger, misunderstanding, and confusion to bring peace. Thich Nhat Hanh of the Zen Buddhist tradition writes: "To develop understanding you have to practice looking at all human beings with the eyes of compassion. When you understand, you love. And when you love, you naturally act in a way that can relieve the suffering of people" (Hanh, 1987, pp. 14–15 in Anderson & Worthen, 1997). Compassion (or *misericordia* in the Western spiritual tradition) involves an active reaching out to the sadness and/or shame of the other to elevate. Compassion cannot come without reflective selves, however, often made possible through a deeper understanding of one's own experience of being the recipient compassion from another.

The Self Is Relational

In the previous chapter and here we reviewed the rich tradition of the now rediscovered relational self. The relational self becomes itself through communication, in the spaces "between" (Buber, 1958, 1965; Josselson, 1992), of human interaction and development. Thich Nhat Hanh (1991, p. 96 in Anderson & Worthen, 1997) explains, "To be is to inter-be. We cannot just be by ourselves alone. We have to inter-be with every other thing." Compassion provides the link between ourselves and others.

The Internal Family System

From Richard Schwartz's perspective,[2] reflecting Assagioli (1975) and Gazzaniga (1985), the mind is an internal family of parts and a self. The parts are like subpersonalities; sometimes they are in contention, sometimes in agreement, sometimes balanced with different parts, sometimes in extreme positions. They are sometimes confused and uncertain, sometimes riotous. Sometimes they are stuck in a very young phase, needing to grow up, to become stronger and more worldly wise. Schwartz writes about the leadership part, "the self," which has the clarity of perspective to lead effectively. When the self is fully differentiated—for example, when persons are asked to climb a mountain in their minds, leaving their parts in the valley—they describe feeling "centered," a state of calm well-being and light-heartedness, confident, free, and open hearted (Schwartz, 1995, p. 37).

RELATIONAL TASKS

Relational tasks develop the connection of the relational self with its necessary context. These tasks are inherent in sociality for every person growing in a family. They are in one sense personal tasks, but they are also tasks done with the other, tasks of the couple, and later of the family. Out of these tasks the family is constructed. Persons form social units (couples, families) through relational tasks. These tasks are geared to action with others, and they can lead to the reconstruction of the relationship or to its destruction. Accomplishment of these relational tasks depends as much on the other(s) as on the self, and the uncertainty of the other's real involvement makes them unpredictable and difficult. There are many obstacles to this accomplishment: fears, disappointments, legacies from the past, problems with the other, environmental deficits, and so on. The tasks and the obstacles become the focus of the helping relationship.

A number of family therapists include multiple generations as the context for relational tasks. Ivan Boszormenyi-Nagy takes such a contextual approach to problems occurring in the present generation. There is really no self-made person, and the helping process cannot remain fixed in the present. There are issues of loyalty between generations and there is also a need for an ethical balance of give and take among persons in a family. This creates a pull between one's learned patterns, hidden "loyalties" and legacies from family of origin, and the give and take with one's partner, who also has hidden loyalties and bonds (Boszormenyi-Nagy & Spark, 1973). Disconnection from family of origin can result in loyalties becoming invisible and bonds unacknowledged. It can result in self-defeating or destructive behavior in one's own life (Fishbane, 2001). An example can be taken from the need

---

[2]For more extensive discussion of this theoretical base, see Nichols and Schwartz (2001), pp. 427–433.

of each person of the new couple unit to rework ties to his or her family of origin. This is work that can only be done with one's *own* family. The partner would do best to take only a supportive role in this. Reworking ties to each family of origin, they can then begin to integrate some of their separate patterns with each other.

Murray Bowen developed the concepts of self-differentiation and connectedness as the keys to his theory of family intervention.[3] Bowen, a psychiatrist, saw anxiety as the key to the fusion of thinking and feeling he observed in disturbed states. From his perspective, the degree to which self-differentiation occurs in a person reflects the extent to which that person is able to distinguish between the intellectual process and feeling process he or she is experiencing without the paralysis anxiety brings. Self-differentiation is demonstrated by the degree to which a person is able to avoid having his or her behavior automatically driven by feelings. This should lead not to a denial of feelings, but a balance of thinking and feeling. The person's thinking is not limited by feelings. The person is able to express feelings spontaneously and appropriately. Such differentiation—more of a process than an attainable goal (Goldenberg & Goldenberg, 1996)—is tested in the presence of anxiety and strong feeling, particularly in family relationships. Although self-differentiation is given emphasis in Bowen's schema, there is also a type of higher-level, unfused connectedness with others' experience that accompanies differentiation. For Bowen, family of origin work is crucial to self-differentiation and connectedness. Can a person creatively partake of family relationships without getting drawn into the feelings of others and taken over by a shared anxiety? As persons make forays into the family of origin, can they remain nonreactive but reconnect and, when necessary, challenge old rules (Fishbane, 2001)? Goodrich (1991, p. 21) with a particular interest in women's development, clarifies that this differentiation is not disconnection. Rather it is an aspect of connectedness, a differentiation *with* rather than differentiation *from*.

Attachment and membership are two related concepts that, with relational tasks, bridge the relation of persons with their environment. They are the product of relational tasks performed in interaction with others. Using attachment theory, psychiatrist Jerry Lewis understands relationships through qualities of connectedness and separateness. Connectedness involves the commitment of one person to another, that is, its priority over other relations and involvements; closeness, a sharing of values, interests, activities and friends; and psychological intimacy. Psychological intimacy is the mutual sharing of vulnerabilities. It is the ability of persons to talk directly and openly with each other about very personal experiences and feelings that rarely are discussed with anyone else. It involves most of all the ability to listen to each other, to feel understood and safe, and ultimately to trust another with vulnerable parts of one's self. Separateness involves the capacity to experience one's self as a distinct person with a unique blend of both assets and liabilities, to manage one's life effectively independently of others, and to appreciate solitude as well as togetherness with others (Lewis & Gossett, 1999)

---

[3]See more extensive discussion of Bowen's Theory in Nichols and Schwartz (2001), chapter 5 and Goldenberg and Goldenberg (1996), chapter 8.

The concepts of connectedness and separateness (or autonomy) are profoundly related to culture. Tamura and Lau (1992), two Asian psychiatrists, discuss the contrasting relational value systems of Japan and Britain.The most significant difference in value systems between the two cultures is the Japanese preference for connectedness and the Western preference for separateness. The Japanese person is seen as a part of the embedded interconnectedness of relationships, whereas British norms prioritize separateness and clear boundaries in relationships, individuality, and autonomy. This value orientation is manifested in the Japanese language, the hierarchical nature of the family structure, the family life cycle, and the implicit communication style. According to Tamura and Lau, the preferred direction of change for Japanese families in therapy is toward a process of integration—how a person can be effectively integrated into the given system—rather than the process of differentiation popular in the West. Different cultures may emphasize the communal or the individual (human agency and communion), human relational capacity and capacity to act together(see table 2.1). In the human condition both are necessary and interdependent. Rather than an absolute dichotomy, it is a matter of cultural meanings and emphasis.

Table 2.1

Contrasting British and Japanese Families

	Britain	Japan
Value System	SEPARATENESS	CONNECTEDNESS
World View	Dualism (Cartesian split)	Holism (Buddhism)
Family Strucrure	Egalitarian Nuclear family	Hierarchical Extended family
Emphasized Relationship	Husband–Wife	Mother–Child
Family Life Cycle	Process of individuation Leaving home	Process of integration Arranged marriage Reunion w/elderly parents
Communication	Verbal Explicit (maximize the difference)	Nonverbal Implicit (minimize the difference)
Direction of Change (solution)	DIFFERENTIATION Individuality Autonomy	INTEGRATION Support network Sensitivity
Role of Therapist	Third Party "Neutral"	Connected directive, authoritative
Mode of Psychotherapy	Verbal Talking through Therapeutic debate Externalize Unconscious->Conscious	Nonverbal Mediation Silence Internalize Conscious->Unconscious

SOURCE: Tamura and Lau (1992), used with permission.

ATTACHMENT THEORY

Attachment is an essential part of the human condition, a precondition for human agency. Attachment theory is a theory of the essentials of human development. An understanding of these essentials, remaining in memory long after the developmental event and influencing further development, supply the context for a theory of corrective intervention. Attachment builds on the assumption that attaching behaviors, bringing developing persons closer to their caregivers, are prerequisites to every person's security, safety and further development (Ainsworth, Bleher, Waters, Wall, 1978; Bowlby, 1969). When a child experiences sufficient reciprocal, affectionate reactions with a caregiver who is available and responsive to the child's appropriate needs, the bond that is formed between them is described as *secure attachment*. Secure attachment develops as the result of thousands of daily interactions in which the caregiver achieves affective attunement with the child, eventually becoming a secure base from which the child can tackle new tasks and new relationships with the consistent expectation of being successful and loved (Ladnier & Massanari, 2000; Hughes, 1997). A child attaches not only to his or her primary caretaker(s), but also attaches through the primary caretaker(s) to the total network of relationships of which the mother and child are a part (Donley, 1993). John Byng-Hall (1995), emphasizing the network concept, defines a secure family base:

> A secure family base is a family that provides a reliable network of attachment relationships in which all family members of whatever age are able to feel sufficiently secure to explore. The term "network" implies a shared family responsibility that assures everyone that any member who is in need of help will be cared for. For small children, it means an expectation of reliable handover and hand-back within the family network, or with appropriate outside carers. Children need a sense that relationships between the adults are sufficiently collaborative to insure that care is available at all times. A secure family base involves a shared awareness that attachment relationships need to be protected and not undermined. The shared working model of the secure family base is of family members supporting each other to care for their members.

Patterns of secure attachment, carried into further development, result in two crucial sets of skills: self-regulation and relationship skills:

Self-regulation Skills	Relationship Skills
• impulse control	• empathy
• self-soothing	• trust
• initiative	• affection
• perseverance	• reciprocity
• inhibition	• expression
• patience	• respect (Ladnier & Massanari, 2000, p. 36).

Children who fail to receive consistent, predictable, reassuring responses from their primary caregivers are considered to be likely to learn insecure patterns of attachment. The child who does not learn to use his or her caregiver as a secure base for exploring the world could be at risk for problems in social relationships, emotional development, behavioral control, and cognitive capacity (Hughes, 1997).

Three subtypes of insecure attachment have been identified in work with infants. These are characterized as: Ambivalent, Avoidant, and Disorganized Attachments. *Ambivalent* attachment involves confusion over how to feel safe and secure (Lewis & Gossett 1999). Infants whose attachment was considered ambivalent were, in general, more likely to cling to their mothers in an unfamiliar environment and less willing to explore on their own. When separated from her they appeared anxious, agitated, and tearful. When the mother returned, they tended to seek contact with her, but simultaneously rejected her attempts to soothe them. Infants considered *avoidant* generally gave the impression of being independent and self-sufficient. They tended to explore the unfamiliar environment with little concern for their mother's whereabouts, just like children who were considered to be securely attached. They differed, however, from the securely attached children in that they seemed unaffected by separation from the mother and either rejected or avoided her when she returned (Ladnier & Massanari, 2000). Infants with *disorganized* attachments lacked a consistent strategy for organizing their comfort-seeking behaviors in times of stressful separation or reunion with the mother. Their disorganized reactions would include such things as apprehension, helplessness, and depression. Some would demonstrate desperate reactions such as prolonged motor freezing or dissociation alternating with agitation in unpredictable ways (Ladnier & Massanari, 2000).

Adult Attachment

Adult attachment involves working models—mental representations of the attachment relationships a person experiences throughout his or her life span. These working models organize interpersonal cognition, affect, and behavior; guide affect regulation; shape self-image; and are the definitional component of the person's attachment style (Baldwin, Keelen, Fehr, et al., 1996 in Mikulincer & Florian, 1999a). As a person grows and develops more complex attachment with significant others, the social relational dimensions of reciprocity and commitment become more important. Reciprocity implies a more complex exchange. The development of commitment to the other extends reciprocity to a type of guarantee of the relationship continuing in good times and in bad. The relationship, strengthened by trust and mutual commitment, becomes a secure base for development (Mikulincer, Florian, Cowan, & Cowan, 2002).

The adult with a secure style of adult attachment demonstrates confidence in the availability of attachment figures in times of need, and comfort with closeness and interdependence. The avoidant style involves insecurity at others' responses and a desire for emotional distance. The anxious ambivalent style shows similar insecurity, but also has a strong desire for intimacy and a high fear of rejection (Hazan & Shaver, 1987).

However, for some persons, attachment does not automatically mean commitment. Commitment is a learned and socially constructed sentiment. It is not necessarily mutual, but there are norms that it be mutual. Recognition of lack of mutuality, can lead to a rapid deterioration of the relationship. On the other hand, as we will discuss in chapter 3, a productive relationship continually works with the difference that is a natural and real part of the relationship. A person with mature commitment loves the other for what the other *is*, not for what I may want the other to be for one's self. This deepening of the attachment relationship is a natural process that, when it takes place, can stabilize the relationship into faithful, unqualified, mutual attachment sentiments: love and fidelity. To be able to love the other as other, not simply as a reflection of the self, is an important step in interpersonal maturity (Shivanadan, 2001). Opinion surveys of married and single respondents place "trustworthy/faithful" as by far the most important trait of a marriage partner over other traits: intelligent, romantic, thoughtful, handsome, pretty, wealthy, and so on. (Bayley, 2003). Since change and growth is essential to being a person, mutual fidelity in a personal context becomes a mutual openness of two selves to the changing and unfolding reality of the other, a reality that never can be known in advance (Grisez, n.d.). Constructing this type of relational openness, authentic delight in what is new with the other, is a lifetime project, that changes with the developmental tasks that emerge. Such constructed and differentiated fidelity to a parent, a spouse, a friend, a sibling continues the protection of attachment through adulthood. It is essential to the architecture of effective relationships. Nevertheless, the human condition is filled with losses, betrayals, inadequate resources, unequal power, and poverty. Through memory these also can have a lasting influence on one's perceptions and patterns. The strengths-based social worker seeks to support a prudent and resilient human response to difficult and inherently insecure conditions.

Reworking Attachments

The process of reworking attachment and commitment is crucial to an understanding of relational tasks working out separateness and connectedness. As we will see in our discussion of the shifts in relations that come with developmental stages, the shifts in relationship, going from one stage to another, are shifts in attachment. These shifts, anticipated, perhaps dreaded, by ego, perhaps avoided by alter create the friction, the light, and the heat of a developmental stage.

CASE STUDY 2.2

Marisa Antonelli, seventeen years old, rocketed herself into pseudo-independence by enmeshing herself into relationships and risky practices with friends. Her parents see that the enmeshed closeness and intimacy they have always had with their only child will change. They feel they have lost her. They react with the watchful, protective behavior, that seemed to work when she was younger. Now their watchfulness becomes extreme. They police her behavior, record her phone messages, and check her purse when she is out. The daughter's response is to continue her risky behavior, now at a further extreme. The resulting cat-and-mouse game takes over the normal processes that work out family relationships when

a member is developing. It prevents family members from dealing with the underlying issues of her steps toward a revised bond with her parents and toward adult relationships and responsibility. The game puts aside their historic commitment to each other. For the relationship to continue in any real sense, commitment will need redefinition.

There is a connection of attachment theory to family development in the process of formation of bonds, discussed in the next chapter. The issues, which have become part of an earlier bonding process, can be re-experienced with formation of a new bond. On the other hand, the new bonding process may allow reworking of some of the attachment issues.

Membership is a type of socialized connectedness. It assumes commitment and a normative context for relationships. In contrast to the notion of individuality, which emphasizes separation, the human condition is one of membership. Membership denotes a continuous interaction with others who are parts of the self "both seen and unseen," that is in current experience and in memory (Falck, 1988, p. 30). Each person's membership spans many normative contexts: family of origin, immediate family, extended family, occupational groups, friendships, neighborhood ties, religion, culture, ethnicity, and so on. (Carlton, 1984). Social workers render professional aid to manage the complexities of membership (Falck, 1988, p. 56). The existence of a member is inconceivable without others; the actions of a member are derived from and contribute to a social bond; the identity of a member is bound up with that of others. An individual's differences lead to separation. A member's differences create tensions that lead to growth, group cohesion, and group conflict. An individual's freedom may be considered the absence of constraint. A member's freedom is not the absence of constraint, but a bond of simultaneous concern for oneself and others (Falck, 1976).

A picture emerges of a systemic dance of change taking place at each different family life-cycle stage. Family structures develop and change as the persons within them develop and change. Structural changes and personal development of family members are keyed to each other. Structural changes and personal changes create tasks for family members at each stage. These tasks are both relational and personal. The social worker intervenes within the family structure and with family members around these tasks. Working between individual members and the particular family unit in formation at any stage of family development, the social worker is a mentor for the accomplishment of these tasks when their accomplishment is at risk. The task concept supplies the connection between two simultaneous processes of change: *between* family members and *within* the family as a structure in its own right.

RELATIONAL TASKS AT FAMILY LIFE-CYCLE STAGES

Among emergent families today, a blend of communication and accepted tradition more and more becomes the key to the development and establishment of relationships. When families are governed by a blend of communication and accepted tradition, members' transactions with each other communicate a type of mutual understanding of expectations. Through this communication they develop relational patterns, lasting structures, and, ultimately, larger relational units. These transactions in family are governed by needs characteristic of a particular stage of the family life cycle. At each stage, different family structures are created to meet these emergent needs. The link between family units and persons is established through relational tasks. Table 2.2 illustrates this connection. The second-order changes in the third column are relational tasks.

Each stage of family development has its own personal and relational tasks. These establish internal and external patterns and prepare for the accomplishment of the next stage. *Relational tasks* have to do with interactive relationships with others that establish interpersonal patterns. These are the more difficult, complex, and uncertain tasks of second-order change shown in table 2.2. They involve the reworking of connectedness and separateness in current relationships with others. Since we also are creatures of our past relationships, as we rework connectedness and separateness in present important relationships, we are also reworking attachment—thus the connection between attachment and relational tasks. However, the relational architecture of every stage may be different in response to the needs and narratives of family members and the external environment. These tasks are similar to personal developmental tasks, except that they range through adult development. They are constructed with others in the family unit. They aim at the development of family structure through different phases according to the needs of its members. Relational tasks are carried out by a couple or larger family in order to cope with what is necessary for the development of a workable family structure at a particular stage of development and in relation to a particular set of circumstances.

Personal Tasks

Personal tasks have to do with what each person does within himself or herself to "get ready" for the task ahead or to respond to the implicit expectations of the family life-cycle stage. Personal tasks come from an internal conversation in relation to our perception of the outside relational world of persons, of units of belonging, of institutions, of expectations, and of potential resources. Our memories of significant relationships, our anticipation of the future, and our present interaction with the other(s) is linked with an internal conversation with the "I" and the "me," the self and its parts. Through this conversation of the "I" with the "me," the person can delay responses, attempt to see himself or herself from the perspective of the other, review the past, and envision the future. Because of these capacities, the creative acting self or "I" can make choices between alternatives and direct thinking

Table 2.2
Stages of the Family Life Cycle

Family Life Cycle Stage	Emotional Process of Transition: Key Principles	Second-Order Changes in Family Status Required to Proceed Developmentally
Leaving home: single young adults	Accepting emotional and financial responsibility for self	a. Differentiation of self in relation to family of origin b. Development of intimate peer relationships c. Establishment of self in respect to work ans financial independence
The joining of families through marriage: the new couple	Commitment to new system	a. Formation of marital system b. Realignment of relationships with extended families and friends to include spouse
Families with young children	Accepting new members into the system	a. Adjusting marital system to make space for children b. Joining in child rearing, financial and household tasks c. Realignment of relationships with extended family to include parenting and grand-parenting roles
Families with adolescents	Increasing flexibility of family boundaries to permit children's independence and grandparent's frailties	a. Shifting of parent/child relationships to permit adolescent to move into and out of system b. Refocus on midlife marital and career issues c. Beginning shift toward caring for older generation
Launching children and moving on	Accepting a multitude of exits from and entries into the family system	a. Renegotiation of marital system as a dyad b. Development of adult-to-adult relationships between grown children and their parents c. Realignment of relationships to include in-laws and grandchildren d. Dealing with disabilities and death of parents (grandparents)
Families in later life	Accepting the shifting generational roles	a. Maintaining own and/or couple functioning and interests in face of physiological decline: exploration of new familial and social role options b. Support for more central role of middle generation c. Making room in the system for the wisdom and experience of the elderly, supporting the older generation without overfunctioning for them d. Dealing with loss of spouse, siblings, and other peers and preparation for death

SOURCE: Carter & McGoldrick, 1999. Used with permission.

and behavior accordingly (Shibutani, 1961; Schwartz, 1995). Persons are often similar to discordant families. Parts of us may believe we can or should do something; other parts may take a different tack (Schwartz, 1995). The leadership part, the "I," can mediate between these parts and join with others on the outside for support. The person may in fact not believe that he or she is able to do all this. A person who is overwhelmed by sadness, fear, anger, or obsessions, such as Gloria (see case study 2.1), clearly does not believe it is possible. Gloria's reflective understanding of herself, however, strengthened certain other capacities. She gradually began to be able to deal with her obsessions.

Each person who develops a relationship with another that may eventuate in the development of a new relational structure, such as a new family or a new structure in an already-existing family, is beginning a series of relational tasks with another. Since understandings and patterns need to be established jointly, the process depends on that other person as much as on the self. As such, the relational tasks of the couple forming themselves, and later the couple plus children can be accomplished only interpersonally. Because of this, these tasks take time and it is uncertain that they will be accomplished.

CASE STUDY 2.3

Sarah and Phil have been married for fifteen years. Sarah's recent severe back ailment demanded that she and Phil rearrange household tasks and the jobs of ferrying two adolescents and two preteens from one activity to another. In addition, Sarah is showing early signs of the reccurring depression with which she has struggled since adolescence. It was only with the onset of Sarah's back trouble that both realized that they had taken much for granted from previous experience. They had assumed that the house should always be kept as immaculately as Phil, who grew up as an only child surrounded by helpful aunts and uncles, had experienced. They had assumed that their children had a natural right to be taxied any place where they had an activity, regardless of the difficulty involved. Their children had assumed the same. If they were going to develop their own patterns and adapt expectations to the realities of their resources of energy and time, they needed to communicate with other members of the family and work out the resulting issues with each other. They needed to ask their children to help, and with the children's participation, to work out priorities for transportation as part of an exchange. They had no language of meanings or communication patterns to accomplish this. It took a good deal of work for family members to find words and a language to use with each other for these unfamiliar transactions. In the process of developing a common pattern, there was a concrete shift in power from "the way Phil's family did it" to "the way we want to do it, given our needs and circumstances." They needed to develop their own pattern over time, rather than adopt Phil's family patterns without further discussion.

Family Resilience

Research confirms the implications of this case study: that interactional processes, such as cohesion, flexibility, open communication, and problem-solving skills, are essential in facilitating basic family functioning and the well-being of members (Walsh, 1996, 1999). It took fifteen years and a back ailment for Sarah and Phil to discover the imbalances in their relationship and to begin to work things out with each other. The problem is that the importance of cohesion, flexibility, communication, and problem solving may suggest that there is only one way for a family to be resilient. Celia Falicov (1995) suggests that resilience is a matter of internal fit of members with each other, rather than a model for all families. Froma Walsh, reviewing this research (1996), suggests that there are many pathways to relational resilience and these vary to fit diverse family forms, psychosocial challenges, resources, and constraints. Shared beliefs and narratives that foster a sense of coherence, collaboration, competence, and confidence are vital in coping and mastery. There is a balance established at each family developmental stage, shifting between stressful events that heighten vulnerability and protective processes that enhance resilience, as well as a balance in the relative influence of family, peers, and other social forces (Walsh, 2003, p. 4). Table 1.3 in the previous chapter illustrates the personal and family resources that resilient families call upon at every life-cycle stage to cope with stressful events. Harry Aponte (1994) makes the point that, in poor communities, where often families lack institutional or societal support, and deal with racism, poverty, dangerous, and dehumanizing conditions, resilience is a matter of spirit. It is a question of building a sense of dignity, purpose, and future in families that have surrendered hope, meaning, and self-worth to despair. Optimism and hope become core elements in resilience. Families also however, require a responsive society and community to improve their conditions and prospects.

STAGES OF FAMILY DEVELOPMENT

An overall picture of the stages of family development emerges from a consideration of adult developmental tasks taken in a relational sense. The demands of developmental change unfold different stages where the family unit may optimally evolve a secure base for what is emerging. Each stage denotes a shift to the construction of a new relational structure—thus there is always difficulty translating an earlier stage to a later one. Family members don't have a clear picture of what new structure is emerging. All of the patterns used to manage the earlier stage, even if successful, will seem obsolete in relation to the new stage. The new stage will at least demand some accomplishment of the earlier one, however. In any case, the tasks of the earlier stage are experienced again in relation to the newer stage. From the point of view of an individual, and later a couple, the possible stages in the life of one couple involve relational processes of:

- Differentiating and reengaging with the family of origin
- Planning for marriage and getting married
- Developing a family system that accommodates children
- Developing a family system that accommodates adolescents; dealing with the needs of aarents growing older
- Developing a family system that allows young adults to leave and reengage; accommodating themselves to a gradually emptying nest
- Reengaging as a couple with each other, with adult children and their partners and with grandchildren; dealing with losses and illness.

A stage is created by family members in particular contexts of cultural meanings. These stages are not necessarily linear. Not every person or family unit goes through all of these, not in the same way and not with the same cultural meanings. Not everyone differentiates and reengages with family of origin in the same way. Not everyone gets married, and there are very different meanings for marriage experienced by family members. Not everyone raises adolescents or takes care of the elderly, and not in the same way. What is common to all persons are the issues of attachment, differentiation, and creation of a secure base for development. The following case studies illustrate some of the ways development is accommodated. Chapter 8 describes the helping process with a few of the many variations on this theme: families going through divorce, single parents, and blended families, each reconstructing relationships in their own way and in relation to concrete circumstances.

Each stage of family development involves development of new relational architecture. A new relational unit must emerge, but it can emerge only through the communication and interaction of the people involved in the new relational unit. At each stage, the attachment patterns, deep in each person's beginnings and later growth, are revisited, then related to the other person's changing physical and relational attachment patterns. In some ways, this co-construction of attachment patterns into a new unit can provide a wonderful opportunity to revise these patterns. To do this, the relationship developed needs to be able to transcend these patterns in a real way. As with the challenge Sarah and Phil faced in adapting to their own realities, these can be difficult moments. Perhaps this is one reason traditional religions do not consider marriage to be an arrangement subject to continuous negotiation. Many religions enshrine commitment and fidelity in a sacrament. The sacrament, an entirely different arrangement from a purely negotiable agreement, transcends certain individual considerations. Paradoxically, it may be easier to work out particular differences and functional patterns within the security of a relationship, that is already well-defined, committed, respectful, and personal—one that is already a secure base to develop further on the inside and to explore the world.

Relational Architecture: Transitions to Personal Communication

Families do not necessarily spend a great deal of time working out these relational arrangements. Sarah and Phil, a reasonably flexible, independent, and well-educated middle-class couple, found that there were many arrangements in their marriage that they hadn't discussed with each other or with their children. Although they had been married for fifteen years, they hadn't developed the language or the communication patterns to do so. Many families are not so much based on friendship, communication, or role flexibility as on tradition. As cultures shift at a glacial pace from fixed-role expectations to negotiated understandings and companionship, a combination of patterns often develops. Some understandings remain externally fixed by culture; some are worked out within the family. Elizabeth Bott (1971), in her study of East London working-class families, found the husband-wife relationship to be not particularly close or important. Husbands had their own friends and family of origin. Wives had theirs. The relationship, guided by some traditional beliefs, was almost taken for granted. It was not as *personal* as might be expected by the modern, individualistic, middle-class mentality. Such an arrangement continues in a variety of cultures, particularly among working-class families. The arrangement can be quite stable as long as the surrounding kinship and friendship support systems are available to uphold the relational arrangement, now taken for granted, and the spousal system is not challenged. When it is challenged, the structure needs to shift to accommodate the challenge (Minuchin, 1974). If the unit is to survive the challenge, a more balanced structure, based on friendship and communication, needs to be developed. The following case study illustrates the development of a more balanced structure. Miguel and Juana, born in Mexico and living in a modern North American metropolis, are gradually moving from traditional understandings of family to a more relational one.

CASE STUDY 2.4

Miguel and Juana have been married twelve years. Miguel, a construction worker, works hard in his father's business. When he is with his friends, he drinks fairly heavily. His mother runs much of his life and advises him on how to deal with Juana. He is often out with his friends. He gives his paycheck to Juana and leaves the child rearing to her. Juana is in control at home. Miguel frequently lies to Juana. When it becomes obvious, he simply smiles and admits he lied. What else could any man do? He takes it for granted that Juana will forgive him, and she usually does. He assumes that giving her the check and his support when she requests it should be enough. Juana, a skilled technician whose parents are still in Mexico, feels isolated. She is alienated from her mother-in-law, whom she sees as hostile to her. She feels Miguel allows his mother to direct their marriage. She is concerned with Miguel's drinking, which is getting out of control. Most recently their son, Jorge, eleven year old, has been challenging her with impunity. From her perspective, Jorge challenges her and disregards her in the same way that Miguel challenges and disregards her. Miguel seems to be supporting Jorge.

Their insurance program had limited them to seven sessions of marital counseling at the company's expense. After that, they would have to pay the costs of marital counseling. From Miguel's initial perspective, married relationships were parallel relationships. He would have his role and Juana hers. Juana disagrees, partly because the relationship is unbalanced with her bearing the brunt of their problems. However, she saw few other possibilities. Juana and Miguel did work together to develop communication both could trust, to help Miguel start to do something about his drinking, to sort out issues around Miguel's mother, and to develop a common strategy around Jorge. In the beginning, Miguel didn't take Juana's determination to see change seriously. When she held her ground, he responded. They worked fairly quickly over several months and seven sessions, and did make some progress on all of these issues. Miguel took more responsibility for Jorge, but only after discussing it with Juana. He now has a program to deal with his drinking and a sponsor. Juana began to trust Miguel more, as it became more important to Miguel to be trustworthy. Miguel set some boundaries on his mother's involvement in their marriage, and Juana worked on developing a better relationship with her mother-in-law. As long as they could see the relational issues as tasks, they were willing to do them and enjoyed the process. They were pleased by the changes they experienced in their family. The development of a common pattern meant that Miguel had to be involved. He couldn't privilege himself in the relationship. Their relationship was slowly growing and a new balance was emerging between them. The balance of their relationship, however, was never their major concern. For the most part, they preferred to see their work as tasks that they had completed successfully within the seven sessions allotted by the insurance company. They did recognize that they had made changes for the better.

A Well-Differentiated Family

James Framo has developed Bowen's concept of self-differentiation and connectedness into principles of healthy family functioning. Few families could meet these criteria. Indeed, most marriages are like Sarah and Phil's: somewhere in process, moving toward achieving these standards in the continuing drama of family life. Framo distills from common experience what family development can aim for. The value of his criteria is that they are useful to understand what goals can be set. Families who arrive at these goals in their daily living would easily be at the upper quartile of self-differentiation/connectedness:

1. Parents, each be well-differentiated, having developed a sense of self before separating from family of origin
2. Generational boundaries within the family cleary separated; the children are free of the role of saving the parent or the parental marriage
3. Perceptions and expectations by parents of each other and of their children
4. Loyalty to the family of procreation is greater than to the family of origin

5. The spouses put themselves and each other before anyone else, including the children; the marriage, however, is not a symbiotic one that excludes the children; the children do not feel that to be close to one parent they are alienating the other
6. Identity development and autonomy for all family members is encouraged; successful development in the children will mean that they will leave home at some point to start families of their own
7. Nonpossessive warmth and affection is expressed between parents, between parents and children, and among the siblings
8. The capacity to have open, honest, and clear communication and to deal with issues with each other is evident
9. There is a realistic, adult-to-adult caring relationship between each parent and his or her parents and siblings
10. An open family in the sense of involvement with others outside the family, including extended family and friends. Outsiders are allowed inside the family (adapted from Framo, 1981, pp. 139–140).

Framo developed a similar picture of a healthy marital relationship, only achieved through the normal developmental challenges over a number of years. After fifteen years, Phil and Sarah are working on all of these.

1. The partners are more personally differentiated, and dependency on each other is voluntary
2. They have come to terms with the roots of their irrational expectations of marriage and of the spouse derived from the family of origin
3. They have developed a more empathic understanding of their mate
4. They can meet each other's realistic needs in the face of their differentness
5. They can communicate more clearly and openly
6. They like each other more and they enjoy sex with each other
7. They have learned to deal with the issues between them
8. They can enjoy life more and get pleasure from their work and their children
9. They have developed flexibility in dealing with situational stresses and crises
10. They have adjusted to the disenchantment of romantic love and have more realistic appraisals of the vicissitudes of mature de-idealized love (Framo, 1981, pp. 139–149)

Personal Components of Process and Structure

Miguel and Juana saw their work as solving problems and carrying out tasks. It was only at the end that they began to see some of the relational changes, that had taken place in this process. Phil and Sarah did not consciously set out to change their relationship as they wanted it to be. The changes became necessary when Sarah's back went out. There is opportunity at each stage of family development for the emergent family to define together the personal components of structure. These are autonomy and independence, vulnerability and obligation, and gender relations. The underlying issues are attachment and bonding, connectedness and separateness, and the light and heat that is generated as these get redefined and bonds need to be elaborated or to shift. This always takes place in the context of broader societal meanings and the social institutions that reinforce them. What gets defined then is not simply structure, but the values and norms that will govern relationships. Once they are defined, can they be taken for granted? Social institutions, such as religion, law and justice, education, and health care systems, will reinforce the emergent structure or possibly create challenges. Each stage carries with it a certain risk that it will be accomplished badly, or not accomplished at all, or that family members will need assistance in its accomplishment. These risks increase when previous stages have not been accomplished well, when a family structure is rigid and unwilling to accommodate change, or when previous generations have had difficulty with a particular stage.

In addition, circumstances such as losses through death or divorce, a stepfamily, premature parenthood, an affair, mental illness, addictions, the birth of a child with a disability—all of these create risks and potential crises. There is often a need for social work intervention with the family on the relational structure. The goal would be that the stuck relational tasks be accomplished in a way that accommodates every member's developmental needs and facilitates family functioning.

We now briefly examine the two earliest stages of family formation, the young person's differentiation and reengagement with the family of origin, and the related processes of two people planning for marriage and getting married. As we move through the book, we will use as examples case studies of different families transacting at different life stages, and of social workers assisting them in beginning and mid-stage relational work related to these stages.

DIFFERENTIATION FROM AND REENGAGEMENT WITH THE FAMILY OF ORIGIN

The first stage of family development we consider is differentiation from and reengagement with the family of origin on the part of young people in their twenties. The personal task is one of getting ready to revise the previous parent-child relationship in the direction of independence and greater self responsibility. In some ways, this task of getting ready is the obsession of adolescence, rarely fully realized since the adolescent is usually not in any position to take effective care of himself or herself. Indeed, there is often a prolongation of adolescence in various ways until the young person is ready to complete an education and establish himself or herself occupationally, financially, and in some countries through separate living arrangements. Interpersonal tasks at this stage are:

- Differentiating oneself in relation to family of origin
- Completing an education

- Establishing oneself occupationally
- Establishing oneself financially
- Developing close peer relationships
- Reengaging with family of origin with a different level of dependence/independence

In some societies, for many persons an often symbolic part of this personal and relational process is the concrete moving out of the home. In any case, for many young people, who may lack alternative housing arrangements, this stage can also be accomplished at home, with the family respecting the new boundary that develops and relying on the young person in a different way. If the process is not accomplished, the move into the next stage is much more difficult, since the previous relational tasks are now involved and implicit in another more complex set of personal and relational tasks.

Family-of-Origin Work

Family of origin work can be done at every stage of development, but it is at periods of sharp developmental transition that the work takes on paramount importance. This is particularly true at the stage of early adulthood and formation of a new family, or at a stage of loss of a family member. During "normal" times, James Framo routinely prescribes this work for couples experiencing marital problems. According to Framo (1981), when there is a focus on past and present issues in the family of origin, often the marital problems recede in importance. These are replaced by the dawning realization that maybe something can be done about that long-standing guilt over closeness or alienation from a mother, father, or sibling. Working out a better relationship with the family of origin frequently becomes a goal in its own right.

Getting Married

The next possible stage for some would be that of planning for marriage and getting married. After the previous stage of differentiation from and reengagement with family of origin, there may be a number of years before the person may decide that he or she is ready to form a more permanent couple bond with another, which would lead to a family. Prior to marriage, many of the personal tasks (getting ready to . . .) are contained within the relational tasks of preparing for marriage as they understand it. It is a shift from an appropriate self-orientation characteristic of the previous stage to a level of mutuality with appropriate boundaries. An example of this would be making oneself ready to take over the role of husband or wife (first as each conceives it, then as they gradually work it out together). The outlines of what the institution and the role is may still be vague at this time. The relational tasks are:

- Disengaging (or altering the form of engagement of) oneself from especially close relationships that compete or interfere with commitment to the new marital relationships

- Accommodating patterns of gratifications of premarital life to patterns of the newly formed couple (marital) relationship
- Establishing a couple identity
- Establishing a mutually workable and satisfactory system of communication between the pair
- Developing mutually workable and satisfactory patterns of decision-making
- Establishing a mutually workable and satisfactory pattern with regard to relatives
- Establishing a mutually workable and satisfactory pattern with regard to friends
- Developing a mutually workable and satisfactory pattern with regard to employment
- Developing a mutually satisfactory set of expectations of marriage and children
- Developing mutually satisfactory pattern and sets of expectations regarding religious practice, ethical values of each, and education of children
- Planning specifically for the wedding, honeymoon, and the early months of marriage that lie ahead (Rapaport, 1963).

These tasks continue into later stages. For Miguel and Juana at a later stage these tasks were implicit in Juana's desire to establish their own couple unit with its own patterns separate from Miguel's mother's expectations, and Miguel's mild resistance to this.

This is complicated and difficult work. Expectations of each member are often different. Real communication about differences may not take place. When one realizes these differences, there is often a jarring personal crisis. The change process often goes slowly. The "I," who may want this relationship, converses with the "me" of one's set patterns. Different parts of the self may take different positions. For this new relationship with a new person, previous patterns will not suffice, even (especially) if one has had a previous relationship with another. Each person is different. No one person can substitute for another. The process proceeds unevenly as both future partners struggle to communicate their expectations and needs and adapt to the other's. At the same time, there is a process of disengagement and reengagement with other meaningful relationships in one's life situation. In Western society, the closeness, even negative closeness, of relations with family of origin has to change to accommodate the relationship of the emergent couple. These patterns remain at least partially unresolved and carried into marriage. It can easily take half a decade to "get married." Miguel and Juana had been married for twelve years; Phil and Sarah for fifteen. Some couples may never alter their previous personal patterns and accommodate each other's sufficiently to do this.

DOES LOVE CONQUER ALL?

In Western European cultures and increasingly throughout a modernizing world, the process of developing a relationship leading to marriage is made much more complex by distorted societal beliefs about romantic love and marriage. Couples' counselors often see people who fall in love believing that love alone will keep them together and that nothing else matters (Bayley, 2003). In contrast to the romantic search for one's self, one's desires, and one's preoccupations with the other, love and fidelity imply a realistic discovery of the other *as other*. This discovery is a process that will gradually unfold over a lifetime of mutual commitment. Couples quickly discover that their real experiences of working out their relationships do not match their beliefs. They may feel disappointed and think that there is something "wrong with us." Romantic beliefs say they should be soulmates. If this is not quickly accomplished, it becomes a sign that they are not really in love, and so on. Let us examine some clusters of popular marriage myths:

- I am in love, and that is enough. Don't bother me with the details. It is not important to learn to communicate, solve problems, and understand differences. If you are really in love, it is enough.
- If we have conflict, if you or I get angry, we must not be in love. If you don't know what I am thinking, you must not understand or really love me.
- If marriage is to succeed, it must meet all my needs. There is a "right person" someplace out there who will do that.

These deny the everyday, hard work of developing and maintaining a good relationship in favor of a type of culturally acceptable narcissism attached to love beliefs. As couples test these myths and their expectations against the realities of their relationship, they often need professional help sorting them out and discerning their real relationship with each other as concrete persons. They often have very little frame of reference for this discovery, thus the need for a guided professional experience.

The following case study illustrates the process of sorting out the myth from the reality.

CASE STUDY 2.5

Brian and Lisa are an engaged couple in their late twenties. Brian is an only child. He has close relations with his parents, an older couple who dote on him. He is just beginning to establish himself in advertising, a high-pressure competitive occupation. His patterns are of hard work and all-night partying. He enjoys many close male friends and enjoys them tremendously. He binge drinks with his friends with weeks of abstinence in between. Before he met Lisa, he had a close relationship with Bonnie, which never gelled. Brian returns to this relationship when he is feeling sad. Lisa is the oldest of six children, accustomed to taking responsibility, and accustomed to being in control. She is a lawyer, just beginning in her profession but quite unhappy with her current job in the district attorney's office. When Brian and Lisa announced their engagement, no one would take Brian seriously. Even Lisa had her nagging doubts about his seriousness. Lisa dealt with this by managing all the small details of planning for the wedding, and Brian was happy to let her do it her way. Brian and Lisa wanted marriage. Each felt the other met their requirements for a spouse, but they kept getting surprised by characteristics of the other they hadn't anticipated. It was a learning process, but they wondered about it as they got closer to marriage. Brian liked Lisa's clear ideas of what she wanted and her sense of control. This was very different from his other flames. Parts of Brian felt ready to marry. However, he also found himself reacting to her set ideas and going back to one of his old friends for relief. His drinking continued off and on. He might take a weekend with his friends, or talk things over with Bonnie. For her part, every time Lisa felt everything was settled, Brian would unsettle things with something she didn't anticipate. Lisa remembered her father, who was a lot of fun, never predictable, but also had had a drinking problem. She was terrified that these patterns she knew so well would repeat themselves. They broke off their engagement several times before coming to counseling. During sessions, Brian agreed to stop drinking altogether, and did. He was tired of his lifestyle and didn't want to lose Lisa.

The social worker helped both to communicate better and develop plans mutually. They had to make an assessment on the basis of their real communication as to whether they wanted to continue the relationship toward greater commitment. Brian had to let go of Bonnie if Lisa was to feel a sense of trust in his commitment and the relationship. Lisa had to back down from making decisions, even petty ones, for Brian. Brian needed to become more active in the relationship. Both needed to change and support the other's changes. They found some mutual friends both could enjoy without the pressure on Brian to drink. As they began to communicate around plans for the wedding, some of the different patterns that had ruled their families of origin came out. Both needed to form a third pattern together, and in the process of doing that, revise some of their previous patterns and relationships. Both had to work out their own friendship with each other and at the same time new relationships with parents, and in Lisa's case, with her siblings as well.

Brian and Lisa are essentially establishing a new set of patterns to govern their future common relationship. It is a type of dance with each other where simultaneously they establish their own pattern and work out different patterns with families of origin and with friends. These are very important for many reasons, not the least of which is that Brian and Lisa need the concrete support of family and friends to establish this new relationship. Things also could go badly on the inside of the relationship. Brian and Lisa could develop extremely distorted communication patterns. Brian might be unable to manage his binge drinking. Lisa could go into a serious depression. They might not be able, or it might not be advisable, to move to the next stage of their relationship: a deeper, exclusive, and more permanent commitment. On the other hand, external factors, such as war, unemployment, death of a parent, or pregnancy could change the process also, delaying it or speeding it up. These could place so much pressure on the couple that they would be unable to continue their plans.

There are several ways to examine Brian and Lisa's worlds. First of all, their interaction is not linear or mechanical. Rather it is recursive and it needs to be seen from the systems perspective. Second, the normal relational work they do, accommodating two worlds in one, will have to go slowly. There will be plenty of fits and starts, even for this relatively well-adjusted couple. This is because the work has to proceed on two levels—personally and systemically. The process continues whether the social worker is working with the family or not. In the authors' experience, often a couple or family will break off contact after one or two sessions, only to reappear months or years later, continuing to work (sometimes quite successfully) on the tasks and concerns identified in the first contact. In this chapter we look at personal work in a relational context. In the next we will examine the architecture of family relationships—structure.

THE SYSTEMS PERSPECTIVE APPLIED TO PERSONS IN FAMILIES

The systems perspective for understanding process and structure has proven itself to be a rich and powerful tool for understanding process and structure and thus for understanding family interaction. The use of the systems perspective, particularly in the family area, has led to the evolution and use of common definitions, that have theoretical implications (Walsh, 1982, 1993). Fundamental principles of systems functioning are:

1. *Circular Process* This term defines the underlying recursive organization of all family systems. In any system, change in any one member affects other members and the group as a whole; this in turn affects the first individual in a circular chain of influence. Every action in this sequence is also a reaction. Causality is fundamentally circular rather than linear (Everett, Russell & Keller, 1992).

2. *Communication* Communication refers to behavior, both verbal and nonverbal, by which people share meaning with each other (Bateson, 1936). Every communication has two functions: a "content" (report) aspect, conveying factual information, opinions, or feelings, and a "relationship" command aspect, which, in conveying how the information is to be taken, defines the nature of the relationship (Watzlawick, Beavin & Jackson, 1967).

3. *Homeostasis* Systems maintain dynamic balances among themselves. All systems members contribute to the balance through mutually reinforcing feedback. When there is too much deviation from the system's norm, the negative feedback process regulates tension and attempts to restore a family equilibrium (Walsh, 1982). An example: if the environment is changed (e.g., via an effective therapist) the family's stable (homeostatic) functioning will be necessarily disrupted (Everett, Russell & Keller, 1992; Dell, 1982).

4. *Family Rules* Family rules are shared norms and values and mutual agreements that define relationships (Everett, Russell & Keller, 1992). Rules are necessarily limited so that the family system is patterned and predictable to

its members. These rules, both implicit and explicit, organize system interaction and function to maintain stability. They provide expectations about roles, actions, and consequences that guide the life of a system and its interaction (Walsh, 1982).

5. *Equifinality* Living systems differ from mechanical systems and are governed by a certain "biology of purpose" (Sinnott, 1961). No matter how the seed is planted, one part of the plant grows toward the sun; the other sends roots to the soil. Similar outcomes may result from different initial conditions (Von Bertalanffy, 1974; Everett, Russell & Keller, 1992). Two-well functioning family systems may have come from different initial conditions, or the same origin may lead to different outcomes. One family system may disintegrate, the other come together in response to a similar stressor. The system's ongoing interactional patterns and responses to stress make the difference (Walsh, 1982).

6. *Nonsummativity* The system as a whole is greater than the sum of its parts. It cannot be described simply by summing up characteristics of individual members. The system's organization and interaction involves interlocking patterns of behavior of its members and the patterns connect the members with each other (Walsh, 1982).

All of these concepts of social interaction: circular process, nonsummativity, equifinality, and so on, apply to Brian and Lisa's relationship. The dynamic content of the relationship, the direction the relationship could best be heading if it is to develop and grow, can be explained by personal and relational tasks. The tasks with which Brian and Lisa are dealing will become very familiar, since they repeat themselves in different ways at every stage of family development. In some ways these tasks are typical to the stage of getting ready for marriage. In other ways, it may seem as if they are doing similar tasks but in a different way, as they prepare for and accommodate children, adolescents, as the children mature and develop their own relationships, and as Brian and Lisa become an empty-nest couple.

In addition to the normal stresses and uncertainties of developmental shifts, there were other stresses in Brian's and Lisa's relationship. These add some personal tasks for each. Brian had an alcohol problem with which he had to deal. Lisa's own history would make this a particularly difficult area for her. She also had a need for a very ordered world controlled by her, and she had to allow Brian some control. These personal tasks would make the relational shifts more risky and difficult. Brian would have to take responsibility for his binge-drinking problem. It would be almost impossible for them to form a real relationship if Brian remains "engaged" to alcohol. Lisa could complicate the situation by her own anxiety and need to control the problem, rather than insisting that this was Brian's domain but she expected change if they were to build their dreams together. She needs to deal with her own anxiety and need for control of things, that can't be controlled the way she wants. Together they also need to sort out some of these issues before they move on. They also need to make their relationship secure, developing trust and fidelity. Working on these additional stresses becomes part of the relational work.

LANGUAGE AND COMMUNICATION: THE NEWLY MARRIED COUPLE

The issues that Brian and Lisa had to face before marriage become even more important in the first years following marriage. They now must develop a real and workable relationship and an understanding of each other, including ways of resolving normal differences. They must develop the common patterns that balance their relationship. They must truly make a permanent commitment to each other as "other," that is, as not self, not a reflection of one's desires and experiences, not as the "heavenly twins," but as real human beings. There is an other who is different, has needs and can contribute something to the relationship. In the beginning, the young couple, full of romantic feelings, marry their desires and illusions, and in this respect marry themselves. Depending on their experience and maturity, they may often be disappointed when their partner is not their expected image. Only later may they discover and hopefully begin to appreciate the "otherness" of their partner. They can then make the discovery and a commitment to the other as "other," and then to the "we" that eventually emerges (Hargrave, 2000). The process takes time. In some cases it never takes place.

Language and communication are the key vehicles for developing the common patterns necessary for sharing a common life and a "we" relationship. This is true at every stage, but it is particularly important at the beginning. To carry out relational tasks, the couple needs to develop a relational language of meanings and to communicate with each other. For reasons having to do with socialization, family experience, and cultural meanings, this is difficult for men and women in a society dominated by competition, work, and a globalized economy, but where paradoxically the demands for relational closeness have never been higher. These tasks are particularly difficult for men, whose goals and life patterns may be often geared to achievement, competition, and the work world and to denial of feelings,. Each person's experience, language, meanings, and communication skills are profoundly shaped by his or her experience in the family of origin. Without language and communication, it may feel as if one has married a stranger. Intimacy may feel like exploitation. For the beginning social worker working with the newly married couple, development of language, meanings and communication skills becomes the pathway eventually to assist couples at any family life-cycle stage to construct and reconstruct a relationship. Social worker Virginia Satir (1988), in her powerful discussions insisted that language and communication, are the chief tools of relational change. When the couple learns to use these tools well, the effect is profound. Good communication acts as a catalyst for rapid change. On the other hand, the expectation of honest communication in a helping relationship, when unfulfilled, can also lead to a degeneration of the relationship. When one or other partner is dishonest, the expectation of honest communication and its disappointment can shut down the relationship and can be a catalyst for rapid emotional divorce.

Communication is at best difficult. It is a learned skill, socially constructed as part of a relationship. Rather than really communicate, people often just talk to themselves in the presence of the other. Sometimes it takes a crisis to begin to have genuine communication. When communication takes place at all between two people, it always consists of two processes: an expression of thought and feeling by an initiator and a reflective response to the expression by a receiver. Then the process reverses, with an expression by the receiver and a reflective response by the initiator, until the issue reaches some resolution. In everyday discussion, the process often gets sidetracked for several reasons. First, the expressor may not have the language to be able to say what he or she is thinking and/or feeling. Second, the expressor may not fully intend to communicate. The expression becomes a smokescreen or it is a self-justifying expression for him or herself rather than a genuine attempt at communication with the other. Receiving communication is even more difficult than expressing because it involves careful listening to the other and an ability to respond without one's own feelings and preconceptions getting in the way. It involves an empathic ability to take the position of the other, to take some of the other's language, and then to respond to the other in that language. Most conversations go much too quickly for anything to get accomplished. The expression or the language may come too fast for the receiver to absorb. The receiver may be preparing a response to what he or she thinks the initiator is saying, rather than listening. There may be too much emotion, too great a merger of thoughts and feelings, even too much noise from the outside for any genuine communication. "Noise from the outside" can take many forms—actual noise (such as traffic), but also interruptions (children, telephone) and even general societal pressure ("I know my father wants me to do well at this, I'd better. . .).

There has been a considerable amount of work in the areas of language, expression, response, and the use of real communication to develop a relationship. In the area of language, persons who have experienced post traumatic stress or sexual abuse, who are dealing with cancer, or who come from families where language was hardly used except for control, often have great difficulty finding language to express feelings and thoughts. This blockage can block the relationship in the area affected. Kathy Weingarten (2000), Peggy Penn (2001), and others from the Ackerman Institute for the Family have done a good deal of work in this area. It is becoming recognized that people struggling with the suffering of end-stage cancer, for example, need to find different voices and languages to reflect their feelings and thoughts accurately. In the beginning, they may have no language to speak about personal suffering. What makes the suffering even more painful is that the perceived injustice of it takes over all other considerations. It is just as difficult for the helper to respond to a person speaking about suffering. At best, the initial response may simply be silence rather than empty words. The helper also must find a voice and a language to help the suffering person to express and reflect. There is a growth process on the part of the helper that parallels that of the suffering person (Reich, 1989). This is a process that every social worker needs to experience if he or she is to be effective with situations where language cannot be found to express thoughts. Empathy, put to words, demands reflective, meditative habits, but the rewards of this process go far beyond words.

Developing Language and Communication

Bernard Guerney (1977; 1982) has developed a process he calls "Relationship Enhancement" over almost fifty years. This is a controlled process of expressing and empathic responding that can be taught to couples. It can be quite helpful. An initiator starts the conversation by some positive reflection on what they will be discussing. He or she then moves to "I" messages (Gordon, 1970) that describe in a non-accusatory way the impact of something to do with the other person on him or her. The "you" message, which focuses on an accusation of the other (you do . . .), rarely works. The receiver and responder needs to suspend his or her own reactions to what is being said and focus intensely on understanding the thoughts, wishes, desires, intentions, motives and inner emotional experience (be it fear, sadness, joy, anger, irritation, or any other emotion) of the speaker. The responder in some ways "becomes" the other and conveys this deep understanding to the speaker. He or she reserves one's personal responses, thoughts, and feelings until it is his or her turn to become the speaker and receive the gift of this same deep empathy from the other (Santana-Grace, 2002). When this communication emerges, the effect is relaxation on the part of both and often a reframing of the whole context for discussion. Sometimes, when one or the other has difficulty expressing or responding, the social worker—with permission—takes the role of the speaker or responder, "becomes" the person, expresses or responds for that person, and checks to see whether the person agrees or disagrees with the expression. If the "becoming" is accurate, the person agrees with the social worker's expression, and this is usually the case. This process is a powerful tool for deepening and teaching empathic accuracy (Snyder, 1995). The response to this expression by the other moves the process along and avoids possible impasses.

The following case study illustrates this process.

CASE STUDY 2.6

Jim and Cheryl, both twenty-one years old, had been married for five months. Already they were having severe arguments with verbal abuse and the eventual possibility of physical abuse. Jim has a physically and verbally abusive mother, and was protected from

her only by his relationship with his father. Cheryl, together with her older sisters, constantly experienced physical and verbal abuse from both father and mother until she left home to marry. In their conversation, Jim tended to ignore Cheryl. Cheryl had great difficulty finding language to express herself and tended to get into circular discussions with herself where she saw herself inevitably at fault, expected to be "wrong," but also angry about it. She said directly and in many different ways, "I'm not good enough." Jim had difficulty penetrating this conviction. Her posture was hunched forward, almost to deflect a blow, while Jim looked sideways at her, never directly. Neither could connect with each other, and this was frustrating to both. The social worker began the session by asking them to talk to each other about what they felt needed changing in their relationship and what they felt they could change. The person who would initiate, the "speaker," has a floor tile, "the floor," while the other reflected the speaker. Jim initiated the conversation. The social worker needed to help him to attend to Cheryl, use "I" messages, and start softly and positively. He shifted to look intently toward Cheryl and talked with her seriously without criticizing her. He needed to help her to find a language to respond to him. She was taking whatever he said as criticism. With the social worker's

help, he challenged what she was hearing—that somehow she was not good enough. When Cheryl finally responded accurately (with the worker's help) to Jim, she took "the floor." Jim gradually was able to learn to reflect her expressions. Midway in a two-hour session, Cheryl visibly relaxed. Her posture changed to attend to Jim. She took his hand, and in the discussion she said that after twenty-one years she suddenly realized that things could be different and that she could do something about her relationship. It wasn't hopeless. In fact it looked doable. Their relationship now felt like it could be a "craft project" to her. She had never understood this before and was delighted. The couple would continue on this basis over a number of sessions, building their relationship and doing family-of-origin work. It was a very difficult process. Cheryl began therapy for herself. Very close to divorce in the beginning, they stabilized their marriage and recommended marriage counseling to their friends having difficulty.

Additional Circumstances: Stress and Relational Tasks

Situational Stress   The stress and complexity of family development is often compounded by situational stress. Situational stress can delay or prevent the accomplishment of family developmental tasks. Social workers are often involved with families when there are other things complicating the completion of family life tasks. With Brian and Lisa, it was some of their older family issues and his binge drinking. In other cases, there are losses carried into the present tasks: hospitalizations and illness, issues of abuse, divorce, suicide, imprisonment, and poverty, all of which put a good deal of pressure on these relational tasks.

Loss of a family member is one example of such stress. Loss includes death, particularly suicide or homicide, but also loss through divorce, illness, hospitalization, or separation through war, prison, or search of employment. Family members will struggle to replace the lost functioning and the lost relationship. In some ways, an ambiguous loss, where the person is at times available or could return, may even be more difficult than the finality of death.

Part of this is the problem of change, which itself may feel like a loss. The unanticipated addition of a family member, whether coming home from prison or from war, the blending of stepfamilies, or even a child coming at a difficult time also can create stress and relational tasks for family members. Family members may need to cope with external stresses such as school problems, lack of health care, probation, parole or court supervision, or community conditions. Internal pressures on family members can arise from a mental or physical illness of a member, alcoholism, or internal conflicts between spouses or between parents and children (see Janzon & Harris, 1997). When these stresses and pressures occur, the social worker often works not only with the family but also with a school, a hospital, a court, and/or a child welfare agency to help the family manage these additional stresses and reorganize themselves when necessary. This work is described in greater detail in chapter 9 of this book.

Some deeper stresses are particularly devastating to the ability to communicate in a real sense with the other, to relate with intimacy and trust, or to take reciprocal roles with one another. An affair is destructive to trust and intimacy. In this case, the social worker needs to help the couple through the personal and relational tasks of repairing the damage and restoring trust, intimacy, and a balanced, collaborative relationship. With alcoholism and other addictions, the partner is in some ways "married" to the addiction, and so the partner must divorce the addiction and re-marry the spouse with all of its implications of restoring trust, intimacy and a balanced collaborative relationship. Similarly a spouse who re-emerges from depression or mental illness needs to help develop a restored relationship from the time he or she was "away." The birth of a child with a disability places the couple in a new and unanticipated situation, that may last their whole lives. They have to shift their relationship, balance their care-giving roles and their relations with other children and their familes of origin, and mourn the loss of an expected child. All of these, and other similar circumstances, generate new tasks, that must be attended to if the couple is to survive. They place particular pressure on the couple's bond, and then on others in the family. A good example of this is found in chapter 5 in the story of the social worker working with Rita and Joav Green, who are dealing with the birth of a child with Down's Syndrome.

There are other stresses that are felt by the couple and, almost at the same level and intensity, by everyone in the family. These are issues, that, if they are unresolved, may stop the family in its relational tracks. Death, particularly the unanticipated, early death of a family member, is an example of this. Every family member mourns the lost and unsubstitutable attachments to the person who died, their relationship with that person, and the meanings of that person's life to them. Every family member has to consider the personal and relational meanings of their death. The personal work of mourning is accompanied by a shifting dance in relationships of every member of the family. A suicide is particularly difficult to accommodate in one's personal world and the relational world of a family. Divorce also brings about personal tasks of mourning and continuing relational shifts of every family member. The formation of a stepfamily is another example of relational shifts, that are superimposed on the loss of a member. Often the stepfamily gets stuck between incomplete mourning for the lost member, the tasks connected with accommodation of the new member, and the development of new relationships. Risk comes when the tasks are not done well or geared toward any resolution of the problems. In this case, the entire family carries the constant weight of unresolved issues into its daily living and work situations. The weight is an unseen presence, that cuts off members from the possible support of each other. Relationships can become ritualized and the family a hollow shell.

Poverty and Discrimination   Another profound influence on family life is poverty and discrimination. Harry Aponte, a Puerto-Rican social worker who has done a great deal of work with poor families experiencing discrimination, writes about the underorganized family discussed in the previous section. Not all underorganized families are poor, the circumstances of poverty and discrimination can affect a family's organization and structure. An underorganized family has a limited number of structures to solve problems, its members may be rigid in the way they employ the structures they have, and may be inconsistent in the use of these structures. (Aponte & Van Deusen, 1981; Aponte, 1986: Aponte, 1994). The underorganized family needs to develop greater complexity of structures, and thus may need to develop structures that it never previously had. The family cannot survive without a supportive external environment. Its members need resources to feel safe, to know that the children are taught well, to be healthy, to have a good place to live, to have good and rewarding jobs, to be able to launch the children into a good environment, and so on—to have some control over the outside world. When the family lacks any of these foundations it may not develop the internal structure to deal differentially with the environment—to have different ways of working with different parts of the environment and with its own internal processes. The family, experiencing poverty and/or discrimination, may feel no ownership or association, may lack resources and be unable to draw upon or trust its surrounding institutional environment. No one from the police, the justice system, the schools, the health system, or from the employment system may have workable relationships with the family. Lacking a way to interact positively with people from these external systems, the family can lose some of its effective internal functioning as well (Aponte, 1986).

ASSESSMENT

Assessment involves an understanding of what is affecting the family and what needs to be done. Understanding the family dynamics of relational tasks and the additional stresses placed on the family members by external events and family history is essential. Relational tasks are geared to personal and relational action on the part of all members of the relational set. The social worker needs to decide who to include in a collaborative assessment and intervention process. When Brian and Lisa understand what they need to do individually and collectively, they can do something about it. When Brian stopped drinking altogether, and when he let go of some of the relationships and patterns characteristic of his bachelorhood, Lisa began to feel more secure. Both began to learn a different way of communicating in a real way with each other. Their commitment to each other did transcend some of the other issues. It was an opportunity for both to change. The actions they performed with each other and their personal work changed their individual patterns and reassured both that they could succeed in their relationship, although the fault lines would remain and would probably come up again at different times. The paradox is that when there is real action on the part of both to develop a new relational system, there is a certain capacity to transcend some of the individual issues through the relational work being done. Both Brian and Lisa did things for each other and for the emergent relationship, that they would have never done for themselves. Brian could now let go of personal feelings of emptiness, that led to binge drinking. Lisa could now let go of the anxieties, that led to a need to control. It is important for the social worker to assess both the persons (for personal tasks) and the emergent relationship (for relational tasks). To intervene in one is to intervene in the other. The social worker does not need control of the helping relationship and its outcomes. The social worker neither judges them as persons nor guarantees an outcome. The focus is rather to introduce them to their own potential and that of their relationship, and to help them to experience this potential to the point of change.

Another very powerful tool, that goes with the family developmental perspective is the concept that the problem can be normalized. The social worker can help the couple normalize what they are experiencing and what they might want to do about it. The problem is demystified when it is understood in terms of normal development and relational tasks needed for a lasting relationship. Even in extreme conditions, such as war, a normalized problem is something, that can be expected, given the circumstances. There is a non-blaming language for normalized problems, one that can more easily be converted into personal and relational tasks. The normalizing framework carries with it the expectations that people will cope and eventually have some control over the problem, (or live with the problem if that is appropriate), through their own shared and individual resources. Fear and uncertainty of something out of control often paralyzes coping. Brian's reaction to this discussion was simple: "I guess I just have to stop binge drinking, or any drinking for that matter." And he did, because Lisa was important to him. Lisa let go of her anxious need to control. At the same time she had to expect something of Brian. Both learned to communicate with each other, developing a better, more human understanding of each other, reassuring each other and helping each other to soothe their own anxieties. Brian and Lisa could each let go because the other was there for them.

SUMMARY

Relational tasks are energized by the needs, listed in the previous chapter, that family life can satisfy. Social workers work with family members who carry out these tasks together and, together with relevant social institutions, re-create workable relational structures. There is no quick or easy way to carry out a relational task. Indeed, it cannot be done except with another person—and therein lies the complexity. There are always older tasks buried in the newer ones. What is remarkable is that they get done at all. To the extent that they do get done, it is helpful to identify patterns, predict next steps to be done, and assist family members to take these steps with each other. Relational time and space are the dimensions of family process. This chapter has explored systematic, life-cycle change processes in families and their vehicle in communication. In the next chapter we move to a deeper understanding of social interaction that develops a relational architecture within families.

REFERENCES

Ainsworth, M. D. S., Bleher, M. C., Waters, E., & Wall, S. (1978). *Patterns of attachment: A psychological study of the strange situation.* Hillsdale, NJ: Erlbaum.

Allen, F. (1942). *Psychotherapy with children.* New York: Norton.

Anderson, D. A., & Worthen, D. (1997). Exploring a fourth dimension: Spirituality as a resource for the couple therapist. *Journal of Marital and Family Therapy, 23*(11), 3–12.

Assagioli, R. (1975). *Psychosynthesis: A manual of principles and techniques.* London:Turnstone Press.

Aponte, H. J. (1986). "If I don't get simple, I cry." *Family process, 25*(4), 531–548.

Aponte, H. (1994). *Bread and spirit: Therapy with the new poor.* New York: Norton.

Aponte, H. J., & Van Deusen, J. M. (1981). Structural family therapy. In A. S. Gurman & D. P., Kniskern (Eds.), *Handbook of family therapy* (pp. 310–360). New York: Brunner-Mazel.

Augustine. (1960). *The confessions of St. Augustine.* Garden City, NY: Image Books.

Baldwin, M. W., Keelan, J. P. R., Fehr, B., Enns, V., & Koo-Rangarajoo, E. (1996). Social cognitive conceptualization of attachment working models: Availability and accessability of effects. *Journal of Personality and Social Psychology, 71,* 94–109.

Bateson, G. (1936). *Navan.* Cambridge, UK: Cambridge University Press.

Bayley, M. (2003, April 7). Ten point marriage test. *London Daily Mail,* reprinted in smartmarriages.com, 7 April 2003.

Bott, E. (1971). *Family and social network: Norms and external social relationships in ordinary urban families.* London: Tavistock.

Boszormenyi-Nagy, I., & Spark, G. (1973). *Invisible loyalties: Reciprocity in intergenerational family therapy.* New York: Harper & Row.

Boszormenyi-Nagy, I., Grunebaum, A., & Ulrich, D. (1991). Contextual therapy. In A. S. Gurman & D. P. Kniskern, *Handbook of family therapy II* (pp. 200–238), New York: Brunner-Mazel.

Bowen, M. (1978). *Family therapy in clinical practice.* New York: Jason Aronson.

Bowlby, J. (1969). *Attachment and loss: Vol. 1, Attachment*. New York: Basic Books.

Buber, M. (1958). *I and thou*. New York: Scribners

Buber, M. (1965). *The knowledge of man*. New York: Harper-Collins.

Burr, W., Hill, R., Nye, F. I., & Reiss, I. L. (1979). *Contemporary theories about the family*. New York: Free Press.

Byng-Hall, J. (1995). Creating a secure family base. *Family Process*, 34(1), 45.

Canda, E. (1986). *A conceptualization of spirituality for social work: Its issues and implications*. Unpublished doctoral dissertation, Ohio State University.

Carlton, T. O. (1984). *Clinical social work in health settings: A guide to profesional practice with exemplars*. New York: Springer.

Carter, E. A., & McGoldrick, M. (1999). *The expanded family life cycle: Individual, family and social perspectives* (3rd ed.). New York: Allyn & Bacon.

Dell, P. (1982). Beyond homeostasis: Toward a concept of coherence. *Family Process*, 21(1), 21–41.

Donley, M. (1993). Attachment and the emotional unit. *Family Process*, 32(1).

Everett, C. A., Russell, C. S., & Keller, J. (1992). *Family therapy glossary*. Washington, DC: American Association for Marriage and Family Therapy.

Falck, H. S. (1988). *Social work: The membership perspective*. New York: Springer.

Falck, H. S. (1976). Individualism and communalism: Two or one? *Social Thought*, 2(3), 27–44.

Falicov, C. (1995). Training to think culturally: A multidimensional comparative framework. *Family Process*, 34, 373–388.

Fishbane, M. D. (2001). Relational narratives of the self. *Family Process*, 40(3), 273–293.

Framo, J. L. (1981). The integration of marital therapy with sessions with family of origin. In A. E., Gurman & D. P., Knishkern, (Eds.), *Handbook of family therapy*. New York: Brunner-Mazel.

Gazzaniga, M. (1985). *The social brain*. New York: Basic Books.

Goldenberg, I., & Goldenberg, H. (1996). *Family therapy: An overview*. Pacific Grove, CA: Brooks-Cole.

Goldstein, E. (1995). Psychosocial approach. In J. G. Hopps (Ed.), *Encyclopedia of social work* (19th ed., pp. 1948–1954). Washington, DC: National Association of Social Workers.

Gordon, T. (1970). *Parent effectiveness training*. New York: P. H. Wyden.

Goodrich, T. J. (1991). Women, power and family therapy: What's wrong with this picture? In T. J. Goodrich, (Ed.), *Women and Power: Perspectives for family therapy*. New York: Norton.

Grisez, G., n.d. *Fidelity today*. Privately printed document.

Guerney, B. G., Jr. (1977). *Relationship enhancement: Skill training program for therapy, problem prevention and enrichment*. San Francisco: Jossey-Bass.

Guerney, B. G., Jr. (1982). Relationship enhancement. In E. K. Marshall & P.D. Kurtz, (Eds.), *Interpersonal helping skills* (pp. 482–518). San Francisco: Jossey-Bass.

Hanh, T. N. (1987). *Being peace.* Berkeley, CA: Parallax.

Hanh, T. N. (1991). *Peace is every step: The path of mindfulness in everyday life.* New York: Bantam.

Hargrave, T. (2000). *The essential humility of marriage: Honoring the third identity in couple therapy.* Phoenix, AZ: Zeig, Tucker & Theisen.

Hazan, C., & Shaver, P. (1987). Romantic love conceptualized as an attribution process. *Journal of personality and social psychology, 52,* 511–524.

Hollis, F. (1972). *Casework: A psychosocial therapy.* New York: Random House.

Hughes, D. (1997). *Facilitating developmental attachment: The road to emotional recovery and behavioral change in foster and adopted children.* Northvale, NJ: Jason Aronson.

Janzen, C., & Harris, O. (1997). *Family treatment in social work practice.* (3rd ed.). Itaska, IL: Peacock.

Josselson, R. (1992). *The space between us: Exploring the dimensions of human relationships.* San Francisco: Jossey Bass.

Ladnier, R. D., & Massanari, A. E. (2000). Treating ADHD as attachment deficit hyperactivity disorder. In T. M. Levy (Ed.), *Handbook of attachment interventions.* San Diego: Academic Press.

Lewis, J. M., & Gossett, J. T. (1999). *Disarming the past: How an intimate relationship can heal old wounds.* Phoenix, AZ: Zeig & Tucker.

Mikulincer, M., & Florian, V. (1999a). The association between parental reports of attachment style and family dynamics and offspring's reports of adult attachment style. *Family Process, 38*(2), 243–257.

Mikulincer, M., & Florian., V. (1999b). The association between spouses' self-reports of attachment styles and representations of family dynamics. *Family Process, 38*(1), 69–84.

Mikulincer, M., Florian, V., Cowan, P. A., & Cowan, C. P. (2002). Attachment security in couple relationships: A systemic model and its implications for family dynamics. *Family Process, 41*(3), 405–434.

Minuchin, S. (1974). *Families and family therapy.* Cambridge, MA: Harvard University Press.

Nichols, M. P., & Schwartz, R. C. (2001). *Family therapy: Concepts and methods.* Boston: Allyn & Bacon.

Parad, H. (1958). *Ego psychology and dynamic casework.* New York: Family Service Association of America.

Penn, P. (2001). Chronic illness, trauma, language and writing: Breaking the silence. *Family Process, 40*(1), 33–51.

Rapoport, R. (1963). Normal crises, family structure and mental health. *Family Process, 2*(1), 76.

Reich, W. (1989). Speaking of suffering: A moral account of compassion. *Soundings: An Interdisciplinary Journal, 72*(1), 83–108.

Santana-Grace, E. (2002). Correspondence on e-responding between Santana-Grace and Guerney. In http://www.smartmarriages.com www.smartmarriages.com 11 June 2002.

Satir, V. (1988). *The new peoplemaking*. Palo Alto, CA: Science and Behavior Books.

Schwartz, R. (1995). *Internal family systems therapy*. New York: Guilford.

Shibutani, T. (1961). *Society and personality*. Englewood Cliffs, NJ: Prentice-Hall.

Shivanandan, M. (2001). Subjectivity and the order of love. *Fides quaerens intellectum, 1*(2), 251–274.

Simon, B. (1960). Ego supportive casework treatment. In *Relationship between theory and practice in social work* (pp. 26–55). New York: NASW.

Sinnott, E. (1961). *Cell and psyche: The biology of purpose*. New York: Harper.

Snyder, M. (1995). "Becoming": A method for expanding systemic thinking and deepening empathic accuracy. *Family Process, 35*(2), 241–253.

Smalley, R. (1967). *Theory for social work practice*. New York: Columbia.

Sullivan, H. S. (1938–39). A note on formulating the relationship of the individual and the group. *American Journal of Sociology, 4*, 932–937.

Tamura, T., & Lau, A. (1992). Connectedness vs. separateness: Applicability of family therapy to Japanese-families. *Family Process, 31*.

Von Bertalanffy, L. (1969). *General systems theory*. New York: Braziller.

Walsh, F. (1982). Conceptualizations of normal family functioning.In F. Walsh (Ed.), *Normal family processes* (pp. 3–44). New York: Guilford.

Walsh, F., (1993). *Normal family processes*. (2nd ed.). New York: Guilford.

Walsh, F. (1996). The concept of family resilience. *Family Process, 35*(4).

Walsh, F. (2003). Family resilience: A framework for current practice. *Family Process, 42*(1), 4.

Watzlawick, P., Beavin, J., & Jackson, D. (1967). *The pragmatics of human communication*. New York: Norton.

Weingarten, K. (2000). Witnessing, wonder and hope. *Family Process, 39*(4), 389–402.

CHAPTER 3

Family Interaction and
Family Intervention

This chapter explores the person-environment relation experienced in families. As families go through life-cycle changes, their beliefs, perceptions, and communication process create a relational architecture (family structure) continued through self-reinforcing patterns. Themes developed in this chapter are drawn from symbolic-interactionist social psychology, structural family therapy, and behavioral research on family communication and bonding.

THE BIRTH OF FAMILY STRUCTURES:
PERCEPTIONS AND INTERACTION

Both social work and the family therapy movement assume there is integrity and validity to the way people see themselves and the way they see others. These perceptions become buried in their interaction sequences and relationship patterns. The milieu and each person's perceptions of it comprise an inseparable psychosocial phenomenon (Hoffman, 1981). Salvador Minuchin's comment (1981), "Patients come to therapy because reality, as they have construed it, is unworkable," pointed out what became a new paradigm in the understanding of family intervention. It would recognize the validity of human subjective experience, its relation to an outside world, and the tension often inherent in this relation.

The symbolic interactionist school of social psychology (Cooley, 1922; Mead, 1934; Shibutani, 1962; Blumer, 1969; Burr, Hill, Nye & Reiss, 1979) has struggled for over a century with the same problem. Social relationships are created out of human experience and interaction. There are relations between the way people perceive reality, the way people act, their patterns of action, and the structures of relationships that they create. These structures in turn stabilize personal patterns and perceptions in a dense, complex recursive relationship. There are three central assumptions of the school:

1. People act on the basis of the meanings things have for them
2. Meanings emerge through social interaction
3. Meanings are managed through an interpretive process[1]

---

[1]For a full description and development of this theoretical base, see Blumer, (1971, p. 163); also Burr, Hill, Nye, and Reiss (1979) and Shibutani (1962), (1979).

The relation between people's patterns of behavior and their constructions of their world does not necessarily make behavior predictable in any linear or mechanical way. On the contrary, when we allow for differing perceptions, behavior becomes somewhat indeterminate. An indeterminate social world is open to reconstruction through mutual communication and mutual action. In the world of practice, therapists intervene in people's interchanges and interactions—in the patterns and sequences, in communication, in the way relations with others are construed, and in what people are accustomed to doing. Through these guided interventions in human interaction, the phenomenal world is altered. Assisting family members to communicate appropriately and creatively is the key to helping them to preserve relationships and restructure their worlds, to restructure how they respond to each other and what they do with each other.

GENERAL CONCEPTS ABOUT SOCIAL INTERACTION

Social Process

People's self-consciousness, responsiveness, actions, and interactions proceed from their evaluations of themselves, their surroundings, and the significant others in their environment. These evaluations are perceived and communicated in different ways. Social agreements form and grow in this way. William I. Thomas' (Thomas & Thomas) 1928 dictum, "What men perceive as real are real in their consequences," brings together the interdependent realities of social structure and personality in social interaction. Social interaction, communication, and the development of social agreements are processes. Processes are interruptible and partially undetermined sequences, moving in their own direction within which crucial events and turning points can occur (Turner, 1970, p.12). Each event is less important for its immediate effects than for its contribution to cumulative developments (Turner, 1970, p. 8). An episode of interaction leaves a residue in the attitudes and memories of the participants. It makes a difference. With the passage of time, these episodes determine cumulatively whether a couple, for example, stays together or breaks up (Turner, 1970, p. 20).

The Active, Constructive Self

Concepts of the active, constructive self, of social interaction, process, growth, the relative indeterminacy of the social world; and of the social nature of mind have long been recognized in social work, at least implicitly. Many leading social workers were familiar with the more complex conceptions of social reality of the early social psychologists. However, in a positivist century, there was a struggle between the more complex conceptions and mechanistic conceptions of social reality, that could be more easily reduced to experience and measured. The latter appeared to have greater scientific weight.

The person is active, coping, adaptive, and to some extent self-directed. The conception of the active person, currently becoming accepted in the field of developmental psychology (Rank, 1964; Angyal, 1940; Hartmann, 1958; White, 1959; Coelho, Hamburg & Adams, 1974; Stern, 1985; Brazelton & Cramer, 1990) has a long history. A leading social work theorist, Jessie Taft, in 1926 discussing the active, constructive self and the social nature of mind, quoted her mentor, George Herbert Mead: "The conscious self arises out of its own social responses and . . . continues to exist as social process, an index of its changing relationships" (p. 10). The quote demonstrates a use of social psychological theory to illustrate and explain what practitioners were experiencing. Taft rejected determinism and the simpler idea that persons would be "molded" by their environment in favor of the idea that they are active in their responses to it. They do not simply take roles, but "make" them within and sometimes beyond the limits of current social expectations.

Reflecting Taft's conceptions of social work, Ruth Smalley saw the human being as potentially able to be, within limits, an agent of one's own development, to become a person within a concrete environment of constraints and possibilities. According to Smalley, the person has a biological will to live, to grow, and to solve problems. There is a psychological urge to be a whole person, to be consistent with one's self, and there is also a capacity to take from the outside and use what he or she takes for the experience of the creation of personhood (Smalley, n.d.). Engaging persons to discover and use their capacities for agency and communion within the limits given in themselves and in their circumstances is a goal of social work.

BEHAVIORAL RESEARCH ON COUPLES' RELATIONSHIPS

Over the past thirty years there has developed a body of research on how couples behave with each other. Previous assumptions about couple interaction were constructed out of therapeutic experience with families, but they had little basis in observed interaction of "average" familes. Nor was there a focus on the relationship rather than simply individuals in relationships (Gottman & Notarius, 2002). For many years, John M. Gottman and others observed couples' interaction as couples. On that basis they began to form different hypotheses about couples' relationships. Because they focused primarily on interaction, their findings had interesting parallels with explanations of interaction provided by symbolic interactionist social psychology. In this chapter we will connect Gottman's findings with symbolic interactionist theory and attachment theory. These theory bases give explanatory power both to the research findings and to social work practice theory.

Gottman's research shifts the focus from treating differences as a problem to the question of how couples process their differences. He found that a certain level of difference and conflict is quite normal in a relationship (1999). The majority (69 percent) of couples experience and deal with issues with no resolution over many years. Whatever the context of the problem immediately experienced, it will also include 1) basic differences in the partners' personalities, and 2) basic differences in needs that are central to their concepts of who they are as people. These differences and "perpetual problems" did not mean that the couple was unhappy. Happily married couples and unhappily married couples had about the same number of differences. What distinguished them was their ability to repair these differences satisfactorily. Romance, however, does have its place in this. Happily married couples had positive feelings about each other, and these overrode incidents of negative interaction. Even where there were few incidents of negative interaction, the absence of positive feelings about the other person predicted divorce within a North American context (Gottman & Levenson, 2000). Gottman concluded from his research that, for marital quality and stability, the positive listening and expressing behaviors had to outweigh the negative by five to one. When negative behaviors and memories prevail, new communications and behaviors tend to be interpreted negatively. A cascade of increasing distance and isolation is established, and the marriage will move to a split (Gottman, 1999).

COMMUNICATION PROCESSES AND SOCIAL INTERACTION

Gottman's research into couple interaction points out the need for the development of explanatory theories of communication processes and social interaction in the family. As a first step, let us examine both of these concretely in the following episode of communication (c.f. Turner, 1970). It involves a married couple in their forties, Mark and Leslie; their daughter, Amber; and her college friend, Julie. They are having dinner together, and this is Julie's first meal with the family. On the previous day, Andrea, a friend of the family, had suffered a heart attack and was taken to the hospital. Mark had heard about the situation before dinner, but Leslie is hearing about it for the first time:

CASE STUDY 3.1

Mark: John called me today.

Leslie: I made the pasta sauce vegetarian this time. Is it OK?

Mark: [taking a breath] It's great, but wait, Leslie. John told me Andrea had a heart attack. She regained consciousness in the hospital, but she is paralyzed.

Leslie: What? Is she really paralyzed? How far paralyzed?

Mark: Well, she can't talk but. . . .

Leslie: Then she's really in a bad way. Will she recover? How much does it cost for her care with a specialist and all?

Mark: Well, it's. . .

Leslie: Will she be in the hospital long? I hope she gets better. Will she get any better, or is there a chance she'll die? Does the doctor know how much longer she"ll be paralyzed? How does she eat?

Mark: She can't swallow, so they are feeding her intravenously, but. . .

Leslie: How much longer will she be in this condition? Did the doctor say? Why can't she swallow?

Mark: [getting angry] For heaven's sake, Leslie, please stop rattling away! How can I answer so many questions? You don't even let me talk.

Amber: [laughing] You're both getting crazy. How can Dad get a word in edgewise, Mom, if you just keep asking questions?

Julie: [laughing] Please. Tell us what happened. I'm dying of curiosity now.

Mark remains silent and just frowns for a few seconds, looking as if he is swallowing something painful. Suddenly he relaxes and smiles. The two girls burst out laughing, especially because of the way Mark looked when he was about to lose his temper. Leslie, who looked quite tense when Mark said she "rattled off," stopped, looked at the girls and Mark, put on a half smile, and then, shaking her head, started laughing herself.

Leslie: Julie, I do this all the time when I get worried about something. Mark is used to it. I'm sorry, Mark, I do talk fast, but I didn't think I was rattling.

Mark: [smiling] It's OK, and I'm sorry it got under my skin this time. And in front of the girls too. Sometimes you just won't stop talking, asking questions. I can't get a word in edgewise when you do that. You don't let me talk.

Leslie: [leaning over and giving Mark a little hug] Yes. I know it gets to you when I do that. But I was terribly worried about Andrea. I just wanted to know as quickly as possible about everything. I'm sorry.

The conversation about Andrea continues comfortably.

The above episode is one of a long series of events in the progressive story of Mark and Leslie's marriage. While there are tension points, Mark and Leslie have a workable marriage and are accustomed to dealing with these points. Mark begins with a "gesture," his statement about John's phone call. Leslie didn't want to discuss something that excluded the girls. Her first response was to ignore Mark's opening gesture and shift the discussion to the vegetarian pasta sauce. She had worked on the sauce and was very pleased with the result. Julie, their guest, is vegetarian. She was concerned that Mark seemed to be ignoring Julie and Amber. She felt this topic of conversation would recognize the girls as well as her work. She was also slightly irritated that Mark hadn't noticed and that he had started in this way with their guests present. Mark persists, making a brief repair effort, because he knows this information is important. Leslie reacts with concern when she realizes the importance of the news. She interrupts Mark and cuts him off several times. Mark's response is frustration. He is on the verge of anger. The daughter, Amber, softens the interaction and the friend joins in the softening. Mark struggles with his anger and Leslie struggles at her hurt and embarrassment at Mark's talk of her "rattling away." Both know this is a hot-button term for her. The girls soften Mark and Leslie's interpretations of the others' gestures and responses.

Both Mark and Leslie have had many more positive than negative interactions in the past. As a consequence of this, neither one is overly watchful for responses of the other that they might take personally (Gottman, 1999). Also the presence of the girls prevents the episode from deteriorating. Otherwise Mark and Leslie might have gone further into reflections on past interactions and intensified criticism or defensiveness on either one's part (Gottman, 1999). The repair efforts are accepted for the moment. The episode is reinterpreted, and family and guest proceed with dinner conversation.

Later, in private, Mark and Leslie will still probably need to repair any leftover issues from the incident so that it doesn't carry over into future communication patterns and ultimately into the relationship. Leslie remembers Mark's remark about her "rattling away." She will think about it and remind him of his remark at an appropriate time. Mark remembers that Leslie cuts him off in different ways when he is trying to say something and doesn't always listen well. But neither does he. Both also remember that that they mostly have a good relationship. Their meanings are eventually understood by the other. Their conversation "makes sense," and these little difficulties won't interrupt their mostly positive feelings. They can joke about them, but there are deeper meanings as well.

Mark and Leslie's episode is extremely important theoretically for several reasons. First of all, it is through interaction such as this that families construct or dismantle their relationships. We see the couple struggling with present communication and with memories of how they have communicated. There are differences, but research points out that this is less important than their ability to repair differences (Gottman, 1999). Simply put, Mark and Leslie communicate with each other as real persons, giving and receiving confirmation most of the time. The key is communication. Communication makes it possible to alter their picture of themselves and their roles in relation to each other. If they elect not to communicate about themselves or their conceptions of their roles, they are then conversing with themselves or with their picture of the other person. Both the need for a better relationship and today's demand for communication about everything will push them to communicate and alter their pictures of themselves and their roles.

However, there is another choice. The couple can also develop a parallel relationship, much as Elizabeth Botts (1971) found in East London marriages. They may communicate about practical necessities and allow cultural influences and family experience to dictate their role conceptions. In these circumstances, men are closer to other men and women to women. This arrangement can be quite stable. It will not work, however, when role conceptions are in conflict or the circumstances of their relationship demands communication. The social worker has the choice of supporting a parallel arrangement, when it is workable, or of helping the couple modify their relationship through developing communication skills.

In Mark and Leslie's episode, Mark retreats from his picture of Leslie "rattling away"; Leslie modifies her original redirection of Mark's gesture. It is very important that they are able to modify their understandings and interaction. Not all couples are able to do this readily or at all. Mark and Leslie do listen to each other. Communication builds in a constructive process. It is real, rather than being circular, with Mark talking to Mark's picture of Leslie but ignoring the real Leslie, and Leslie talking to her picture of Mark. As pointed out previously, Mark and Leslie have had many more positive than negative episodes and they can joke about the negative ones. This is the music of their couple communication.

John Gottman's "Four Horsemen"

Left unrepaired, the episode between Mark and Leslie could have deteriorated into cascading dysfunctional patterns. The research of John Gottman (1999, pp.

41–47) points out that four negative patterns of communication criticism, defensiveness, contempt, and stonewalling ("the four horsemen of the Apocalypse")—if prolonged, almost unfailingly predict marital split. On the other hand, without the above four indicators of negativity, emotional disengagement also predicted a split (Gottman, Driver & Tabares, 2002). Mark might not bother to tell Leslie about Andrea or might completely stand apart from Leslie's reactions. Leslie might take the news without any relational comment or feeling at all.

Criticism

Criticism is any statement that implies that there is something globally wrong with the other, something that is probably a lasting aspect of the partner's character. "You always . . . rattle away, cut me off," and so on, are criticisms rather than constructive complaints. An "I" message is better. It can repair criticism, because it is not an attack on the other person, "Please wait, Leslie. When I was trying to say something about John, it confused me for a moment. It felt like you were going off with your own concerns before I could get back to what I was trying to say." Actually most couples would not be so diplomatic in real life. But then there may be less to repair, or the repair may not be made, eventually leading to bad memories. The antidote to criticism is making any statement of the problem that does not criticize (Gottman, Driver & Tabares, 2002, p. 393), such as an "I" statement.

Defensiveness

Defensiveness is an attempt to defend oneself from a perceived attack. In marital interaction, it takes the form of the innocent victim posture. The message is, "What are you picking on me for? I didn't do anything wrong."

Mark: You interrupted me, Leslie. I was trying to tell you something.
Leslie: Why not? You always do that to me.

The antidote to defensiveness is accepting responsibility for even a part of the problem (Gottman, Driver & Tabares, 2002, p. 393). The couple then can go back to the original communication and repair it.

Contempt

Gottman considers the third horseman, contempt, the "sulphuric acid" of a marriage. Contempt is any statement of nonverbal behavior that puts oneself on a higher plane than one's partner. It often sounds like mockery with a contemptuous facial expression. It stops positive communication completely because it is directly aimed at the other. According to Gottman's research, the amount of contempt in stable, happy marriages is essentially zero (Gottman, 1999, p. 47).

Leslie: I made the sauce vegetarian today. Is it OK?

Mark: There she goes again. Mrs. Rattle away. Amber, notice she never follows what I'm saying and I can't get a word in edgewise.

Leslie: [smiling tensely and bitterly] OK, Mr. Know-it-all. If you were really so smart, you might have noticed Amber's guest sitting over there.

The antidote to contempt is creating a culture of appreciation in the marriage (Gottman, Driver & Tabares, 2002, p. 393). It is difficult to repair contempt except through a long period of positive work on the part of both partners on a greatly revised relationship. In this case, the matter gets complicated when Mark quickly moves to a possible alliance with Amber, who gets triangulated into the conflict with Mark and Leslie competing for the alliance with her. When couples come to this point, it is difficult to move back, and the move backward is a dance of three: Mark, Leslie, and Amber. As we will see at a later point, such alliances can both strengthen the dysfunctional couple patterns and at the same time foster serious problems in children.

Stonewalling

The fourth horseman, stonewalling, occurs when the listener withdraws from the interaction, shuts down, and is chronically unwilling to return to interact with the partner.

Mark: [Getting angry] For heaven's sake, Leslie, please stop rattling away. How can I answer so many questions? You don't even let me talk.

Leslie: [smiling coolly] Mrs. Rattle-away will just shut up and find out for herself what happened, thank you. (pause) Amber, how was your English class today? Did you and Julie go together?

Mark: Do whatever you want. I'm done.

Leslie shuts down the conversation with Mark, switches the subject, and the focus shifts to the girls. In doing this she reinforces an implicit alliance with Amber and further isolates Mark. His complaint, although badly phrased, just wasn't important enough to deal with at all. Mark replies by stonewalling also, and both are competing to shut things down now. Generally stonewalling is such an embedded pattern that the stonewaller is hardly aware of what he or she is doing. The antidote for stonewalling is self-soothing, taking productive breaks, and staying connected (not leaving) (Gottman, Driver & Tabares, 2002, p. 394). It takes a great deal of repeated relational work and a real revision of the relationship to rectify stonewalling (Gottman, 1999).

There are some gender correlates in negative couple communication in North American samples. Research suggests that women tend to use criticism in a conflict; men tend to use defensiveness and stonewalling. In this connection, Gottman found that, in happy marriages, men to listen to women. Everything is fueled by the positive feelings about the other that we identify as love. Repairs are more important than the original problem and couples can learn to change negative communication patterns. Among newlyweds, even with high negativity, if they were able to learn to make effective repairs, 85 percent experienced happy, stable marriages six years later (Gottman, Driver & Tabares, 2002).

In the last two examples of problematic exchange, the dysfunctional communication between Mark and Leslie is reinforced by attempts to realign with Amber against the other parent. In many ways, regardless of the age of the child (ren), an alignment of a child against a parent what Jay Haley calls a "cross-generational coalition (Haley & Hoffman, 1968; Haley, 1980) seems closely related to problems with children, and, of course, it also undermines the marriage. Reinstating the coalition between the parents so that they form a united front (even if disagreements about the children continue in private) makes socialization of the children possible.

Communication: Repair Patterns and Change

Mark and Leslie actually have relatively healthy communication and most likely could successfully repair and reconstruct their relationship. In case study 3.1 the girls neutralized the issue, and this prevented Mark and Leslie from an immediate repair—Mark and Leslie may have to repair some of it later. In marital counseling, rather than neutralizing and covering over the issue, the social worker would help them work it out using their own natural communication with each other. The focus would be on repairing and stabilizing communication patterns. Through this repair of communication, the couple's processes of decision making and bonding could also be strengthened in a longer and more determinate process.

This type of relational reconstruction demands real interaction both in-session and out-of-session with a professional as a coach for the work to be done. Thus one key to the art of intervention is an understanding of interactive processes, of what needs to be done to repair and reconstruct relationships. Another key is an understanding of how and where to intervene in these processes while they are taking place before the social worker's eyes. One has a grasp of the process and of what needs to be done for a couple or family to reconstruct itself. The couple is in charge of their reconstruction. Then the professional social worker, as a coach, can choose from among a wide variety of methods that can be used to help the couple reconstruct their relationship, just as an artist can choose to work in a particular medium out of many possibilities. The professional could work with Mark and Leslie as a couple on couple issues, or with the whole family on issues involving the whole family.

Mark and Leslie communicate fairly smoothly. In other couples, certain memories of previous interactions, perhaps not even with the same person, may be enough to stall the present interaction. Sometimes there is very little real communication, that is, of real people with each other. Ego communicates with his or her memories or impressions of alter; the conversation is ego with him or herself, and not at all with alter. Alter does the same. Both react to their impressions of each other without really hearing what the other has said. Neither feels understood. Neither feels a genuine friendship. They are, for the most part, communicating with themselves and their communication only reinforces their present beliefs about the situation. To change this condition requires persons to find some real communicaton with each other, and through that, to manage the work they must do together in reconstructing their relationship. The social worker can assist this difficult process.

SOCIAL INTERACTION

Social interaction is communication and action—with and in reference to other persons with whom we have a present or past relationship. Out of social interaction, persons communicate, develop bonds and connections with one another, experience conflict, learn and develop roles, develop expectations for the roles of others, make decisions, and carry out tasks. Not all couples have sufficiently rich verbal interaction to transact all of the above. They can communicate verbally mainly on practical details. They may get along well or poorly, depending on the fit of their interactional patterns. If the couple relationship is less important for both of them than their relationship with their parents, siblings, children, or their friends, conflict with the partner may not be considered a major problem.

For social workers, who have to decide whether or not to support a workable but undeveloped relationship, it is essential to know that social interaction can be modified through communication. To the extent patterns of social interaction can be modified, a relationship also can be modified. Processes of social interaction need to be understood by the social worker as interruptible sequences rather than inevitable events. The sum of these transactional processes—a network of social agreements—is experienced by each person through membership in groups, in families, at work, at play and so forth. This is the work of social interaction, where social workers intevene to reshape its parts.

BONDING PROCESSES AND VULNERABILITY

Bonds are powerful. Both membership and attachment are expressions of the interactive process of bonding. The stages of a bonding process correspond to the different stages of family formation. As illustrated in our earlier episode involving Mark and Leslie (case study 3.1), the bonding process is a reflection of the interaction of both the past and the present. As it is shaped by interaction, subject to continuous change. As Mark and Leslie inevitably change and as their circumstances change, so also must they continually work to stabilize their bond. As we saw from our examples of alternative conversations for Mark and Leslie, a bond could degenerate from clumsy handling, but the clumsiness of the past often can be rectified somewhat. A couple's bond inevitably reflects their past interactions and even their memories of bonding in their families of origin. Indeed, as internal and external changes occur, as the couple faces new circumstances, they must reconstruct this past in relation to their present. They are continually and actively in a bonding process. They cannot stop. If they did, certain bonds would deteriorate. On the other hand, Mark and Leslie already have a whole complex of bonds to each other. The vulnerability and deterioration of one set of bonds does not necessarily prevent other bonds from working. To clarify this point, let us examine the different types of bonds, that exist in Mark and Leslie's case.

Identity bonds are bonds that can be made only with a person. These bonds often demand that a whole complex of sentiments of friendship and/or love be attached to them if they are to be seen as authentic. Not all bonds are so fully personal. Other quite powerful bonds are attached to a position or a task. These status bonds and task bonds may lead to identity bonds. We will discuss status and task bonds before discussing identity bonds.

Status Bonds

Status bonds are inherent to social membership. They come from the status of being married or being a member of a family. The child, born into a family, is born into a status. Only later may more person-oriented bonds develop out of interaction. Nevertheless, the status bond of child to parent and parent to child is quite powerful, even when the relationship is not yet personal. In Western society there is the expectation that the family bond, and in particular the married bond, should be based on love. A marriage for status or position, or a loveless marriage, is considered tragic. Marriage is looked on as a desirable status, implying within many groups a certain level of maturity, of prestige, and of accomplishment. There are societal benefits and even financial benefits to the married state. The attraction of this bond may be such that, rather than marrying another person, a person may simply marry marriage. In traditional societies, (such as those where marriages were arranged), this did take place to some extent, and it was hoped that other bonds related to the other person would later develop. In this sense, the status bond may be a pathway to the later development of more person-oriented bonds. The power of this bond may be seen in that, for example, even in Western society, there are considerable incentives to remain in a married state, even when love is tragically absent. In the case of adoption, the original status bond of parent to child is dissolved, but another parental bond is formed to replace it.

Task Bonds

Collaboration in common or shared tasks is a bond. Although this bond as such dissolves when the task is completed, it is a well-used pathway to deeper bonding processes. Tasks infuse every other aspect of our lives. Being a part of a team or a school class, going through a stressful test together, taking wilderness training, going to summer camp—all of these experiences may lead to deeper and more lasting friendships. Interlocking task roles in families develop interdependence between persons.

Individual developmental tasks and milestones, such as graduation from school, have a particular significance as task bonds and can be reasons for celebration in the family unit. Incomplete action is another type of task bond. Shared tasks and future aspirations, even the bond of having a mortgage to pay off, bring family members together through the powerful bonds of incomplete action in a never-ending search for the achievement of one and then another goal (Turner, 1970).

Response Bonds

The way alter (the other) habitually responds to ego (the self) as a person and ego to alter generates another kind of bond, the response bond. The response bond, the way ego and alter were with each other, is a very important component of the lasting memory of a relationship. The response evokes in ego both a kind of favorable self-image and an identification of "we." In this case, the interaction is continued into a relationship with expectations of continuing positive responses and treatment. The interaction of Mark and Leslie (case study 3.1) can be seen as a continual test of responsiveness and repair so that the meanings of the relationship, the self-conceptions, of one and the other and the relationship itself, the "we," are reinforced. When a relationship is disrupted through death all of the bonds seem to be lost, but the lost "we," the lost response bonds, may be the most deeply felt. This is particularly true when relating to others who have known the "we" and, feeling the loss of the other, they struggle to relate differently to the person remaining.

Identity Bonds

In Western society, with the expectation that the family bond should be based on the complex sentiment of love, the identity bond is extremely important. Identity bonds are bonds to a particular (and unsubstitutable) human being based on an understanding of the other's experience as if that experience were one's own. The complexity of Mark and Leslie's communication had everything to do with maintaining an understanding and acceptance of the other and the other's experience. Mark's hurt by being cut off by Leslie, or her not listening to him, was matched by Leslie's hurt when Mark said she was "rattling away." Both gestures were taken "personally" and thus went beyond the overt meaning of Andrea's hospitalization. Both tried to repair the slight and thus maintain an identity bond, that is to be treated lovingly. If there was no attention to repairing the slight, the relation would become conflictual for each, that is, for their vulnerable identities. Ultimately it could deteriorate systematically into a relationship governed by criticism, defensiveness, contempt, and stonewalling, the four "horsemen" of Gottman. In this sense, identity bonds are quite vulnerable and demand constant relational work. Social workers act as coaches to such relational work.

Identity bonds rest on empathic foundations, an understanding of the other's experience as if it were one's own. These bonds are vulnerable and, because of this, the persons are vulnerable as well. People change in their own experience and in their experience of the other. Gender barriers and the strains between generations inherent in socialization (where one generation takes some responsibility for the other's behavior) create barriers. These barriers can weaken identity bonds. During periods of transition and strain, the status and task bonds become a type of safety net that can stabilize the relationship until the bond is repaired or new identity bonds are formed.

Empathic understanding denotes the ability to know or to imagine what another person is feeling, and to feel with him or her without becoming caught in that feeling and losing perspective. It is the foundation for a powerful bond, that can reinforce a certain mutual understanding of one's worth as a person, and thus has the ability to provoke change. It also can stabilize a relationship. Empathic understanding of the other becomes an important tool in the repair of relationships. Social workers are continually working within the realm of empathic understanding, both in their own practice skills and in helping family members to develop workable bonds with each other.

Breakdown of Identity Bonds

Identity bonds, denoting both connectedness and separateness, can easily turn themselves into the extremes of sympathy on the one hand or disengagement on the other. Sympathy involves feeling like someone without the presence of difference. One shares the same feelings, is identified with the same interests, becomes aligned with the person, and loves and hates the same things. Enmeshed families are excessively involved with each other. The family members are so tightly interlocked in its relationships with each other that boundaries, particularly generational boundaries, do not seem to be functioning. Alliances may exist across generational lines (e.g., cross-generational coalitions) rather than within generational lines. Any conflict or even difference is threatening to the family and is stifled. The extreme versions of this structure can stifle any growth and differentiation of its members.

At the other extreme, the disengaged family, in contrast, appears to be a family of unrelated, atomistic individuals with very little sensitivity to each others' messages or needs. The disengaged family provides few points of reference and very little support for members efforts to cope (Minuchin, 1976). Disengagement denotes the feeling of alienation brought on by a failed identity bond. It involves a much stronger feeling than one might have for a stranger. In this sense, it is also a bond just as persons, who go to great lengths to avoid each other, are bonded. Empathic identity bonds, in contrast, are differentiated and allow for healthy connections and separation. They allow the other to be understood from the position of difference and thus allow flexible role development to proceed within the dyadic units of the family.

The concept of bonds, created through present interaction, is enriched by an understanding of invisible loyalties created out of past bonds, debts, and legacies, handed down over generations (Boszormenyi-Nagy, Grunebaum & Ulrich, 1991). Thus, for the persons in a couple to develop an unimpeded relationship with each other, each may need to deal with the relational legacies from previous generations that affect current relationships. Current relationships are perceived as analogous to a past relationship and responded to accordingly. Personal work on the past relationships can be done in the context of the present relationship and vice versa.

Cross-Generational Coalitions

Since there are a large number of dyadic units in the family, it is probable that identity bonds of different quality will develop. Potentially this could lead to triangulated relations of persons on the inside or on the outside of different relationships. The common element in triangulation is an imbalance in a relationship of three persons, a triad. Two parties may remain close by distancing the third party, or by making the third party an object of common concern. Two partners may remain distant while the third becomes a mediator or forms a coalition with one. Between parents and children, one problem is that a close bond between parent and child, with the other parent on the outside, will undercut the normal hierarchy of generations within the family. It can also affect the marital bond and the child's potential for a constructive relationship with the person on the outside. The child is "pulled in" on the side of one parent. Similarly the child who is a "mediator" stands between both parents, closer to each parent than the parents are to each other (Bell, Bell & Nakita, 2001, p. 176; Vogel & Bell, 1960).

In another configuration, the marital couple's mutual focus on a symptomatic child may conceal strain within the marital relationship and postpone dealing with marital issues. Some research suggests that such triangulation can be unhealthy for the child because it interferes with accurate perception and response to the child's needs by the parents (Bell, Bell & Nakita, 2001, p. 177). On the other hand, a certain level of triangulation is natural to all families with children. Indeed, it is inherent in a gender-identification process. The social worker may need to assist the parent on the outside of a close father–son or mother–daughter relationship, for example, to hold his or her own without getting drawn into needlessly challenging a developmentally healthy relationship.

THE PROCESS OF ROLE DEVELOPMENT

Roles are sets of expected behaviors arrived at and learned through social interaction. Role is often confused with the more static concept of status (Linton, 1936), but as we are using the term, it is a much more dynamic, relational concept, a product of interaction. To the extent that roles are actively taken by persons, they are capable of enormous variability within limits. With the present interlocking complexity of family tasks, roles are not so much prescribed by tradition as taken in relation to another person. That is, in order to take my role, I (ego) must understand it in relation to the other's (alter's) and the other's in relation to me. This demands not only that I learn and take my own role, but that I am also able to "take the role of the other" in relation to my role—to understand the reciprocal role of others in relation to my role. In Phil and Sarah's situation in chapter 2 (case study 2.3), Sarah's back condition demanded that they shift and revise fixed concepts of role to something more adapted to each other's needs and their situation. To do this, they needed to develop communication with each other and with their children. They had to shift from an implicit understanding of roles to one, that is more explicit and based on communication. For the interaction process out of which roles are developed, George Herbert Mead gives the example of ego and alter throwing and catching a ball. To throw a ball is to anticipate the motions of the person catching. To catch is to anticipate the motions of the person throwing (Mead, 1934). Phil has to understand and communicate with Sarah, and Sarah with Phil, if they are to resolve their role discussion brought on by Sarah's back. In these circumstances, the necessary family developmental shifts are made possible through appropriate communication.

An awareness of the roles of others may then lead to an awareness of conflict between one's habitual role expectations and the needs of others, as with Phil and Sarah. Family members often attempt to modify their own roles or innovate to meet the needs of another more accurately. A father may find that his expectations of his own role do not relate to his son's needs, and thus the father may have to modify his role. This modification could create considerable difficulty, and so the father may have to help the son modify his role expectations of him or work out a third solution that is satisfactory to both.

On the assumption that implicit understandings of roles can be modified, role learning and role making proceed reciprocally, involving ego and alter. Out of the principle of reciprocity—that my obligation is contingent on the other person's carrying out his or her own role—grow systems of mutual obligation and rules.

These rules rest on reciprocal relations of ego with alter. A violation of these understandings would release ego from obligations commensurate with the violation. In any case, this mutual agreement on role modification does not take place in a vacuum, since any change will affect and be affected by all relations, such as the father's relation to the mother and the son's relation to his siblings. For interaction to take place smoothly in a family group, clustering and segmentation of the many possible roles a person may carry generally occur. Each family member establishes a cluster of activities as his or her own. These activities often have some relation to each other, such as bookkeeping, tax payment, and bill payment. Each family member is generally expected to stay in his or her cluster and not dabble in the activities approriate to another role (Turner, 1970). Family members often do take the others roles, when needed, but this should be accompanied by a negotiation process with the person who normally has the role.

Role boundaries are developed over time with frequent interaction. These boundaries can become seriously distorted, with one person approaching a role in a rigid, nonadaptive way, the other becoming overadaptive, and both supporting a less workable system of roles or a person can become so absorbed by implicit role expectations that there is no uniqueness or "I" separate from the "me" of network expectations. When this takes place, where relationships are potentially conflictual or risky for some members, the family could cease to be personal—that is, a place where persons can flourish as persons. When one person cannot develop, all the others in the unit are affected in different ways.

Once a system of roles has developed, family processes tend to preserve the balance that this establishes and to exclude the possibility of members playing different roles. If I cultivate the role of mediator in family conflict, others are likely to become even less restrained instigating conflict, depending on me to mediate and restore an accustomed balance. Family interaction and the role system had become balanced and stabilized through my mediation.

In the episode of Mark and Leslie (case study 3.1), Amber, the daughter very quickly moved in to mediate between her parents, although one could also detect some alliance with her father. Her speed and comfort in assuming the role indicate that she had played it previously. However, it is also possible that, as long as Amber is balancing the system in this way, her mediation may be preventing Mark and Leslie from working out the conflict. In this way her mediating role may be stabilizing and maintaining the immediate status quo at the expense of long-run stability. Her influence and standing in the family may depend heavily on her skills as a mediator, and her position might diminish when others do not play antagonist roles. A change in her role would cause normal family operations to slow down, and others could hold her responsible for any consequent breakdown of task accomplishment. If Amber had made herself so essential to her mother and father that without her they would be deadlocked, she also would be locked into the triangle. It could be difficult for her to leave that tight triangle to form a relationship with another. She could lose herself in the role. In a rigid relational system, forming a relationship with another would be very difficult without radically leaving the system. If Amber were to attempt to change, the family would need to endure confusion and misunderstandings until a new agreement on roles was developed and put into action.

FAMILY STRUCTURE AND COMMUNICATION

The pattern of roles adopted by the family has a certain permanence and develops through memory and communication into family structure. *Family structure* is a network of agreements that, once made, become essential for family operations. We can map out these different intensities of communication to form a sociogram of family structure. When we do this, we may locate the interlocking and conflictual three-person and two-person subgroups within the family. With specialization of role, there is often a certain stability of power over particular areas of decision making in this structure. As long as a subgroup can maintain its own internal agreement, it can develop alliances and coalitions and acquire power over decision-making processes in areas considered important.

Since these agreements involve the relatively fixed and expected behaviors of many actors, they are difficult to change. One person's attempts to change his or her role in this structure will inevitably be met with resistance. Others in the family subtly—or not so subtly—attempt to move the person back to his or her accustomed role. Even if the role is detrimental to the individual, family members may attempt to maintain the accustomed role, since their own definitions of family well-being and wholeness depend on the maintenance of family structure.

We often characterize a person in a family as dominant when we believe that person has a heavy influence on certain decision-making processes taking place in the family. The ability to influence decision making is closely tied to communication. Often the dominant person may be dominant only on some issues. This "dominance" may even be maintained by others who actually may have greater power over decision making but wish to preserve a belief in the superior power of one member. In most families, power grows in a more functional way, not as much from inherent authority as from the ability to communicate and develop alliances across the subgroups in the family. The greater the relative ability to communicate across family subgroups, the greater the ability to influence decision making, since a central "switchboard" can amplify or censor a message to manipulate others to go along. Miguel and Juana (case study 2.4) and to some extent Sarah and Phil (case study 2.3) in the previous chapter had to rebalance power and dominance as they rebalanced their patterns, as they were now sensitive to the personal dimensions of their own relationship rather than mainly external criteria.

Cultural values and the inherently conservative nature of family structure can provide a common set of reference points and a point of stability amid changing self-conceptions and behavior of members. Since structure reflects agreements made and power balances of the past, there is usually a lag between family structure and the changing identities of family members. Family structure, maintained through communication, is often a source of conflict between persons who want to change their interpretations of their roles and others in the family who are bent on maintaining an unchanged structure. The struggles between generations, each coping with changing self-definitions and the demands of their life stages, ultimately do create changes in family structure. The struggle may be more likely if there are forces outside the family supporting a different self-conception.

SOCIALIZATION: THE ACQUISITION OF A FRAMEWORK OF MEANINGS

Socialization is the medium through which family members learn to cope with society. From multiple and continuing interaction with significant others, persons organize a framework for the interpretation of reality, values, acceptable motives, and sentiments, and also for the interpretation of the meanings inherent in the actions people take toward them. This framework of meanings is acquired through the process of seeing things, people's actions and roles, from the standpoint of the various actors in the person's experience. The ability to understand the role of the other is suggested by some developmental psychologists to be an important index of maturity (Kohlberg, 1969; Selman, 1976), particularly for developing persons, who are often family members. The framework contains conceptions of the self, of others, and of roles that become generalized into persistent coping patterns. If socialization is to be effective, it pervades all parent–child transactions and thus affects other aspects of family interaction, such as role differentiation and decision making. It also adds some specific sources of family tension and gratification. Socialization is built upon the unequal authority of parents and children (Turner, 1970). A coalition of a parent with a child across generation lines would effectively undermine the other parents's socializing efforts and the hierarchy of the family. Family therapists note an association of the breakdown of appropriate boundaries around the parental dyad, lack of agreement of the dyad on socialization, or subtle alliances of one parent with a child with severe family conflict and breakdown of socialization. The parent, however, does not control all socialization influences on the child, and this is the irony of the parent's position in modern society. The parent is an agent of societal expectations, and is made responsible by relatives, court systems, and children themselves for the results of socialization. The caricature of the uncle or grandparent who can indulge and enjoy the child without the responsibility for socialization is a source of continual triangulation within the family. It points out the pressures on the parents as agents of expectations that may actually be conflicted, contradictory, or impossible to achieve.

THE STRUCTURAL PERSPECTIVE IN FAMILY THERAPY

Family structure is a network of implicit and explicit agreements that, once made, become mutual patterns and eventually become essential for family operations. The concept of family structure was very quickly taken over in the 1960s and1970s by the school of structural family therapy as a way of illustrating and clarifying the implicit understandings, bonds, and relationships that govern the way people behave in families (Minuchin, 1974; Minuchin & Fishman, 1981).[2] Some of the structural family therapy theory base is described here, particularly as developed by Aponte and Van Deusen (1981).

Structures are the implicit understandings that regulate how family members relate to each other, what roles they should take, and so on. These sturctures are used to deal with the complex and changing internal and external worlds that families experience. Families need to manage their own relationships, the changes in individual members wrought by development, and at the same time cope actively with a changing and demanding environment. As a consequence of these changing internal and external tasks, families have to carry out a variety of functions in

---

[2] For more extensive discussion of this approach to family therapy, see Goldenberg and Goldenberg (1996), chapter 9, Nichols and Schwartz (2001) chapter 8, and Aponte and Van Deusen (1981). Harry Aponte is a social worker who continues to be one of the leaders of the structural school of family therapy.

the case of temporary absence or incapacity, members often have to take each other's roles. Thus every family needs to have a repertoire of structures to meet and integrate these complex internal and environmental changes. Some structures are dominant—that is, most family operations are based on a particular relational structure. Other structures are less frequently called upon, and thus are subordinate. The ability of a family to function well depends on the degree to which the family structures are well-defined, elaborated, flexible, and cohesive. A family with a limited number of structures to solve problems, whose members are rigid in the way they employ the structures they have, and who are inconsistent in the use of these structures are, by definition, underorganized (Aponte, 1986). This is a very important set of distinctions. Some families, such as Phil and Sarah (case study 2.3), dealing with somewhat dysfunctional dominant structures, may either modify those structures or call upon less used but available subordinate structures to deal with a problem. Some families on the other hand need to develop greater complexity of structures. These families are underorganized, and thus they may need to develop structures that they never previously had.

Every operation, indeed every transaction of the family, defines structure. Structure involves boundaries, alignment, and power.

Boundaries

Boundaries are the rules defining who participates: who is in and who is out of a family operation. To work in any operation, family boundaries need to be differentiated, relatively flexible, and permeable. The extremes of boundary making are:

1) enmeshment (where the boundaries are too low for an operation to work), and
2) disengagement. (where the boundaries are too high for an operation to work).

There also is a violation of function boundaries where there is inappropriate intrusion of family members in functions that are the domain of other members (Aponte & Van Deusen, 1981).

Alignment

Alignment is the joining with or opposition of one member of the system to another in carrying out an operation. For examples, father may either agree or disagree with mother in relation to deciding where to take a vacation. If he disagrees, he may join with the son in this disagreement. A *coalition* is a joining of two persons in opposition to a third person, as in the above example (Aponte & Van Deusen, 1981). An *alliance* is a joining of two members on the basis of common interests—father and son both enjoy fishing, for example, and form an alliance of fishermen in the family. An alliance is not necessarily energized by opposition to a third member. Breakdowns of alignment can take place through 1) a stable coalition, which is the joining together of two family members against another, so that the pattern becomes a dominant, inflexible characteristic of their relationships; 2) a detouring coalition which occurs when stress between two family members is diffused by designating another party as the source of the problem and assuming an attacking or solicitous attitude toward that person; and 3) triangulation which occurs when each of two opposing parties seeks to join with the same person against the other, with the third party finding it necessary to cooperate, now with one, now with the other of these opposing structures (Aponte & Van Deusen, 1981).

Power

Power, always relative to the family operation, is the influence of a family member on the outcome of an activity. Power is different from authority, since a person in authority may be utterly unable to influence a particular outcome. A baby will have great power over the sleeping and eating routines of family members, although that same baby is low in authority. Children in the family often have considerable power over certain operations. The power of a parent may be seen by who will prevail in a disagreement, and whether both parents can impose an agreed-upon rule on a child. Breakdowns of power in the system can come from disagreements and confusion, reflecting problems of boundaries and alignment. For socialization to work, there must be a certain hierarchy of parental power in relation to the children. Thus a weak executive undermines functional power in the family.

We can take Mark and Leslie, and Amber and Julie (case study 3.1), as simple examples of integration of systems concepts outlined in the previous chapter and also of concepts of interaction and structure outlined in this chapter. The interaction described in the case is a product of all of the persons, not of one involved alone. The causality of interaction and the results of interaction are circular, rather than linear. Furthermore, the total communication episode cannot be understood by a focus on the individuals involved. Together they create something unique (nonsummativity). It is the pattern between Mark and Leslie that is constant, that can characterize them. They are different from each other and come from different backgrounds, but they have learned to heal and repair differences through interaction. On the other hand, if they ceased this pattern of repair, it could quickly break down into the four horsemen (equifinality). Everything that occurs takes place through and is referenced to communication and memory of past communication. There are rules governing their interaction—that is there are implicit understandings—that continue. It is like a predictable dance. Mark and Leslie move to a certain point in their conversation of difference, and then they repair. Amber moves in when she senses tension. In this way, the family system maintains its balance, or steady state, (and is said to be in homeostasis).

System Rules

The family is too complex to do its work as if each instance is a totally new existential happening. There is a need for consistency and predictability in the relations and the sequences of relations in the family. People demand predictable relationships, even if they are adverse. The complex operations of the family in issues such as the socialization of children demand that the family develop patterns in its relationships. These patterns become established as system rules. Such relationship rules, both explicit and implicit, organize the interaction of the family and maintain a stable system by prescribing and limiting a member's behavior. The problem is that sometimes individual developmental needs place members where they see these patterns as inappropriate to their own developmental stage. As with Phil and Sarah (case study 2.3), Mark and Leslie (case study 3.1), Jim and Cheryl (case study 2.6), and Brian and Lisa (case study 2.5), this juxtaposition constantly occurs, prompting the family, time and time again, to develop new ways of affiliating and preserving the essential bonds of membership in the midst of change. The family normally employs homeostatic mechanisms to maintain a steady state in the essential bonding of its members. Often, in instances such as the loss of a member through death, these homeostatic mechanisms break down. When this happens, a new form of family structure is needed to preserve family values and functions. Even the loss of children living at home, bringing couples to an empty-nest period, creates complex demands that the parents develop their relationship in a different way and build on that. They also need to develop their relationships with their children not living at home. The two are interdependent and a new form of family needs to emerge.

Self-reinforcing Patterns

When patterns and structure become dysfunctionally integrated with the daily interactions of a relationship, it may seem as if the relationship has turned into an unreal game. The pattern takes over any real communication or interaction. In the previous chapter, Marisa Antonelli's relationship with her parents (case study 2.2), took on the qualities of a cat-and-mouse game, aimed at avoiding the real issues connected with Marisa's relational maturation. She and her parents were both caught up in this game. The game patterns are self-reinforcing because, from each party's perspective, one's behavior is a reasonable response to the other. Marisa's evasiveness brings on hyper-vigilance on the part of the parents; the parents' hyper-vigilance brings out more evasiveness, and so on. One is behavior brings out an intensification of the other's behavior, until the interaction often goes out of control in a runaway episode. Each player draws oppositional energy from the energy of the other, and the pattern takes on a life of its own. Soon each needs the other to play the game. Unless the game can stop, boundaries get set, or the players simply withdraw from the field, a runaway episode becomes inevitable. The runaway episode confirms each party's picture of the other and the reason for their extreme behavior. The solution would be to gradually make it an "ungame." Restorative and stabilizing work can then take place during the temporary cessation of hostilities that the ungame stimulates. Parents and young adult can work out the terms of their relationship in a way that will gradually assist Marisa to take appropriate responsibility for herself and assist her parents to support her in this. The cat-and-mouse game is then no longer necessary, and the relationship can be stabilized in a more workable structure.

There are many possible forms of self-reinforcing patterns. Indeed, many of these patterns are quite normal in family interaction as long as they do not take over the family structure, polarize family members in extreme positions, prevent effective developmental and relational work from being done, and paralyze the normally benign operations of family relational structure (as in the Antonelli cat-and-mouse game). From the earliest development of family therapy, therapists from various schools—psychodynamic, Bowenian, structural, communication, and behavioral schools—each using somewhat different language, quickly identified a wide range of self-reinforcing patterns. These patterns, once identified, became the object of corrective work. In work with couples, some of the more important self-reinforcing patterns to emerge were the overfunctioning/underfunctioning (or overadequate/underadequate) pattern and the pursuer distancer (or demand/withdraw) pattern (Christenson, 1990). In the overfunctioning/underfunctioning pattern, the overfunctioning of one member in areas normally allocated to another brings out the underfunctioning of the other member, and vice versa. A simple example would be one person's speaking for another. Speaking for another can bring out silence on the part of the person being spoken for, or vigorous protest and conflict. When there is silence, it reinforces the need to speak for the other, and so on. Both move to extreme positions. The speaker overshadows the other with his or her world, but is less and less in contact with the real world of the other. The other is caught up in the speaker's world and loses an ability to speak for him or herself. The relationship becomes artificial and full of anger and disappointment, without any ability to correct itself through communication. Patterns similar to this can extend to every area of family structure, particularly where one member is already vulnerable and another is ready to act for the vulnerable person and in some ways to take over his or her reality. The overfunctioning person becomes dysfunctional; the underfunctioning person loses capacities he or she might otherwise possess or develop, particularly his or her voice in the relationship.

RELATIONAL CHANGE THROUGH INTERACTION AND COMMUNICATION

The pursuer/distancer or demand/withdraw patterns have dynamics somewhat similar to those of the overfunctioning/underfunctioning pattern. When these patterns take place in communication, one person will bring up an issue and the other person will minimize the issue or cut off discussion, or one person will initiate an activity and the other will disqualify or undermine it. The disqualifying response will energize the other to a position of further demand. The demand is disqualified, and both are now in extreme positions. Among couples, the pattern often reverses suddenly. The distancer begins to pursue and the pursuer to distance. The game prevents constructive communication and relational work. As with the Antonellis, (case study 2.2) the solution is to make the game an "ungame"—that is, not to play it. The response will be dramatic attempts to restore the game. Making the game an ungame will not resolve the problem, however. Starting with relational areas not colonized by the game, there needs to be a corresponding effort gradually to begin to work out the underlying issues during the momentary period of confusion when, the other refusing to play, the game has lost its potency.

The following case study illustrates this process of repair.

CASE STUDY 3.2

Armand, an East Indian information technology specialist who shares his hobbies of tennis and cycling with his many male friends, has been married for five years to Rosalind, a medical professional from a large Greek family. They have a four-year-old girl, Anaya, whom Armand worships. In certain areas of their relationship, such as care of Anaya or recreation with each other, they get along quite well, despite the turbulence of other areas. During the early stages of the marriage, their personal relationship was rather undefined. It was as if they were trying to develop a common identity with little room for their own differences. When differences did arise, these immediately became a problem and severe conflict resulted. Fueled by Rosalind's intensity, Armand would take the "rational" side. When the conflict became chronic, Armand withdrew into an affair, which he denied. Suspicious at Armand's new coolness and sensing his ambivalence toward her, Rosalind pursued further. Sometimes they would argue all night. When Rosalind discovered clear evidence of the affair, she responded with extreme anger, severe depression, suicidal threats, and withdrawal from the relationship. Eventually she began an affair of her own. Armand now began to pursue and Rosalind to withdraw, but Rosalind withdrew only until Armand stopped pursuing. In the meantime

both remained together in a precarious relationship. Approximately half of their day-to-day interactions were unhampered, while the other half reflected a demand/withdraw pattern that shuttled back and forth. A discussion of money, or anything involving emotional intensity, brought out the same dominant pattern. With their conflict so painful and unresolved, Rosalind asked Armand to leave and Armand complied. When Armand suggested they begin with a social worker, Rosalind's profound anger prevented her from taking part, but she did go to an individual therapist for her depression. She wasn't yet quite ready to start marital therapy, and promised to come later (implicitly inviting Armand's pursuit of her on this issue). Armand cut off his affair and sought help from a social worker. After a short period, Rosalind invited Armand back on condition they maintain their separation at home. With assistance from the social worker, he came back and went along with Rosalind's condition that they not resume their marital relationship. He slept on the couch, but willingly went along with Rosalind's intermittent desires for intimacy. He did not respond in kind to her anger, which inevitably followed intimacy.

Gradually becoming conscious of the game, Armand was working with his social worker to end his part of it. He began to put names on the sequences of interaction—for example that she would be angry and provocative after any intimacy, and that he shouldn't respond in kind. He had felt badly about the damage his affair had done, and was self-consciously making up. The first step was to build enough boundaries for each within their own home so that the need for a separation, at least for a time, was less pressing. There needed to be some separation in their relationship, so that both would be free. Armand was coached to construct healthy boundaries that respected Rosalind's choices, and to make their game an ungame. He would set goals for himself in his journal. He would be available to her, when she was ready, but wouldn't pursue her. He would want her to make up her own mind. When she needed him, he would be there for her, but wouldn't impose himself. He avoided angry confrontations—"I won't let her use my anger," but learned to find calmer ways to resolve problems when he found them in himself. The social worker worked as a type of guru-coach, teaching him about the game that had dominated their relationship and supporting his positive, constructive, and freeing interaction with Rosalind.

Rosalind's response was to test him, inviting him to the familiar pursuit but ready immediately to pounce on him or withdraw. When there was an opening in their relationship for real communication, he did try to use it as best he could. Only gradually were they able to give up the game and work together more constructively on their relationship. Both had been badly hurt, and both had to relearn trust in each other. At one point a dramatic shift occurred, when Rosalind was able to tell Armand of her ambivalence and hurt. Armand listened, acknowledged her anger and hurt, and wordlessly took her hand. Rosalind responded, "I think I'll keep you." Despite this breakthrough, the work of reconstructing their relationship would take many years.

The case study points out both the persistence of a self-reinforcing pattern in the emergent story of Armand and Rosalind and contextualizes its meaning. It also outlines a process of working with one person to manage relational issues. Although relationally focused, the methods used are somewhat similar to those used in working with Gloria in the previous chapter (case study 2.1), but now in a family systems framework. The family systems framework provides some theoretical predictability and allows the social worker to broaden the focus and act as a mentor to Armand. Armand's more effective communication helps Rosalind to respond differently. Gradually the two develop effective recursive patterns of communication and interaction. The process goes much more slowly than working with both members of a couple together. Eventually the angry confrontations dropped off and the couple was getting along better. But Rosalind was hurt and fearful. She was in no hurry to give up her anger and hurt too quickly, as she felt she would have to in couples' counseling. Armand respected this. The counseling format went at about the right speed for the situation. It was important to use the time to move from an ungame to a real healing relationship. When this took place, Rosalind did want to talk about her own ambivalence and hurt. When Armand listened and validated her feelings, she responded to him and both were able to stabilize their relationship.

LEVELS OF FAMILY FUNCTIONING AND APPROACHES TO FAMILY THERAPY

At this point we can begin to make connections between levels of family functioning, discussed in chapter 1, and different approaches to family therapy, discussed throughout the book. These connections are illustrated in table 3.1. Each approach is a useful abstract, taken from a much richer picture of the whole—the social functioning of persons in families fully considered in all of its aspects and complexity. Social work in an actual practice situation should not be reduced to an abstract methodology or a partial picture of the family functioning. The holistic perspective, which relates to every aspect of human social functioning, has always been a characteristic of social work practice. Each school contributes a great deal to the holistic perspective. This book relates the many schools of family therapy to content and process of social work with families. It cannot, however, cover each school in a comprehensive way. The reader is referred to original work from different schools listed in the reference list or to texts, that cover this vast area in a more comprehensive way.[3]

Table 3.1
Levels of Family Functioning and Approaches to Family Therapy

Personal Development & Interpersonal Process	Family Communication & Meanings	Interpersonal & Spiritual Narratives & Stories	Personal Developmental Processes	Family Structure	Family Environmental Systems
Psychodynamic Approaches	Bernard Guerney	Michael White	Bowen Family Systems	Structural Family Therapy	Ecological Systems Theory
Attachment Theory	MRI Interactional Family Therapy	Froma Walsh			
Object Relations Theory	Strategic Family Therapy	Contextual Therapy			
Cognitive-Behavioral	Experiential Family therapy Virginia Satir				

Integrative Approaches: Gottman (1999), Bruenlin et al. (1992), Pinsof (1995)

---

[3]Among these works would be Goldenberg, I. & Goldenberg, H. 1996. *Family Therapy: An Overview.* fifth edition. Pacific Grove, CA: Brooks-Cole. And Nichols, M. & Schwartz, R. 1998. *Family Therapy concepts and methods.* Boston: Allyn & Bacon.

The key issue considered throughout the remainder of the book, is what the personal and relational tasks as family members see them. The social worker helped Armand and Rosalind to resolve their dysfunctional relational and communication patterns and to construct a concrete attachment relationship (case study 3.2), which each could trust. Thus to reduce Armand's and Rosalind's relational work to communication, to attachment, to narrative, or to structural change is a partial and not fully accurate picture of what actually happened in each of these areas of social functioning when they worked on their relational tasks.

SUMMARY

In the chapters 2 and 3 we have studied the process of family development in time through relational tasks at the personal and at the family level. These tasks, as they are tried and carried out at both levels, create family structure, the spatial dimension. Change often takes place slowly. It is dependent on many common factors. There is an investment in the current homeostasis or balance maintained among all the different elements that comprise the family. Yet, when the time is ripe, change can occur very quickly. The social worker assesses the family in motion: the potential for change, the family process, the relational structure and the personal components. Based on this assessment and his or her agreement with key members of the family, the social worker can be a catalyst for the development of family structure for the benefit of its members, searching for the goods of a secure base: safety, belonging, communication, the capacity to choose, and the capacity to grow, to interact, and to care for one's self and others. These interventions take place within different frameworks of cultural meanings and through different family life-cycle stages, explored in the following chapters.

REFERENCES

Ainsworth, M. D. S., Blehar, M., Waters, E., & Wall, S. (1978). *Patterns of attachment. A psychological study of the strange situation.* Hillsdale, NJ: Erlbaum.

Angyal, A. (1940). *Foundations for a science of personality.* New York: Commonwealth Fund.

Aponte, H. J. (1986). "If I don't get simple, I cry." *Family Process,* 25(4) 531–548.

Aponte, H. J., & Van Deusen, J. M. (1981). Structural family therapy. In A. S. Gurman & D. P. Kniskern (Eds.), *Handbook of family therapy* (pp. 310–360). New York: Brunner-Mazel.

Bell, L. G., Bell, D. C., & Nakata, Y. (2001). Triangulation and adolescent development in the U.S. and Japan. *Family Process,* 40(2), 173–186

Blumer, H. (1969). *Symbolic interactionism: Perspective and method.* Englewood Cliffs, NJ: Prentice Hall.

Boszormenyi-Nagy, I., Grunebaum, J., & Ulrich, D. (1991). Contextual therapy. In A. S. Gurman & D. P. Kniskern (Eds.), *Handbook of family therapy* (pp. 200–238). (Vol. II), New York: Brunner-Mazel.

Bott, E. (1971). *Family and social network: Norms and external social relationships in ordinary urban families.* London: Tavistock.

Bowlby, J. (1969). *Attachment and loss (Vol. 1): Attachment.* New York: Basic Books.

Brazelton, T. B., & Cramer, B. G. (1990). *Earliest relationship: Parents, infants and the dawn of early attachment.* Reading, MA: Addison-Wesley.

Burr, W., Hill, R., Nye, F. I., & Reiss, I. L. (1979). *Contemporary theories about the family.* New York: Free Press.

Christenson, A. (1990). Gender and social structure in the demand-withdraw pattern in marital interaction. *Journal of Personality and Social Psychology, 59,* 73–82.

Coelho, G. B., Hamburg, D., & Adams, J. (1974). *Coping and adaptation.* New York: Basic Books.

Cooley, C. H. (1922). *Human nature and the social order.* New York: Scribner.

Constable, R. T. (1984). Phenomenological foundations for the understanding of family interaction. *Social Service Review, 58*(1), 117–132.

Goldenberg, I., & Goldenberg, H. (1996). *Family therapy: An overview.* Pacific Grove, CA: Brooks-Cole.

Gottman, J. M. (1999). *The marriage clinic.* New York: Norton.

Gottman, J. M., & Notarius, C. I. (2002). Marital research in the 20th century and a research agenda for the 21st century. *Family Process, 41*(2) 159–198.

Gottman, J. M., & Levenson, R. W. (2000). The timing of divorce: Predicting when a couple will divorce over a 14-year period. *Journal of Marriage and the Family, 62,* 737–45.

Haley, J. (1980). *Leaving home: The therapy of disturbed young people.* New York: McGraw-Hill.

Haley, J., & Hoffman, L. (1968). *Techniques of family therapy.* New York: Basic Books.

Hartmann, H. (1958). *Ego psychology and the problem of adaptation.* New York: International Universities Press.

Hoffman, L. (1981). *Foundations of family therapy.* New York: Basic Books.

Kohlberg, L. (1969). Stage and sequence: The cognitive-developmental approach to socialization. In D. Goslin (Ed.), *Handbook of socialization theory and research* (pp. 347–480). Chicago: Rand McNally.

Linton, R. (1936). *The study of man.* New York: Appleton-Century-Crofts.

Mead, G. H. (1934). *Mind, self and society: From the standpoint of a social behaviorist.* Chicago: University of Chicago Press.

Minuchin, S. (1974). *Families and family therapy.* Cambridge, MA: Harvard University Press.

Minuchin, S., & Fishman, C. (1981). *Family therapy techniques.* Cambridge, MA: Harvard University Press.

Nichols, M. B., & Schwartz, R. C. (2001). *Family Therapy: Concepts and methods.* Boston: Allyn & Bacon.

Rank, O. (1964). *Will therapy and truth and reality.* New York: Knopf.

Schwartz, R. (1995). *Internal family systems therapy.* New York: Guilford.

Selman, R. L. (1976). Social-cognitive understanding: A guide to educational and clinical practice. In T. Likona (Ed.), *Moral development and behavior* (pp. 299–316). New York: Holt Rinehart & Winston.

Shibutani, T. (1961). *Society and personality*. Englewood Cliffs, NJ: Prentice-Hall.

Smalley, R. (n.d.). *Mobilization of resources in the individual*. Philadelphia: University of Pennsylvania School of Social Work.

Stern, D. N. (1985). *The interpersonal world of the infant; A view from psycho-analysis and developmental psychology*. New York: Basic Books.

Taft, J. (1926). The effect of an unsatisfactory mother-daughter relationship upon the development of a personality. *The Family, 7*, 10–17.

Thomas, W. I., & Thomas, D. S. (1928). *The child in America*. New York: Knopf.

Turner, R. (1970). *Family interaction*. New York: Wiley

Vogel, E. F., & Bell, N. (1960). The emotionally disturbed child as the family scapegoat. In N. F. Bell & E. F. Vogel (Eds.), *A modern introduction to the family*. New York: The Free Press.

White, R. D. (1959). Motivation reconsidered: The concept of competence. *Psychological Review, 66*, 297–333.

CHAPTER 4

Assessment and Intervention with Families in a Multicultural World

In the previous chapters, we developed a comprehensive frame of reference for social work practice with families (chapter 1), built on the actuality of transactions on the inside and the outside of families. We developed social work theoretical frameworks for concepts of family developmental processes (chapter 2) and family relational structures (chapter 3). The cases in this chapter are examples of transcultural practice, but they also anticipate some of our discussion in the following chapters on assessment and intervention with families.

THE IMPORTANCE OF CULTURE

Relational processes and family structures take place in their own cultural contexts. This chapter adds the complexities of culture in a diverse society to our framework for social work practice. In this complex social environment, family transactions influence the ways people in families communicate and solve problems. Building on the understanding of cultures, which is basic to the education of every social worker, the chapter approaches assessment and intervention with families from a transcultural perspective. The transcultural perspective recognizes the already-existing diversity of transactions within and across cultures. There are thus many paths to developing good family environments. Recognizing the cultural meanings in these different paths, the social worker can assist family members to develop an environment that is workable for all the family's members.

The following cases point out some problems and solutions within a complex, multicultural society.

CASE STUDY 4.1

A Hmong family, who had been relocated as refugees from the mountains of Laos to Columbus, Ohio, learned that their child's cancerous eye needed to be removed to prevent the cancer from spreading. Not understanding the decision or having been involved in it, the father took the child out of the hospital without notification and ran away. The state invoked the child protection law and searched for the family. This event became a top news item. Unfortunately, no helping professionals in the situation had a cross-cultural understanding of the meanings of the family's cultural beliefs and the fear and trauma behind its flight. The surgical removal of the eye, an appropriate course by Western medical treatment standards, would seem to the family like a death sentence for the child. Cross-cultural consultation, carefully combined with spiritual rituals of consolation, psychoeducational approaches to this family, and mediation by the clan group leaders, in addition to modern medical practices, could have prevented the many unfortunate outcomes of the situation.

CASE STUDY 4.2

Samoans from a Pacific Islander community expressed their concerns for spiritual space when one of their family members became sick and was hospitalized in Hawaii. It is their cultural practice that healing take place through joining together with the sick person as a group of extended family and kin. However, the time, the space, and the limited number of visitors allowed in the hospital room prevented this communal practice of spiritual healing from taking place. Although it took some time to change, the hospital later not only modified its regulations for visitation rules, but also made space available for a group visitation and spiritual practice.

RIVERS FLOWING INTO THE SEA

Working with families in a complex, multicultural society is like working with many rivers with different sources. Assessment and intervention within a family's relational structures is intervention within a complex cultural framework. The cases already cited in previous chapters and in the introduction to this chapter involve persons from many different cultures. Yet with all this diversity, there are still common threads. People do things that any person, knowing one's self and one's own relational sources, could understand. In each case, family members struggle to define their family relationships. However, now the struggle takes place in the context of an increasingly media- and market-dominated North American society, which has itself an enormous and diverse cultural substructure. The example of the Hmong family suggests that a process could have taken place with the family and elders of the clan that would have respected their own cultural meanings and the appropriate need for recognition, by the Western medical community, of their status and function and the meanings of the situation. In the second case, a shift in hospital procedures accommodated the needs of Samoan culture.

FUNCTIONAL FAMILY ASSESSMENT

The problem of family assessment in an already complex and multicultural world is balanced with the need to develop a functional assessment. This is an assessment of how (and whether) the family unit is able to construct appropriate responses to the needs mentioned in chapter 1: safety, communication and belonging, appropriate choice, and the conditions conducive to growth within the context of the culturally referenced ways the family has of doing this. Without these reference points, it is easy to get lost in a myriad of differences. Family assessment comes from a consideration of how the family relational structure is working, how its members might construct relationships with each other, the cultural meanings of these relationships, and the relational work to be done. Relational structures, internal to the family, emerge at particular stages of family development. These relational structures can be tremendously varied, additionally reflecting culture and other factors in the environment. Their functions, however—the prerequisites for the optimal development of persons—remain the same. For these relational structures to work inside the family, they need the support of a surrounding complex of family and societal arrangements and these also have their own systems of meaning. Social workers work between the internal relational structures and the external societal arrangements so that family members are able to construct these essential functions and relational qualities in their own way, but with reference to learned cultural patterns.

One of our principal assumptions has been that in a diverse, multicultural society, where economic and political power inevitably privileges certain groups over others, conflicts and discrimination unfortunately do take place. Because social workers are positioned at the juncture of major institutional sectors of society and with families, they have to deal with these multicultural issues even more than members of other helping professions. Where there is pain and discrimination, social workers usually are the first to deal with it and the dilemmas it brings.

Cultural differences between family members and their outside environment, and within the family itself, are powerful determinants of intervention. Given the diversity of the society, the transcultural work of the family members is already embedded in their relational work, in their internal relational work, and in their external work with social institutions. It waits only for recognition and appropriate support. The internal work has to do with family developmental tasks, which are transcultural tasks as well. The external work involves complex transactions with social institutions, which often do not by themselves understand the family. Such work usually involves a diverse, larger community with its political and economic structures. A transcultural perspective integrates into practice multicultural perspectives on the experiences and life ways of different cultural groups. Such practice with the emergent blend of family cultures in North America is already taking place. It is no longer seen simply as a matter of respecting cultural differences and the life ways of different groups. A key to understanding the family from a strengths and resilience perspective is realizing how it deals with its own differences while retaining connectedness. The dialogue of family members at any stage is a dialogue of many types of differences and connections. Many of the effective ways family members have of dealing with other differences can be applied to cultural differences as well.

Because of the nature of the practice situation, the assessment process with couples and families is somewhat different from the process with individuals. The concepts of couple and family developmental tasks and family structure, discussed in earlier chapters, delineate personal, family, institutional, and community tasks. The intertwining of different lives, stories, and meanings, and the coexisting presence of conditions such as depression, anxiety disorders, posttraumatic stress, and substance abuse, brings complexity to the assessment. The passion of a family's struggle with differences, the needs of its members for justification and control, and the possibility that a relational structure may become unsafe for its members can create concern. Such problems are perceived by family members as mystifying, complex to understand, and beyond any personal or family influence. For the social worker, it is easy to get lost in the details without knowing what to look for. Or the social worker, often reflecting the agency, could take over what appears to be unresolvable complexity and try to resolve it "from above" with the power of the social institution. As with the Hmong clan, when the outside, non-Hmong community takes over, the family and clan has to retreat into dysfunction or prepare to resist. The possibility of a productive couple or family process would then no longer exist.

Assessment demands a purpose. Assessment, done with family members and continuing throughout the helping process, is first of all the determination *with the family* of a workable present purpose. Family members need to become active enough to decide what they can and want to do in the light of internal and external realities. There needs to be a focus on the present, with the past as background. The most important part of assessment is assessing conjointly the conditions and tasks a couple or family face, whether they are willing and able to do something about the problem, and how they might do it. What balance needs to be struck between personal and family tasks? How would the social worker work with different units of attention, both within and outside the family, to make a difference?

Since family structures and family needs are so diverse, assessment should provide an emergent general picture in the social worker's mind of what needs to be done if the family is to regain and maintain its balance. What units of attention in the family and in the environment would be most workable? Might one work with one member, such as Armand (case study 3.2), a couple, such as Miguel and Juana (case study 2.4) or Brian and Lisa (case study 2.5), a parent and a child, the whole family in-session (Mario, Renata, and Marisa Antonelli, case study 7.4), and/or a mix of work with family members in different configurations and with an institution, such as the court or the school, as in the J. family (case study 4.7), the Hong family (case study 4.5), or all of the case studies in chapter 9? With the case of Jack and Jung (case study 4.6), there was work with the couple, with Jack's family of origin, and with a sectarian assistance agency. What tasks are most important for what the family needs to do? Where can they begin and what might they aim for?

Developing and ensuring safety will involve a complex of personal and family tasks. For example, persons have to deal with depression and anger and an inability to communicate effectively; couples have to work out boundaries, understandings, ways of communicating, and mechanisms of anger control, and may have to agree on a truce until key issues are worked out, and so on. Rather than talking about communication or history, overwhelming family members with all the aspects of what needs to be done in the abstract, the worker begins by helping family members to test out, with each other and in-session, their picture of the problem, their ability and willingness to do something: to communicate, to develop and respect boundaries, and so on. The worker begins with the family member given the most authority in the culture and then moves to other family members until a picture, with all of its differences, emerges. When this takes place, the assessment and the history usually fall into place as well. In any case, when assessment takes place in this way, it is hoped that the couple or family remain in charge of what needs to be done and can reinforce each other's efforts without intruding on or taking over the personal work of the other.[1]

On the other hand, family members may decide that, in the final analysis, they are unable or unwilling to do what it takes to resolve the problems. This is in itself a most valuable finding, not ultimately undesirable since it frees other members to take appropriate steps for the new and different family structure that then needs to emerge. None of this can be fully predicted. In this sense, rather than a diagnosis— assuming some sort of fixed, underlying reality that needs to be rooted out and displayed—assessment is an ongoing and active testing of possibilities in the context of tasks to be done. The social worker becomes a collaborative coach for the family's active exploration of what it can or cannot do, what it is willing or unwilling to do. Although the worker may first have to make a very rapid tentative assessment to establish a direction for focus and exploration, most of what follows will not be known by anyone in the beginning. Trying to fit everything in at once in a feverish hunt for the problem is the wrong focus. This only overwhelms the family with what it could not do so far, and it prompts the worker to take over. What family members most need is a sense of where they can begin, what they can do, and some realistic hope of improvement coming from their own actions with each other. Often the worker becomes a gentle referee for communication about difficult issues, communication that in many cases may not take place at home. When it does take place in the interview context, the next task is for the couple or family to bring it into their ordinary dealings with each other.

This means that the social worker must actively structure the assessment process, provide a frame of reference, and thus normalize family members' understandings of what is happening while setting boundaries on any possibility for destructive communication, self-harm, or harm to others. Such structuring is done without explosive and dysfunctional exchanges. The couple or family members remain in control of their interaction with each other, they can participate in the initial assessment of the issues and meanings, and they can foresee doing something together about the situation.

---

[1]With the complexity of tasks in the first interview, the authors have found that, when possible, a two-hour first interview often works better and keeps the family appropriately in charge of its realities.

MULTICULTURAL PERSPECTIVES

What does the family social worker need to know to practice competently in a society that is already multicultural and struggling to develop transcultural frameworks? A variety of approaches to practice with families have recognized and built on the specifics of culture (Fong & Furuto, 2001; Ho, 1987; McGoldrick, Giordano, & Pearce, 1996; Lee, 1995). Man Keung Ho (1987) suggests that cross-cultural family practitioners need first of all to have general knowledge about specific ethnic groups. The understanding of persons in specific cultures and the way the cultural themes may be processed by different persons in different cultures is basic to the education of every social worker. There are classic common cultural patterns and themes that arise in any comparative analysis of families in a particular context. Among these classic patterns and themes, themselves changing in the face of a dynamic society, are mate selection and marriage, gender and family roles, child-rearing patterns, acculturation, adaptation and change, and religious practices (Ingoldsby & Smith, 1995; Locke, 1992; Mindel, Habenstein & Wright, 1998). Ho expanded these to include nine further patterns that can be applied to each cultural group. These are: extended family ties, the spousal relationship, the parent–child relationship, sibling interactions, intermarriage, divorce and remarriage, immigration and acculturation, and help-seeking. The social worker can apply these patterns to a deepened understanding of any particular cultural group.

However, in the face of a complex, postmodern society, the interactive and relational patterns of ethnic families are themselves changing. Family members are often faced with adopting new roles that conflict with their traditional cultural norms, and the practitioner can experience confusion regarding what should be supported. A beginning answer to the question of what to support is to build on the strengths and resources that ethnic minority families bring with them. How should this be done in a dynamic, multicultural society? Again, the family itself resolves the dilemma. With the assistance of the social worker, the family arrives at and tests out its own best balance. The greatest danger is the worker taking over, using prescriptive and reductionist approaches (Ho, 1987; Lee, 1989), and making assumptions about the family's experience without checking with them.

The family therapy field has long been characterized by divisions into different approaches. The major emphases of these approaches are related to levels of family functioning, as illustrated in our discussion at the end of the previous chapter. A focus on one sector of family functioning and its related methodology (see table 3.1) implicit in many conventional approaches to family therapy narrows the field of focus, and it often elevates the worker as an expert in the method, shutting down the family's efforts to manage the problems. Surveying conventional approaches to family therapy, Man Keung Ho (1987) pointed out that many of these approaches are insensitive to the indigenous cultural values and structures of ethnic minority families. The family therapy method framework, which divides family functioning into parts, can narrow the focus of assessment. Some family therapists, whose major method focus is personal development, reflect this in their assessment. Others emphasize communication, or narratives, or family structure, and reflect that particular emphasis in their assessment (Cocozzelli & Constable, 1985). A more dynamic and inclusive framework needs to take in all the aspects of family functioning, with intervention geared to the problem. The integrative frameworks of Bruenlin, Schwartz, and MacKune-Karrer (1992) and Pinsof (1995) are meant to do precisely that. As such, these frameworks are major steps forward.

In the field of social work, systems theory has been the source of theoretical integration of method theories dealing with individuals, families and family networks, neighborhoods, organizations, and institutions (Hearn, 1969; Von Bertalanffy, 1968). Ecological systems frameworks, which model relations of person to the family and the outside environment in an effort to explain complexity, have been developing since the early 1970s (Auerswald, 1971; Gordon, 1969; Germain, 1973; Hartman & Laird, 1983; Stein, 1974). These assumptions, detailed in chapter 2, have also framed our discussion of social work with families.

Moving from a focus on a single culture in itself, it is important to account for the dynamics of cultural transition, particularly in the diverse North American society. Using Asian-American families as an example, and recognizing that there are many intra-ethnic differences, Evelyn Lee (1996) attempts to develop a typology of transition, summarized in table 4.1.

The families described in table 4.1 are in transition from patterns that emphasize stability and family connectedness (family members letting go of their individual preferences) to other patterns with more individualistic perspectives. Families who emphasize connectedness and de-emphasize individual preferences are often reluctant to seek help from someone outside the family who might have a different perspective, or to discuss personal issues. They are reluctant to believe that any assistance could be derived from those contacts. The case of the J. Family later in this chapter (case study 4.7) is a good example of dilemmas faced by these families. An external structure, generating relational tasks, was necessary for the family to make real changes.

Discussions of culturally competent practice in a North American context have acknowledged four basic assumptions essential for practice:

1. There is no single North American culture
2. Diversity is to be acknowledged and valued
3. Members of each cultural group are diverse
4. Acculturation is a dynamic process (Caple, Salcido & di Cecco, 1995).

Our focus on family brings two further basic assumptions:

1. Families (and individuals in family units) adapt to their contexts and to their outer environments as well as to their internal relations (Ho, 1987).
2. No single current family therapy model of how families function can account for cultural complexity. Nor can a single model of family therapy adequately account for and treat the complex content of family interaction (Bruenlin, Schwartz and MacKune-Karrer, 1992).

Table 4.1
Five Patterns in Asian American Families

Family Types	Common Characteristics
Traditional Families	—Consist entirely of family members born and raised in Asian countries. —Family members hold strong beliefs in traditional values. —Speak regularly in their native languages and dialects. —Practice still traditional rituals and customs, etc.
Cultural Conflict Families	—Have American-born children. —Arrived a decade ago when the children were young. —Intergenerational conflicts and role confusion are common problems. —A husband may have lived in the U. S. for many years, gone home, and brought back a wife who is not familiar with American culture, etc.
Bicultural Families	—Consist of well-acculturated parents who grew up in major Asian cities and were exposed to urbanization, industrialization, and Western influence. —Some were born in the United States but raised in traditional families. —These parents often hold professional jobs, come from a middle-or- upper-class family backgrounds. —The power structure has moved from a patriarchal to an egalitarian relationship between parents. —Family discussions are allowed between parents and children, etc.
Americanized Families	—Consist of parents and children born and raised in the United States. —Have become largely Americanized. —The roots of the traditional Asian cultures began to slowly disappear. —Communicate in English and adopt a more individualistic and egalitarian orientation, etc.
Interracial Families	—Currently consist about 10–15% of marriages and they are increasing rapidly. —Japanese Americans lead in this trend, with more than half marrying outside their group, followed by Filipino, Chinese, Vietnamese, and Korean Americans. —Some are able to integrate both cultures with a high degree of success. —Others often experience conflicts in values, religious beliefs, communication style, child-rearing issues, in-law problems, and so forth.

SOURCE: E. Lee (1996, pp. 231–233).

A TRANSCULTURAL PERSPECTIVE

The realities and complexities of cultural transition in a diverse society demand a transcultural perspective. Looking for patterns in isolation from their dynamic contexts does not deal fully with the fact that social workers operate in contexts of change, of *becoming*. Cultural values are themselves in process of change. The transcultural perspective uses action and relational tasks as powerful ways to assist family members to make changes. From a systems perspective, changes in any part inevitably affect the whole. In the case studies presented in this chapter, Jack and Jung have to learn that getting a Christmas tree should not conflict with an infant's need for food. Mr. J. needs to find better ways to deal with a disrespectful adolescent than violence and intimidation. Mrs. J. needs to learn that her implicit acceptance of gender dominance can interfere with her dignity, her worth, and her potential contribution to the family and to society.

As the world gradually becomes a global community, its dynamic and inexorable logic is to rethink ethnocentric, regional, or national membership boundaries. This trend toward a global community is inevitable, as technology, trade, communication, civilization, and spirituality become common points of reference, and as migration of peoples across geographical, racial, and religious lines inevitably occurs. Although the trend is inexorable, what will emerge is still unclear in its particulars. The general picture is of many families moving toward enriched relational and community contexts where development is a possibility for every person—a picture of many rivers flowing into the sea. The spirit and principles articulated in the Universal Declaration of Human Rights set some standards for this transition. As such, it is a tremendous resource for social workers.[2]

A transcultural perspective focuses on the possibilities of developing connections between and among family members of diverse cultural experiences and socioeconomic backgrounds. It reaches out toward a vision of what is common to all cultures and what is different, and the communication necessary to manage differences. It assumes that people construct relationships with the hope of securing fulfillment for similar basic needs and relational goods, but may have different understandings and may interact with each other in somewhat different ways. A transcultural perspective also assumes that family members can decide on how much they want or need to modify their roles, and how much personal and feeling-oriented communication they want or need. Rosalind (in case study 3.2), for example, did not want to talk about her vulnerable feelings, and Armand respected that until she finally was able to tell him about them. This was a crucial moment in the helping process. When Armand listened, they resolved the issue for a time.

---

[2]Adopted and proclaimed by General Assembly Resolution 217 (111) of 10 December 1948. See www.un.org/nghts/50/decla/htm (19 July 2003).

The key to a transcultural understanding can be found in the helping process itself. The helping process involves a search for the substantive, the ontological meaning of being with each other, despite many perceived barriers. This transcultural perspective assumes that barriers and differences do exist. However, the values that best undergird family life, the goals sought by family members because they are human, and the relational tasks needed to carry out these goals can inexorably bring members to radical choices: to encounter differences, to resolve them, and to look for appropriate change. The alternative is to face dissolution of functional communication, connectedness, and support for appropriate personal differentiation.

Social workers, working with change processes and differences, can assist family members to deal with the demands of these change processes within the context of transcendent human values and transformed relational systems. Family practice is beginning to assume that there really are commonly shared meanings of our family existence, and that there is a mutual healing process in the context of these emergent common meanings. Paradoxically, these assumptions emerge mainly through encounters with difference and through some sort of communication. These differences, including cultural differences, demand some resolution if any unit is to grow. The transcendence over differences that emerges in a bonding process can also be present in helping relationships. Social workers can help members to create mutual healing processes, with the goal of maximizing the capacity of persons to care, to grow, to choose, and to change—and thus to transform a relational system.

Working from a Transcultural Perspective

A young couple may experience cultural differences with a surrounding environment, or they themselves may come from different cultures. In either case, their tasks are somewhat similar. They need to construct a common family culture, different from its surroundings. In this sense, the normal relational tasks of early marriage also become transcultural tasks. Armand and Rosalind (case study 3.2) combine East Indian and Greek-American cultural backgrounds. Both reconstructed their relationship, blending both personal and cultural patterns into a common relational culture of its own.

Class differences can also operate in a way similar to cultural differences. In the following example, Catherine comes from a middle-class background; Dwain from a working-class background. Both share the same ethnicity. Some of the difference in patterns can be traced to social class of the families of origin.

CASE STUDY 4.3

Catherine and Dwain are an African-American couple who are having difficulty dealing with the differences emerging in their first years of marriage. Catherine, the daughter of two physicians, uses medical concepts to talk about her ups and downs; Dwain, raised "on the streets" thinks Catherine is just not tough enough. She uses general concepts that from Dwain's perspective implicitly criticize him. Dwain understands these concepts, but when he wants to get to her for being "uppity," he responds concretely to her abstractions and makes fun of her. She "doesn't get the joke" and responds with disappointment and hostility. For Dwain, it is a funny compliment to tell her that she is getting a little plump; Catherine feels he rejects her when he does that. Both have trouble dealing with the polarities of their own communication. Abstractions on one side are met with concreteness on the other. The game maintains the distance between them, and they feel a vague lack of intimacy in the marriage. They need to develop common languages and patterns of communication. With help, they begin to work on developing a common understanding, uniquely their own.

Intergenerational Patterns   Relational tasks are not simply experienced on a single generational level. There are clear intergenerational patterns and precedents, as indicated in the following case study.

CASE STUDY 4.4

A woman from North China, an upper-middle-class Catholic refugee with a family fractured by war and resettlement, married a man in Taiwan of peasant stock, a Buddhist with a strong, intact Taiwanese family support system. With her encouragement, he became a highly educated professional. Throughout their marriage, they experienced massive shifts in Taiwan toward a more open society. Their oldest son, Dwight, was educated in the United States from his early adolescence through his Ph.D. He remembers with some pain his struggle as a Chinese-American teenager to become "one of the boys" in the Seattle schools. Dwight married Becky, a North American, Catholic woman of Irish, English, and German extraction with her Ph.D. Becky comes from a large, well-educated, and equally complex family. Despite ethnic differences, their educational backgrounds made them very similar in orientation. Becky grew up in an interracial family, in a very diverse, well-educated urban community. As a child, she devoured books. As a teenager, she traveled and participated in international exchanges. By her university years, her friendship network was international. Together, now with their first child, they bridge massive cultural issues, developing their common family culture.

Relational Tasks in a Transcultural Perspective   When relational tasks break down, they can be recomposed and rectified in the context of a helping relationship with a social worker. Social workers bring their own experience and their ethnicity, as well as the orientation of the sponsoring agency (school, court, family service agency, or hospital) to the transcultural mix. The challenge of such transcultural family work is to channel complex understandings and specific practice approaches into a flow of couple or family energy toward the development of "we-ness" and simultaneously toward a deeper experience of self as a person.

Transcultural Assessment

To aid the transcultural assessment process, social workers need first of all to gain an understanding of the experiences of each cultural group as they have assimilated and adapted to a diverse society while at the same time retaining a distinct identity of their own. It is important to avoid stereotypical and biased generalizations about any particular group. The interaction of culture and personality is complex and difficult to differentiate. The social worker therefore needs to resist looking for simple cultural categories to explain behavior. The following list of strategies, from one social worker's experience with transcultural assessment, brings together research findings with social work practice experience.[3] These strategies provide guideposts to discern both differences and commonalities across cultures.

- Consider all clients as individuals first, then as members of a minority status, and then as members of a specific ethnic group.
- Never assume that a person's ethnic identity tells you everything about his or her cultural values or patterns of behavior.
- Treat all "facts" you have heard or read about cultural values and traits as hypotheses, to be tested anew with each client. Turn facts into questions.
- Remember that all minority group people in this society are at least bicultural. They have had to integrate two value systems that are often in conflict, and these conflicts may override any specific cultural content.
- Some aspects of a client's cultural history, values, and lifestyle are relevant to your work with the client. Others may simply be interesting to you as a professional. Do not prejudge what areas are relevant.
- Identify strengths in the client's cultural orientation that can be built upon. Assist the client in identifying areas that create social or psychological conflict related to biculturalism. Seek to reduce dissonance in those areas.
- Know your own attitudes about cultural pluralism, particularly whether you tend to promote assimilation into the dominant society values or to stress the maintenance of traditional cultural beliefs and practices.
- Engage your client actively in the process of learning what cultural content should be considered.
- Keep in mind that there are no substitutes for good clinical skills, empathy, caring, and a sense of humor.

Transcultural Intervention

The helping process is a search for the ontological meaning of being with each other despite many perceived barriers, and so the key to a transcultural under-

---

[3]These strategies were developed by Helen Brown Miller (1995). Not otherwise published.

standing can be found in the helping process itself. Helping is a process of encounters that themselves can generate energy for change. Through communication, the couple or family learn to redirect the energy from these encounters toward
the transformation of the inevitable impasses in their relational systems. With the
assistance of the social worker, the couple or family's own resolution of these impasses challenges stereotypes; implicit assumptions of dominance; and patterns and
beliefs of race superiority, gender inequality, power abuse, and the personal and institutional exploitation of vulnerable people.

Let us begin with four basic principles of transcultural practice:

1. *Take the position of the other*   The basic understanding of each person as
a subject interacting with others (intersubjectivity) underlies family work, particularly in a transcultural perspective. In real relationships differences already exist. To
model understanding and working with differences, the social worker needs to put
his- or herself in another's shoes and help members of the family to do the same.
In communication, this skill means reflecting accurately the other's meanings (accurate empathy), clearing one's mind of one's own reactions and for the moment
becoming the other in feeling and thought and in dialogue (see further discussion
of this in chapter 5). This powerful tool of communication and mutual understanding is used collaboratively and with the permission of the other. The worker
helps each person to communicate, sometimes even filling in the gaps in communication with another, and doing the same for the other when necessary.

2. *Discover and use the healing power of relationships*   Persons who come
to a helping process have often experienced discrimination and inequality in the
larger society. There are many persons who have never experienced their own
worth and dignity, their radical equality, and the self-responsibility that goes with
being a person. They do not really expect to be treated or accepted as a person. The
alternative experiences of inequality, of dominance and being dominated, and of
nonacceptance are carried into family relationships and even into the helping relationship. Domination is expected to continue. The remedy for the experience of
nonacceptance, inequality, and exploitation is not a technique but a more personal
approach to relational tasks. Relationship building needs to be rich in values that
respect personhood. It must address issues of appropriate process and personhood
when they emerge. The approach cannot be value neutral.

3. *Language and communication are the media of the healing process*   Language and communication are the first elements to suffer from undeveloped or dysfunctional relationships. When cultural and relational difference intrude on personal development and understanding of roles, language can become
impoverished and communication impersonal. There can be a struggle around a
common personal language, the vehicle of communication, that they have yet to
achieve. Catherine and Dwain (case study 4.3) fenced with each other in abstract
and concrete languages respectively. To communicate appropriately, they had to

learn each other's verbal and nonverbal languages. In large part this involves listening, taking in what the other is meaning, and reflecting it accurately back to the other. A smaller part of this learning involves expressing one's self in a way that the other can listen and understand.

4. *Agency and communion resolve themselves more quickly in joint relational work* The couple or family unit, the "we," formed out of difference, learns to act and support each other's agency through communication and relational work. However, a mentality of colonization by what is perceived as the more powerful culture can shut off a person's ability to act as an agent of one's own development. Joint relational work, with each other and with the social worker, can heal some of the mentality of colonization. The social worker/mentor helps the couple or family unit to deal with these issues, which come from both inside and outside the unit.

Working across these cultural divisions within the family and with the outside world, transcultural practice inevitably involves one's own cultural integration. One cannot help others deal with a mentality of colonization if one has the same mentality. These processes of cultural integration, taking place simultaneously with the worker and with the family, deepen the river of the universal emotional system. They move toward higher and more complex resolutions of the developmental needs of persons and family units. When people find genuine connection with each other, the superficial layers of preconceived notions, preconditioned reflexes, and patterns of emotional reactivity lose their disruptive power. The shared energies (synergy) of effective dialogue flow into the core of the relational system, validating the worth of every member of the family. Appropriate communication moves toward the goal of empowering and revising family functioning and dealing with its own generational differences. When it comes together, the family system discovers its ability to deal with its own community of belonging and the outside world.

Froma Walsh (1999, p. 24) points out that the journey into different patterns and meanings has much in common with a spiritual journey. More than symptom reduction, problem solving, or communication skills, people are seeking meaning and deeper connections with others in their lives. There is often spiritual distress at the core of physical, emotional, and relational problems. Making space for spirituality—encouraging spiritual connections in family and community life—adds to the transformational power of the helping process. Making this space can begin a process of healing and overcoming barriers, whether the barriers are socioeconomic, linguistic-symbolic, racial-political, or cultural realities of dominance and discrimination.

Working with Families with Children

Moving from the couple relationship, transcultural family practice has additional dynamics with the family with children. There is now a generational divide. As they encounter another culture in school, children often feel caught between cultures. The transcultural focus needs to include both generations of the family as well as the school or other salient institutions. With the Hong family, in the following example, there was work both on the outside and the inside of the family relational system.

CASE STUDY 4.5

Myong Hong, age sixteen, had just moved with his family to a newly developed Detroit suburb. Myong had consistently been a good student until his sophomore year. His parents were hoping for better education for their children. Soon after he had been transferred to his new school, Myong faced peer pressure to join an ethnic gang group. He was suspended by the school on suspicion of gang membership and activity. The school had a no-tolerance policy for any apparent gang involvement. Myong's suspension brought the Hong family to a crisis that needed professional intervention. His father, a first generation Korean-American radiologist, was very disappointed to find out about the suspension of his eldest son. Myong's mother was also very upset. She was concerned about Myong, but had trusted that her son's longstanding "big brother" relationship with John, the son of mutual friends, would help him to avoid these problems. Both parents were also disturbed by their recent moving process. They moved from an ethnic enclave into a multicultural neighborhood with few members of their group available to them. Myong lost his old neighborhood friends. His

contact with John had become occasional. Myong has a brother, Hoon (twelve), and a sister, Sunyoung (nine), whom both of seemed to adjust better to the family's recent move. They liked their new house and had made some neighborhood connections at a park center. Both parents are very active volunteers in services to the ethnic community and church life. They have maintained their good connections within the Korean-American Community. Nevertheless, the incident was a terrible blow to them.

After an initial meeting with Dr. and Mrs. Hong, a home visit, follow-up family counseling sessions, and individual session with Myong, the social worker sought a joint conference with the school social worker, the academic dean, and the parents over Myong's situation. Out of this collaborative process, Myong returned to school under a set of guidelines established to strengthen his self-esteem and to reduce his level of anxiety associated with peer pressures and alienation. Myong eventually recovered his sense of belonging when the family spent more time together. The school took a more proactive role in accommodating Myong with extracurricular activities, where he was able to find success.

When a child of a recent immigrant family enters the mainstream school system, he or she is at risk of experiencing both anxiety and low self-esteem unless the family/school/neighborhood provides some support and connections. This anxiety can become unresolved emotional reactivity. It can spread to interactions in the family and the larger society (Bowen, 1966). Intervention with Myong, within the family system and with the school, was aimed at reducing anxiety and validating self worth while promoting a secure environment, relational justice, cross-cultural accommodation, and intercultural connections in the family and school community. These goals were accomplished through tasks. Tasks for Myong would assist his family and the school to manage the relationship better. In this way they would help Myong adapt appropriately to his new school and what it was asking from him.

We develop the principles of transcultural practice further through two cases. The first case involves an escalating crisis for Jack and Jung. The crisis could have led to breakdown of the bicultural relationship and child neglect.

CASE STUDY 4.6

Jack, a Caucasian, nonpracticing member of the Church of Jesus Christ of the Latter Day Saints (Mormon), married Jung while he was serving in Korea in the armed forces. They moved to his hometown, Ogden, Utah, after Jack's period of service had ended. Jack, taking college courses in accounting, had been laid off from his job. The couple, now with a six-month-old baby, was experiencing severe financial pressure. Both were very preoccupied with their daily difficulties getting adequate subsistence for the family.

A family crisis was precipitated over whether they should buy a Christmas tree or purchase food for their baby. For Jack, celebrating Christmas without a Christmas tree was inconceivable. He grew up with many fond sentiments associated with the tree during the Christmas season. Jung grew up in a small rural village where her parents worked hard to survive as a family. She feared that Jack's spending habits had not considered her concerns for basic needs. She could not comprehend Jack's sentimental interest in such "a luxurious decoration" during the holidays. Nor was Jack able to attend to the urgency of

obtaining essential food (i.e., milk) for the baby. Jung had recurrent memories of traumatic experiences of hunger and hardship, growing up in a poor family when Korea was suffering from a destructive war. She was increasingly feeling anxious.

These issues and the couple's frustrations and disappointment led to frequent arguments with verbal abuse. Jack's parents had disapproved of their marriage and were unsympathetic to the couple. Jack refused to seek any help from them. Jung had been cut off from her in-laws from the beginning. Jack, going through a periods of transition and doubt, was not at all interested in his family's faith tradition. From the time she had emigrated to the United States, Jung had been emotionally cut off from her family of origin. Although she began taking language courses and showing some interest in involvement in the Church of the Latter Day Saints, the birth of her child and the severed relationship with her in-laws made it difficult for her to connect to supportive social networks. Additionally, Jung's limited English skills and her dependency on Jack for transportation further complicated her ability to access needed support and resources.

The social worker worked with Jack and Jung to help them develop safer and more effective communication patterns, develop problem-solving skills, clarify their goals as a couple, and eventually receive assistance from Jack's church and from his family. Helping Jack to reconnect with his family was a defining moment that opened up both systems to shift in their beliefs and their structure and accommodate each other. It became a metaphor for their changed perceptions of themselves as a family. It took a good deal of work with Jack, with Jung, and with the family to develop a reconciliation where Jung could feel real membership in Jack's family and Jack was able to come to terms with enough of his anger to reconcile with them.

Five Further Practice Principles

We now examine the helping process in this case study to elicit further principles of transcultural practice. The external crisis forced Jack and Jung to begin to deal with parts of their marriage that were profoundly incomplete. The social worker began by exploring with them what their experience was and how they were able to express what they experienced. The social worker needed to avoid imposing his views on them—judging who was right or wrong, and/or explaining why something was taking place. Listening to their inner voices as well as their bodily messages, the worker focused on being together with them as a couple and also with each of them separately as distinct persons. He facilitated the construction of a dialogue between Jack and Jung to bring together their separate energies. Where connections were needed, he helped them make those connections, reaching out where they could be found and reframing and redirecting them. Jack knew his own mind and his preferences, as did Jung. Paradoxically, as this mutual understanding of who they each were and what they valued was accepted as part of a dialogue, they began to free themselves from their own ethnocentric and self-centered rigidity. This rigidity was causing the relationship to lose energy and connectedness, when they fell repeatedly into dehumanizing cycles of evaluating and judging each other. These cycles had become their relational pattern.

5. ***Begin Where the Client Is***   This is the starting point for cross-cultural understanding and culturally sensitive approaches to families. It helps practitioners to avoid any rigidity stemming from their own preconceived notion about who the family members are, and thus it liberates both clients and therapists from victim-blaming preconceptions or assumptions that their interaction is in any way linear. To begin in this way demands an open position. The open position allows participants to explore authentically the core of who they are, as agents of their own development, to discover the true meaning of what they seek to construct, and to discover strengths and resources, in themselves and in others to resolve the challenges of their struggle.

6. ***Respect Individual Perspectives and Choices***   Respect perspectives and choices helps participants to develop a joint perspective: Although the worker put

this principle into action at the onset of his practice with the couple (case study 4.6), it became even more important when it was incorporated into the sequences of family work. The couple realized that both psychological and physical needs were essential to the healthy individual and to family development and social functioning. They decided that the main challenge was not so much deciding who would be right or wrong in a marital dispute, but rather their problems involved lack of resources in meeting both sets of needs at the time of their crisis and an inability to mobilize available external resources. The problem was to choose between a Christmas tree or baby milk. Both were timely and appropriate. If they had enough resources to satisfy both, each could be simultaneously pursued without conflict. When they realized this, the couple began to see more clearly their baby's needs and rights. These had been pushed aside in their tug of war about who was right and who was wrong. The baby's needs took on urgency as the couple determined to seek out the needed resources from both his extended kin and other social service agencies.

7. *Promote Social Belonging: Without Belonging There Is No Survival*   Social work is committed to promote social belonging for clients. Belonging is necessary for group survival. Cross-racial integration has always been a source of tension in North American society, and Jack and Jung (case study 4.6) felt it. Many immigrant families with school-age children and youth encounter and experience hostility when they settle in a mainstream neighborhood. There is a well-known Korean proverb: As fish must live in water, so people must live in a society where they find acceptance. Jack and Jung had experienced social and cultural isolation during courtship and after marriage. Their way of coping with uncomfortable social attitudes toward their interracial marriage was to wall themselves off from the outside world, from Jack's family of origin, and from each other. This self-imposed isolation prevented any meaningful contacts with friends and kinfolk. Jack and Jung needed to expand their socio-cultural boundaries. These included other interracially married couples, Jung's ethnic people, Jack's kin, faith communities, and other friendship groups.

8. *The Ultimate Goal of Family Intervention: Achieve an Optimal Balance of Integration*   In the beginning, Jack and Jung's crisis (case study 4.6) appeared to focus on a conjugal dispute over the resources to satisfy two different needs. However, the problem is more complex and goes beyond any particular individual boundary. It is interwoven with the integrity of family system. The cost of a Christmas tree cannot outweigh the child's needs. Nor can Jung's concerns for the baby obscure the more complex relational issues of her needs, Jack's needs, and their joint concerns and responsibilities for the baby. This total picture would demand more resources and expand the boundaries of the nuclear family system. To integrate each member's needs, one can also move beyond the immediate family toward the boundaries of the community, until an optimal balance between demands and resources is reached. In this case, Jack, Jung, and his family of origin overcame their

initial reluctance to rediscover their connections with each other and the resources of the community where they now have their cultural and religious affiliations.

9. *Change and Adaptation Is an Ongoing Process*   Jack and Jung (case study 4.6) also needed space to accommodate the child of their bicultural bonding. Jung had to adapt herself to her new country: its laws, language, and expectations. Jack and his family needed to facilitate the acculturation processes for Jung by creating a more friendly holding environment of cross-cultural acceptance. Both Jack and Jung needed to provide their child with cross-cultural opportunities to enrich their child's bicultural identity and to integrate the strengths each culture brings to their marriage. The family on both sides needed to develop more supportive roles to bridge the emotional gulf and social distance between the generational lines. Healing the wounds of the past can take place therapeutically through the efforts of a faith community as well as through work with the social worker. Working between different units of attention, social workers also need to assist the outside units to increase their cultural competence and avoid a potentially negative experience with Jack's family of origin or faith community.

TRANSCULTURAL ASSESSMENT AND INTERVENTION: THE J. FAMILY

Assessment assists the practitioner to understand the complexity of a situation and provide a framework for intervention. Tools for assessment include genograms, ecomaps, inventories, home visits, and contracts, among others. The relation between assessment and intervention is illustrated in the case of the J. family.

Mr. J., forty-five years old, born in Singapore of an overseas Chinese family and living in Berkeley, California, was referred by his attorney for individual counseling in relation to a recent episode of child physical abuse involving his thirteen-year-old son, Kwak. At the time of the episode, the police and child protection worker had intervened, responding to a neighbor's complaint. While under an order of protection from the county court pending further hearings, he had contacted a social worker of his ethnic background in private practice for professional help.

The J. family has to develop a safe environment, shift in its ways of communicating expectations and in the socialization process with adolescent children, and rebalance the relationship between father and mother. Members have to resolve their anxiety stemming from Mr. J.'s probationary status and the consequent delay in having their immigration status changed to permanent resident.

During the assessment period, Mr. J. was seen at the social worker's office three times. Then he was joined, in weekly couple sessions, by his wife, also from an overseas Chinese family in Singapore. Followed these initial sessions, a combination of the conjoint family sessions, couple, sibling, and individual sessions were synchronized according to the needs of the therapeutic process and family members' circumstances. Additionally, during the interim intervention period, two home visits were made. Their initial purpose was to assess both the living environment and family atmosphere; later it was to share the therapist's interest in engagement with the family in their own natural family space. The case narrative details work on the inside with the J. family to recompose themselves and then meet the expectations of the court. On the outside, the social worker worked with the court, sending reports to the family and the court.

CASE STUDY 4.7

The J. family is composed of the biological parents and two adolescent children, Chen, a sixteen-year-old girl and Kwak, a thirteen-year-old boy. They were living in Berkeley, California, with a pre-immigration status, and waiting for approval of their permanent residency. Both parents completed university education in Singapore. Mr. J came to the United States several years ago, first as an overseas business assistant manager of a leading transportation company. He moved his family from Michigan to California to manage the area branch office. Their families of origin still live in Singapore, except for Mr. J's younger brother and his wife. These now reside near the J. family. Mrs. J. is a housewife, devoting herself to the care of her family and occasionally helping neighbors with art projects. Chen, the elder child, is in her third year in a private high school with boarding facilities. Her academic achievement is very high. With support from her high school and from her family, she looks forward to admission and scholarship assistance in the best universities in the country. She lives in a school dormitory during the week and spends her weekends with her family. Kwak, the younger child, who is in his eighth grade, had been the victim of his father's severe physical punishment. In the J. family constellation, Mr. J. is closer to his high achieving daughter,

while Mrs. J. is closest to Kwak, who resembles her physically. In the family triangles, Mr. J. was the outside member of a tight bond between Kwak and Mrs. J. Mrs. J. was the outside member of Mr. J's and Chen's bond.

Mr. J. was arraigned under the state child protection law by the police and a child protection team upon a report of child abuse by a neighbor. The son had been severely punished with a broomstick for talking back to his father, and this led to a family altercation. Mr. J. was put on an order of restraint. Subsequently he was forced to separate himself from his family for a period of nearly eight months, until the court order was lifted. The court involvement would severely delay the family's application for permanent resident status.

The issue had begun around Mr. J's concerns that Kwak be ready for college. The parents are very much concerned about the education of their children, particularly as the time for college application approaches. Chen was planning her college application. Mr. J. began to worry about his son's academic performance. He believed that Kwak was not making enough efforts to improve, and instead, appeared to be obsessed with computer games. Usually Kwak is quiet in family gatherings. However, he became quite verbally reactive when he was forced to join a family gathering where Chen would consult with a university professor to develop a study plan to strengthen her essay skills. The father thought this would encourage Kwak to develop some motivation and skills for his future education. In Mr. J.'s youth, "talking back" to his parents or elders would not have been tolerated in any way, nor could Mr. J. tolerate his son's disrespectful behavior. Mr. J. had experienced severe physical punishment from his father. That evening, after the family dinner, he chose to confront and punish his son. As their verbal interaction became more intense, Mr. J. lost his temper and punished his son with a nearby broomstick. Kwak had been defiant to his father and disregarded the cultural norm of obedience. For Kwak, his father's action with the broomstick was unacceptable in their new country. Mr. J. lacked any other means of resolving his anger and his son's behavior. This conflict between cultural expectations in a country of origin and the child protection law takes place with many recent immigrants from many Asian countries. In these countries, corporal punishment is still widely tolerated as the parents' right to discipline their children. Kwak's injury was mild enough. The bruises, cuts, and a fractured finger were treated and healed quickly. However, the image of Mr. J., the father and husband, needed rehabilitation with family members. The family also needed to be able to manage issues without intimidation and violence. Psychological residues of the incident remained in the memories of each family member. The guilt, the resentment, and the secrecy, as well as other residues of the incident needed to be examined for cleansing and healing. There were strained relationships both inside and outside of the family system.

The family also experienced the institutional constraints on Mr. J. The court's expectations had been humiliating and imposed public shame on the family. The application process for their permanent resident status had to be temporarily suspended on the advice of their immigration lawyer. The family court had demanded concerted efforts from the family members toward accommodating each other. In this sense, the court was reconstructing their interactive patterns and their socio-cultural realities. The court was concerned that the healthy growth and development of the J. family members be promoted. Chen, in particular, who had more quickly assimilated North American values, had a heightened sensitivity toward family violence but also a strong connection with her father. She reacted to the incident more profoundly than others in the family.

Genogram Assessment

A genogram is a generational family map that allows a person to see a family system historically.[4] Assessing previous life-cycle transitions, the social worker can present issues in the context of the family's evolutionary patterns. The genogram in-

---

[4]For a more detailed discussion of genograms, see McGoldrick, Gerson and Shellenberger (1999); Nichols and Schwartz (2001, pp. 160–162); Goldenberg and Goldenberg (1996, pp. 181–183); and Hartman and Laird (1983).

cludes at least three generations of family members, as well as nodal and critical events in the family's history as related to the life cycle. When family members are questioned about the present situation in relation to the themes, myths, rules, and emotionally charged issues of previous generations, repetitive patterns become clear. Genograms suggest possible connections between family events over time. Patterns of previous illness and earlier shifts in family relationships brought about through changes in family structure and other critical life changes can easily be noted. The genogram provides a framework for reconstructing what may be currently influencing a crisis in a particular family (McGoldrick, Gerson & Shellenberger, 1999, p. 3).

The J. family genogram is constructed in figure 4.1 to demonstrate a transcultural perspective toward assessment and intervention within intergenerational family emotional systems. It provides a model that can be generalized to other multigenerational family situations. Circles donote females; squares, males. An X in the figure denotes a deceased family member.

Figure 4.1
Genogram of the J. Family

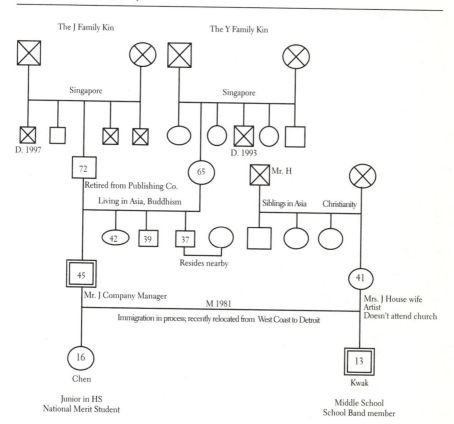

Ecomap Assessment

An Ecomap is widely used as a tool to assess the level of social support inherent in family members' transactions with possible environment resources and connections. Hartman and Laird (1983) and others have elaborated its clinical use in assessing environmental resources, including significant others, social institutions, and spiritual resources available to families. The quality of resource mobilization, external to the immediate family structure, is diagrammed according to the connective lines. These lines symbolize various types of connections (see figure 4.2).

On the basis of the initial assessment, Kwak had stressful relations with his father and was overclose with his mother. He had positive relations with his paternal uncle and the school band. He had tenuous relations with school and stressful relations with the court. Chen had positive relations with her father, her friends, school, and camp; tenuous relations with college admission offices and her uncle; and stressful relations with court. Mr. J. had positive relations with his company and his brother; tenuous relations with neighbors; and stressful relations with the court, his separate residence, and the immigration lawyer. Mrs. J. had positive relations with her art work; tenuous relations with her brother-in-law; and stressful relations with court, her husband's separate residence, her

Figure 4.2
Ecomap Assessment of the J. Family

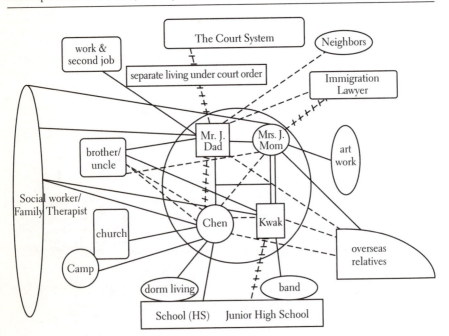

neighbor, and the immigration lawyer. All family members had positive relations with the social worker. The ecological sources of stress for this family came directly from the court, the separate living arrangement for Mr. J., and the immigration lawyer.

Despite these strained interactions between the family and the legal system, they were able to maintain some positive relations with their school and work situations, the exception being Chen's concern with college admission and Kwak's academic progress at school. Mr. J.'s younger brother is the only close relative available to the family members.

Other than her art work, Mrs. J. has few social outlets. Both of Mrs. J.'s parents had died recently. She was unable to be with them in their illnesses or attend the funerals. Additionally, she had deferred to Mr. J. and stopped practicing her religion. Mr. J. has tended to downplay her sadness.

Chen finds her friends and opportunities to volunteer at camp satisfactory. Kwak had a limited amount of social interaction with his band group. Mr. J. finds his social outlet in his contact with colleagues at work. Both Kwak and Mrs. J. seem to lack much of a social support network. Kwak seemed to understand his mother and she felt close to him, defending him against his father. During the incident they both gained more weight than they would like to keep.

The Intervention Phase

Sessions with the J. family were arranged jointly. During the initial phase, the sessions were scheduled more regularly. Later they were scheduled less often, according to their needs and the time demands experienced by family members and by the social worker.

Most standard clinical procedures will work for culturally diverse families. It is important, however, for practitioners to respect the readiness of these families for clinical intervention. Recent immigrants from non-Western countries may perceive professional (and psychological) intervention in their families as intrusive. Depending on their pre-therapeutic history and the circumstances leading to professional intervention, they are often suspicious. Research on help-seeking behavior and premature termination indicates that the initial period of intervention is the most critical. Transactions with the family need to be sensitive and carefully monitored from a transcultural perspective. For those who can benefit from psychoeducational approaches, clinical procedures should be explained in linguistically and visually understandable ways. In the process of early engagement, spiritual and symbolic ways to integrate trust, humor to break the ice, or other tested ways to build relationships are useful. When and where necessary, mutually trusted persons may be utilized as buffers and mediators for the purpose of connecting and contractual development. Sometimes working through the context of a church, school, or another trusted institution makes a big difference in the family's receptivity to the helping process.

Goal Setting and Intervention Strategies

From the onset of the helping relationship, clients are responsible for taking part actively in the tasks leading to the expected outcomes. For the J. family, there were specific therapy goals for individual members and general goals for the entire family system. The overall context of these goals was one of relational justice. From Mr. J.'s perspective, Kwak's talking back demanded of him the same measures his own father had used. However, Mr. J.'s act failed to accomplish its intent. It made the family unsafe for Kwak and in different ways worrisome for the others. It cemented Kwak's anger, disrupted Mr. J.'s relationships with the others in the family, and diminished Mr. J.'s stature. If he were to defend his actions, he would have had to develop a culture of further dominance and ineffective communication patterns in the family. The result would have been that members would become afraid. Communication around certain realities would go underground or break forth in uncontrolled outbursts. Mrs. J. would be further diminished in her alliance with her husband. Chen would look elsewhere to satisfy her hunger for relational justice. The family would become less effective for its members.

The J. family needed to restore its own safety and harmony. It needed to develop the means and patterns that could accommodate the different needs, possibilities, and aptitudes of each of its members. It needed to release itself from court supervision and move on with the process of application for permanent resident status. Mr. J. needed to repair and restructure his damaged relationship with his wife and children, as did each family member with each other member. Following the ecomap, each family member needed to work out a change process in relation to each of the other members of the family. With the information already presented, a list of concrete goals and the process needed to meet these goals can be established.

Intervention strategies become the definitive means to achieve these goals in the course of the helping process. Although communication techniques and cognitive-behavioral strategies have a proven effectiveness in resolving many family problems, transcultural practice principles serve as general guideposts in utilizing intervention methodologies and techniques.

The social worker for the J. family was bilingual, bicultural, and known for his expertise in such situations. Mr. J. had initiated his contact for social work services on the referral of a lawyer who had confidence in this social worker's work. Mr. J. was tense and reserved in the beginning. He faced unknown possibilities of professional engagement for himself and his family. It was important for the social worker to centralize Mr. J.'s control of his destiny, even under the constrained circumstance of receiving assistance and being under court supervision. Individual, couple, and family sessions were charted out with specific goals and a specific agenda. Contacts involved homework between sessions, periodic reviews of therapeutic progress, court hearings, home visits, information/referral services, and consultation. Mr. J. and his family became central to the hoped-for movement from a state of vulnerability and dysfunctionality to a more defined and renewed level of social functioning. All the assessment data, including the genogram, the ecomap and other inventories—journal essays and professional progress reports—were made transparent to the clients as means of ensuring that transcultural principles would be realized.

The goals for the J. family in the helping process were tied to clinical procedures and intervention strategies as well as to principles of transcultural practice. These goals were achieved not merely by means of techniques, but also by the mutual engagement in co-creating new realities of effective living and parenting.

When Mr. J. re-examined his traditional patterns of control and came to a new understanding of relational justice, he became more open to a developed appreciation of the meanings inherent in parenting and individualization in growth and development. He saw himself changing and realized that he could regulate his stress and impulses. Seeing more options for himself, he became more open to meeting the challenges of life differently. Mrs. J. also began to free herself. She moved away from her earlier depression and began to regulate her activities to strengthen family cohesion and to reduce the stress generated by her own anxiety. Although Western values might have expected even more independence, these were enormous moves for Mrs. J. Chen began concentrating her energy on her college admission. She involved herself in volunteer services and began to expand her extracurricular activities. She reconnected with her father and brother. Kwak began healing the physical, psychological, and relational wounds caused by his father's punishment. He gained back his self-esteem and was able to reach out more to his father, his sister, and his friends. Both Kwak and Chen felt comfortable enough to contact the social worker voluntarily; Chen even brought her close friends to be introduced to the social worker. Kwak would use e-mail now and then to share his feelings with the social worker. Mr. and Mrs. J. regained their balance as they were reunited and freed from the restraining order. Mr. J. began to listen to his wife's feelings and encouraged her to practice her religion. They had learned to support each other. This support could help heal Kwak's and Chen's pain associated with their father's abusive episode. It also would help heal the family crisis resulting from court supervision. The family's reactive emotionality (anger), their anxiety, and their stress-producing patterns were eased. Intergenerational cultural conflicts—family members' struggles to adapt to the expectations of society—were eventually alleviated.

The Use of Metaphors and Culturally Congruent Approaches

Metaphors and maxims are very helpful for directing a family's attention to emerging phenomenological realities that cannot easily be articulated in cross-cultural transactions. Family therapists frequently use metaphors to communicate about current family dynamics without taking the risks that may come with more direct language. Well-known maxims and metaphors, handed down from sages through many civilizations over the course of time, attest to their lasting effects on problem solving. Strategic (paradoxical) and solution-focused brief family therapists, among others, often use these intervention strategies. Transcultural therapists often find parables and metaphoric messages either from a particular culture or more universally known sources (such as Aesop's fables). These parables have useful, culturally transcendent, and generative meanings. Their use could bring more congruence to therapeutic interaction. There are rich sources of stories and parables in the Talmud, the Bible, and other religious texts. There are sayings with similar meanings across cultures. The Western saying *"There is a shadow under the lamp"* and the Eastern saying, *"A monk can't cut his own hair"* are understood similarly. They can be metaphorically used to explain that both clients and therapists have blind spots and need help at different times. Edwin Friedman, a family therapist and rabbi, has made extensive use of metaphoric stories (Friedman, 1990), as has Carl Whitaker. These stories become useful in moving families beyond their impasses and in unlocking cognitive and emotive issues deeply veiled with covert, secret awareness. These issues could involve extramarital affairs, rumors of incest, and so on. Hawaiian ways of resolving family illness often necessitate calling their ancestral ghosts or spirits to reveal the secrecy hidden in the family circle (Hurdle, 2002).

In the case study (7.7) of John, Mary, and Stephen Maxwell, the story of Pinocchio was used to deal with the attachment issues created by Stephen's running away. Also, certain aspects of a case can become metaphorical. Sarah's back (case study 2.3) becomes a metaphor for issues to be resolved in her relationship with Phil. Jack and Jung's reconciliation process with Jack's family becomes a metaphor for the acceptance of their marriage in their society. Joseph and Paula construct a temporary "wall" to protect each from the other's verbal abuse. Ashford and Louise (case study 6.6) take a trailer trip through the West, a metaphor for their growing comfort with each other in their empty nest.

Mr. J. did not realize, except through discussion, that he was projecting his unresolved hostility toward his own abusive father onto his son, Kwak, and using the issue of academic performance to do so. The metaphor that helped him see his own projective anger came from a familiar saying: *You can burn down your entire house to kill bugs.* When the roots of his hidden anger were externalized, Mr. J. was able to differentiate Kwak's needs from his own emotional reactivity. He began to see other ways to deal personally with his projections from his father and to develop effective parenting skills. Many of the individual sessions with Mr. J. were focused on these issues. Similar to the ego-oriented approach with Gloria in chapter 2 (case study 2.1), they assisted him to deal with anxiety and achieve differentiation. They drew from the family systems perspective of Murray Bowen (1966). At the same time, family sessions were used to reinforce structural boundary making and effective communication, using both structural family therapy and narrative perspectives. Different techniques were used in different formats to achieve related goals.

Home Visits

In their earliest work with families, social workers were "friendly visitors." Home visitation is one of the most distinctive outreach activities in social work. Although for safety and other reasons, home visits are challenging to do, they can provide many therapeutic advantages. Family members can be better accommodated in the natural setting of their daily lives. Home visits make an assessment of the ecological contexts of client's neighborhood environment and dwelling quarters possible. They widen the scope of clinical observation by making the home atmosphere and living arrangements a part of the work. They often allow clients both flexibility and control. Family pictures and other significant cultural icons can be more readily accessed for assessment and intervention. They also help social workers to become more aware of human geography and space from a cross-cultural perspective. Young people and children often have more open space for therapeutic engagement when they are given opportunities to participate in a more creative way.

The worker made a home visit in the middle phase of work with the J. family. The purpose of this visit was to understand their family's ways of accommodating familial needs and to celebrate their efforts to develop a certain quality of life and relationships. He found that the J. family was living in a modest, three-bedroom rental apartment in a large, racially integrated complex in Berkeley. The family atmosphere was hospitable. Their daily life was largely and noticeably centered on the children's educational achievements. They believed this affordable location could best help them to accommodate the children's education. Chen and Kwak each had their own private room and the parents occupied the master bedroom. Their dream is that some day they would have their own single-family home. A noise factor, due both to the building structure and nearby traffic, disturbed some of its peace and created some anxiety.

The family session was informally conducted and free ranging. This informality allowed a great variety of themes to emerge. There was some focus on the roles each member takes with others; the television programs they watch together; their levels of inclusiveness, control, and affection; intergenerational linkages; their ethnic support system; and daily schedules. There was also discussion of questions of neighborhood attitudes, public facilities, public transportation, issues of religion, social contacts, health care, and dietary, cultural, and family heritage, and so on. Mr. J., although actually living outside, took part comfortably. They were relaxed, interactive, and eager to share personal things of interest to them. The experience and understanding from this visit helped the worker to focus more on family cohesion and developmental tasks of each family member from each one's own personal and cultural points of view. Thus the family's strengths and their sense of control were accentuated.

Between-session Activities

Much of the actual family work takes place outside of the formal sessions. Assignments and between-session activities are arranged around the goals and progress of the work with the family. These activities are a real test for family members' level of commitment to and competence in taking control of their situation and making their therapeutic engagement work effectively. A variety of therapeutic homework assignments can be used. Journal or letter writing, inventories, behavioral tasks, genogram construction, drawing, and communication exercises are most frequently used, in addition to a host of creative activities. These activities help both social workers and clients to be on a forward track toward the goals of family work and toward implementation of their initial agreements. They reinforce and fortify therapeutic and healing processes. They strengthen the family's control and competence in mastering the social functioning skills and tasks connected with meeting needs, solving problems, and resolving conflict. These activities should be linked to the phases of family work, including diagnosis and evaluation.

For the J. family, there were a number of between-session activities and individualized assignments for each member of the family. At the initial stage, Mr. J. was asked to provide preliminary data for genogram construction. He also got involved in writing his own reflective, bilingual letter. In this letter, he assessed his role in the family crisis from both narrative and cultural value perspectives. These two assignments enriched family intergenerational assessment data. Even more important was their reinforcement of the new concepts and new language he incorporated in his narratives. They helped him to construct a more holistic meaning of the change taking place.

Mrs. J. began writing a journal, focusing on her thoughts and feelings about different things. She needed to be able to recognize her feelings and thoughts, find a language for them, deal with each of them, and find a way to balance and accommodate both to each other. Her journal was meant to increase her awareness of depressive ways of thinking, feeling, and reacting. In the face of these older ways of thinking, she would search for constructive connections and linkages, changing her feelings of helplessness and her self-blaming communication patterns. This helped her to focus on her strengths. It began to rebalance her functioning with Mr. J. and with the family toward equilibrium.

Chen continued focusing on her college admission process, volunteer work, outings with her mother, dialoguing with her father, playing with her brother, and so on. As a more competent bilingual person, she was asked to take a more proactive role in representing the best interests of her family in dealing with the court system and in reaching out to colleges and universities for scholarship. She attempted to serve as a role model for her brother in achieving academic success while recognizing his own unique strengths. She successfully wrote a very convincing letter to the judge requesting that the restraining order for her father be lifted.

Kwak was asked to send e-mail messages to the therapist as frequently as he felt he needed to express his inner struggle in dealing with his recent experience of abuse and its associated mixed emotions of guilt, anger, confusion, and low self-esteem. He got involved in school extracurricular activities including band, and watched his eating habits carefully. He set priorities, balancing the demands of his schooling with family needs, personal health care, recreational and social activities, and computer games. He made greater effort to express himself in both verbal and written communication with his father. He appreciated what his sister was going through and learned from her success. He visited his paternal uncle on his own and maintained a close adult relationship with him. These activities were reported verbally and through telephone contacts, written letters, and e-mail messages. Each family member made an inventory of conflict tactics, using an instrument already developed. They also made their own progress reports during this period.

Linkage to Cultural and Spiritual Resources

It is critically important for social workers carefully to attend to a contextual understanding of clients' cultural resources, including spirituality, ethnic support systems, historic patterns of assimilation and adaptation, and formal and informal social service structures of the host or majority community. Ethnic families need to maintain linkages with their own cultural and spiritual resources. Such linkages often bring healing and social support. They buffer the stresses of acculturation. They assist family members to recover their sense of wholeness, purpose, and meaning. They become sources of synergy, enriching the family's transcultural meanings. These meanings are particularly important with interracial married couples.

Although the J. family did not belong to any particular faith community, Chen actively linked herself to a local Chinese church as a summer camp volunteer, helping the adoptive families of Asian-born children. Mr. J. involved his family with his Singapore-based transportation company staff and their families during a Chinese festival. He maintained contact with his family of origin back home by phone and letters. Mrs. J. maintained contact with her relatives in Singapore through her art work. Kwak had a few friends of Chinese ancestry at school. The family had sought therapy from a bilingual person who could relate to their cultural roots.

THE ENDING PHASE

In the ending phase, normal clinical procedures should be followed in working with families in a multicultural setting. When they have achieved the goals of therapy, it is important that clients be set free to advance their life course with a sense of empowerment and completion. In this process, feedback and validation are directed to affirm their readiness to terminate, and an evaluation checklist can be used as a tool to facilitate the ending process. As clients depart from one's office, metaphors of their own changes can be developed to celebrate their achievements.

In some cultures, the ending needs to be stretched out with some relationships continuing. Asian-American families often believe that "once you become connected as friends, your friendship should prevail in good faith over all other circumstances." They tend to maintain their relationships far beyond the time and space of therapy. Nevertheless, the focus of the ending is on ending, showing the social worker that they have changed and are able to handle new realities. They are grateful for all the social worker has done. In the family members' minds, he or she has become like a member of the family. The ending phase with the J. family, discussed in greater detail in chapter 9, was not an ending in the Western sense but a continuation. Each member of the family "checked in" with the social worker in different ways over the next two years to point out that they were maintaining their gains.

What Brought about Change in the J. Family?

Given that Asian families often are quite reluctant to talk about personal and familial issues, the J. family had made considerable lasting personal and relational changes while still retaining their cultural identity. It was not so much communication in itself, but relational tasks and then some communication, that assisted the J. family to accomplish a major relational shift. There are a number of reasons for this:

1. *External Necessity*: There was a difficult external situation with which to deal. The court had set expectations that the family could not accomplish without help. Their immigration application was also dependent on a resolution of the court's expectations.
2. *Focus on Relational Tasks*: The focus of the worker remained on the relational tasks connected with dealing with the demands of a concrete situation. This was reinforced by the use of assignments and a mentoring relationship with family members in relation to their relational tasks. When this took place, their understanding of themselves and the others gradually also changed and they were able to talk about it to a certain extent.
3. *Culturally Congruent Meanings*: The social worker's use of culturally congruent metaphors established a framework of meanings that made sense to the family but was not personalized.
4. *Internal Shifts Depend on External Work*: The internal forces in the family—the unstable triangles of Mr. and Mrs. J., Kwak, and Chen—were pressing for resolution. However, given the cultural situation, these internal forces alone probably would not have brought the family to seek help.

Family work allows for an opening for every member to greater possibilities. The social nature of family relationships may allow members to move from the outside in, each transcending some of the limits of their situations. An ethnocentric worldview broadens and the rivers move inexorably to the sea. The following Buddhist parable tells the story:

If you take a tablespoon full of salt, put it into a glass of water, stir it and drink, the water will taste quite bitter because of the salt. But take the same tablespoon of salt and stir it into a large, clear, pure mountain lake, then take a handful of that water and drink it. You won't taste the salt at all. (Wolin et al., 1999, p. 126)

The lake is the living, cultural environment of the outside world, complex, full of difference, full of stories, a precious heritage for each person. It is also the world of common understandings and meanings and the functional patterns that can emerge from the productive interaction of differences.

SUMMARY

How may persons and family units retain cultural uniqueness in a diverse and changing society? The transcultural perspective addresses the relational task of managing personal meaning and difference in a situation of diversity and change. The following chapters take the task perspective further into life-cycle tasks faced by couples and elaborated families.

REFERENCES

Auerswald, E. (1971). Interdisciplinary versus ecological perspective. *Family Process, 10,* 202–215.

Bowen, M. (1966). The use of family theory in clinical practice. *Contemporary Psychiatry, 7,* 345–374.

Bruenlin, D., Schwartz, R., & MacKune-Karrer, B. (1992). *Metaframeworks: Transcending the models of family therapy.* San Francisco: Jossey-Bass.

Caple, F. S., Salcido, R. M., & di Cecco, J. (1995). Engaging effectively with culturally diverse families and children. *Social Work in Education, 17,* 159–170.

Cocozzelli, C., & Constable, R. T. (1985). An empirical analysis of the relation between theory and practice in social work. *Journal of Social Service Research, 9*(1), 47–64.

Fong, R., & Furuto, S. (Eds.). (2001). *Culturally competent practice: Skills, interventions, and evaluations.* Boston, MA: Person Custom Publishers.

Friedman, E. (1990). *Friedman's fables.* New York: Guilford.

Germain, C. (1973). An ecological perspective in casework practice. *Social Casework, 54,* 325–330.

Goldenberg, I., & Goldenberg, H. (1996). *Family therapy: An overview.* Pacific Grove, CA: Brooks Cole.

Gordon, W. (1969). Basic constructs for an integrative and generative conception of social work. In G. Hearn (Ed.), *The general systems approach: Contributions toward an holistic conception of social work.* Newbury Park, CA: Sage.

Hartman, A., & Laird, J. (1983). *Family-centered social work practice.* New York: Free Press.

Hearn, G. (Ed.). (1969). *The general systems approach: Contributions toward an holistic conception of social work.* Newbury Park, CA: Sage.

Hurdle, D. H. (2002). Native Hawaiian traditional healing: Culturally based interventions for social work practice. *Social Work, 47*(2), 183–192.

Ho, M. K. (1987). *Family therapy with ethnic minorities.* Newbury Park, CA: Sage.

Ingoldsby, B., & Smith, S. (1995). *Families in multicultural perspective*. New York: Guilford.

Lee, D. (1989). Book review. [Review of the book *Family therapy with ethnic minorities*]. *Social Casework, 70,* 517–519.

Lee, D. (1995). The Korean perspective on death and dying. In J. Parry, A. Ryan (Eds.), *A cross-cultural look at death, dying, and religion* (pp. 193–214). Chicago: Nelson-Hall.

Lee, E. (1996). Asian-American families: An overview. In M. McGoldrick, J. Giordano, & J. Pearce (Eds.), *Ethnicity and family therapy* (pp. 227–248). New York: Guilford.

Locke, D. (1992). *Increasing multicultural understanding*. New York: Guilford.

Marlin, E. (1989). *Genograms*. Chicago, Contemporary Books.

McGoldrick, M., Gerson, R., & Shellenberger, S. (1999). *Genograms: Assessment and intervention* (2nd ed.). New York: Norton.

McGoldrick, M., Giordano, J., & Pearce, J. (Eds.). (1996). *Ethnicity and family therapy* (2nd ed.). New York: Guilford.

Miller, B. (1995). Personal communication.

Mindel, K., Habenstein, R., & Wright, R. (1998). *Ethnic families in America: Patterns and variations* (4th ed.). New York: Prentice Hall.

Pinsoff, W. (1995). *Integrative, problem-centered therapy*. New York: Basic Books.

Stein, I. (1974). *Systems, theory, science, and social work*. Metuchen, NJ: Scarecrow Press.

United Nations. (1948). *Universal Declaration of Human Rights*. Adopted and proclaimed by General assembly resolution 217 (111) of 10 December, 1948. See www.un.org/overview/rights/.

Von Bertalanffy, L. (1968). *General systems theory*. New York: George Braziller.

Walsh, F. (Ed.). (1999). *Spiritual resources in family therapy*. New York: Guilford.

Wolin, S. (1999). Three spiritual perspectives on resilience: Buddhism, Christianity, and Judaism. In F Walsh (Ed.), *Spiritual resources in family therapy* (pp. 121–135). New York: Guilford.

CHAPTER 5

Beginning Phases with Couples: Process and Theory

In discussing beginning and middle phases of social work with couples, we develop related themes from family developmental theory, from family therapy, and from social work practice theory. In this chapter, we use examples of couples dealing with developmental issues of early marriage. We also explore the creation of boundaries and intimacy through communication and the concept of projective identification in couples as developed by object relations family therapists. We explore the beginning phase of work with couples and issues of commitment and gender inequalities in couple relationships.

The couple is the executive subsystem at every stage of the family in formation. For this reason, our discussion of work with couples is also applicable to work with larger family units in later chapters. The social worker addresses the couple first of all, and then the other parts of the family complex, whether these comprise children or the extended family structures, such as grandchildren, in-laws, and so on. As the family becomes more complex, the couple may find itself having to develop further what brought them together in the first place. Thus, as the family structure elaborates itself, relational tasks connected with the couple's beginnings repeat themselves in different ways.

THE NEWLY MARRIED COUPLE

To understand the newly married couple, we need to imagine Brian and Lisa (case study 2.5) now experiencing the *actuality* of a committed relationship: the need to communicate and develop common patterns of managing their relationship, to manage everyday decision making about issues such as about money, and their intimacy. All of the tasks of the engaged couple apply to the newly married couple as well. They need to establish their communication and relational patterns. Many of the issues put off in the engagement period can no longer be put aside once they are actually married. They now need to develop common patterns of dealing with their common life and still preserve differences and appropriate ways of managing personal issues. These personal issues are no longer private and cannot be walled off, away from the other, nor are they common property. Rather, they are somewhere in between.

Some of the most profound issues faced by the newly married couple have to do with the fact that the couple needs to develop compatible patterns of managing their common living situation, while at the same time they are becoming a separate unit from their families of origin. This raises all sorts of personal and relational issues. Each person learns relationships and patterns of living from their family of origin, even in opposition to what was expected. There is a certain transfer of these learned patterns and remembered relationships from each person in the marriage to the new couple as a unit, but there is not an orderly or predictable way for this transfer to take place.

In Western culture, there is a demand that the marital friendship be stronger than earlier connections with parents and siblings. However, the process of actually becoming the "number one friend" to the other and melding particular patterns is at best a lifetime process. At the same time, the son or daughter, with some secondary assistance from the spouse, needs to redefine the relationship with his or her own family and with others. This can happen only at the point where the new couple has really developed their relationship and ownership of their common patterns. This redefinition of relationships with families of origin demands some development of the marital friendship, but the reverse is also true. The development of the marital friendship demands some redefinition with the families of origin.

These patterns from the family of origin get right in the middle of the couple's own experiences and perceptions of things. Learned from their own families, the patterns are taken for granted until something comes up where they may be questioned. One example would be Phil and Sarah's assumption of Phil's family patterns and beliefs in relation to household chores and other issues (case study 2.3). When Sarah's back went out, they had to develop different, compatible, and balanced patterns of managing household chores and making decisions about money and family resources. Armand and Rosalind's different cultural and familial ideas of intimate relationships, together with the immediate pressure of salvaging their relationship from their respective affairs, brought them to attempt to work out their boundaries and the patterns of intimacy in their relationship (case study 3.2). In an earlier period, when they were single, they had personal tasks of making decisions and managing resources. In early adulthood they may have struggled with depression or anxiety as they redefined their relationships with their families of origin. As they become a couple, these remain personal tasks because they have to do with personal agency, but also to some extent they become relational tasks, because they have to do with communion. Part of the problem is distinguishing between the personal and the relational. Two individual and personal patterns need to be made compatible in the development of a third pattern. Each needs to deal with their own feelings around money, their own experiences, and their own developed patterns from their families of origin. Each needs to strive to develop a common approach. The common approach should also preserve individual initiatives and decision making. These tasks continue throughout the couple's relationship.

All of these relational tasks demand the development of common communication patterns. The shift in communication depends on a profound relational shift. Communicating as a couple demands the development of the reciprocal ability of ego to express feelings and perceptions and of alter to listen and reflect. In turn, alter needs to express and ego to listen. The two processes should lead to a common understanding and a common vocabulary of accepted meanings. This is more than a development of expressive and empathic skills on the part of the couple—it demands a recognition of and care for the other *as other*, that is, as not part of the self.

What then needs to be learned if a relationship is to endure through all of the changes and developmental stages that family members will encounter in each other over a lifetime? In contrast to the romantic search for one's self, one's desires, one's preconceptions in the other, John Gottman's (1999; Gottman & Tabares, 2002) research would suggest that happily married couples embrace a realistic philosophy of persons and differences. Persons do change. On what basis can the relationship continue as a secure base while change is taking place? What is needed if the relationship is to accommodate persons and their needs?

Love and Fidelity: The Construction of a Secure Relational Base

Recent developments in philosophy, influenced by existential personalism (Wojtyla, 1981), have provided some responses to these questions in a realistic construction of love and fidelity (Grisez, n.d.; Rousseau, 1995; Shivananden, 1999, 2001). In Western society, the sentiment of love, fueled by romantic beliefs, nevertheless has to become an ongoing discovery and appreciation of the other *as other*. This discovery becomes a relational process that, as love in a personal context becomes fidelity, can gradually unfold over a lifetime of changes. Fidelity to the other as a person would provide a secure base for the continuity of family and for safety, belonging, communication and other relational goods, despite inevitable change, growth, and the vulnerabilities implicit in any personal relationship. This is the basis for the importance of the bonding processes (see chapter 3), the social and personal processes that construct and maintain fidelity and that grow with the growth of the couple. In this sense, fidelity is not simply the avoidance of infidelity. It is a learned and socially constructed sentiment. It requires an openness to the reality of the other, a reality that never can be fully known in advance. It is the will to accept the true self of the other as it emerges over time (Grisez, n.d.). This true self is partially unknown, even to ourselves. Our relational deficits may be surprising to us when they emerge. But we are also surprised by the good that can emerge from us in the presence of the noncritical acceptance and care of the other.

Fidelity takes for granted that both persons are changing, discovering who they really are, and letting go of false selves, but that each is faithful to the changes in the other. Indeed this secure base in the relationship allows each person to grow and differentiate one's self as a person. In the face of the other's personal changes, fidelity becomes a continual choice of this person in preference to any other. Each choice of this person means that certain parts of ego, no longer relevant to their emergent relationship, may have to change. One discovers in one's self a will to accept the other in loving kindness and to become the person one will have to become if communion is to last and to flourish (Grisez, n.d.). To restore the trust broken after their affairs, Armand and Rosalind (case study 3.2) had to reconstruct concretely and test a relationship that could become a secure base for each other, now faithful to each other as persons. Armand had to wait and accept Rosalind's hurt and anger before she could discover her positive feelings below the anger, and then her gradually emergent trust. The process repeats itself in a thousand ways in couples' encounters.

From this mutual care of the other, there emerges a transcendent "us" (Hargrave, 2000). This transcendence is deeply connected with the spiritual side of our nature. The "us" has to be a truly differentiated and developed self. It cannot be either a mirror of the other or of the self, a romantic "heavenly twin." Transcending some of our limits, the relationship—the "us"—allows each to come to be more than what they are while at the same time remaining what they are (Rousseau, 1995, p. 152). In this narrow sense, the couple can revise their separate heritage and, together, can become agents of their own development (Shivananden, 2001).

The reality is that couples struggle to know each other all their lives, often through the fog of their projections. Without this real connection, the couple would love only themselves in the other. As one grows and develops, one might discover (and then reject) a once-denied and unacceptable part of the self in the other. In any case, the couple would not have truly known each other.

Object Relations

Object relations family therapists,[1] operating from a psychodynamic orientation, contribute the concepts, originally from Melanie Klein, of introjective identification and projective identification. In *introjective identification*, the other is introjected, that is, assumed whole and entire by ego, which then identifies with some or all of the other's characteristics (Segal, 1973, p. 126; Scharff & Scharff, 1991). In *projective identification*, marital partners unconsciously project or externalize certain split-off or unwanted parts of themselves onto their partners, who in turn are manipulated to behave in accordance with this projection. As a consequence, each person attempts to reestablish contact with missing, repudiated, or unwanted parts of themselves (Dicks, 1967; Goldenberg & Goldenberg, 1996). The other person is accepted or rejected on this basis. The well-known family therapist Carl Whitaker trenchantly commented on a couple getting divorced: "Find out who's getting divorced." A partner may be divorcing an unwanted part of the self, or even a part of the other, without ever taking in the otherness of the real spouse. In this case, the person has never made the personal and relational shifts involved in "getting married."

Relational tasks provide some escape into reality from initial constructions of the relationship envisioned and induced by one or both partners. If the relationship reflects only the self, it could become a trap. Built into the relational tasks there

---

[1]For further discussion of this school of family therapy, see Nichols and Schwartz (1998, chapter 7), Goldenberg and Goldenberg (1996, chapter 6), and Scharf & Scharf (1991).

needs to be some recognition of the other. Recognizing the reality of Sarah's back (case study 2.3), if nothing else, can bring her and Phil to let go of patterns from Phil's family that both had taken for granted. When we begin to form a relationship with the other as other, not as a reflection of the self, it has to include both individuals as persons and thus transcend the initial expectations. It is possible that it may no longer be a trap. Ideally, a couple, such as Brian and Lisa (case study 2.5), could transform unneeded parts of themselves in the light of their emerging relationship.

The heart of the work of the couple with the social worker is the couple's work with each other. Using couple communication as the medium for change, this work ranges from a focus on themselves as persons to the relationships they have, now as a couple, to the worlds of their families of origin, to their work, and to other social institutions, all of which they now confront together. As they restructure communications, little by little the couple can reconstruct the understandings and behaviors on which their relationship is based, and thus on which the structure of their relationship is based. The social worker can help the couple to transform communication and discover their relationship with its profound implications for themselves as persons.

Personal Tasks and Couple Tasks

Personal tasks and couple tasks have a reciprocal, recursive relationship with each other. Working to develop communication, to develop compatible relationship patterns, and to become a functional couple (or family), each member works on personal tasks at the same time. Often the focus on couple tasks is also the most effective way to work on personal tasks. On the other hand, it is also often possible to help a member to work directly on personal tasks in the context of the relationship, and with the other member(s) assisting, as Armand did with Rosalind (case study 3.2).

Personal work and relational work is essentially a two-step process. First the focal member needs to take charge of what he or she has to do to deal with a personal problem or concern. Then the relational effects of the decision need to be discussed; this discussion often leads to modification of the personal task or goal, as seen in the following two case studies.

CASE STUDY 5.1

Jerry decided to do something about his drinking and save his marriage. Jerry had to take charge of this problem and do something about it. Kathy, his wife, couldn't intrude in this and, in her anxiety about his drinking, take charge of it.

Jerry had to learn to manage his problem without inappropriately involving Kathy; Kathy had to learn to support Jerry's efforts to become responsible without taking over by nagging him when he fails or absorbing the consequences for him. In their ongoing work over a number of sessions, the social worker started by helping Jerry, in Kathy's presence, to make resolutions and a concrete plan to deal with the drinking, and to find a group and sponsor. Then the worker encouraged Jerry to talk with Kathy about how she could help him with this without taking over. Over multiple sessions, the couple worked on communication and other problems while Jerry's changes and Kathy's support went on in the background. Kathy, for her part, struggled with depression, but she developed a plan, worked with a therapist, and got medication. As she took action on her depression, Jerry supported her. Both continued to deal with the implications of these personal changes for their couple issues.

CASE STUDY 5.2

All of his life Bill had patterns of attention deficit disorder. As an adult, he found it very difficult to remain focused, to work consistently, and to achieve in work as well as in other areas. His wife, Jane, a super-organized planner, struggled with other issues. She was very self-critical, had low self-esteem, and tended toward depression. She relied on Bill's sense of humor and constant energy to cheer her up. When she was unhappy with his inconsistency or when he failed, however, she became an over-responsible parent figure to him and took over his work. When Bill was marginalized in this way, he would withdraw and become less adequate. This confirmed Jane's concerns about him. In a joint session with Bill and Jane, the worker helped Bill to identify his patterns (without giving them a name), and asked him how he had compensated for them when he was in school. He responded that he always did better when the parameters were clearly set. Building on this, Bill developed his own five-point plan to deal with his patterns. When he had come to the point of taking charge of this, he was able, with the worker's help, to ask Jane to help keep him on track without taking over his tasks. They talked about this in detail and agreed. The remaining sessions, were focused, among other issues, on helping them to carry this out, with Bill in charge of his personal tasks and Jane beginning to involve herself in a different way. The circular patterns began to reverse themselves.

None of this work is easy. Jerry may not succeed in doing something about his drinking, and Bill will continue to struggle with his difficulty in remaining focused. To persevere in the framework of the relationship demands a second step. Jerry will need Kathy's support and Bill will need Jane's, and vice versa. The tasks that come out of this work will last a lifetime.

A COUPLE WITH FAMILY OF ORIGIN AND COMMUNICATION ISSUES

We now examine an overview of the helping process with couples by looking at the case of Rafael and Angie Vega.

CASE STUDY 5.3

Rafael and Angie Vega, married four years with no children, have experienced increasing arguments, particularly about Angie's perceived rejection by Rafael's family. Rafael is the oldest of a large and boisterous Mexican-American family. His mother constantly involves him as the problem solver with this or that family situation as if he were not married at all. Rafael is spending many of his weekends and evenings on these missions. Also, when Rafael's family gets together, he is the center of rather loud interchanges with his brothers and his mother. Angie is feeling rudely ignored, left out, and lonely on all counts. Rafael is vaguely aware of Angie's feelings. He feels caught between loyalties to his wife and to his family and helpless to change the situation. Angie is the youngest and only girl of three children of a middle-class, Polish-American family. Initially she was vague in depicting her family of origin, saying that everyone got along and they were certainly not like Rafael's wild family.

Rafael and Angie have different ways of communicating with each other. There is a demand/withdraw quality to their relationship. Angie pursues Rafael with her complaints and Rafael responds by being full of words and generalities. Rafael has great difficulty getting to the point of his feelings and thoughts. Angie doesn't really engage with Rafael, except in terms of what she expects of him. She seems to have "married marriage" in Rafael, but has not yet married Rafael as a person. She has few words to say to Raphael, but usually comes directly to the point. Her trenchant criticism is totally devastating to him. She is frustrated that she must be the demanding one and that Rafael isn't direct with her and that he tries to avoid her feelings. She is feeling trapped in a family she never married, without a relationship with Rafael, whom she did marry. The problems they have around communication reflect themselves also in their discussions around money. They have not worked out an agreement about money. Rafael wants to get a home above everything, and so he saves everything he can. Angie wants a home also, but not at the sacrifice of a good life now. She usually wins any discussion, since she is more direct and fluent with communication. Rafael is starting to resent this. Their marriage has been in this holding pattern for four years. In a pervasive climate of tentativeness, neither are able to make any plans for the future. In many ways they have not yet gone through the process of "getting married."

RELATIONAL TASKS

Personal Tasks

- Rafael needs to come to terms with the fact that he has married Angie and that he will need to become more active.
- Rafael will need to make changes in his accustomed relations and patterns with his family of origin and with Angie to make the marriage work.

- Angie needs to disengage from the rigidity and abstractness of her own expectations of her relationship with Rafael, from her chronic disappointment and comparison of Rafael's family with what she expects a family should be and what she feels entitled to.

Couple Tasks

- Rafael and Angie need to develop different patterns of listening and expressing, of communication with each other.
- They both need to discuss productively their expectations of their own marriage and arrive at some conclusion that both can support.
- Rafael needs to disengage from his family and reengage with them in a way that includes Angie as his "best friend."
- Rafael and Angie need to develop the uniqueness of their own relationship as different from either of their families of origin.
- Angie needs join with Rafael, putting herself into the picture in a different way; she needs to find a "third way" with Rafael that can be their own.
- They both need to work out a common pattern in relation to managing money.

Rafael and Angie did attempt these tasks in marriage counseling. The process took about six months of weekly sessions. Rafael did listen to Angie's concerns, and he agreed with them. He decided that he had married Angie and she would have first place in his life. He had an opportunity to demonstrate this when one of his brothers got married and he was to be the best man. A bachelor party was scheduled on the weekend that he and Angie had planned to take a short and much-needed vacation. He felt an obligation to attend, but this would violate his understanding that he wanted to put his relationship with Angie in first place. After discussing this with Angie in their weekly counseling sessions, he told his family that he would not attend the party unless they rescheduled it at a better time. They did reschedule. Rafael did rework his relationships correspondingly with his family. Over time, they gradually did accept

Angie's position in his life and thus in theirs. In their sessions, Rafael was discovering that he could be much more direct with Angie. Rafael's pursuit of Angie reversed the pattern and Angie began to withdraw. Angie at first felt unable to respond immediately and personally to Rafael's new directness. Instead she kept raising her expectations of him, passing the task baton back to him. This was discouraging to Rafael, and there were times when both wondered whether it was all worth it.

Eventually Angie began to let go of her expectations of an abstract person in a spousal role and commit herself to Rafael as a real person, and Rafael to her. As this took place, they were able to develop a different and mutually compatible communication pattern. Paradoxically, what Angie would never reveal previously came out only as she became more confident in her relationship with Rafael as a person. She had been deeply disappointed by her father's alcoholism. In many ways, she had placed Rafael in the impossible position of having to be the person that her father never had been to her. When she could let this go, she discovered Rafael to be a lovable, fallible human being who loved her. She found herself now able to respond to him as never before. When she did this, she became aware of her disappointment with her father. She was able to unburden herself about it to Rafael. As they completed the helping relationship, many of their issues were well on the path to resolution. At this point, they were in the process of buying a home and thinking about children.

For Angie and Rafael their early period of marriage eventually became a choice of each other in preference to images left over from other experiences. These would pass away as their relationship became personal. They could then begin to plan and think of next steps.

BEGINNING WITH COUPLES

Nowhere is the struggle of the social worker and the couple to find a collaborative stance clearer than in the beginning phase of the helping process. The time needed for the beginning phase may vary from one session to many more than one. The process can be quite difficult, both for the couple and for the social worker, partly because of the obvious uncertainties inherent in it. It is important for the social worker at least to have some sense of the overall process, of what may be possible to help the couple (Rafael and Angie) make a beginning. Although couples make very different uses of the social worker, and thus the process differs greatly in each case, the social worker needs first of all to help the couple develop a sense of what needs to be done and a sense that, with some direction and help, they can do it. The couple often feels utterly defeated. They keep coming back to their old adversarial and withdrawn patterns. They feel they are in a "mess" that only some expert can sort out. The social worker, little by little, begins to help them see this "mess" as a problem that is something that is not necessarily out of control. One can deal with a problem. Then, in a more concrete way, in the initial and ongoing sessions, the problem becomes "tasks" to work on. These tasks inevitably involve communication, since without communication it is difficult to make other changes.

An assessment is made with the couple. The problem is partialized with tasks. There are session-by-session objectives, otherwise the social worker is reinforcing the couple's sense of loss of control. It would be as if they were walking together through a strange and uninhabited forest with no map or trail, with no idea of where they are going or what they are trying to achieve. To bring back the sense of control, the social worker normalizes the problem. That is, the social worker puts it into the context of what could be expected, given the circumstances; then places it into the framework of personal and relational tasks, and places the tasks in some initial time framework.

Understanding personal and relational tasks and the differences between them, will help a good deal. Tasks clarify goals, sort out what each needs to do, and clarify what each needs to do with each other to reach them. Such goals give direction to the couple's beginning, to the tasks of each session and between sessions, and to the later, middle-stage content of sessions with the couple. They clarify what the work will be. They indicate where to start and what the process might be like. Working together on the tasks, it is hoped that the couple's communication changes as well.

Couples in the beginning stage are usually not ready to begin. There is often too much hurt. They are afraid that if they risk openness, they will be hurt again. They wait for the partner to fulfill their expectations of change before they will venture out. Furthermore, communication patterns have usually become quite dysfunctional. To avoid the needed personal and relational work, each will often attempt to shift the onus to the partner and argue about who is to blame, setting the social worker up as a judge. To avoid this, it is best to help them immediately get focused on and discuss what they think can or should be different about their relationship, including what they bring to it. The social worker can help them to structure the communication so that each is able to listen to the other. The social worker can reframe the communication from an initial blame of the other to a more workable focus on what is possible and what needs to be done. A premature focus on trying to understand the problem can take the couple away from the prior question of what they think they can and want to achieve through their work together. It also can take the social worker away from a strengths-based beginning. In any case, the question of their goals is the key to the assessment process. Social workers can quietly gather history as they observe communication and listen to the couple discuss what they want to deal with. The following case study is an example of a beginning.

CASE STUDY 5.4

Sherry and Bill, both successful, high-powered lawyers, were experiencing increasing conflict around finances, their search for a house, and plans to accommodate their third child, due in four months. They "review options" with each other as if talking to a client. Their discussion is almost devoid of feelings until there is a sudden explosion and breakdown. Five months pregnant, Sherry is tired. She wants to participate, but shuts down quickly. At the same time she resents the fact that she is implicitly giving the power to Bill. Bill feels shut down, cut off from Sherry, and in a dilemma. Buying a house will demand that someone take over on their finances. He will be wrong if he takes over without Sherry's consent, but he wants to get a house to accommodate their growing family and he is not certain how long he can wait.

It took Sherry and Bill two sessions to make a beginning. Both needed help to listen to them other. When they cleared the air, both discovered that it was easier to communicate. They then moved on to deal with finances and their basic issue of how they as a couple together were to accommodate their third child.

As a result of the beginning session, the couple should have together developed some common understanding of the problem, seen it as something they could work on with each other, made a joint beginning on it, and agreed to continue to work on it in a specific way at home and in their sessions. The social worker's role is to help the couple do this—that is, to move from the phase of beginning and contracting to the next phase, the work phase. To do this, there is a joint process of assessment and actively testing out possibilities. The beginning place for this assessment is in the here and now—the tasks confronting the couple where they are—although the past is important and also needs to be addressed.

A great deal needs to take place at once within the agency's regular intake procedures. This can be enormously confusing to the social work practitioner, and indirectly confusing to the couple. The control of the process is quite different from casework. The social worker is helping two people to come to an understanding, develop an agreement, begin a process together, and do this in the context of the agency's procedures. Sometimes the process can take two sessions. One author routinely does a two-hour intake, which generally works very well. The couple or whole family finishes with a fairly clear idea of what they need to do and remain in charge of their situation.

Let us imagine the process of Rafael and Angie's beginning (case study 5.3).

The Very Beginning

The Phone Call Angie calls the family agency after going around in circles once more with Rafael about his family. She is getting tired of it and feels trapped and not hopeful. But at least she could try. Lynn, a social worker, calls back. After hearing briefly about the situation she makes the initial assessment with Angie that she is not asking for help with individual problems (her anxiety and/or sadness about a situation). The problem could best dealt with in a couple's counseling format. Could Angie and Rafael come in together to look at the possibility of working on this? Angie agrees to talk with Rafael and confirm if they were interested. Lynn is very careful to ask Angie to come in with Rafael for the first session, since if Angie came in alone, Rafael might later feel an alliance between Lynn and Angie and be reluctant to come in. Lynn knows that she can't accomplish much without the two starting together. Later she may want to see one or the other alone, but they need to begin the process together and eventually come to a similar understanding of things.

The Opening The room is set up comfortably, with two large chairs a quarter turn toward each other and a small table with a lamp and a clock on it in the middle. There is a small swivel chair facing the two chairs. Lynn greets Rafael and Angie in the waiting room, introducing herself and shaking the hand of each. She makes brief personal contact. They go into her office, and she asks them to sit in the large chairs, so that they face each other and Lynn. Some workers make small talk at this point to get the couple relaxed. Lynn is actually fairly relaxed already, and she finds that when she helps them to get to the issues in her own relaxed, but focused style, the couple also relaxes reasonably well. She reviews some of the face-sheet information with them that provides the concrete details that they have already given over the phone. She may set a fee at this time, if it has not been already discussed over the phone. They will have to set an agreement by the end of the session. Acknowledging with Angie that they talked over the phone, she moves briefly to Rafael and joins with both about whether they have talked about some of these marriage issues in counseling before. She asks them to pretend that she is a distant relative who doesn't know much about their situation. They work out whether they will use last names or first in their session.

Getting Them Started and Making an Initial Assessment Lynn wants Rafael and Angie to take control of the situation as quickly as possible and to get in communication with each other. She doesn't start by taking down a lot of details. Instead she helps them start their story with the question of what changes they would like to see take place through marriage counseling, and what they think could take place. It is important that they start by focusing on possible changes. As they talk about the situation she will ask them about it, and they will fill in the details for her. Rafael asks Angie to go first. Angie tells her story about Rafael's family. Lynn listens carefully, reflecting what Angie is saying, normalizing the family of origin issues and asking a few questions about her point of view. Rafael tells his story, talking about how he feels caught in the middle and pointing out his difficulty communicating with Angie. Lynn reflects that, normalizing it for Rafael and asking him some questions, filling in a concrete picture of the couple with them. She is beginning to get a picture of concerns about Rafael's family and about their communication. She identifies this to them and they agree that these are real concerns they need to work on.

Sampling Rafael and Angie's Communication Lynn starts by getting them started talking with each other. They have real difficulty communicating, so Lynn works directly with them on this, coaching them on positive communication, listening techniques, and so on. Lynn knows how easily she can get pulled into their adversarial or withdrawn cycles, but she cannot be aloof from their interaction either. It is a difficult balance. She actively works with them, setting enough structure so that each is able to express their different perceptions as well as their agreement, and the experience moves in a positive direction.

Agreeing on Personal and Relational Tasks; Defining a Possible Focus Lynn asks Rafael and Angie how the communication felt and gives some feedback. Out of this they identify some overall goals dealing with family-of-origin and communication issues. They feel they can work on these and want to get started.

Reaching a Contract, Agreeing on Next Steps and Ending Reflecting some of their communication work, Rafael and Angie contract for further sessions with these goals. They now have some sense of what it is going to be like. Lynn gives them some communication tasks to try the first week, together with some ways of repairing communication when it breaks down. She points out that the first time they try these they will have difficulty and they shouldn't get discouraged. They set an appointment for the next week, and Lynn shakes the hand of each as they say goodbye.

Rafael and Angie's case is not particularly complicated. Because of that, it allows us to identify a couple's process of beginning. What is important here is that Rafael and Angie take charge of their process together and Lynn helps them to do it. They make an assessment together, and it comes out in a language of tasks and goals—what they may need to work on. Rather than steering the couple toward some goal of the worker, Lynn helps them to find what is do-able, and gets them started. There is a real parallel with what she would do with an individual client in the beginning. The difference is that her focus is on the couple beginning work primarily with each other rather than primarily with her. She intervenes in the couple's work to facilitate it, and in this sense the work goes much faster than work with individuals.

What the Worker Does: Skills

Using a classic listing[2] (Shulman, 1992) of beginning and contracting skills for working with individuals, we may reframe these skills in relation to working with couples.

- *Clarifying Worker's Purpose and Role.* The skill of clarifying purpose and role is essential with couples, but the worker is more decentralized in work with couples than in casework; the focus for activity and the work is that of the couple with each other with the worker as coach.
- *Reaching for Feelings.* The worker reflects thoughts and feelings of each partner in the beginning and when they get stuck, but as soon as possible helps the partners to do this themselves with each other.
- *Putting a Client's Feelings into Words.* This is the skill of articulating feelings in response to tuning in to indirect and direct communication. The couples social worker works actively between the partners, helping them to recognize implicit messages without becoming too centralized and shutting down their communication.
- *Reaching Inside of Silences.* Silence in couples work can be an extremely powerful tool, used to "wait out" the couple's struggle to deal with some of their issues. With certain cultures, such as Native American cultures, silence may be an indication of personal work. When silence seems to feel uncomfortable to the couple, the worker may ask them to talk about their uncomfortable silence and actively help them reach into that.

---

[2]These skills are developed in greater detail in Shulman (1992), and in a slightly different format in Hepworth, Mooney, and Larson (1997).

- *Partializing Concerns.* Partializing concerns is very important in couples work. The key to this is to move from a "mess" to a problem, to relational tasks, and to specific session-by-session objectives. Helping the couple set goals, differentiating personal and relational tasks, and setting specific assignments all help to do this, but the primary means of partializing concerns is the communication of the couple skillfully focused by the worker. The couple is working in-session on the relationship.

- *Assessment.* The goal of assessment is for the couple and worker together to understand the problem and then to set objectives and plan the intervention (Johnson, 1981). It is important that assessment be focused on possible change rather than on all that went wrong. The beginning assessment should generate some ideas from the couple for personal and relational tasks: ideas of what *should* be changed and of what *can* be changed. The process takes place through reflective communication by the couple, with the social worker actively moving back and forth between them.

- *Contracting.* Contracting is an effort to establish the purpose of the work, to establish appropriate roles, to give feedback, and to deal with issues of authority. Out of a tentative assessment, an initial agreement with each other and with the social worker should emerge. In couples work, the purpose and contract is established first of all *with each other*, and then with the social worker and agency. What the worker needs to do is to listen carefully, reflect, and help the couple when there is hesitancy or ambivalence about the process. Identifying hesitancy often opens up issues they were afraid to bring up: doubts, concerns, reluctance to get involved, or a need to have the social worker take charge of the problem. What do they think they can do to accomplish these changes?

Rafael and Angie's situation (case study 5.3) is useful for its simplicity as a clear illustration of beginning work on the couple relationship. Most situations are more complex. Social workers work with many couples where there is stress on the bond from several fronts at once. Perhaps there is a new child and one of the parents is very ill. Perhaps the husband has an addictions problem, or there has been an affair, or one of the grandparents dies. Perhaps the parents are age sixteen and seventeen, without good employment and unable to support themselves, and with a very uncertain relationship. Perhaps one of the parents becomes severely depressed, or a baby, expected to be "perfect," is born with a disability. The dynamics of Brian and Lisa's (case study 2.5) and Rafael and Angie's (case study 5.3) situation, which border on normal, are also present in these instances, but in greater complexity.

The Miracle Question   The emphasis on changes that accompanies assessment and contracting has set an important tone. Problems are seen in the light of the family's desired changes. When the beginning is difficult, several solution-focused techniques are often quite useful to get the process moving in a good direction (deShazer, 1985, 1988, 1991). One technique is a variant of the miracle question. The miracle question is: "Suppose one night when you were asleep, there was a miracle and the problem was solved by morning. How would you know? What would be different?" This question switches the focus from negative to the positive. It also asks each partner to think about what differences would tell them the problem was solved. Another similar approach is the exception question. Rather than focusing on the problem, this focuses on the times the couple didn't have the problem when ordinarily they would. By exploring the differences (exceptions), they can discuss how these exceptions can be expanded. This also makes the problem seem less overwhelming, and it can lead from an initial agreement to beginning work together on the problem. We will see an example of middle-stage use of some of these techniques in the Kowalski case study in (6.5) the next chapter.

Unrecognized Gender Inequalities   Developing effective communication means reciprocal and equitable recognition of the other as a person. Communication about relational tasks thus often automatically demands an internal rebalancing of inequitable relationships. In examples given so far Phil and Sarah (case study 2.3), Miguel and Juana (case study 2.4), Brian and Lisa (case study 2.5), and Rafael and Angie (case study 5.3), the couples developed their own balances. Often, as with Miguel and Juana and also with Phil and Sarah, the internal rebalancing in relation to family of origin, roles, or other issues also rebalanced gender inequalities without much discussion other than recognizing what had happened. Sometimes, however, the inequalities so profoundly influence the couple's relational work that the automatic rebalancing does not seem to be taking place, and the social worker may need to get more active. Nichols and Schwartz (2002, p. 97) point out the single most useful question to ask about gender inequality is "How does each partner experience the fairness of give-and-take in their relationship?" Built on this question, all of the relational tasks can be reconfigured in a way that is compatible with the couple's perceptions and with a more balanced relationship.

PROBLEMS IN DEVELOPING COMMITMENT

Frequently the social worker's involvement is sought to shore up a failing structure where the unacknowledged problem is commitment to the relationship as a relationship. In the following case, personal tasks and issues have overshadowed any ability to construct love and fidelity in a relationship.

CASE STUDY 5.5

John and Eileen were referred to a family service agency by the court, which was supervising John for substance abuse. The couple, married for four years and with a three-year-old child, has been separated for a year. The marital history has been stormy. Eileen, the "perfect" child with an opinionated mother and a weak, silent father, married John as an act of rebellion and moved out of state with him. John's heavy drinking and drug habits were evident from the beginning of the relationship. Their relationship never developed further or dealt effectively with this problem. During the first years, there were numerous separations and instances of violence, culminating in an incident where John threw a knife at Eileen and severed a tendon in her arm. John was periodically unemployed. Eileen, who has had very little experience managing for herself, finally was able to leave after three years of "hell." Eileen, now living on her own, with the support of a local church, family members, and a part-time job, is managing a precarious independence with her child. John came back two months ago with the expectation of a reunion. He stopped his drug use two months ago and his heavy drinking two weeks ago.

He gets about twelve to twenty hours of construction work a week, and his family continues to take care of him. He attends AA now, but isn't sure he is ready for either the program or a sponsor. He doesn't seem to be too concerned about his probation. He rejects the idea of doing work on his addictions program, but doesn't understand why Eileen is fearful and uncertain about getting back together. In the joint interview both talk about themselves, but there is very little mutual communication. Eileen withdraws quickly when he makes a demand, and that only draws out his incredulity. He openly questions why Eileen is so fearful, but it seems as if he knows the answer already.

In this case, the social worker heard Eileen's grave doubts and concerns about working on the relationship, and reflected them back to the couple. They decided not to initiate work on their relationship until and unless they had done something about their pressing personal issues. Eileen decided to work individually on her issues. When offered further help with his concerns, John said he would think about it and call back, but never did.

Sometimes the problem is that the couple has not yet made a commitment to each other. They haven't really "gotten married." In the following case, only one partner was seen. Although having both available might have been likely to be more effective, in this case one person became anxious around communication and the possibilities of relational change. He would not be directly available to participate in the helping process. Nevertheless, the tasks remained if they were to construct a secure base for the relationship. The social worker did work with the other partner, helping her to deal with the situation as best she could. As in the case of Armand and Rosalind (case study 3.2), Sandy's systemic work assists Sheldon to make a commitment. They were able to begin to construct a secure enough base to move on in their relationship.

CASE STUDY 5.6

Over their year of marriage, Sheldon, an engineer, has been chronically uncertain about his commitment to Sandy, a nurse. They have had severe marital conflict whenever the question of his commitment is raised. He says he married only because he felt he couldn't call off the ceremony, but he never made a permanent commitment. He is uncertain that he wants to stay married and has excluded any thought of children. He was particularly shaken when he heard that Sandy had briefly used drugs in college. He felt that she was "damaged goods" and on "probation" with him. He will decide whether they should continue their marriage or not. His life patterns of chronic ambivalence suggests obsessive compulsive disorder (OCD) and depression, but he keeps delaying getting help. He terminated marital counseling after two contacts because he was overwhelmed with the idea of talking to Sandy about his feelings and listening to her feelings.

Sandy continued using counseling. She decided to work on her part of the relationship with the aim of giving six months for them to either make a permanent commitment to each other or break up. As she learned to manage the situation better, conflict did drop off. They got along fairly well as long as the issue of his commitment didn't come up. He decided to let go of his concerns about her past, but remained uncertain about commitment. In her work alone with Sandy, the social worker coached her to help Sheldon test out his commitment to her without demanding that he put feelings into words. Their communication took place in a more concrete way, through what was taking place in the relationship. With Sandy's patience, Sheldon eventually resolved his chronic ambivalence. They jointly recognized these changes in his feelings about trust and relationships and decided to recommit their marriage promises to each other in a private ceremony.

In the beginning of the case, Sheldon had not yet made a commitment to Sandy. There seemed to be only a slight chance that Sheldon would ever make a commitment. Sheldon could have been asking for individual help, but he refused any initiatives in this direction. Sheldon has great difficulty communicating. He found tasks of communicating with Sandy about feelings and changing their relationship overwhelming. Similar to Armand and Rosalind (case study 3.2), Sandy decided to work individually on the relationship. With Sheldon's anxiety around communication and explicit change, the emphasis had to be on tasks and emergent implicit understandings.

The paradox is that, when it came to day-to-day issues, with very limited communication their relationship did work. Sandy asked for Sheldon's commitment within six months as the price for hers. She worked on being available to him in his limited efforts to communicate, without pursuing him. This put Sheldon in a situation where Sandy touched on what both needed if their relationship was to grow. There would be a certain amount of time for Sheldon to respond. In any case, the work with Sandy continued with personal and relational tasks. She remained available to him, but she would not merely accept Sheldon's noncommitment. She expected more. When Sheldon did take the step of recognizing his real commitment to her, she was able with help to support him without making his decision her decision. When the relational tasks are identified in the beginning stage there may be a variety of ways for the couple or family to accomplish them (equifinality).

SUMMARY

Beginning with couples is complex because the tasks of gaining an understanding of the problem (assessment) and helping the couple make their own beginning may seem to be in conflict. However, as the social worker assists the couple to make this beginning, so will the middle stage go. The following chapter looks at middle-stage work, relating social work practice theory at middle stages to the developmental and personal issues of couples.

REFERENCES

Dicks, H. V. (1967). *Marital tensions*. New York: Basic Books.

deShazer, S. (1985). *Keys to a solution in brief therapy*. New York: Norton.

deShazer, S. (1988). *Clues: Investigating solutions in brief therapy*. New York: Norton.

deShazer, S. (1991). *Putting differences to work*. New York: Norton.

Goldenberg, I., & Goldenberg, H. (1996). *Family therapy: An overview* (4th ed.). Pacific Grove, CA: Brooks-Cole.

Gottman, J. M. (1999). *The marriage clinic*. New York: Norton.

Gottman, J. M., Driver, J., & Tabares, A. (2002). Building the sound marital house: An empirically derived couple therapy. In A. S. Gurman & N. S. Jacobson (Eds.), *Clinical handbook of couple therapy* (3rd ed., pp. 00–00). New York: Guilford. AU: pag

Grisez, G. (n.d.) *Fidelity today*. Privately published.

Hargrave, T. (2000). *The essential humility of marriage: Honoring the third identity in couple therapy*. Phoenix, AZ: Zeig, Tucker & Theisen.

Hepworth, D. H., Mooney, R. H., & Larson, J. A. (1997). *Direct social work practice* (4th ed.). Belmont, CA: Brooks-Cole.

Nichols, M., & Schwartz, R. (2002). *Family therapy: Concepts and methods* (4th ed.). New York: Allyn & Bacon.

Rousseau, M. F. (1995). Fairest love: John Paul II on the family. *Anthropotes, 11*(2), 167–183.

Scharff, D. E., & Scharff, J. S. (1991). *Object relations family therapy*. New York: Jason Aronson.

Segal, H. (1973). *Introduction to the work of Melanie Klein*. London: Heinemann.

Shivananden, M. (1999). *Crossing the threshhold of love: A new vision of marriage*. Washington, DC: Catholic University of America Press.

Shivananden, M. (2001). Subjectivity and the order of love. *Fides Quaerens Intellectum, 1*(2), 251–274.

Shulman, L. (1992). *The skills of helping: Individuals, families and groups* (3rd ed.). Itaska, IL: Peacock.

Wojtyla, K. (Pope John Paul II). (1981). *Love and responsibility*. New York: Farrer, Strous, Giroux.

CHAPTER 6

Middle Phases with Couples

This chapter relates social work practice theory at the middle phase to the life-cycle and personal issues of couples and to development of their own problem-solving and relational capacities. The discussion of middle-phase skills focuses on intimacy, boundaries, communication, decision making and task prescription. These themes are developed through cases. The chapter ends with focus on the qualities needed in the social worker to sustain middle-phase work.

MIDDLE-STAGE COUPLES WORK

In some cases, the beginning goes slowly, by fits and starts, beginning again and again until the couple is able to make headway together. The middle stage is more accurately called the "work phase" (Shulman, 1992), because this is the phase when the couple is actually engaging in the work promised by their beginning. The beginning and contracting work should contain all the necessary tasks and issues that might prevent the couple from reaching their goals. Obviously, the better the beginning, the better the middle stage and the better the possible outcome. The authors have often encountered situations where the couple made such a good beginning in one or two interviews that they moved to the middle stage quickly. They were able to take ownership of the situation and continue on their relational tasks by themselves without further help, or with the social worker available just as a "consultant" if they ran into trouble.

DEVELOPMENT OF THE COUPLE'S PROBLEM-SOLVING AND RELATIONAL CAPACITIES

In the middle stage, the couples' unresolved issues become clearer and repeat themselves time after time. The social worker is often tempted to impatience or despair at the couple's failing efforts. The polarization seems as if it will never end. It is important not to get discouraged at this time, and also to keep the couple in ownership of the problem and the tasks, not to take over the problem. The stage sometimes seems interminable, when in effect a good deal of work may be taking place.

The first process of middle-stage work is the development of the couple's problem-solving and relational capacities. When the couple is actively working on relational tasks with the social worker as coach, some of the most demonstrably powerful and effective tools of therapeutic change are being used. The conversation of the couple focuses on life problems, core personal relationships, and feelings (affective responses to) these problems and relationships (Orlinsky, Grawe & Parks, 1994, p. 359). It is direct and experiential as the couple together in the session alter their relationships. It is supportive and reassuring, drawing on the therapist's qualities of empathy, genuineness, and warmth. The therapist teaches this response to the couple in their transactions with each other. The conversation of the couple involves learning (cognitions) of different points of view and new skills. It involves action—that is, couples managing their behavior and responses, facing fears with support, modeling behaviors, taking risks, testing new realities, and working through issues (Lambert & Bergin, 1994, p. 163). As long as the social worker has a clear professional focus on persons acting in relationships, and as long as the couple is in charge of the problem, the social worker can use a wide range of tools to help the couple accomplish these goals. There is no confinement to a particular method or tool of helping, since the worker is only, like a good coach, discovering resources in the couple and bringing out ways to help *them* accomplish something with each other (Lazarus, 1981).

Intimacy, Boundaries, and Communication Processes

The theme of the next case studies is the development of relational closeness (connectedness) and boundaries (separateness) through communication. The relationship of a couple in the early phase of marriage is expected to be close and intimate, but it is most difficult to achieve this—to know the other as other, to be known by another, to feel respected and to respect, and to solve problems without fear in a trusting relationship. Although sex is a form of communication, intimacy means more than sex.

The key to this growth to intimacy will be found in the relationship developed between the couple. Few theoretical approaches capture the complexity of the closeness-distance cycling in adult intimacy. A major task in work with couples is to help the couple build and maintain empathy with each other. Each needs to understand the other well enough "to discern transactional cues signaling desired distance or intimacy." They need to be able to communicate productively about these cues. They also need to be able to maintain a necessary distance without either the marriage or one of the couple losing their ability to function and cope adequately. To build and maintain emotional intimacy, the couple must be able to approach each other without feeling anxious. Spouses must be able to be empathically attuned to each other without losing self and becoming enmeshed (Kheshgi-Genovese & Constable, 1995).

In a concrete sense, this can take place in two ways. Relatedness to the other and differentiation of self take place, first of all, in the process of appropriate engagement with the other—the processes of communicating, making decisions, and performing relational tasks. Second, this takes place in the mutual learning of empathic accuracy in couples' counseling sessions. A variety of tools have been developed to do this (Snyder, 1995: Wile, 1992; Guerney, 1977).[1] As couples communicate, each is taught in turn to take different roles in relation to the other, the

---

[1]Communications theory and existential theory are discussed in Nichols and Schwartz (2002, chapter 6), Goldenberg and Goldenberg (1996, chapter 7), B. Guerney (1977), and Snyder (1995).

expressive role and the empathic role. When I am in the expressive role, I can give "I" messages to the other, that is, express how something affects me without placing the other on the defensive through the "you" message (you do . . .). The other reflects what I said without adding further input. When that happens, the other goes into an expressive mode and I will go into empathic mode (Guerney, 1977). The therapist moves back and forth between the two, facilitating communication. When things get stuck, the therapist will, with permission, reflect the other or, again with permission, speak for the other (Snyder, 1995).

The point is not simply an exercise in communication. In a profound way, it is taking the attitude of the other (Mead, 1932, 1934) and teaching partners to do that with each other. It becomes a mutual process of accurate empathy. Maryhelen Snyder (1995) draws from experiential-humanistic family therapy to define this mutual process. It is not simply a matter of being understanding and benign. To take on the life-world of another (Grunebaum, 1990; Habermas, 1987), to take on his or her lived experience in a particular social and psychological context, is a very special skill. Nor is it simply a matter of reflecting what has been said. Without this form of empathy, no real meeting between human beings occurs (Snyder, 1995, p. 318). In the presence of adequate empathy as Snyder defines it (1995, p. 242), "typically . . . the empathizer as a person 'disappears,' and both persons are simultaneously in the same experiential world."

Communication, Empathic Accuracy, and Relational Reconstruction

The following case is adapted to illustrate the power of empathic accuracy to help the couple reconstruct itself (Ables, 1977).[2] Nicholas and Johanna are a couple with a great deal of anger for each other. Their hurt feelings and their ways of dealing with problems are very much a part of them. During the first part of the session, Nicholas has been complaining that he feels "left out" from the family, unappreciated, and unimportant. We pick up with the social worker in the middle of the third session as they are beginning to get to the relational tasks they face:

CASE STUDY 6.1

Social Worker (to Nicholas): And you're telling Johanna that somehow you feel you're not included in things.

Nicholas: Johanna, I'm not. . . . I'm not.

Johanna: When you go through that routine, Nick, you don't know how much it annoys me. I give you every chance to be a part of things. You don't take the opportunity, and someone has to make a decision. So I do. Does anyone have a problem with that? We'd be out on the street if I didn't.

Social Worker: Wait. Nick and Johanna. Is this what happens at home when things get tense? (They nod to the social worker, but don't look at each other.) Johanna, I know you have a lot

---

[2]This example of couple communication, adapted by the authors, is taken from Ables (1977) and used with permission.

of things that get you upset, and you have a tough job. And Nick, I know you get upset too, and you need to hear each other. But Johanna, let's just stay with this a minute. Because I hear something coming from Nick constantly as if he's neglected. And what I'm asking you, Nick, now, is would you like Johanna to include you more in decision making—to pay more attention to you?

Nicholas: It doesn't make any difference. There's no way it'll ever happen. . . ever.

Social Worker: Would you like it?

Nicholas: Yes! But I might as well wait for the next millennium.

Social Worker: Could you ask Johanna now what she's willing to do now to help you with this?

Nicholas: I could, but . . . it'll never work.

Social Worker: Well, let's try it.

Johanna: What are you willing to do? The checks?

Nicholas: Well, it's not a matter of the checks. You're in control and I'd like to just have a vote on some things.

Johanna: I'd give you a vote on anything you wanted, if you just didn't fly off the handle. I can't even talk to you, so I just do what I have to do.

Social Worker: Johanna, would you like to be able to talk with each other?

Johanna: That's why we're here.

Social Worker: I'd like to try this with you, if you're both willing. (Nicholas nods, Johanna shrugs. Social worker gives a ceramic floor tile to Johanna.) Johanna, you have the floor for the moment, so I want you to talk to Nick. Start with something positive, and only "I" messages after that. Nick, I want you to just walk around in Johanna's head and reflect what you think she is

trying to say. Don't add any of your own thoughts or reactions. Just what she is thinking. You'll have your chance at the floor as soon as you have reflected what she is saying. OK? [Both nod.]

[Johanna starts by saying Nick never listens to her anyway. The social worker goes to where she is sitting and sits next to her. She helps Johanna to start with a positive ("Nick, I'm really happy we're working on this, but I don't have a lot of hope") and make the message into an "I" message. Eventually after a few false starts, where the social worker reflects her thinking as an "I" message, she says, "It's hard for me, Nick. I never see you when I need you, so I have to take over." She looks away because a tear is starting down her cheek. She quickly regains her composure. "See what you do to me!"]

Nicholas: [at first Nick doesn't take in the tear] What you do to me!

Social Worker: [she moves next to Nick's chair] Wait, Nick. You need to reflect what she's saying. [to Johanna]: Could you say it again, Johanna? [Johanna says it again, but in a slightly hurt, angry tone, and adds, "There we go again."]

Nicholas: What you're saying is I'm not around, and that's just not true! (The social worker coaches Nick to wait on his own response until he gets the floor, and try to reflect what Johanna is feeling.)

Nicholas: You're feeling that even when I'm around I haven't been there to help you when you need me.

Social Worker: That's real good, Nick!

[The couple begins haltingly to express and reflect feelings. When the floor tile comes to Nick, he talks about how left out he feels, but also acknowledges that Johanna does do a good job when she does take over. Bills get paid. Johanna starts to cry and blurts out, "That's the first time you ever said that." The rest of the session they both start talking about how left out, isolated, and lonely they feel. They feel stuck in the roles that they generate for and with each other. When things slow down or get stuck, the social worker reaches into either's feelings, and develops each one's feelings of loneliness, of being trapped in their anger, using reflection, sometimes speaking for one or the other when they feel stuck. She works out with them a between-session task of having dinner together at a favorite restaurant, with Nick paying, and planning a weekend at Lake Delavan with each other. They will save the intense talk for their next session next week.)

This was a good session. It is probable that Nick and Johanna will revert for a time to their old, hurtful patterns. However, both now see other possibilities, and with lots of repetition they begin to develop different communication patterns, different behavioral patterns, and, finally, reflecting together on these changes (which neither anticipated), a different relationship. As long as they have developed some level of communication skills and willingness to engage positively with each other, all of the relational tasks—whether they revolve around developing new patterns of money management, family-of-origin work, issues around children, and so on—can be processed by many couples in a manner somewhat similar to that used by Nick and Johanna.

MIDDLE-STAGE SKILLS: THE WORK PHASE

For the middle stage, or, more precisely, the work phase, we can use approximately the same framework for helping skills that we had developed in relation to helping the couple begin. The difference is that in the middle stage there is a focus on relational work with each other. The process can easily get stuck, and so the skills are used to help the couple remain on task and get unstuck when needed. The worker needs to tune in, contract for each session, and help the couple elaborate a focus. This is active work in the first sessions, but when the couple becomes more accustomed to the helping process they begin to take more responsibility for beginning the session. Johanna and Nicholas are ready to focus, but they are utterly lost in the complexity of their relationship when they start trying to communicate. Here the social worker becomes very active, helping the couple with each other to:

- Elaborate a focus
- Express feelings and thoughts so they can be heard and discussed
- Listen to the other and reflect the other's thoughts and feelings
- Take the viewpoint of the other
- Respond to the other's needs
- Separate personal from relational tasks
- Solve problems together

To do these things, the social worker is constantly clarifying focus and tasks, partializing this focus in relation to time and resources (what can be done in this interview), and helping the couple elaborate their direction in relation to these tasks and goals. She is sharing data from her observations of the couple, from her understanding of good relational skills, from research, and from her experience, but she is sharing it in the way the couple can use it at this point in their process. She is reaching for feelings and putting feelings into words (Shulman, 1992), and often actively teaching relational and communication skills. She partially manages the process until the couple is ready to manage it for themselves. When this takes place, she assists them in identifying and summarizing what has taken place. She will help the couple generalize their learning to other situations and begin to manage issues by themselves.

A key question at this time is how much understanding the couple needs to have about what is happening, the roots of their problems, their attachment styles, issues passed down through families of origin, and so on. The answer to this question gets more complex and nuanced as practitioners draw from a variety of family therapy approaches, some of which emphasize insight as the major goal and some of which emphasize behavioral and relational change. Workers have traditionally tended to emphasize either one or the other (Constable & Cocozzelli, 1989). However, it seems clear that both reflection (meanings) and action (behavior change) are necessary and interrelated the one to the other. Successful change is a matter of developing the connection, in theory and in practice, between the two.

Let us use our example of Nicholas and Johanna (case study 6.1) to clarify the relation between reflection and action. Clearly Nicholas and Johanna have a very complicated relationship. Both feel trapped in it, but both are beginning to see the position of the other, and to some extent both are beginning to see their own patterns. The social worker teaches them different skills of communication, expression, and empathy, and as they operationalize this learning, they see more. Learning and insight proceed along with interaction. As their relationship changes, understanding changes and vice versa. Some couples will immediately see relational and attachment connections and use them to sustain and reflect on their work. Others will be mainly interested in the changes that take place. The two are interdependent. The social worker works concretely with the tasks of relational change, helping clients come to a deepened understanding to sustain the process and to maintain gains. Understanding cannot be effectively reached without the experience of interaction, and interaction cannot take place without some level of understanding and ability to reflect on the process.

The Use of Tasks and Assignments

When relational tasks are central to the helping process, then understanding, reflection, and the helping process are no longer removed from the realities with which the couple is dealing. Personal and couple tasks are what they need to work on in any case. However, this is precisely where the couple is often stuck. The use of a natural focus (relational tasks) helps them experience themselves and each other differently. The tasks, once identified, sustain and help the couple take ownership of the work. Tasks provide the criteria, the bases for ongoing evaluation. These criteria make it clear and evident when it comes time to end. The tasks already exist; they are simply there to be done. It is a question of partializing the tasks, helping the couple to perform the tasks and then identifying and sustaining what they have accomplished with each other. They are in charge and the social worker is a coach to help them do this in their own way.

The tasks already exist, but they need to be identified. The more complex question is how the worker handles these already-existing tasks. Does the social worker prescribe tasks for the couple to do in session or out of session? Does the social worker take control of the process in this way? What would be a reason to prescribe a task? What theory would justify it? How would it work?

In our case studies so far, the social worker is continually prescribing tasks both in session and out of session. The social worker prescribed communication tasks for Nicholas and Johanna (case study 6.1), and taught them to use empathic accuracy as a powerful tool of relational understanding and change.[3] The worker prescribed a between-session task (take her to dinner and pay the bill, plan a weekend, and so on) that had a slightly paradoxical flavor to it (save the intense talk for our next session).

The first principle behind task construction is that the most powerful tool of learning is doing. The rationale for this approach is similar to the rationale in the discussion of "working from the outside-in" in ego–oriented casework (chapter 2). The difference is that some of the doing takes place in session with the partner, and so it can go relatively quickly in comparison with the longer time frames often associated with individual work. As with the J. family in chapter 4 (case study 4.7), family members often work on these tasks between sessions. Doing the well-constructed task both recognizes the basic relational realities and also changes them slightly in the process. Thus Johanna and Nicholas are seeing their relationship and the position of the other differently through their communication. They are also seeing themselves differently, and this can be a source of profound personal change. Nicholas shows a more active side of himself, Johanna a more thoughtful, vulnerable side. The worker extends this into their everyday week through the assignment.

The task concept has gradually clarified itself among family therapists over a number of years. There are four types of directives in cascading order, going from prescribing the tasks inherent in the situation to reconstructing the relationship (Haley, 1976). These are:

- *Straightforward Directives.* These are directives inherent to the situation. The relational work the couple has to do is simply assigned. Most directives are like this. Nicholas and Johanna should go out to dinner. If a straightforward directive will achieve its end, it's not necessary to go further.

---

[3]The use of a concrete focus on behaviors and tasks is well developed in behavioral approaches. See Nichols and Schwartz (2002, chapter 9), and Goldenberg and Goldenberg (1996, chapter 12).

- *Remedial Directives.* The remedial directive is the first of three reconstructive directives, that is, its intent is to reconstruct a relational pattern. Remedial directives prescribe doing something different from the normal pattern. Nicholas will pay the bill when they go out for dinner. If mother is customarily the disciplinarian, she will take a well-deserved "vacation," and father will take charge. One version of this was developed by Steve deShazer (1988) in the "solution-focused" approach. The worker looks for exceptions to the dominant pattern and prescribes the exception.
- *Metaphorical Directives.* These directives assign a metaphorical task for the relational issue. A boy, having issues around adoption, adopts a dog. The adoptive father (a mailman) knows a lot about dogs and the two share this project together.
- *Paradoxical Directives.* These directives essentially prescribe the problem, the way the family has been acting to date, or restrain the couple from change. Nicholas and Johanna should not talk intensely about their problems over dinner.

By prescribing that they *not* talk intensely about their problems over dinner (a mildly paradoxical instruction for them)[4] the social worker is doing several things at once. She is first of all urging that they do have an enjoyable dinner and weekend without falling into their destructive patterns, which come with intensity. Second, she is restraining them from change, thus indirectly encouraging change but in a way that they can control, and in a way that is related to their sessional work. Finally, if they do have some intense conversations (as they well may) and these break down into recriminations (also probable at this early stage), she is giving them a way of interpreting what happened in a benign way (we went too fast). For this to work, the social worker needs to be comfortable with paradox as a truthful communication, since the paradox identifies the reverse side of Nicholas and Johanna's actual intentions. By urging that they avoid intense discussion, she is siding with their real denial until their relationship becomes more manageable. Social workers should never prescribe a paradoxical directive they are uncomfortable with, and should never prescribe one without a clear understanding of how the relationship (and the reverse side of their intentions) operates. For the most part working with straightforward tasks and directives may well be enough to accomplish their goals.

Middle-Stage Work

The following three case studies are examples of middle-stage work with relational tasks of couples at different stages of the family life cycle. In the first case study, Rita and Joav Green are a young couple struggling with the decision of whether to take their child with Down's syndrome home. The couple is having a

---

[4]The use of paradoxical directives is well developed in Haley (1976), Stanton (1981), Goldenberg and Goldenberg (1996, chapter 10), and Nichols and Schwartz (2002, chapter 11).

great deal of difficulty deciding. The worker uses a variety of techniques to help them to make a decision.

A Couple Decides to Accommodate Their Baby with Down's Syndrome

The theme of the case focuses on tasks and assignments, now with a couple dealing with their newborn baby with Down's syndrome. They can't make a decision. How does the social worker help them break the impasse? What is the relation of process, understanding, and task? What is the relation of the decision-making process to the use of paradoxical tasks?

In the months of anticipation before the arrival of a baby, couples are usually beginning to think of how they will accommodate their life and work patterns (and their living unit) to what they anticipate of the baby's needs. The unfolding process of accommodation and change continues through all of the child's developmental stages. The dance of the couple is paralleled by the dance of the broader family and relatives as the accommodation continues. However, it is usually expected the baby will be "perfect"—that is, not have a disability. When the baby has a serious disability, the expectation of the perfect child vanishes. It is the loss of the expected "perfect child" who never came, a loss that needs to be mourned. When these tasks of coming to the reality of their child are not accomplished, the couple may be dealing mainly with hidden disappointment or fears. They may never know the child who actually comes for the person he or she is. Furthermore, complex and lifelong care-giving responsibilities can create heavy stress on the marital unit. If the couple does not share this responsibility, one person can become the "expert" on the child. The more one parent is absorbed by this role, the less the other may be involved, creating a serious fissure in the marriage (Beckman, 1991; Seybold, Flitz & McFee, 1991; Bernier, 1990; Davis, 1987). Consequently, as Voysey found in her research on a British sample, the child may be constructed as "a constant burden" (Voysey, 1975) rather than as a person who can bring something to his or her surroundings. When a baby is born with a disability, the couple has much to struggle with and the event can derail their normal processes of anticipation and acceptance.

CASE STUDY 6.2

Rita and Joav Green, a creative, well-educated Israeli couple in their thirties, came to a child welfare agency in Jerusalem. Three weeks earlier their second child had been born with Down's syndrome. The baby was now in temporary care, and the Greens could not decide whether to bring him home or to give him up. The Greens had al-

ready developed a comfortable, respectful relationship with each other. They had one other child, a bright eight-year-old girl. Joav had a limited and unsteady income, but his business was growing. Rita, a professional, provided the primary income and had begun to move up the career ladder. She had tried to nurse the baby in the hospital, but he had poor sucking reflexes. She then left his care to the hospital staff and some of them hinted at the possibility that she might refuse to take him home. Family members advised them to leave the baby. They knew social services would find a foster home if they abandoned the child. They feared that if they took the baby home and decided not to keep him, they would have a hard time placing him on their own. They were paralyzed with the decision they had to make, and if one of the couple indicated a decision in one direction, the other would take the other side. In some ways the idea that this was their decision, a decision they could control, made it all the more difficult to make. In one way or another, the couple could see difficulties: professional and economic limitations, the energy the child would draw from the whole family, their other child, and pressure from their families and even the hospital staff. All of the options were so painful that it immobilized the Green's ability to make decisions. As long as the baby did not exist in their perceptions as a couple, they didn't have act on their perceptions and their values. The work they needed to do and therefore the impossible decision could be forestalled.

The work of the couple was to make a decision and a commitment at the same time. If they took the baby home, they would only want to do it mutually. When they couldn't do this, they became paralyzed. The social worker took an approach that emphasized familiarizing the parents with the child and getting information to help them make an informed decision. She said they could do that only through some hands-on experience with the baby and through supportive involvement of the temporary care facility presently caring for the baby. They had to know what they were losing, but part of each of them didn't want to know this because they would then feel obligated to take the baby home, and so on.

The worker encouraged them to explore the implications of both possibilities; to visit the child with an experienced child-care worker, who gently helped them with certain details of care; and to discuss the situation with her over the time the agency allowed. She encouraged the couple to evaluate their ability to bond with their child and directly confronted the problems of caring for him. She asked them about other special-needs children in their respective families, and asked about family beliefs and legacies about such children. How did they ordinarily react to crises? How would their parents react if they decided to keep their baby? She encouraged them to grieve, normalizing for them the grieving process for the perfect child, whom they expected, but who never came. When they still made no decision after several weeks, she paradoxically tested the possibility with them of letting the child go, but also reviewed the supportive and special services that would be available if they took him home. She said that it sounded as if they had already made the decision to let the child go, and the worker was only recognizing it. They cried with the worker as they resisted the idea of abandoning their child. They then visited the child, and in two more sessions decided to take the child home. They came to the next session like two changed people. With a warm and mischievous smile the husband told the social worker his baby was "ugly as hell." In their final session they brought the baby, now three-and-a-half months old, dressed in bright, new clothes, the parents relaxed and attractive. They were getting specialized help and had even succeeded in making arrangements so that, in the end, neither of them had to sacrifice his or her career to care for the baby (adapted from Bardin, 1992).

Decision-Making Processes and the Family

There is a direct relation between decision-making and bonding processes. After all, the decision-making process has to reflect already-existing bonds. Additionally, the product of the decision-making process may be a commitment to change, a changed structure, an altered bond, a different way of viewing another person or network, or a different way of acting with the other. These are continuous processes leading to assent and commitment. Commitment is the irrevocability of consent (Turner, 1970). Sandy and Sheldon (case study 5.6) had made somewhat different decisions when they went through the marriage ceremony. It took them much longer to reach a mutual commitment. John and Eileen (case study 5.5) apparently never did.

Decision making ideally moves toward a consensus, that is, all give equal assent and all feel equally committed without private reservation or personal resentment. This is infrequently achieved, particularly across the dividing lines of generation and gender. Members give assent in order to allow a decision to be reached, and not because they are privately convinced that the decision in question is best. This assent is an *accommodation*. Agreement is achieved by the adjustment of some or all of the members to the irreconcilability of their views (Turner, 1970).

Rita and Joav (case study 6.2) see clearly that they could have a lifelong commitment to their son that could unbalance everything they had planned. They also see that they could easily control this possibility, and were pressured to do so by relatives, nurses, and hospital staff. It took them time to resolve the conflict between an underdeveloped, disregarded status bond with their son, the obligations going with it, and the question of whether they wanted to recognize it. Fortunately, the social worker gave them time to go through this decision-making process and arrive at the consensual decision that they needed to go forward with such a serious commitment.

Their relationship demanded that they pursue consensus rather than accommodation. From their perspective, accommodation would be a decision reflective of a type of dominance of one partner over the other. Drawing from this discussion, Turner builds an intriguing hypothesis on this very point:

> The more extensive the common values of family members or the more extensive the understanding that members have of one anothers' values, the less often will decision making contribute to unequal domination in the family, the less often will commitment to group decisions be conditional or ambiguous (Turner, 1970, p. 104).

Their love and respect for each other and the undeveloped bond with their child made the decision difficult. As they began to deal concretely with this with the paradoxical help of the social worker, their common values brought them to a consensual decision.

Personal Tasks: Joseph and Paula

The major themes of the following case study are *personal work* and *genograms* (see figure 4.1) in the context of relational work. Joseph and Paula have a lot of personal work to do. In the beginning, their personal work keeps getting enmeshed and confused with their relational work and vice versa. They cannot do personal work either without dealing with their relationship. On the other hand, redeveloping their relationship will presuppose the accomplishment of personal tasks. In Joseph and Paula's case, they agreed to reduce dysfunctional communication (to "construct a wall") so that they could deal with personal tasks and then reconstruct their relationship. Every couple faces a dilemma between the pull of personal and relational tasks, although Joseph and Paula expressed it more dramatically than most.

Several things helped them to do this work. First of all, rather than opening up the possibility of communication as with Nicholas and Johanna (case study 6.1), the social worker prescribed a partial shutdown. The shutdown was a somewhat paradoxical task that also allowed both to separate their respective issues of near-alcoholism, and depression from each other. As they dealt with these problems personally and apart from each other, positive communication could be relearned and cautiously resumed.

Joseph and Paula have chronic marital problems. In addition, Joseph is on the fringes of alcoholism and Paula has struggled with depression most of her life. They will return for help periodically in their lives. The example is useful to see a couple with serious problems fully using the opportunity to make changes in what appeared to be an impossible situation.

CASE STUDY 6.3

When they came to their first interview together, Joseph and Paula presented as a chronically contentious couple in their late thirties who were disagreeing sharply in almost all of their communication to the point of verbal and some physical abuse. Paula tended to criticize Joseph incessantly for everything, making him responsible for anything that went wrong or even her fears of something going wrong. Joseph, who had good verbal skills, would respond by making fun of Paula. Everything was going wrong in their relationship. The

---

[5] For a more detailed discussion of genograms, see McGoldrick, Gerson & Shellenberger (1999), Nichols and Schwartz (2002, pp. 160–162); Goldenberg and Goldenberg (1996, pp. 181–183), and Hartman and Laird (1983).

only positive points were that Joseph held down a very good job as a factory manager. Despite their conflict, they were able to agree on their parenting of their twin thirteen-year-old girls. They were both ready for divorce and marriage counseling was to be their last step.

Both had previous marriages that had ended in divorce. An immigrant from Romania, Joseph began his first marriage shortly after his immigration to the United States. Both had married hastily the first time. Paula had a three-month marriage to a man who was alcoholic, constantly physically abusive to her, and unable to leave his family of origin.

Joseph was on the fringes of alcoholism. When drinking, he would explode in verbal abuse of Paula, and she would respond in the same way. Paula had struggled with depression all of her life. When she was depressed she would become extremely blameful, and Joseph was an obvious target. Both would trigger each other's responses and fence with each other until the communication became explosive. Both, on the other hand, had a heavy investment in their marriage, partially because their first marriages had failed. They needed, however, to separate their individual problems from their relational problems and begin to work on individual problems without making the other responsible for those problems. They needed radically to change their communication patterns so that the patterns became supportive of the other rather than hostile. If they made and stabilized these changes, they could begin to think of developing a forgiveness process between them. The

negative communication patterns, however, were strongly established.

After making an assessment together of the situation, they decided on an initial threefold focus:

- Joseph would take responsibility for his binge drinking and its effects on the relationship. This was a disease as fatal as cancer unless he did something about it. He agreed to stop drinking entirely and go to Alcoholics Anonymous for help.
- Paula would take responsibility for her depression and its effect on the relationship. She would go back to her medication, begin a journal where she differentiated her thinking from her feelings, and do some other things that could be effective against depression.
- Both were to limit communication with each other to things that could be managed: the children, the news of the day, describing what happened at the factory or home, and so on. They should save the serious or contentious issues for sessions together with the social worker. They needed to construct a "wall" around any issues that would create problems.

They agreed to this, and in fact did do all of these things. During the following sessions they kept up the wall of communication, with Joseph and Paula communicating with each other only through the social worker. Each took turns talking about their situations to the social worker in the presence of the other. There was a focus on genogram work at this time. They found it very interesting to see the flow of their lives and their very different heritages. The focus of the work on individual genograms was on the roots of their problems as they had experienced them in their families of origin. Paula came from several generations of very strong women who took over, while their husbands were somewhat dysfunctional alcoholics. The failure of the first marriage was a deep shock to her, which made her all the more fearful that her second marriage would also fail. She would not be taken advantage of again and would remain on the defense against this. Joseph also came from a family of very strong women, who had complete control of their sons but whose husbands paid no attention at all to them. The shift from Romanian to North American society was very difficult, but he was proud that he had always been able to work and be well paid. Work was his only route to success, and in his previous marriage he was hardly aware of a relationship. He had his work and so he could fit into North American society. The first marriage had deteriorated over several years

and he hardly was aware of it when it ended.

Over the following months Joseph and Paula listened to each other's stories. Each took personal responsibility for working on their own alcoholism and depression. They began to attribute these problems less to each other and to take action on them themselves. The physical and verbal abuse stopped completely. Joseph did maintain complete sobriety, even when pressed by his Romanian friends to drink. Paula's depression began to lift as she took more responsibility for working on it. They each then could gradually let some of the wall down, and they began communication with each other in a completely different way—no criticism, no mocking. It was like learning to communicate when they had never communicated before. A warmer relationship emerged to the extent that, during the Christmas holidays, their twin daughters showed mock disgust that their mother and father were now treating each other so well. With their ability to maintain better communication stabilized, Joseph and Paula were able to manage to their satisfaction without further help.

The task model allows us to differentiate personal from relational tasks. In Joseph and Paula's case, it allowed personal work by both to take place in the presence of the other with some protective barrier to destructive communication in the meantime. As both would progress in personal tasks, they eventually could move to relational tasks. A balance then would emerge between personal and relational work.

Boundaries Protecting Personal Work

Communication is obviously important and is a major tool in helping couples reconstruct relationships. However, we have already seen a number of cases where verbal communication remained very limited (Armand and Rosalind (case study

3.2) and Sandy and Sheldon (case study 5.6)) so that the social worker worked only with one partner with the focus on relational tasks and communication, not with words but with action. In several cases (Jack and Jung (case study 4.6) and the J. family (case study 4.7)), cultural values put communication of feelings and meanings in second place to relational change. Joseph and Paula (case study 6.3) created a "wall" so that they could work on personal tasks and then shift to relational tasks. In the following case study, Edward and Joyce also needed a "wall" but for them the purpose was to stabilize their respective areas of competence from interference.

CASE STUDY 6.4

Edward is much older than Joyce, very bright, thoughtful, and not verbally aggressive. In some ways, Edward's consistency anchors Joyce's unpredictability, but this unpredictability keeps Edward on the alert with Joyce, ready to take over. He will tell her only what he feels she can manage to deal with. This shuts down much of what he would want to say and keeps him patronizing Joyce. Joyce shows symptoms of bipolar mood disorder, and she is getting psychiatric help and medication for this. She oscillates between reasonableness and becoming overwhelmed and explosive with him and with the children. Her unpredictability in her treatment of the children is a source of constant concern to Edward, so that he is losing a great deal of time in his home business. Edward tries to compensate when she is upset, taking over with the children, but this feels paternalistic to Joyce. In some ways she feels free to explode when Edward is so available. She shuts down when he goes into his long, quiet explanations. Edward feels he is a hostage of the situation.

In their work with the social worker, Joyce gradually took more responsibility for managing her outbursts. When she did that, they would construct a partial "wall." Joyce was more comfortable when she was in charge of her role and herself, but she had to work to achieve this internal balance. Her care for Edward and for the children motivated her as nothing else could. Edward's involvement and communication was taking over her responsibility, felt "touchy-feely" to Joyce, and didn't always help. They agreed to communicate on a regular basis on practical issues. Each could be in charge of their own area, but available to the other when needed. They were both relieved to operate in their own spheres, check in with each other on a regular basis, and arrange immediate communication if there was a need. Further relational goals would depend on their stabilizing their own areas.

Reconstruction: Societal Narratives and Couple Narratives

Social constructionist intervention focuses on changing contexts for meaning. In some cases, the target is the couple's context of meanings. This context needs to be reconstructed so that appropriate, relational tasks can proceed. Changing culturally constructed words and language makes way for the family's appropriate con-

structions. Words derive their meanings from the contexts in which they are produced or constructed. Language emerges from the cultural practices that give
shape to human interaction. It constructs the means by which thoughts, feelings,
and behaviors are produced (Monk & Gehart, 2003; Gergen, 1999). Foucault
(1972, 1979, 1980) discusses how a society's dominant narratives and discourses
marginalize some groups and empower others. Michael White took Foucault's discussion of dominant societal narratives and translated it into an approach to changing the way the family processes these narratives. The narratives were often the
basis for the family's own current balances or status quo (White & Epston, 1990).
Many of these dominant narratives are narratives of political oppression that people internalize, but also there are narratives of ideal beauty, of physical attributes,
of gender, of age, of able-bodiedness, of success, of children, of mental health, of
sexuality, and so on. These narratives, often taken for granted, are equally oppressive and equally denigrating to the real people experiencing them. Rather than
drawing from the effects of dominant narratives, social constructionists focus on
construction of local meaning. Freed from the effects of dominant narratives, the
construction of local meanings can release the couple to focus on workable and appropriate relational tasks rather than being drawn into impossible narratives drawn
from the broader society. Since social workers represent many of the societal institutions that create some of these dominant narratives, they are in a good position to
assist both the institution and the family to manage their part in them. Rita and Joav
Green (case study 6.2) had to develop a discourse with each other, and with society's dominant narratives around disability. The Kowalskis had to let go of a variety
of societal scripts, which had emptied their relationship.

CASE STUDY 6.5

Bogoslawa (Bonnie) and Andrzej
(Andy) Kowalski both are second-gener-
ation Polish Americans whose parents
arrived as refugees, having experienced
enormous losses to their families in
World War II. Bonnie and Andy were
the next generation, retreating from
very painful family experiences and
conforming to their new society. In their
university experiences they found their
identities and each other as antiwar
rebels of the generation of 1968. Extended intellectual conversations were
interlaced with considerable alcohol
and marijuana consumption. They
eventually married, struggled with their

addictions and let them go, and settled
down to a middle-class existence. Somehow their own relationship, the conversations and the addictions, were replaced by work, children, and other
things propagated by the media.

Bonnie became absorbed by her
jobs as a freelance computer consultant
and more recently by their son, Paul,
age four. She finds it very difficult to say
"no" to him. When Paul is not sleeping,
he controls Bonnie. Lately she has had
difficulty working because of Paul's increasing demands. Bonnie sees herself
as seriously overweight, is preoccupied
about eating and dieting, and shows
symptoms of major depression. Andy
has been similarly absorbed by his job as

an accountant. They are civil to each other. There is little overt conflict, but both feel that the relationship after eighteen years is "nearly dead." Now they find only emptiness when they look at their relationship, and plan to divorce if nothing else happens. Both feel trapped by their work, and Bonnie by their son, Paul. Sex has become a non-occurrence. Their communication and the overall relationship are extremely undeveloped. They have to work hard to make their interaction personal. Bonnie tends to talk about herself in a somewhat impersonal way and has very little "voice" to ask anything from Andy. When Bonnie and Andy do try to make contact, Bonnie remembers past hurts and becomes very impatient and reactive so that Andy is discouraged. Andy is quiet, feels it is difficult for him fully to comprehend Bonnie, feels lost for words with her, but actually does reasonably well in their discussion. Bonnie has great difficulty responding to Andy in any way. Bonnie feels entitled to more sensitive behavior on Andy's part. She becomes hyper-alert to any evidence of his insensitivity and tends to depreciate his efforts to be more sensitive to her: "You are sensitive only because I pointed out your insensitivity." Andy, feeling trapped by her logic, acknowledges that he has been insensitive, but feels he can never win and wonders whether it is worth trying. Bonnie does, however, appreciate his willing and competent help with Paul. He does prevent her from losing herself in Paul. Both feel close to hopeless about their relationship, but are willing to work on it "for one last time."

Bonnie's depression was identified in their first contacts. She started work-ing on it with an individual therapist. The marriage problems were connected with her depression (and vice versa). She continued to work with Andy on the marriage. Their emptiness and hopelessness was partially being fueled by outside investments of themselves and outside criteria governing their meaning systems, on their (local) experience of each other. Both had lost important parts of themselves and were colonized by work and standard images of success. Bonnie had lost herself in Paul, in her feelings about her weight and dieting, and in her depression. Could Bonnie deal with her depression without medicalizing her life? Andy found some success only in his work. Both had little hope their sexual relationship would be "successful," and were very reluctant even to try. The more they focused on their present relationship, the emptier they felt.

Their first step was to reestablish communication, particularly around their most pressing immediate concern, Paul. They did this. Andy enjoyed taking over with Paul as soon as he came home. Bonnie had some time to let go and recover, and Paul got better and less demanding. Building on that improvement, the social worker coached them to look for the exceptions to the negative picture of their relationship they had adopted. They could find these exceptions only in their past. Bonnie loved the heady, intellectual conversations they once had with each other, and Andy remembered them fondly as well. Could they bring them back again? They began to see how external definitions of work and success, societal ideas of some ideal weight, and Bonnie's concerns about being a perfect parent had robbed them of their care for each other as unique persons, of their real priorities, and even of their time with each other. Indeed it was shutting Paul down from his own struggle to develop. The worker encouraged them to write their own stories of their relationship, set their own priorities, and de-velop these stories together in the way they wanted. Removing their relationship from the partially self-imposed op-pression of societal criteria became a key to the unique relational tasks of re-discovering a friendship and an appreci-ation of each other, which did eventu-ally emerge.

THE POST-PARENTAL STAGE

The post-parental stage is sometimes called the empty nest, dramatizing a loss of active responsibility for children as they gradually become independent. Actually, the nest is not always empty. Often there is still the need to care for elderly parents as they become less able to care for themselves. Adult children also have a way of returning from a divorce or some other difficulty. Increasingly often these days, there may be a grandchild living at home. In addition, the relationship with adult children often remains quite active. Shorn of its responsibility to socialize, make decisions and carry responsibility for them, it often becomes quite a bit more com-fortable. In any case, much more couple work rather than child-oriented work is done. The post-parental couple remains quite active as long as they remain healthy. They are often the center of a very complex network of children, grandchildren, their own parents, and friends, and now they have some leisure time. The shift from a work role to retirement could be a crisis if work has been the only source of iden-tity and pleasure. It is the season of life to call upon one's inner resources to ap-preciate art and beauty, and often to be a support to a very complex network of friends and family. This needs to be well understood. When this personal shift has not occurred, or where there are losses or relational absences of the people with whom one would ordinarily share this, there can be bitterness, loneliness, and de-spair. Older men with losses, cut off from family, sometimes with drinking prob-lems, can be at risk for suicide.

The major shift inside the family is that the couple needs to move some way back toward its original structure, prior to the arrival of children (as long as that structure was functional)—but now with a very different history and outlook on the future. They may prevent this from happening out of fear of intimacy. They may try to remain in an earlier, child-centered stage. Although there are many distrac-tions of a complex network, the couple needs to rediscover the dyadic relationship and its potential for them at this point in their lives. Another danger is enmeshment with each other. The loss of work and of direct parental roles could throw them much closer into each others' orbits than they may have been accustomed to. They may become quite critical of each other, dabbling in each other's affairs, or explo-sive, as the Caldwell family (described in the following case study) experienced. Another extreme, if they have never really developed a relationship with their spouse, is the loneliness that comes with disengagement. Illness is always a real possibility at this time. Illness can cut off any possibilities of development. It can lead to loss and be a great source of stress. In addition, there can be an accumulation of real losses that leaves the older person bereft and detached from life. Older men are one of the most suicide-prone groups of all, partially because losses of work and those closest to them may leave them less able to create new networks.

CASE STUDY 6.6

Ashford and Louise Caldwell, a retired African-American couple in their late sixties, are a study in contrasts, although they do have some common values and beliefs. Ashford is a retired ironworker, a foreman. He did his job well, "managing men," as he puts it. It was a source of great pride to him and he misses it greatly. Although he hasn't changed his waking habits, he has less to do. Louise manages his senile mother, something she is very willing to do, but it is a full-time job, and sometimes she wonders how she ever got into this. On the other hand, she considers it *her* work and hardly lets Ashford in on any of it. When she has time at all, she loves her garden, although with her arthritis she needs Ashford's help to manage it. She will get help only grudgingly, and so she doesn't ask any more. It is one of a number of issues that bring her to the "slow burn" she carries into many relationships. Both are very religious, but have affiliated with different religions. Ashford constantly criticizes Louise's religious practices as if they were his own. He has also become quite critical of Louise's housekeeping. Louise's slow burn seems to be constantly with her these days, and she appears to be depressed. Ashford takes the slow burn seriously, since he (somewhat correctly) sees that it comes from a long

list of Louise's disappointments with him. Louise never easily forgot things.

They have very different communication styles. Louise is quite verbal. She easily overcomes Ashford with her words. When Ashford feels overwhelmed by Louise or by a situation, he becomes quite explosive. This occurred when he was working at the mill, with their children, and with Louise. There have been increasing explosions between Ashford and Louise. Ashford never was subtle in his relations with their four children. Louise says that he would tell you to do it and how to do it, and you would do it that way, or else. He managed to alienate all three sons when they were in their late teens or early twenties. They left home prematurely and with controversy. They couldn't take his constant direction. Louise always had the stronger relationship with the children, and this somewhat undercut Ashford's relationship with them. It irritated Ashford, and he felt isolated from his children. At one point many years ago, when his fifteen-year-old second son, Chad, talked back to him, Ashford exploded and beat him. Chad ran away to a friend's house, but quietly returned after a week. Louise "let him in the back door." Ashford was embarrassed at his behavior with Chad, but never dealt with it. Neither apologized to the other, and there are lasting, uncomfortable feelings between the two. Louise, concerned about an explosion, has taken pains never to remind him of it.

Louise was the oldest girl in a family of five. She has always been placed in something of a caretaker role, and has long had mixed feelings about the role. When she was sixteen, she found herself pregnant. Without much discussion, her mother made her place the child, a boy she named Joey, for adoption. She considered abortion, is happy she didn't have one, and is happy that Joey is alive somewhere. She remembers his birthday and wonders how he is doing now, at age fifty. When she looks quiet and sits away from him sometimes, Ashford knows she is talking to Joey, and respects that. Other than Ashford, no one knows this family secret.

Louise and Ashford came to Lutheran Family Services for help after a particularly explosive week. They were increasingly uncomfortable with the constant arguments, and now, after forty-two years marriage, threats of divorce. Ashford was still reactive from the last argument and Louise carried her slow burn, so it was most difficult to get the couple talking with each other at all. They seemed simultaneously to occupy different universes, but also appeared overinvolved with everything the other was doing. From Ashford's perspective, the problem was religion and Louise's involvement with a Pentecostal group, while he is Lutheran. From Louise's perspective, the problem is Ashford's need to control everything she does, even things of which she was previously in control. On the other hand, she would pursue him incessantly whenever a difference came up until he exploded. She didn't seem to be able to stop. She was also showing signs of

some mild to moderate depression. In the initial contract, they identified Ashford's need for anger management and Louise's depression, together with what were problems in communication and differentiation of one from the other's areas. Their in-session communication with each other bore out all of this. They set personal and relational goals dealing with anger management, depression, and "time out." They identified their mutual patterns of pursuit, withdrawal, and explosion. They needed to find different ways to communicate and set boundaries on some of their involvement with one another.

There were a total of fourteen sessions over a total of five months, with the social worker's vacation in the middle. During the first six weekly sessions, they identified patterns of communication, set boundaries on things that lead to explosions, helped Ashford to deal with his anger and Louise with her slow burn, depression, and tendency to pursue. Ashford got a job cleaning the church and began to do some volunteer work. Louise, with Ashford's more willing help, got involved with her garden again. Both began to "date," partially to rebuild their relationship and partially to get respite from the constant chore of caring for Louise's mother-in-law. Louise gradually permitted Ashford to take more care of his mother, something Ashford was quite willing to do. Arguments began to lessen, although they still occurred, and Ashford began to say positive, loving things to Louise. Louise was surprised. Most of the sessions involved communication between the two. It was difficult, but getting somewhat better. One of the things they were able to talk about was Louise's continued hurt and slow burn, something she was totally unaware of. She began to use this insight to deal with it as a personal task. This made a great difference when she began to get some grasp of it.

When the worker returned from a one-month vacation, they had gone back to many of their older patterns but had also held on to some gains. After three weekly interviews, they had recouped their earlier losses and were making further progress. In addition, Ashford was beginning to be able to repair the relationship with his son, Chad. There was a potential point of controversy between Ashford and Chad at a family picnic. Ashford took him aside, and they were able to talk it out, something they had never done previously. Ashford was surprised that Chad was so willing to accept his relationship and implicit apology. His eyes filled with tears as he described the incident. Louise talked about her recollections of her early life and of Joey. She made some connections of these incidents with her slow burn, while Ashford listened respectfully. Louise was feeling far less depressed as she began to un-

burden herself and as she saw concrete improvement in her relationship with Ashford.

In three more weekly interviews, they came to the point where they were ready to go on a biweekly and then monthly maintenance schedule. They were close to termination. In the meantime, they had bought a travel trailer and were fulfilling a lifelong dream of touring the West. Someone was taking care of Ashford's mother at home. The worker received a postcard from them. They were having a wonderful time but they noted that they would still argue once in a while. They used the techniques they had learned and were mostly enjoying a new freedom and closeness they had never dreamed of before. They thanked the worker for the help. In one further session on returning, they talked about their new patterns. Louise had gone back to her garden, Ashford to his church work, and both in their own ways were including their adult children in their lives. They were excited about all of this and felt comfortable in what they had achieved.

The case of Ashford and Louise, while not a complicated one, is an example of all the principles we have been discussing in this chapter. The couple learned to reconstruct their relationship through communication. Although the relational tasks are typical of the post-parental stage, there is a parallel with the case of Joseph and Paula (case study 6.3) in that both were overinvolved with the other in some ways, and very separate from the other in other ways. They needed to separate personal from relational tasks. If they were to be successful, work had to proceed on both levels at once

THE NEEDS OF FAMILIES, THE SOCIAL WORKER AS A PERSON, AND THE HELPING PROCESS

In the first chapter we examined a model of the interaction between human needs of people in families, such as safety, belonging, communication, and so on; the response of the social worker; the response of the family; and general principles of practice. The theory reviewed in this chapter on beginning and middle phases of the helping process can be summed up in the Caldwell's story (case study 6.6). Families are assisted at different stages of development to carry out relational tasks. Techniques, which assist them to do this, have similarities to each other. The differences in the content and process of helping are contained in the stage of development, the personal realities of family members, and to some extent the process.

The family becomes a place where identity bonds are respected and can develop, where members can act appropriately in relation to others' needs and in relation to self. Knowing this, the social worker assists the family to develop this moral unity through the repairs needed in carrying out personal and relational tasks. The response of the social worker generates values in the performance of tasks. The family responds by carrying out these values in their communication, in their relations and in their action. The practice principles, listed in Fourth Direction column of table 1.2, are essentially complex values placed into specific action by the family through the worker's response.

In the Caldwell family (case study 6.6), Louise and Ashford learned to differentiate themselves from each other, to respect each others' uniqueness, and to reconnect with each other as they are now, with their own respective developmental issues. They had something on which to build from the beginning. Louise was able to trust Ashford with the secret of Joey, knowing that it would not be violated. Ashford's guilt and delicate relationship with Chad was never used by Louise to hurt him or harden him. In the sessions they learned to communicate, to express feelings and thoughts, and to respond in an entirely different way. They carried over these new patterns into their relationship. They learned to repair areas of difficulty. Both Louise and Ashford did different things for themselves, knowing that they had the other's support. Ashford took on a part-time job and did volunteer work. Louise spent time with her beloved garden. They also were able to do things together, such as their dates and finally their trip West. In the end, their relationship became a relationship where they were each free to be the person they are with the other, and to choose this comfortably.

The principles generate a picture of the social worker not simply carrying out effective techniques but actually becoming them in his or her interaction with the family, and thus helping the family to carry them out. They generate a normative interaction with the family, and a type of "virtue orientation" to practice. These principles become qualities of the worker and from these there come qualities, in their own way, of the family, to the extent that the family is willing to process them. Given this model and the discussion of the book, what qualities of the worker result?

- The ability to take the role of each family member in relation to the other(s)
- The ability to visualize the possible good connections of family members with each other
- The ability to develop the listening language of empathy as a tool for growth and to teach others to use this tool according to their needs and capabilities

- The ability to express feelings and needs, respecting the other(s) and without being hurtful
- The ability to accept and value the other(s), including their potential to contribute that they, themselves, may be unaware of
- The ability to use this acceptance and good vision of the other(s) possibilities as a teaching tool
- The ability to help people in families to choose appropriately, respecting themselves and others, without being swayed by external pressure
- The ability to maintain safety and discretion, protecting the fragile identities of others, and teach others to do so
- The ability to be honest with oneself and with others

These qualities are qualities of the social worker that underly techniques. There is a strong research tradition that connects therapist qualities, such as empathy, genuineness, and warmth, with therapeutic effectiveness (Truax & Carkhuff, 1967; Orlinsky, 1994), far more than allegiance to a particular school or technique. The relationship is, at least in part, created by the beliefs and values to which the social worker has come and that he or she is willing to help the family learn through coping with personal and relational tasks, with all of the implicit values contained within these tasks if they are to be done well.

SUMMARY

Work with couples is important. Recent research points out that clinicians work with about twice as many couples as elaborated families—taking care of children or elderly persons (Doherty & Simmons, 1996). Moreover, work with the couple within the elaborated family is also the key to working with the elaborated family. The following chapters develop the themes of middle-stage work with elaborated families, work with families reconstructing themselves, and work between families and social institutions. Since the couple is the center of the family, the principles from work with couples in this chapter can be carried over into work with elaborated families.

REFERENCES

Ables, B. S. (1977). *Therapy for couples*. San Francisco: Jossey-Bass.

Bardin, A. (1992). Less than perfect: A couple's struggle to accept their Down's syndrome baby. *Family Therapy Networker*, November-December, 75–76.

Beckman, P. (1991). Comparison of mother's and father's perceptions of the effect of young children, with and without disabilities. *American Journal on Mental Retardation, 95*, 585–595.

Bernier, J. (1990). Parental adjustment to a disabled child: A family system perspective. *Families in society, 71*, 589–596.

Biestek, F. J. (1954). *The casework relationship*. Chicago: Loyola University Press.

Constable, R. T., & Cocozzelli, C. (1989). Common themes and polarities in social work practice theory development. *Social Thought*, Spring, 14–24.

Davis, B. (1987). Disability and grief. *Social Casework*, 68, 352–57.

deShazer, S. (1988). *Clues: Investigating solutions in brief therapy*. New York: Norton.

Doherty, W. J., & Simmons, D. S. (1996). Clinical practice pictures of marriage
and family therapists: A national survey of therapists and their clients. *Journal
of Marital and Family Therapy*, 22, 9–25.

Foucault, M. (1972). *The archeology of knowledge*. New York: Harper & Row.

Foucault, M. (1979). *Discipline and punish: The birth of the prison*. Middlesex,
UK: Peregrine Books.

Foucault, M. (1980). *Power/knowledge: Selected interviews and other writings*. New
York: Pantheon Books.

Gergen, K. (1999). *An invitation to social construction*. Newbury Park, CA: Sage.

Goldenberg, I., & Goldenberg, H. (1996). *Family therapy: An overview*. Pacific
Grove, CA: Brooks-Cole.

Grunebaum, J. (1990). From discourse to dialogue: The power of fairness in therapy with couples. In R. Chasin, H. Grunebaum, & Herzig (Eds.), *One couple,
four realities: Multiple perspectives in couple therapy* (pp. 191–228). New York:
Guilford Press.

Guerney, B. L. (1977). *Relationship enhancement*. San Francisco: Jossey-Bass.

Habermas, J. (1987). *The theory of communicative action (Vol. 2), Lifeworld and system: A critique of functionalist reason*. Boston: Beacon Press.

Haley, J. (1976). *Problem-solving therapy*. San Francisco: Jossey-Bass.

Johnson, L. (1981). *Social work practice: A generalist approach*. Boston: Allyn &
Bacon.

Kheshgi-Genovese, Z., & Constable, R. T. (1995). Marital practice in social work.
Families in Society, 76(9), 559–566.

Lambert, M. J., & Bergin, A. E. (1994). The effectiveness of psychotherapy. In A. AU: page
E. Bergin & S. L. Garfield (Eds.), *Handbook of psychotherapy and behavior
change* (pp. 00–00). New York: Wiley.

Lazarus, A. (1981). *The practice of multimodal therapy*. New York: McGraw-Hill.

Mead, G. H. (1932). *The philosophy of the present*. Chicago: University of Chicago
Press.

Mead, G. H. (1934). *Mind, self and society*. Chicago: University of Chicago Press.

McGoldrick, M., Gerson, R., & Shellenberger, S. (1999). *Genograms: Assessment
and intervention* (2nd ed.). New York: Norton.

Monk, G., & Gehart, D. R. (2003). Sociopolitical activist or conversational partner? Distinguishing the position of the therapist in narrative and collaborative
therapies. *Family Process*, 42(1), 19–30.

Nicholas, M., & Schwartz, R. C. (2002). *Family therapy: Concepts and methods*.
New York: Allyn & Bacon.

Orlinsky, D. E., Grawe, K., & Parks, B. P. (1994). Process and outcome in psy- AU: pag
chotherapy—noch einmal. In A. E. Bergin & S. L. Garfield (Eds.), *Handbook
of psychotherapy and behavior change* (pp. 00–00). New York: Wiley.

Seybold, J., Flitz, J., & McPhee, D. (1991). Relation of social support to the self perceptions of mothers with delayed children. *Journal of Community Psychology, 19*, 29–36.

Shulman, L. (1992). *The skills of helping: Individuals, families and groups* (3rd ed.). Itaska, IL: Peacock.

Snyder, M. (1995). "Becoming": A method for expanding systemic thinking and deepening empathic accuracy. *Family Process, 34*(2), 241–253.

Stanton, M. D. (1981). Strategic approaches to family therapy. In A. S. Gurman & D. P. Kniskern (Eds.), *Handbook of family therapy*. New York: Brunner-Mazel.

Truax, C. B., & Carkhuff, R. R. (1967). *Toward effective counseling and psychotherapy*. Chicago: Aldine.

Turner, R. (1970). *Family interaction*. New York: Wiley.

Voysey, M. (1975). *A constant burden: The reconstitution of family life*. London: Routledge & Paul.

White, M., & Epston, D. (1990). *Narrative means to therapeutic ends*. New York: Norton.

Wile, D. B. (1992). *Couples therapy: A nontraditional approach*. New York: Wiley.

CHAPTER 7

Beginnings and Middle Phases with Families of Two or More Generations

The focus of this chapter and the following one moves from working with the couples to working with elaborated family units involving two and three generations. These elaborated families are families of parent(s) and children and possibly an older generation. Elaborated families may have experienced disruption and loss, and so we include in the next chapter families where parents are divorcing, families blending through remarriage, and underorganized families. The task framework is particularly useful amidst complex arrangements and disrupted arrangements.

ELABORATED FAMILIES

Families Comprised of Parent(s) and Children

We will examine beginning and middle-stage social work practice with a number of families, some with school-age children and some with adolescents. These families involve at two or more generations: the parents, the children, and grandparents and other relatives involved in the picture. There are several stages of family development here. We have already seen a glimpse of the decision-making process used to accommodate a child with apparent severe disability in Rita and Joav Green's family (case study 6.2). The emergent structure demands a strengthening of the couple relationship in a new set of tasks. As the child grows, the relationship of socialization and responsibility for the child demands inequality of power between parents and children. It demands a functional hierarchy. The parents need to be in charge.

There is an unstable shift in the hierarchy in adolescence, as the adolescent brings in reference groups other than the parents and challenges the family structure. On the other hand, the risky behaviors of which adolescents are capable still demand some external controls. These behaviors are also often seen as a challenge to the perceived structure and a move toward power. The challenge for both parents and children is how to move from power and control to a more functional relationship, a relationship that respects the adolescent's growing self-responsibility. This movement is what much of the discourse between parents and adolescents is about. There needs to be a qualitative change in communication, which may become less formal as power may be less frequently called upon by both generations. Ultimately, friendship, attachment, membership, and belonging should operate more frequently than power. Ideally, the transition in adolescence moves from a power struggle to a cooperative effort. Parents remain secure attachment figures, and the adolescent explores his or her appropriate competency and autonomy. When this transition appears to be impeded, the frequent result is family conflict and negative developmental outcomes (Diamond & Liddle, 1999, p. 9).

Families Where Parents are Divorcing; Families Blending Through Remarriage

In chapter 8 we will examine practice with families in the process of divorce and its aftermath. In the case of the divorcing family, there are two structures, often at war or in conflict. One is the family as it was (with two parents), the other is the family as it now must be, if the custodial parent is to take charge. Because a transition from one to another structure takes time and needs to be tested, these family forms (divorcing or blending families) can be chaotic and full of confusion, with members having different or mixed allegiances, now to one parent, now to another (Montalvo, 1982). Remarriage brings in another set of allegiances.

Underorganized Families

Families that are underorganized often have experienced poverty and societal neglect, but they also may be chronically stuck in a transition. These are families of two or more generations, unable fully to carry out the socialization of children and other family functions. We rely on Harry Aponte's (1986) developed discussion of this type of family structure, together with a case study illustration of work with these families.

Couples in Elaborated Families

The basics of working with couples, of course, are still important. The couple is the executive subsystem of the family. Many of the basic issues within elaborated families are still couple issues. The parents of the young child need to come to an agreement around socialization and what they should expect of the child and of each other. They need to preserve and develop their own relationship at the same time. If one spouse's alliance with a child is stronger than his or her alliance with the other spouse, parents will not be able to manage relational tasks of socialization or of couple formation. They will be undercutting each other, with one parent experiencing greater closeness to the child, one experiencing distance, and their conflicts are played out through this triangle.

As the child reaches adolescence and encounters a more complex world, the couple will need to shift their relationship again to the adolescent's changing needs and world. They need gradually to encourage responsibility on the youngster's part.

Even if they privately disagree, the couple need to support each other. Adolescents are legendary in their skills at gaining power by setting up cross-generational triangles, pitting one parent against another. This is stressful for the couple and tests their own relationship. Paradoxically, this move can also provide some distraction to the couple and relief from their own developmental issues. To cope with this potential stress on their relationship, the couple needs to form a united front while dealing appropriately, lovingly, and firmly with the needs of the adolescent. Such circumstances force parents to come together or face chaos. Eventually the adolescent we knew, with all of his or her creativity, will disappear, replaced by a young adult with different relationship and attachment needs. The problem is that some of the damage to the adolescent, left by the risks taken, may remain.

BEGINNING WITH ELABORATED FAMILIES

Work with elaborated families is different from work with couples. The task focus is no longer primarily a search for boundaries and intimacy in the couple relationship. Instead, the focus is on finding ways to manage the complexity and the changes in an elaborated structure, retaining a feeling of solidarity, and managing the needs of the child and the couple relationship at the same time. In the Peterson example (case study 7.5), involving a ten-year-old child, the focus was mainly on the child and secondarily and implicitly on the couple's relationship. The Maxwell example (case study 7.7) involved an adolescent. Here the focus on the chronic marital problems of the couple alternated with the focus on Stephen Maxwell, who was running away from home. The parents had great difficulty relating to his needs in the throes of their chronic marital difficulty.

There are several related sets of tasks. One set deals with the couple as a couple. The other deals with the couple as socializing agents, and with the youngster in relation to all others in the family. These multiple sets of tasks generate a complex picture. However, as long as one is taking a systems approach to family relationships, each set of tasks tends to be implicit in the other. Doing one task with the couple on socialization issues can also mean working on their couple issues at the same time. This means that, working with the couple on socialization issues and tasks, one is also working with the adolescent, and at the same time helping the couple strengthen their marital relationship. In the same vein, by working with the adolescent, helping him to sort out his issues of enmeshment and disengagement with either or both parents, one is also setting up the conditions for a possible reaction on the part of the couple to these changes in the relationship with their child. The couple, without the demands of a cross-generational coalition, without the "distraction" of an enmeshed or disengaged relationship with their son or daughter (which the adolescent was supplying), would have difficulty working on their own relational realities. The distraction may have conveniently prevented them from working on their own relationship. On the other hand, without the distraction there is now an opportunity for the couple to resolve the relationship issues. If the couple does unite in the face of the problem, this unity may help resolve the dilemma they face.

Beginning with elaborated families is always complex and difficult. Coexisting couple and parental problems create different agendas, and often the agendas are conflicted or hidden. It is possible that the couple may find it more acceptable to work on a problem with a child than to acknowledge a marital problem and deal with it. Issues involved with marital breakdown are very personal. It may be hard to admit that the marriage is failing. The couple may perceive less shame in having problems with their children than in having problems with each other. The perceived next step—the threat of divorce and the possible loss of the relationship—may seem drastic.

The Skills of Beginning

In any case, as with couples' experiences, the family's perception is that things are out of control. The family sees itself in a mess. It is important that what family members perceive as a mess be transformed into a problem, and then into workable tasks. It is important that, without any premature reassurance, the family see the process as hopeful, as something in which they can engage. A focus needs to be defined, a contract be reached, and a personal connection to be made with the social worker as a possible helper. As with couples' counseling, this may be reached through a phone contact and two to three interviews. The difference is that there are now more people involved in the process and thus more uncertainty. Although the process may take longer, the steps are similar. The dance needs to start with those who should be involved (given the tasks). Whether to begin with the couple or the whole family is itself a complex question. The parents and others need to agree on tasks, define a focus, reach a contract they can trust, and agree on next steps. The skills listed for beginnings with more elaborated families (Shulman, 1992) are similar to the skills we reviewed in beginnings with couples:

- *Clarifying the social worker's purpose and role*, now with two generations.
- *Reaching for feelings* of a more complex network with multiple perceptions, interests, and tasks.
- *Putting feelings into words* when there is an unequal relationship of parent and child, and when there is a different language of feelings between the generations and different reference groups.
- *Reaching inside silences* when the silence has been set up on both sides by fears of revealing parts of self.
- *Partializing concerns* when concerns get distorted and are translated into privileged demands on both sides, or when some concerns are unrevealed.
- *Contracting* under conditions of generational inequality.
- *Assessing* more complex structures and more complex tasks, often involving the world of social institutions.

All of this needs to be done between family members involved in the helping process, not simply with the worker as in individual counseling. This process and these skills will be illustrated in greater detail in case examples.

Respecting Hierarchies

In working with elaborated families, the major difference from working with couples is that, rather than a focus on equals, the *hierarchy* of the family needs to be respected. The parents need to be in charge, and this is often the problem. How does the social worker avoid taking over the process and thus displacing the parents? When what is happening in the family appears dysfunctional, as it will, the temptation will be very strong for the social worker to enter the family as an "expert" and undercut the already tottering parental power. When the "expert" takes over, both parents and child(ren) either move into dysfunction or fight the agency and social worker in order to remain in control. It may be better to for them disagree with the agency and the worker, since moving into dysfunction eliminates any possibility of betterment. Energy is then simply invested elsewhere.

Safety

Safety is particularly problematic where there has been abuse or the threat of abuse. Nothing can proceed if there is violence in the family, or if people don't feel safe. The only solution to problems with safety is to start with an enforceable agreement with the parents around their tasks of creating safety and a well-understood safety plan. These tasks, worked out in detail, will be the key to any other tasks that follow. The social worker is there to help the parents carry out these tasks. This is, then, the basis for the contract. The social worker will need to use all of the beginning process skills listed above to help the parents assess the problem, contract on this basis, and begin. The parents' efforts to create safety are supported, but if safety cannot be created and maintained by the parents, then the community and the legal system will have to intervene. In situations where safety is not an issue, the social worker still must work delicately to preserve the hierarchy of responsibility of parents and children. This is particularly a problem where parents or child(ren) would prefer to hand over the power to the social worker.

One-Step or Two-Step Beginnings

Beginnings with the entire family are often quite complex. For this reason, it might be quite effective to work with the parents as a couple on developing a united approach to the needs of the child (and implicitly to their own needs) without the child or adolescent being involved at all. If this is a possibility, the process can go much faster. In any case, the issue of focus needs to be resolved fairly quickly, although at the beginning it is necessarily a tentative focus. Is this to be a one-step beginning—that is, the social worker sees the parents and not the child(ren)? Or is this to be a two-step beginning—that is, the social worker has one session with the parents, and then a family session with parents and child(ren)? This can be determined with the client either at the stage of the initial phone inquiry or in a first session with the parents alone. As with couples counseling, it is important to listen to the request and determine with the person calling whether it is 1) an individual problem that can best be dealt with individually; 2) a problem best dealt with by beginning with the couple alone, the one-step beginning; or 3) something best dealt with in the whole family, with parents and child(ren) together in a session.

Beginning with One Parent

When the problem has to do with parenting issues, it is generally best to start with the couple together or the couple and children. Usually, if the couple can be helped to agree on specifically what the problem is and how to deal with it, they can be a support to each other and their approach to the problem can be more effective. On the other hand, a parent with a spouse obdurately opposed to coming in for help, or a person clearly identifying a personal problem or need, will need an approach tailored to the situation. Although it is generally preferable to start with both parents, it may not be possible to do this. If beginning with both parents is not possible, working with one parent still can have impact on the total system. A single parent needing to take over the parenting role can also begin without involving the child(ren). The parent may change and the system might be expected to adjust to these changes. The following case study is an example of the social worker working with single-parent issues.

CASE STUDY 7.1

Joan, a single parent, is dealing with a chaotic home situation immediately after her divorce. She had never wanted to be a single parent and has difficulty accepting the implications of the role. No one—not her children, her mother, or her former spouse—take her seriously, and she is having great difficulty exerting any control at all. The social worker works with Joan over four months, helping her to differentiate herself in relation to her family so that she can meet the demands of this new role. With her children, she eventually takes charge. With her former spouse, she sets limits. With her mother, she clarifies that she will manage her problems. She is in control, but she would accept help from her mother. She strengthens her approach with her children, her mother, and her former spouse. These respond by changing their own expectations and relationship with her, allowing her to take her role. In this particular case, it was unnecessary and would be dysfunctional to see any person other than Joan for working with her parenting issues. With support and extensive work she became strong enough to manage the situation.

A One-Step Beginning with a Couple

One parent may call with a problem. When the social worker returns the call, she briefly helps the parent to clarify the problem and arrange to come in with the partner to see how she might help them to manage the problem. To avoid an implicit alliance with one partner, she doesn't spend a lot of time over the phone. They both come in and, as a result of the session, resolve together to try a different approach to the problem. The worker keeps them in charge. The approach works to the point of resolving the issue without further involving other parts of the family. The couple may come in a number of times with different issues. The focus is always on helping them to clarify their roles and strategy in relation to the problem — that is, on empowering the parents as parents while helping them to respond in a differentiated way to situations where their normal responses seem to fail. The approach takes some experience on the part of the social worker to make the assessment, to deal with parents' problems with relational tasks, and to begin the process of coaching parents on dealing with these tasks without the children present.

The Kim family was able to manage without bringing in their teenage son, Justin. From the parents' perspective, bringing him in would have empowered Justin (with his verbal skills in English) and undermined their delicate sense of control in a different culture.

CASE STUDY 7.2

Mrs. Bernice Kim called Methodist Youth Services on the advice of their minister at the Korean Methodist Church about the problems she and her husband, Dr. Peter Kim, were having with Justin, age fifteen. She had some reluctance to come in with her husband, but assumed that an expert from the agency could just tell them what they should do better. Both were born in Korea and had emigrated as employees of a multinational company. All of their kin on both sides of the family are in Korea. Recently there has been a problem between Justin and his father. Dr. Kim feels that Justin, born in the United States, no longer respects his father as a Korean boy should. He spends a lot of time with his American friends, even sleeping at their houses when he can. He is not doing as well in high school as Dr. Kim thinks he could. He will not study more than a few hours a night. He refuses to go to Korean Saturday School and spends his weekends watching videos with his friends. Dr. Kim has been restrained with Justin. His father would have used physical punishment on Justin for being lazy. He knows he cannot do that in the United States. Mrs. Kim tends to see Justin's side of the problem, saying that he is growing up as any other American boy. As long as they live here, they must adapt. Justin is adapting more than they are. They can expect nothing more from Justin.

The previous night Dr. Kim and Justin had an argument. Rather than Justin listening to his father, he left home to spend the night with his best friend, Kerry and his family. Kerry's family seems to be a rather disorganized American family with no clear hours or well-defined relations. For example, they never have any meal together. Kerry tells Justin how unfair and repressive Justin's family is. Justin told his father this. His father was so angry and ashamed of him that he told him to go and stay with Kerry. Justin left to stay with Kerry. Dr. Kim now regrets his outburst. Justin may be getting tired of being a long-term guest, but neither of the two will back down.

The social worker suggested that this couldn't be resolved over the phone and suggested that Dr. and Mrs. Kim come to the agency to discuss it further. They need to develop a plan. They made an appointment to get together in a few days. In the session, the social worker was fairly formal, addressing them as Dr. and Mrs. Kim, and asked Dr. Kim to identify his concerns to see whether they could develop a strategy together. As Dr. Kim described the situation, she responded by reflecting his narrative and commented that that "It sounds as if you feel that you are losing your son." Dr. Kim's chin quivered as he said "yes." Mrs. Kim, seeing Dr. Kim's emotion, moved in to say that she doesn't think they are losing Justin, but that he is like an American boy now. It is a shame, but what else could we expect? We have done it (looking at her husband). The social worker encouraged them to talk about how they saw the problems. Summarizing their discussion, she reflected each's point of view, the concerns about loss of cultural heritage and connections with family, some of the reality of Justin's present high school and friends. Both saw their common point of view in this, together with some of their different perceptions, and agreed with the picture. The problem was how to help Justin to rejoin the family without either his father or him feeling shame.

They worked out a plan for his mother to call Justin on the weekend and invite him for dinner with them in a good Korean restaurant. The worker coached Dr. Kim on helping Justin to tell his story, just as they had just done, this time about how things were at the house of his friend. She coached him on how to invite Justin back without criticism. They agreed to follow the strategy. At the same time, how could Justin learn more about his Korean heritage? The outcome of this discussion was that Dr. Kim would wait for Justin to settle comfortably at home again. When things had settled, he could take a two-month vacation from the company and invite Justin to come back with him to Korea to spend some time with his relatives. At the end of the session they agreed to try this strategy and to stay in contact. They would get together with the social worker again, but this would get it started. The dinner was initially somewhat tense, as Justin expected his father to reprove him for his behavior. When this didn't happen, his mother wondered if he was ready to return. He said he was. His father welcomed him and Justin apologized to his father on his own. His father accepted his apology. Later his father invited him to take a trip with him to Korea and Justin accepted the offer. They had more sessions with the worker discussing some of their own differences with North American culture, and some of Mrs. Kim's issues to which she had not previously been able to give voice.

As communication got better between Justin and his father and the tension lessened, Justin's grades improved somewhat. The Kims stayed in touch with the social worker and had a final couple's session before Dr. Kim left with his son for the two to make connections with Dr. Kim's family again. She gave them a genogram assignment to do when they were visiting his family, and they agreed to come back, when they returned, to share the genogram and what they had discovered about their families.

The Kims did not have a cultural expectation of extended work with the social worker, particularly around their feelings. Clarifying purpose and role, partializing concerns, assessing and contracting were skills that helped develop the framework of the worker's approach to the Kims. Feelings were mostly implied, evident to everyone, but not centralized in the discussion. Dr. Kim's quivering chin as he spoke of possibly losing Justin, and Mrs. Kim's move to protect him from sharing feelings further were understood by everyone. Later Mrs. Kim could express some of her own feelings about herself, which up to this moment she was living out through Justin. The worker does not need to reach out aggressively for these feelings. They are already understood, and they will emerge through further process. To go faster would be to frighten the Kims away from the work. They responded well to the worker's coaching and task approach, which kept them fully in charge of their concerns.

In other cases, the one-step approach may involve extended work with the parent(s) and without the children. This may be particularly useful where the major focus is marriage counseling or individual counseling, and the issues can be managed, with coaching, between the parent(s) and the child(ren) without the social worker present.

CASE STUDY 7.3

Dave Harrison, a recovering alcoholic, worked with his wife, Becky, on issues stemming from his years of alcoholism. She had become the central support and director of the family during those years. It was difficult for both to move to a more balanced position. At the same time, their four boys were out of control, supported by the position Dave had taken as "one of the boys" and against Becky during his drinking years. Dave and Becky worked for nine months on these issues. They were able to do most of the work with the boys on their own, talking about it in their weekly couple's sessions. It was not necessary for the boys to take part in family sessions.

A Two-Step Beginning

In many cases there is a two-step beginning. Sometimes the patterns are very entrenched and there are reasons for eventually involving the youngster(s) in family sessions, or the parents may expect and want the youngster to be involved. In the following case, in the initial phone contact, the worker determines that this is a possible direction and schedules an initial session with the parents with the goal of having a family session following the initial session. As in the Antonelli family situation, originally cited in chapter 2 (case study 2.2), the social worker sets this up from the first phone call, when it becomes clear that this is the best direction.

CASE STUDY 7.4

Renata Antonelli called about her only child, Marisa, who is two months short of eighteen. Marisa was originally a compliant child, the center of attention of her parents and extended family. For three years, she has been rebelling against the family strictures, particularly around dating and boyfriends. Her mother Renata has taken responsibility for discipline. Renata's husband, Mario, a bookish man absorbed in his small business, is not as definite as she is with Marisa. Renata learned of Marisa's sexual activity with her boyfriend about five months ago by listening to and tape recording her phone conversations with her girlfriends. The parents had previously been quite restrictive of her activity, but now the restrictions and Marisa's rebellious response have escalated to extreme positions on both sides. Marisa could not make a phone call. Marisa avoided any of her mother's restrictions at school, and her mother found herself, in her own words, "micromanaging" all of Marisa's affairs, going through her purse regularly and engaging in a "cat-and-mouse" game with her. Marisa has run away for a day at a time, but was brought back by the police. Marisa was winning the game in any case, but the parents were very concerned that she did not seem at all to be aware of the risks she was taking. She will be eighteen in two months and firmly plans to move out on her birthday.

The situation had moved to a point of seriousness. Parents' and child's positions had rigidified. Marisa was close to emancipation. The parents wanted whole-family work. For all of these reasons the social worker opted for a whole-family approach. Over the phone, the social worker promptly set up an interview for Renata and Mario to discuss the situation and plan for a family session that week. Renata seemed to be aware that she had trapped herself into a cat-and-mouse game with her daughter, that both were now at extreme positions, and that her daughter seemed so

invested in the game that she was unaware of some of the risks she was taking. She knew that there would have to be some change in their approach, but couldn't find a safe alternative to what they were doing. Marisa's rebellion and the corresponding restrictions had escalated to the point where she was permanently grounded. She had little to lose.

The initial interview with Mario and Renata started a working relationship and confirmed the initial assessment that parents and daughter were caught in the cat-and-mouse pattern. It was decided to change the pattern by shifting the primary responsibility of working with Marisa to Mario. Renata would be Mario's closest adviser. This was discussed in some detail. Mario was willing to do this, and Renata was willing to step back, since she had borne the bruising conflict until now. She could see that she had lost effectiveness. They also needed to shift from their extreme restrictiveness, if the daughter could make a corresponding shift toward a degree of self-responsibility. Her privileges could come back gradually, but she had to merit them in some way also. It was decided that they would ask her to write down what *she* should do to regain privileges, and work out an agreement with her in their next family session with her included. They would also be thinking about her thinking systematically about her planned emancipation in two months. Mario agreed to talk with her. They would remain in touch by conference call prior to the family session in two days.

Mario took Marisa out to dinner, where they talked over the situation. Instead of writing what she would do, Marisa wrote what they should do for her, including buying her a car and providing an allowance of $300.00 a month, so that she could manage her up-coming emancipation. It was decided by phone that this was a good beginning and that it would all be worked out at the family session. Rather than getting caught up on Marisa's concrete expectations of $300, the process of beginning would be more impartant.

In the family session, the room was comfortably set up with seven chairs arranged around a low table. The family sat so that they could have eye contact with each other, with the social worker sitting in one place or moving next to one or another family member to facilitate communication between them. The social worker began by connecting with each family member, then setting the focus; the purpose of the meeting was to help Marisa and the family to deal with the difficult situation they were all in, with all of its risks for Marisa. He started sitting next to Mario and helped him to get things started with Marisa. Mario started reasonably well with concern for Marisa, but tended to preach a bit as soon as he sensed Marisa's resistance. Without undermining Mario, the social worker supported Mario's efforts to reach out to Marisa and her concerns. The mother, as agreed in the previous session and over the phone, made a heroic (and successful) effort to sit back and let the father take over. The social worker moved to sit next to Marisa as soon as he sensed Mario was comfortable with what he was doing, and Marisa was responding. Initially she threw obstacles up to her father, but softened her position with some support. Several times later in the discussion she began to cry as she continued softening her stance in the face of her parents softening their own stance.

They worked out a beginning agreement where privileges would be restored under certain conditions. The family agreed to meet weekly to monitor this and move to the next restoration of privilege. The social worker warned that there would be difficulties on both sides, and shifted the focus to Marisa's plans to emancipate in two months. At a certain point, the social worker moved in and began a dialogue with her in the context of her discussion with her father. When the social worker reached for her feelings, she really opened up about her uncertainty about her planned emancipation. When this came from Marisa, it was accepted by all without any preaching. It had become obvious to all, including her, that her plans were unclear. If she emancipated, Mario and Renata would continue to care about her, but would not support her financially, providing a car and so on. She would have to get a job, possibly at K-mart, to manage things, and it would be hard to manage that and college at the same time. After some further discussion, Marisa admitted that she had been "just as stubborn as her parents," and that she might want to defer this plan a bit. Renata joined in at this point, supporting the direction the family was taking. The ending task was for Marisa to work out on paper a plan for what she should do to get her privileges back. On a separate piece of paper, she was to write her dreams and aspirations for the time in her life following high school. She agreed with that. As the family was ready to leave, the mother Renata rejoined Marisa in an accustomed enmeshed position when she reminded her that Marisa ought to go to the bathroom before they went on the road. Marisa dutifully complied.

During the following sessions, Mario remained in charge, now with Renata sharing his position. Marisa relaxed somewhat and was able to show a softer side of herself. The family became able to discuss their concerns with each other without an explosion and without punishment. Marisa is beginning to take a longer-term perspective and talk of her dreams of further education and a career working with teenagers in trouble in a school.

The Antonelli family still has a good deal of work to do. The focus of the work of the interview was clear and all were engaged in it. The worker could decentralize himself and help the family to engage with each other. They did come up with an agreement and a shift in the structure. There was a good deal of work with Marisa, reaching for her feelings and some of her silences, and helping her to bring them into her discussion with her father. By the end of the interview, the contract had a more specific focus on the immediate arrangements at home, on her planned emancipation, and on her dreams. She may be sacrificing her dreams for an emancipation, but she also needed to know how her parents could appropriately support her reaching for her dreams. This would then be some of the work for the following sessions. Using all of the skills listed, a beginning had been made sufficient for the family to move on to middle-stage work.

MIDDLE-STAGE WORK WITH ELABORATED FAMILIES

The Family with School-Age Children

The family with school-age children is now accommodating the reality that another agent of socialization, the school, will share in their responsibility. When the child is having difficulty in his or her psychosocial functioning in school, school social workers will work with child's teachers, the family, and the child so that, on an individual basis, the difficulty is alleviated. At the same time, the child is growing and his or her relations with the siblings and parents are becoming more complex. Within the couple relationship, the arrangement has to shift to make space for the developing needs of their children. They need to take on appropriate parental roles. On the other hand, they also need to maintain their spousal roles. Sometimes, as in the Peterson family in the following case study, the child feels cut off from one parent and begins to develop problems that demand a shift in the family relations. In the case of Jerry Peterson, he wanted more connection with his father as he was growing up.

CASE STUDY 7.5

Larry and Jennifer Peterson, a couple in their early thirties, are concerned about their oldest son Jerry, age ten. Jerry is having daily screaming tantrums when he is frustrated about anything. These occur mainly at home in the presence of his mother. He presents no problem at school and is doing well academically. The mother feels she has lost control of him and brings in his father from his work to deal with him. Jerry has always been very close to his mother, who has elected to remain at home with her children. He particularly appreciates his mother's cooking, and can name every dish she has cooked over the past several weeks, describing each with great relish. His younger brother, Craig, age eight, is close to his father; the two brothers have differentiated themselves in this way. Both Craig and his father spend a lot of time together and love outdoor activities, such as hunting and fishing. The family now has a baby girl, Karen. Jerry has less time with his mother, and he is growing up into a boy's world. Larry feels trapped in his job in the family business. He had been a rebellious son as a teenager and now feels the need to make up for his past mistakes. Larry's relationship with Jennifer, although it appears somewhat unconflicted, also appears undeveloped. They carry out their roles as they individually conceive of them, but they are not necessarily close in their friendship. They were eager to get help with Jerry, but their own spousal relationship was not part of the bargain.

The initial interview was a family session with the mother, the father, and Jerry. It was clear that the first task was for Jerry to get control over his tantrums. Both the mother and father needed to support that control with a positive approach. Jerry needed a better relationship with his father. Jennifer and Larry needed to accommodate that relationship shift without upsetting the balances of their own marital relationship.

The first task was for Jerry to begin to manage his tantrums. In the first session he talked about them. He agreed to keep track of them on a calendar, which he would fill out every night before going to bed. With a focus on his good days, his father would reward him when he had a good day. Also Larry and Jerry would spend time together doing activities that Jerry enjoyed. These days with his father were not to be used as rewards. The mother would stay out of the arrangement between Larry and Jerry, but encourage it. If Jerry caused her problems, she would deal with him herself rather than call in Larry to punish him. Mother and father would communicate on a regular basis about how things were going with the children, including Jerry. They would also use their weekly sessions for this communication, with Jerry taking responsibility for how he was managing his tantrums.

The first session had begun with the family. The social worker made an assessment, developed a plan, worked out the agreed arrangements, and began with Jerry so that Jerry could take charge, as much as possible, of his part in the situation. A plan emerged and was agreed upon in the first session. As they moved to the following sessions and the middle stage, the father and Jerry would need to communicate with each other in the sessions about how things were going with these arrangements. The mother would encourage them, but not interfere.

Jerry was immediately responsive and loved the opportunity to have some access to his father. Larry had much greater difficulty finding ways of relating to Jerry, finding words to say, being consistent with his rewards, and finding ways to have a relationship with Jerry that was different from his relationship with Craig. Jerry didn't seem to mind or to notice that his father was having difficulty. For the sessions following, as they had previously arranged, Jerry brought his calendar with the good days and bad days marked on it. The first week he had more good days than bad days. Jennifer tended to get overinvolved with this, and the worker had to help concretely shift the focus from the mother to the father and to Jerry. The father tended to focus on the bad days, and so he needed help to focus more on the good days. As Jerry recounted the days in the family sessions, he also would recount with great relish every meal his mother had cooked that week. He had noted them on the calendar. The sessions following had fewer and fewer bad days until they completely disappeared over the period of a month. The parents also began to notice that Craig, formerly the good boy in the family, did some things to get himself in trouble, and that Jerry had some really helpful qualities in these situations. However, the majority of the time together was focused on the time spent between the father and Jerry, encouraging their developing relationship. This was again more difficult for the father than for Jerry. The whole process took place over six weekly sessions, and, with change stabilized, the family was able to end the process.

The focus of Jerry taking charge of his tantrums was elaborated throughout the middle stage. In order for him to accomplish this, the family shifted; the mother let the father get closer to Jerry, and the father discovered that he could have a relationship with his oldest son. There was not the framework of intimacy one would have in couples' counseling. There was a certain level of focus on feelings, but in accordance with what the family wanted, there was a primary focus on behavior. The social worker was continually clarifying the focus and partializing it in relation to what could be done within the space of a week. The social worker shared data, provided support for Jerry's good response, and helped the family deal with problems when they occurred. The worker was actively teaching communication and relational skills as the structure changed. When Jerry could maintain his changes and begin to generalize them, the process could end.

Three-Step Processes

If one strategy is not working, the worker may need to go to another within the same framework of relational tasks. Jerry's problem (case study 7.5) could have proved to be unmanageable, or the parents could have begun to show couple issues. The process with Jerry would then have to take one further step, becoming a three-step process. What was started with the family would continue, but in this context it might also be necessary to see Jerry alone for him to process further his work on his tantrums. Another possibility is that the parents could have become aware of their marital issues behind the focus on Jerry. What if the cross-generational coalition of mother and son is so strong that, when they try to change it, it becomes stronger? Then the third step would be to work with the couple. In the

Maxwell case discussed later (case study 7.7), this is what happened. At different times the social worker did family work, couple work, and individual work with the son and with the father.

What would trigger the further steps is that, from the social worker's assessment, the simpler one- and two-step alternatives do not work. Parts of the family begin asking for a more individualized approach. The social worker needs to decide whether this can be done without losing the family work that has already been started. Since the tasks are embedded in one another, the same family work can be done in different ways, now working with a couple or an individual. In any case, a good assessment will determine the direction taken. Whatever options seem best, there needs to be a good understanding of the dynamics of the family as a whole and of family tasks.

The Family with Adolescents

The adolescent usually challenges the family system. The family with adolescents needs a combination of firmness, ability to communicate, flexibility, and the wisdom to know when to be firm and when to be flexible. The couple must be able to resolve any differences around childrearing, since any perceived division can be fatally exploited by the adolescent. A good example of this was seen in the Antonelli family (case study 7.4) earlier in the chapter.

As discussed earlier, personal tasks are sometimes buried in the relational tasks of the couple dealing with parental responsibilities. In these cases, there is again a two-step process: first helping the member to own the task and do something about it, then helping the partner to assist in this without taking over or reacting inappropriately to the other's efforts. Some of these issues can be profound, as in the case of George, Marian, and seventeen-year-old Sean. The parental and couple relational tasks inherent in raising an adolescent become the context for some resolution of George's personal issues. Much of this particular work was done in a couple's counseling framework.

CASE STUDY 7.6

George and Marian had been having great difficulty with their oldest son, Sean, age seventeen, who was displaying out-of-control behavior, particularly around drinking and drugs. The family has a number of boys. George has been quite close with his sons, and in particular with Sean as a younger child. As Sean reached adolescence, George began to withdraw and became very inconsistent, sometimes harshly punishing him for small infractions, sometimes being indulgent. In the face of his father's withdrawal, Sean retreated into a relationship with his generally indulgent mother. In this triangulated situation, a high level of marital conflict over Sean developed between George and Marian. Sean would either play one against the other or ignore them both. George and Marian felt helpless in the face of Sean's behavior and their emergent marital conflicts.

As part of a broader process of help-ing George and Marian to come to some agreement on how to treat Sean's in-creasingly self-destructive behavior, George pointed out that he had lost his father through divorce when he was six-teen. As a consequence, he feels para-lyzed when he tries to be a father to a boy this age. He gets overwhelmed with the same helpless feelings he had when his father left him. The focus of the work in the couple's sessions then switched to George. The theme to be explored and developed in their work together be-came: You can be the father to your son, that your father never was to you. George accepted this and worked on it. At the social worker's instigation, George asked Marian to help him with this, since she had had a different experience with her father in her family. George and Marian were able then to come to a common agreement on how to manage the situation with Sean.

Building on George and Marian's agreement, as in the Antonelli family in case study 7.4, one further step was to include Sean in the process. Involving Sean, the focus on George and Marian as a couple shifted to a focus on their relationship with Sean and Sean's with them. There would be an opportunity to shift from a power struggle to a discussion of themes of attachment—trust, commitment, power, protection, and love (Diamond & Liddle, 1999). With the more secure base settling some of the problems the attachment issues might bring, it was possible for Sean to begin an appropriate and real exploration of connectedness and autonomy. For parents and adolescents, this is a difficult path, accomplished in spurts, not re-ally at once.

When Sean came to the sessions with George and Marian, there was a gradual shift in focus. Initially the struggle was over whether parents still had the power to influence a seventeen-year-old boy while still at home. Over several ses-sions, a truce was developed on this dis-cussion. As long as Sean lived at home, George and Marian did have the right to set some standards, but ultimately Sean was in charge of his future. The social worker attempted to shift the focus to attachment and relational themes. Did George and/or Marian have regrets about the way things had gone with Sean? Did Sean know of these regrets? Does Sean have regrets? Would he have liked things to have been different? If there were a miracle and things were different tomorrow, how would he like them to be? This was difficult work, but it succeeded in shift-ing the focus from power to attachment issues. The social worker was particu-larly focused on developing father–son dialogue. Over the following sessions, George felt himself to be less responsi-ble for Sean's choices. He was able to get more get more consistently involved with Sean as a friend as well as his fa-ther. In what would have to be a con-tinuing process, Sean began to take some responsibility for dealing with his emergent addictions.

A Three-Step Process: The Maxwell Family

The Maxwell family is far more complex in its needs, so the social worker found himself working at different times with every part of the family to help them carry out the relational tasks. The family faced issues similar to those faced by the Antonellis (case study 7.4). However, the parents had a long and chronic history of marital conflict and it was difficult for them to agree on anything. Both had previous marriages and had adult children from these marriages. Mr. Maxwell, in his late sixties, was dealing with retirement issues at the same time he was raising two adolescent boys. An uncontrolled diabetic, his circulatory problems were at the point of chronicity and possible collapse. Although often in contact with reality, at times his own private demons tended to take over and he would appear to distort reality profoundly. When challenged in a humorous way, he would cycle back into reality contact. The social worker learned to do this repeatedly, reinforcing his grasp of reality so that, at least in sessions, his outbursts of profound reality distortion receded. The family system was rigid. Paradoxically, Stephen's runaway episodes were the one thing that eventually brought his parents to find some agreement at least on how to deal with him. Both eventually learned to put away their private demons in the interests of Stephen. This eventually reinforced a certain calmness and unity in their approach to each other.

CASE STUDY 7.7

John and Mary Maxwell came to a family service agency when their sixteen-year-old son, Stephen, had run away from home to live with the family of his girlfriend, Jodi Smith. The Maxwell family had experienced continual conflict for many years. It was the second marriage for both. John, age sixty-six, and Mary, age forty-five, had experienced conflict since the beginning of their relationship. This conflict was now aggravated by John's retirement from his position as a supervisor in a factory. John was frequently verbally abusive. He regularly related to Mary as if she were his abusive and hated grandmother, who had raised him. This association was very close to the surface in his mind and in his verbalizations. John had grown up in South Dakota with roots in the Sioux culture of his ex-

tended family. He ran away to the city when he was sixteen. Later he joined the Army and worked his way up to master sergeant and drill instructor before his discharge. Mary, of Lithuanian ancestry, had a drinking problem, which she would not discuss with anyone. The family living with John and Mary at the time the case began comprised Leon, age thirty; Stephen, age sixteen; and Mike, age fourteen. Leon is Mary's son from her first marriage. He is mentally retarded and extremely dependent on her. Mike, a remarkably resilient youngster, escaped his parents' focus as long as he could bury himself in his beloved computer. Occasionally in the process, the social worker had to protect Mike from his parents' focus when they were looking for a substitute for Stephen. From the social worker's earlier assessment, he decided that it would be better to leave Mike out of family sessions. Including him might actually unnecessarily create dysfunction, by burdening Mike with family triangles he had skillfully opted out of in favor of Stephen. He did see Mike twice over two years however, and worked with him indirectly through the parents. Mike continued to function reasonably well outside of the family triangles, and the assessment in retrospect seemed correct.

Stephen had been a somewhat naïve youngster, a good student who was very much a focus of the family triangles. He was alternately overprotected and the object of conflict between John and Mary. He could not easily break free. When he met Jodi Smith, he met an entire family, profoundly disturbed, who allowed and encouraged him to have sex with Jodi on the condition that he in effect become a member of their family. This attraction was the equivalent of joining a cult with sex as a bait. He was running away from the tense, conflictual enmeshment of his own family to the loose and pleasureful enmeshment of the Smith family. Regular access to Jodi was an incentive for a sixteen-year-old, for whom the attraction of sex became like an addiction. Over two years Stephen ran away four times and stayed with the Smiths for months at a time. Partially because Stephen was close to eighteen and partially because the Smiths seemed to have a certain amount of power with the police, the police colluded with the Smiths in this. Finally, Stephen became able to mature beyond the attraction of the Smith family for him. He was able to discuss this in individual work when he eventually became ready to let it go.

The Maxwell family initially presented as both rigid and out of control. The relationship between the mother and father was chronically conflicted. Any communication between them was difficult and subject to distortion. The father would take over an entire interview ventilating about his earlier abuse and traumatic memories. Any focus on Stephen or Mary would be lost. The mother enmeshed herself with Stephen in the interviews, thinking for him and speaking for him. Stephen would come with a list of how cruel and unfair his parents were. None had any experience of listening to the other and so their communication tended to be reactive — acting out rather than expressing their thoughts and feelings through words and listening to the other person. It was clear that the process would have to move slowly, and it was unclear how much the family would tolerate before they summarily ended their contact with the social worker, and how much they might be able to accomplish together. However, John, with his Native American background, understood the value of silence. In any case, words or explanations were not particularly effective. Some of the most productive work was done slowly and in relative silence. The family was eventually able to develop ways of communicating, but good, uninterrupted, sustained communication was rare. For John and Mary, Stephen's acting out tended to distract from their problems with each other. Without Stephen's dramatic problems, their marital problems escalated.

Members of the Maxwell family were seen in different combinations for approximately two years. During this period there were also contacts with a counselor from the school Stephen attended and with an officer of the Juvenile Court. In the initial phase, the social worker worked with Stephen and his parents together on issues of differentiation. Then, when he would run away to the Smiths, she worked with the parents alone on communication, problem-solving, and relationship building in their efforts to bring him back. When he returned home, they would work in joint family sessions on differentiation of self in the family. There was some progress in both sets of tasks, but never enough to stabilize the situation until the last six months of the case. By this time, they had made enough progress in family work to move to a third step — seeing the parents separately on couple issues and Stephen on differentiation issues. Although the situation remained unstable, Stephen did fully separate from the Smiths, graduated from high school and had a period of reworking his relationships with his parents before he joined the Army, where he did very well. Both parents were pleased and appropriately involved with this step toward emancipation. As Stephen moved toward differentiation, the parents worked on their marital issues and made some progress on them. The social worker ended with some individual sessions with the father working on personal and couple issues.

The tasks of the Maxwell parents and of Stephen are dramatically interrelated. Stephen needed to disengage from Jodi and the Smith family and reengage with his parents enough to complete schooling and eventually emancipate. At the same time, he needed to differentiate himself from enmeshed relationships with each of his parents and with their marriage. Then he needed to develop appropriate plans for his further education or his work. His mother and father needed to learn to communicate and work together in the difficult and stressful situation of Stephen's runaway episodes. They needed to begin to manage some of their chronic marital and personal issues without involving Stephen. For Stephen to let go of the Smith family and reengage with his own family enough to emancipate, there had to be an appropriate relationship at home. The mother and father could not use Stephen as a distraction. They had to manage their marital issues without Stephen.

The focus with the Maxwells was always complex. There were two sets of tasks of different generations that were interdependent and therefore needed to be worked on at the same time. Communication had to take place if they were to cope with the issues, but both Stephen and his parents had a tendency to act rather than work out issues in this way. Only toward the end did they show any ability to communicate effectively. To the extent that they did develop these skills, the problems slowly alleviated. The most important point is that the assessment perspective and intervention focus had to remain with each person in the family and with the family as a whole in its interactive processes at the same time. Based on this perspective, a three-step process could take place, with the social worker working with the family as a whole and all of its parts in different ways until there was sufficient improvement for Stephen to emancipate, the couple and individual problems alleviate somewhat, and Mike survive adolescence with the protections he had already ably constructed for himself. A useful metaphor for the complex transaction between Stephen, the Maxwells, and the Smiths was the story of Pinocchio, with his recruitment to and escape from donkey island (where boys became donkeys). This was used at different times with the mother, the father, and Stephen to give a context for their emerging story and Stephen's transformations. The metaphor became quite meaningful to all, especially Stephen. He would be in charge of his transformation. Once he was ready to take himself willingly out of donkey island, he could develop a different relationship with his mother and father.

FAMILY TASKS AND STRUCTURE IN EARLY ADULTHOOD

In some ways the Maxwells, as a couple, were experiencing the same issues of the post-parental stage that the Caldwells were experiencing in the previous chapter (case study 6.6). Retirement had brought the spouses face to face with each other without a well-developed relationship. In the Maxwell's situation, there were serious mental and physical health problems and their relationship was actually far less well developed or resilient than that of the Caldwells. In addition, the Maxwells had two adolescents. The combination of ingredients could lead to breakdown. Corrective family work was needed on all fronts.

The Ambach Family: Separating and Relating Generational Tasks

In the Ambach family, a relationship with an older child needed to be reworked in order for the structure to shift and all the family members to carry out their own developmental tasks.

CASE STUDY 7.8

The Ambach family is a rural family with seven children. All of the children — except for Walter, twenty-six years old, the second youngest — have left home to make their way in the neighboring metropolis. The family is very success oriented. The father, John, and the mother, Loretta, have advanced educational degrees, but continue farming, anticipating retirement when Walter leaves home. All of the children have at least graduated from college. Some have completed graduate school and, except for Walter, project a strong image of success. Walter has made a number of efforts to keep a steady job

and to live elsewhere. He has never been satisfied with his work. He feels he is a failure compared with his brothers and sisters. His mild obsessive compulsive and depressed life patterns have brought him to quit the jobs he had. He is now at home, with a part-time job, that he will soon have to give up with nothing in prospect. He evidences no thought of doing anything. His mother Loretta has been his support through all his ups and downs, but she is losing her patience. John would like to travel with Loretta. They are both waiting for Walter to launch himself before they attempt this next phase in their life together. Walter is a concern for all his brothers and sisters, but they differ in what they would suggest, some urging more patience and protection for Walter; some urging that he be put on his own. Previous efforts to help him have been defeated. The helping process initially involved the whole family and then shifted to Walter.

In the initial sessions, after the social worker connected with all the family members and Walter, she moved to focus the process through Walter. Walter was able to tell his family that he did want to find a job for himself and get out on his own. The process shifted to how he could take charge of this and what certain family members could do to help him with this. With some individual sessions and group sessions, a plan was worked out involving mom and dad not

getting involved, very temporary housing with a sister, a mentoring relationship with an older brother he admired, a job search plan, and a plan to get back on medication and receive some mental health services. The family should relax and let Walter do what he needed to do. Walter was then seen with his "landlady" sister and his mentor brother and briefly by himself. He needed some help coming to terms with a less-than-perfect job, with his new life in the city, and with sorting out his own direction from those of his brothers and sisters. With the family less involved with him, he did get a job, and an apartment, went on medication and got further help, and, with some support from his siblings, gradually adapted to the city.

The O'Conner Family: Breakdown in Later Adulthood

The Ambach (case study 7.8), the Maxwells (case study 7.7), and the Caldwells (case study 6.6) still have some health and independence. They have not yet come to the point of being dependent on another generation for survival. The O'Conner family are at a later stage of family development. They are at the point of experiencing disability and the family relational shifts that come with this. They need to draw in a younger generation to help them but are having difficulty doing this, so that relations at every generational level are not working well. The family is a three-generation family that needs to become elaborated and complex in its ability to assist each other, but so far has not been able to find a way to do this. It is a good example of relational tasks at the stage of family development when the founding generation faces disability. It is also a further example of focusing both on the family as a whole and on the persons within it.

CASE STUDY 7.9

Maura O'Conner, age seventy-two, is involved in the older adults program of a community family service and mental health agency. She has recently been diagnosed with early-stage Parkinson's disease, which may not progress beyond

its present point. Her mobility is somewhat limited and she is now afraid of driving. She will be having cataract surgery soon. She was born in Ireland into a family of fourteen children, ten of whom were girls. Her mother, who lived to be ninety-eight, was cared for by the daughters who remained in Ireland.

When Maura was fifteen, she moved to the United States with her sister, Kate, who is five years older than she is. Maura has suffered from depression and anxiety attacks off and on much of her life. Now she is fearful of being alone. Her depression has been intensified by recent life events. She has been living alone for a year now. Her husband, Peter, was placed in a nursing home by the family, working with the agency. They had been a socially active couple. Both Peter and Maura had been teachers, active in the teachers union and committees. They would travel together to conventions, had a wide circle of friends, and had planned to retire with several of those friends to Florida. Peter had had brain surgery for removal of a tumor six years ago. Before his surgery, he had been the active one of the couple. Maura had depended on him to keep her going. When she was feeling sad, he would take her to a movie or for a drive to take her mind off things. She would then feel better. After his surgery Peter rapidly became depressed, withdrawn, and noncommunicative. He was exhibiting inappropriate behavior, such as exposing himself in front of the window of their home. Their friends stopped visiting when Peter declined. He went into the nursing home a year ago. Maura visits him once a week with her only son, Jack. Now he does not carry on a conversation, responds with a yes or no answer, and cries when he is visited. Maura feels Peter is "like dead." The experience of these visits immobilizes all three — Maura, Peter, and Jack.

Maura's older sister, Kate, lives in the area and stays with her periodically for several days at a time. Although Maura is grateful for Kate's companionship, she feels that Kate nags at her and doesn't understand her depression. Kate tends to ally herself with Jack by saying that Maura is asking too much of him when he drives her every week to see Peter. She feels that Peter could have been kept out of a nursing home for longer. Maura feels Kate is resentful that she can no longer drive and be as active as she had been in the past. Kate always depended on Maura for these things and can no longer do so. Indeed, she may need to take care of Maura someday.

Maura's only child, Jack, his wife Nancy, and their four children, ages fifteen, thirteen, ten and six, live in a suburb forty-five minutes away from her. She is frustrated with the relationship she has with Jack and his family because she feels that they do not give her the emotional support that she needs. She feels they are too busy with their own lives and she cannot really talk to them about her problems. Jack takes Maura to her monthly appointments with her psychiatrist, and he occasionally sits in on the sessions. She states that her son's presence inhibits her from being completely open with the psychiatrist, that she "isn't a strong enough person to totally tell her son everything." The relationship with Jack seems formal and obligatory. She wants emotional and "moral" support from Jack, but finds it difficult to open up to him saying "sons aren't aware of feelings and personal problems like women are." On the other hand, Maura's relationship with Nancy is also not very close. She believes that Nancy has no time for her because she is involved with her own mother and sisters who live in the same area. Maura considers Nancy closeminded and conservative. She doesn't call to see how she is doing and rarely invites her out to their home. Maura appears to have a standard as to how a daughter-in-law "ought" to behave toward her, but she is unable to communicate this openly. Maura had always wished she had had a daughter and is disappointed that Nancy doesn't fill this position as a daughter-in-law. The grandchildren are growing up in their own worlds. They are extremely busy with sports activities in their suburb, as are their parents. They rarely visit except on holidays. They have never visited Peter since he went into the nursing home. But who would want to visit him? Maura feels it is an obligation and a chore. It is enough for her to do it. Peter just looks at her and Jack and cries. What can they say? Nobody has the heart to say anything. "I just wonder when I will be like that. It won't be long now. What did I do to deserve this? I think God is punishing me."

Figure 7.1
Genogram of the O'Connor Family

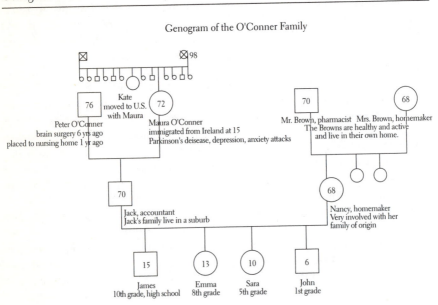

Genogram of the O'Conner Family

To understand the O'Conner family, one needs to see the entire family in relation to Peter and Maura's situations with their disabilities. A genogram (figure 7.1) allows the reader to see the complexities of this family more clearly. The disabilities involve a role shift and a demand on each of the members for a corresponding shift. Carlos Sluzki (2000) discusses the necessary transformation of social networks of the elderly, with relational networks already attenuated by losses. The entire family needs to construct in different ways a secure base for Peter and Maura and ultimately for themselves. This is precisely what is *not* happening in this family. The paralysis of the O'Conner family toward the first generation affects the other generations as well. Family members seem afraid to care for each other, and so they seem paralyzed to act at all, to become a network in relation to the needs of the first generation. The presence in all three generations of a family network of care would prevent the burden from falling on one person. Importantly, this does not mean that the O'Conners necessarily should personally take care of Peter and Maura. Even if an institution is included in the network, the issues of connection and membership are still the same — the institution is included in care, but it is not a substitute for family membership. The first generation — Peter, Maura, and Kate — is also paralyzed in a type of denial of any ability to be a family for each other and fear that all the burden will fall upon one person. Paradoxically, the fear is realistic in a culture that values autonomous individuals and has fewer developed patterns for solidarity in the face of weakness or dependency.

The major issue is whether members can adapt to each other's needs, and thus whether a change in personal circumstances — struggling with the possibility or actuality of disability — really changes relationships. In this case it does. In the absence of an ethic of care for each other, relationships become somewhat unreal and artificial. The family becomes a collection of ice statues. Change is equated with loss. Peter is not really "dead," but he can't take care of Maura anymore. Actually, his situation is a metaphor for the whole family's inability to function effectively as a family. He now needs loving care and concern for his lost role and capabilities. He is very sad about his losses, but he is still a most important family member. Maura cannot take care of Kate in the same way as she always did, and so Kate acts as if a seventy-two-year-old relationship, which includes emigration together, is gone. Jack is losing some of the relationship to his father he previously had. He might try to have some relationship with him, although it would be different from what he had known. He might try to listen to his mother's feelings, and Maura might try to find a different relationship with her son. Men often have some capacity to listen to feelings and understand, if asked. Maura is afraid of a relationship with Nancy, and Nancy is afraid of being obliged to Maura, (of "being the daughter" and taking on the needs of the whole O'Conner family).

The children are absorbed in their sports activities and their achievement, so they are not learning the implications of family membership. Jack and Nancy's energies are absorbed in making it possible for them to pursue their activities without reference to the larger family. Everyone is missing the opportunity to change slightly and to come together around the needs of Maura and Peter. Maura and Peter need to draw in a younger generation to help them, but they are having difficulty doing this. Maura is afraid to ask them. The legitimate fear of the younger generation, as in the case of Nancy, that one person will have to take all of the burden, is preventing anyone from doing anything. For Maura and Kate, who could be beginning to face disability, the anxiety about facing disability in these circumstances, alone, may be more paralyzing than the disability itself. They know that there should be some way to manage it, as in the case of their mother in Ireland. The availability of nursing care facilities, when needed, may ease some of the difficult aspects of care, but this should not obliterate the family issues of membership and care in changing circumstances. The availability of nursing home care may only alter the way membership is managed.

Maura and Kate's implicit assumptions are that disability has to be managed alone, and that men (Jack) cannot manage relationships. Their roles are fixed on these abstract assumptions, rather than interpersonally and in relation to each other's need. The absence of adaptive roles proclaims a functional breakdown of the family *as a family*. If the O'Conner family members are to be a family at all, they need to be concerned and help take care of each other when members, such as Peter and Maura, are in need. There should be enough flexibility in roles that a role shift—that is, a functional shift in the way members are able to relate to each other, should not obliterate membership. Yet this is precisely what is not happening. The key task of the O'Conner family is to become elaborated and complex in its ability to assist each other to develop workable and balanced patterns of solidarilty and caring for members in weakness and need. A whole range of relational and personal tasks would emerge from this, but so far the family has not been able to find a way to do this.

The social worker from the community family service and mental health agency has as clients Maura and Peter O'Conner, but then also with the needs of the founding generation, has the entire family as clients. Keeping Maura and Peter central, she needs to involve Jack in a different way, and then Kate, with the needs of the situation. This could be done perhaps in family sessions with Maura and Jack and then Kate, and then possibly Nancy. Nancy may be more willing to be involved if Jack and Kate are involved and carrying what they can. The children also have roles to play in this opportunity to learn about family taking care of one another. Much of the hard work is already being done by the nursing facility. It is basically a matter of family shifting in their roles. They need to communicate and listen to each other, to make requests and work out problems, to support the older generation's efforts to remain independent as long as possible, but also to feel membership in the family they have fostered. With this taking place, the central focus of the family would eventually shift to Jack and Nancy.

Middle-stage work, then, would involve the social worker taking this broader perspective on family relational tasks and personal tasks that arise from disability in the founding generation. The focus needs to be elaborated and adopted by agreement of key members of the family in family sessions. There will need to be a great deal of work on communication, on helping members to express feelings and thoughts so they can be heard and discussed, on listening and reflecting. Each needs to appreciate the viewpoint of the others. From this appreciation they may respond to the others' needs through developing a family plan, separating personal from relational tasks, and solving problems together.

SUMMARY

The O'Conner family is a relatively simple example of work with elaborated families. It can get even more complex. The multiple focus for work on both the persons in the family and the family as a whole needs to be maintained. The basic task for elaborated families is to help them elaborate in an appropriate way. In order to live out her dreams Marisa Antonelli reworks a rigid and enmeshed relationship with her parents (case studies 2.2 and 7.4). Jerry Peterson moves from an exclusive relationship with his mother to a relationship that includes his father and his mother (case study 7.5). Stephen Maxwell emancipates, but remains in appropriate contact with both parents and his brothers (case study 7.7). His father and mother no longer need him to take them away from their couple issues, nor will they use Mike. To do this, both John and Mary will separate personal issues from their relationship. The O'Conners (case study 7.9) begin to include each other, using community resources, when needed, to keep membership bonds alive in the face of disability. In this sense, using the nursing home still necessitates a whole range of family membership work; the work of sharing the memories and dreams that keep the family alive and carries on its traditions and bonds.

One primary reality in family work is that its members will change — indeed must change at every stage to meet the internal demands of development. The work of the family, the relational tasks and the personal tasks that flow from developmental needs, becomes the medium that makes these changes possible. The family continues in its essential role, supporting solidarity in the face of change and in the face of its members' needs. It would best make change possible in a way that most respects the common humanity, the dignity, and the dreams of its members. The social worker's role is to help the family and its members to do this. In the next chapter, we add a further set of tasks in middle-stage work with elaborated families where the family structure itself has been disrupted and demands reconstruction.

REFERENCES

Aponte, H. (1986). If I don't get simple, I cry. *Family Process, 25*(4), 531–58.

Diamond, G. S., & Liddle, H. R. (1999). Transforming negative parent-adolescent interactions in family therapy: From impasse to dialogue. *Family Process, 38*(1), 5–26.

Montalvo, B. (1982). Interpersonal arrangements in disrupted families. In F. Walsh (Ed.), *Normal family processes* (pp. 277–296). New York: Guilford.

Shulman, L. (1992.). *The skills of helping: Individuals, families and groups* (3rd ed.). Itaska, IL: Peacock.

CHAPTER 8

Radical Family Reconstruction: Toward Middle-Stage Work

This chapter focuses on families in the process of structural change and reconstruction, on assessing underorganized families, and helping them to reorganize.

FAMILY RECONSTRUCTION

In this chapter we move to a further level of complexity: that of the family experiencing serious relational deficits and needing to reconstruct itself in some form if it is to survive. Actually, the process of relational reconstruction takes place for all families at every family life transition. After all, this is what relational tasks for all family members are all about. However, for some families that are losing members, the changes are more radical. These families have children, and are experiencing relational losses through death or divorce. Some of these become single-parent families, while other single-parent families, such as the Hannon's, discussed later (in case study 8.4), have always been that way. Families who have experienced relational losses frequently remarry and form stepfamilies.

The formation of a stepfamily is a further process. But the work of stepfamily formation often gets confused with the personal work of dealing with a loss. The stepfamily could become an illusory attempt to substitute for the different losses the family members have experienced. Family members who experience losses cannot really go back to the relational structure they have known. Often family members have hardly any effective patterns for dealing with the change that has taken place. They need to understand that they are simultaneously developing a new unit retaining workable patterns from the previous unit. Without this understanding, the relational shifts, if they are accomplished at all, will take much longer than other, expected family life transitions. They will be more difficult, and in some ways they will continue on through each member's life span (Wallerstein, Lewis & Blakeslee, 2000). There may well be conflict and blaming. There is often less support than in other circumstances from the extended family for members going through these transitions.

Some families are simply chronically underorganized, without being able to point to any one event, such as a divorce, related to their underorganization. Over many generations, these families have been unable to deal both with their own internal tensions and with the outside world, particularly with necessary social institutions of employment, school, courts, police, the welfare system, and so on (Aponte, 1986). There is no abrupt break or loss in the family history to explain their problems relating internally or with external institutions. Often these problems are associated with chronic poverty. There is a chronic inability to influence external institutions or utilize their support for their functions connected with education and socialization, health care, security, or work and income. The loss or dysfunction of their relations with potential external supports can lead to a type of internal starvation and limited effective patterns of dealing with each other. Similarly, internal dysfunctions can generate external dysfunctions in a never-ending cycle, with profound effects on the self-image of each person. These families are often involved with multiple social institutions, community resources, and social workers. They present problems that go much deeper than the immediate difficulties and concerns of the school, the clinic, the court, or the child welfare agency, among others. The long-term job of the social worker is to interrupt the cycle and help the family reconstruct both internal relationships and external relationships with their environment at the same time. This takes considerable time and the ability to overcome the inevitable barriers of mistrust. We will discuss this type of work in the later section of this chapter and in the chapter following.

In chapter 5, we saw couples whose relationships were very incomplete from the beginning. In John and Eileen's case (case study 5.5), the severe immaturity of one partner, the addiction of the other, and the constant threat of violence since the beginning of the marriage raises questions about whether they made a basic agreement to marry and understood what they were doing. For Eileen, it may have been more a matter of reacting to and running away from her strict and closeted family. John was already "married" to addictive substances, which were in firm control of his life. Whether he ever detached himself enough from drugs and alcohol to commit himself to Eileen as a person, to take in her needs, (or Eileen his needs as a person), is questionable. In Sheldon and Sandy's case (case study 5.6), there was a question of mutuality of consent and also of what they were consenting to. One partner essentially said, "I didn't consent to marry, but I didn't want to disappoint people, but let's stay together for a time and see what happens." For both John and Eileen and Sheldon and Sandy, to survive as a couple they would not simply have to correct dysfunctional patterns and remedy serious structural deficits, but they would have to reconstruct their relationship and the understandings on which it was based.

For John and Eileen, the relationship itself continued to seem full of risk. Other than John's family's pressure, there seemed little motivation to form a stable union. John's efforts to deal with his addictions did not so far seem to promise success. Eileen had scarcely become more of a person in her own right and showed no signs of wanting to revisit the relationship. For both, their own emotional processes seemed to overwhelm any possibility of accommodating the other in at all, much less the complexity of the other's emotional process. For Sheldon and Sandy there was more hope. There was at least the opportunity to work things out. They did not have a dangerous relationship, and on some levels it was working. There was some time to work; Sheldon was responding somewhat, although communication of any depth was very limited. It would be a difficult challenge for everyone involved, and it would be unlikely to succeed. However, for Sandy it was worth trying for a limited time. From her perspective, the costs of not trying might be even greater, and in the end the relationship did succeed.

Membership Losses and Transitions

Losses are the most serious issue faced by members of blended or reconstructed families. Families establish a network of relationships, validate those relationships through interpersonal patterns, and then lose a crucial member. These losses have multiple implications. There are families who have lost a member through death, those in the process of divorce, and those in the process of blending with another family or parent. Dealing with membership losses, they often experience their current relationships as incomplete. The person bonds, the identity bonds, can never be the same as the bonds with the person lost, no matter how problematic these bonds have actually been. At the same time, they are in transition to a new and untried set of relationships and a new set of interpersonal patterns of doing things with each other. Members are asked to adopt new patterns and relationships without first coping with losses from the old ones. Worse still is when a member feels asked to substitute a new relationship for an older one. From an identity bond perspective this is impossible, since any bond to a person as a person is unsubstitutable. On the other hand, a new relationship can still bring good things without threatening the older bonds.

During the transition period there inevitably will be great confusion. Many of the older interaction and communication patterns of relationships discussed in chapter 3: socialization, boundaries, alignment and power, and so on, will have to change. Often there will be efforts to shorten the painful relational work and become "like other families" through new marriage, as if one person could substitute for another. There may be little awareness that older patterns and preferences do not change so easily. In any case, for success, an entirely new set of relationships—not a substitute for the old relationships but a new set of relationships that does not compete with the older ones—will have to emerge. Families are usually quite unprepared for this. When they have difficulty they will often experience breakdown and find themselves working with schools, courts, family counseling, child welfare, or other agencies. Particularly if the referral comes from a concern of the agency and is involuntary, social workers from these agencies find themselves working between the particular agency, the court, the school, the child welfare agency, and the family. They are probation officers, school social workers, and so on. They do not always see themselves as doing family work, helping families to restructure their relationships and become effective again. Work with families in the context of these agencies will be discussed in chapter 9, but for the moment we discuss families coming voluntarily to a family counseling agency or private practitioner to find some resolution for their relational difficulties.

Tom Fields' family is dealing with the recent loss of Meg, wife and mother.

CASE STUDY 8.1

Tom and Meg Fields had a very traditional but relaxed marriage. When Meg started her fight with cancer, Tom retreated into his work, which consumed him, and into his fishing, his outlet from work. The death of Meg was a double loss for the four children, since they also lost communication with their father. Eventually, as Meg got worse, they would get housekeepers, but none could manage this impossible situation. Over the course of the year before her death, Meg gradually weakened, taking on different regimens of chemotherapy. They took her energy, but none worked. As Meg gradually withdrew, the oldest, thirteen-year-old Ashley, took over, becoming a link between Meg, Tom, the housekeeper, and Ashley's brothers and sisters. Power struggles centered on Ashley. Housekeepers left, some after a few days, and the family descended into chaos. After Meg's death, Tom retreated further into his work and his fishing. Ashley would take over sporadically with the same relaxed firmness she remembered from her mother, but then she would get into conflict with the housekeeper and withdraw. Finally one housekeeper stayed and tried with a will to shape the family up. However, the more she tried, the less successful she was. In the meantime, Ashley's grades slipped dramatically and she started hanging with a drug crowd. Each of the other children were also having their own, similar difficulties, some with school, some with behavior problems, some with depression. After an explosion, the housekeeper left and Tom went to the family service agency. The family was in chaos, and he was at a loss.

The social worker worked with Tom to bring him back to the family, then Ashley, and later the other children. She helped to normalize and connect the problems they were experiencing, individually and as a family, to unresolved mourning and family work needed after Meg's death that had been left undone. There was a need of each, especially the father, to take charge of what he or she could and to connect with the others. The family needed to develop a more appropriate set of patterns to fit the new situation. The work with the social worker took approximately a year and a half to get to the point where they felt ready to manage on their own.

The Fields family did begin, over time, to overcome its chaotic and wounded state. Families in this situation do this best when there are spiritual resources and a supportive network, although depression, associated with loss, can prolong the healing process.

Family Processes of Divorce

The divorce rate grew exponentially from 1960 through the late 1970s (Glick, 1979). It stabilized in the early 1980s and has been dropping slightly since then. At today's rate, the chances that a marriage contracted this year will end in divorce before one partner dies has been estimated to be between 40 and 45 percent (Popenoe, 2001; Goldstein, 1999; Norton & Miller, 1992).

Virtually all discussions of divorce point out that its effects on families and children are complex. Divorce should not be approached as a single event, but as a process, and indeed a painful and long lasting one for children (Amato & Booth, 1997; Wallerstein et al., 2000). Although approximately 75 percent of children experiencing divorce do eventually cope with it, the process is painful and there is a considerable remainder who are quite damaged by it (Hetherington, 2002). Rather than an event, divorce needs to be seen as a family transaction with very uncertain outcome, and which always demands coping skills on the part of every member.

Children begin to have to cope with the effects of severe marital conflict before the divorce. This coping must continue long after the split (Amato & Booth, 1997). Wallerstein and Kelly's initial findings (1980) on children of divorce were confirmed over a ten-year longitudinal study following 116 children (Wallerstein & Blakeslee, 1989). The divorce is just one step in a series of consequent family transitions: prior to the divorce, the divorce itself, the one-parent family, remarriage, the stepfamily, and so on. In one study, five years after a divorce, one-third of the children were still functioning more poorly than they had been at the time of the divorce. One of three children found themselves still embroiled in the ongoing bitterness of their two battling parents (Bryner, 2001). Wallerstein's and Blakeslee's (1989) ten-year follow-up found half of the women and one-third of the men studied still intensely angry at their former spouses. Children felt caught in the crossfire.

The systems principle of equifinality is well illustrated in the child's response to divorce. The child who shows little response at the time of the divorce may react quite severely many years later as his or her relational needs become different. As in the case of Alan in case study 9.1, the child who is initially quite reactive to the divorce may eventually find ways to cope and adapt (Wallerstein et al., 2000).

Paul Amato (Amato & Booth, 1997) studied 2,000 married adults and 700 of their children over twenty years. There were approximately 300 divorces in the group during the study. Amato and Booth found that divorcing families could be divided into those with low-satisfaction/high-conflict marriages and low-conflict marriages. Amato and Booth (1997, p. 197) suggest that children for whom divorce is an opportunity to escape from a highly conflictual, hostile, and abusive home may be better off in a well-functioning single parent household. Low-conflict marriages looked very much like many other marriages in terms of satisfaction and conflict one and a half years prior to the divorce. They were quiescent, but less than fully satisfactory. Parents might divorce for reasons of self-fulfillment or the presence of a more attractive partner (Amato & Booth, 1997, p. 197). There may have been very little discussion of the divorce with the children. Divorces in low-conflict marriages, comprising around two-thirds of the divorces Amato and Booth studied, had a broad negative impact on virtually every dimension of their children's well-being. On the other hand, recent research, using a large national sample, indicated that 86 percent of people who were unhappily married in the late 1980s but stayed with their marriage indicated five years later that they were happier. Sixty percent of these formerly unhappily married couples rated their marriages five years later as either very happy or quite happy (Popenoe, 2001: Waite & Gallagher, 2000).

The divorcing family has suffered losses often without the support and the compensations available when a family member dies. When a parent is lost through divorce, the family needs to go through a realignment of relations similar to what the Fields went through (case study 8.1), only the process is generally more difficult due to a number of fairly well accepted factors (Herzog & Sudia, 1973). Most important is the understanding from attachment theory that relationships do become parts of every person, and that, although persons have the capability of adapting to relational changes and losses, they do not do it readily. When they experience such change, they often need help to deal with it. In the divorce process there is often considerable painful marital conflict. Often there are children involved on one side or the other. Conflict precedes the divorce, and it continues in different ways during the divorce and after the divorce. The voluntary separation is often taken by family members as a personal rejection of each of them. Even with joint custody, there can be a perceived loss of one parent, frequently over the years turning into a diminished relationship and a real loss. There is often loss of relationships with one side of the family, as one parent's ties weaken. This is often profoundly resented. Finally there is almost inevitable economic insecurity.

Social workers inevitably become a part of these processes, working with the spouses, with the children, and with schools, health care agencies, courts, child welfare agencies, and other social institutions. These agencies inevitably are drawn in different ways into a difficult divorce process and/or its aftermath. There are a number of dangers in this process.

Dangers of Triangulation The first task of the social worker is to avoid triangulation into the family system, and to help the parents discover whatever possibility there is of working together. This may seem like an oxymoron. When there is sufficient marital tension for one or both partners to consider divorce, the parents are gradually moving to an adversarial role. This is supported by a legal system whose main concern will not be the complexity of relationships, but the settlement of property rights. Involvement in an affair, alcoholism, depression, a history of constant conflict, simple anxiety, and the need to justify oneself all reinforce the adversarial position of the spouses beginning with the social worker. Each will try to align the social worker with his or her position in a type of rehearsal for a divorce court, with the social worker in the position of judge. Furthermore, the children are often drawn into the conflict and either aligned with one parent against another or, with the family in confusion, they may hold more power than either parent.

If the social worker is to be successful at all, he or she needs to support the appropriate functioning of both parents whenever possible, to the extent that they allow themselves to be involved with the helping process. The social worker should immediately avoid the shadow of alignment with one parent over another. Unless there is a question of the protection of a vulnerable person, he or she should gently refuse to become triangulate, on one side or another of the conflict. In the first interview, the social worker should redirect interaction toward the partners taking responsibility for whatever they best can do about the situation with its emergent relational realignment that comes with divorce. A further problem is that a school, child welfare agency, a court, or other agency often already has a particular client. Unless the social worker is able to address the whole family from the beginning and skillfully include both parents in working on the problem, a premature alignment with one or another in the family, whether parent or child, could prevent productive work from being done.

During the divorce process itself, so such energy is taken up with the legal issues that there may be very little time or energy available for a helping process. Moreover, there is always concern that getting help may be taken by the other contending party as a sign of inadequacy. The legal necessities often trump the social and emotional issues. The emotional issues are usually much broader than the divorce, so that for each partner the divorce becomes a symbol of many other issues that have nothing to do with the divorce. If this is the case, the underlying issues might not be resolved by the divorce. There is also the myth that relationships can be easily (or ever) dissolved. Attachment theory and object relations theory suggest that relationships remain a part of each person in different ways.

Dysfunctional Beliefs and Cognitions   Will the problem really be resolved by the divorce process? Family therapist E. W. Beal (1980) suggests that subscribing to the following beliefs may indicate that the problem or dysfunction will not be resolved by the divorce:

1. A belief that the problem lies in the current relationship and is not likely to be found in subsequent relationships
2. A belief that a divorce will produce a long-term rather than short-term serious loss in the sense of self or sense of identity
3. A high level of denial about the possibility of loss in the divorce process
4. A belief that the only important thing is to get away from the other
5. Making a decision solely on what "feels" right or what is legally possible for the purpose of revenge (Beal, 1980, p. 248).

Assisting divorcing spouses may be a matter of helping them to sort out the broader processes and beliefs or thinking patterns that have led to the divorce decision. Each cognition denotes an unresolved problem in the current marriage that divorce probably will not resolve. Unresolved, the cognition is faced again in the post-divorce period. It could lead to serious post-divorce problems or an attempt to resolve the divorce issues through remarriage.

The first several years after the divorce are predictably chaotic and difficult. Family functioning is worse twelve to eighteen months after the divorce than at the time immediately surrounding the divorce. Five years later, one-third of the children were functioning more poorly than they did at the time of the divorce (Bryner,

2001). Eighty percent of children have severe and increasing difficulties with the process (Wallerstein et al., 2000). Ten years afterward, significant numbers of former partners report intense anger (Wallerstein & Blakeslee, 1989). When there is single custody, there is the risk of a diminished relationship with the non-custodial parent. Children of divorce seem to fare better if there is a joint custody agreement, unless there is intense parental conflict or an abusive or mentally ill parent (Bauserman, 2002). However, the joint-custody agreement may be difficult for the estranged parents to manage and may demand professional intervention. There is considerable concern for the children who do not make an adjustment to divorce. These often show difficulties, are involved with courts and child welfare agencies, or have difficulty at school and are seen by social workers or others.

Realignment of Relational Architecture

By definition, divorce creates a vacuum in the relational structure of the executive subsystem of the family and also in each member. One parent leaves; the other must take charge. A joint-custody arrangement alternately empowers one and then the other to take charge. Both must learn a new role, play it, and then, when the other's period of custody comes, turn it over to the former spouse for him or her to play. Boundaries are inevitably confused in the beginning, with family members getting involved in areas no longer open to them. Extremes of enmeshment with one parent bring about disengagement with the other. Overfunctioning in one partner brings about either conflict or underfunctioning on the part of the other. Alignment problems are legendary. Children become triangulated into the parental conflicts and resentments. Moving from one parent to another brings about constant shifts. Power becomes diffuse. Parents can become helpless and dysfunctional. Often the children step into the power vacuum, becoming a type of guidance system for their parents (Montalvo, 1982). Sometimes there is massive confusion, compounded by the other problems of single parenthood. The communication skills and relational investment demanded by the co-parental relationship, favored by joint-custody arrangements, may be in short supply. In many ways, the joint custody arrangement, while it may be a partial solution to some of the child-caring problems divorce brings, is quite difficult to implement. This arrangement will probably require better communication, relational and problem-solving skills, and interpersonal maturity than a marriage with a moderate amount of conflict. The only solution possible is the gradual and painful realignment of boundaries, alignment, and power in favor of the parent with custody, withdrawal of the non-custodial parent from authority while the custodial parent is in control. There needs to be some communication, agreement, and a well articulated shift between the parents as the child moves from one orbit to another. This could be done with good will on the part of both parents and some guidance from a disinterested party. Small wonder that families have painful experiences and post-divorce child care appears dysfunctional, as seen in the following case study.

CASE STUDY 8.2

Edna Friedman came to Jewish Family Services with her daughter, Renee, age fifteen. The family had been through a very conflictual divorce several years ago. Renee regularly visits her father, Hal, telling him about her problems with her mother. Mrs. Friedman has very little control over Renee. The number of screaming fights with each other has increased dramatically since Mrs. Friedman began talking about marrying her boyfriend, Lloyd C. At this point, the triangle of Renee with her mother and father has become quite rigid and is aggravated by the oncoming marriage to Lloyd C. and the emergent triangles implicit in this relationship. Whatever Mrs. Friedman will say, Renee will say the opposite. If Mrs. Friedman ignores Renee, Renee will scream at the top of her lungs for hours. Mr. C's daughter, Allison, age eighteen, has already moved in with them. Although Allison plans to move out as soon as she can find a place, Mr. C. will be moving in after they get married in three months. Renee is opposed to all of this and wants to prevent it from happening. Mr. C. is reluctant to involve himself in the problems with Renee. He believes that if Renee was nice to him, she would feel like a traitor to her father. Mrs. Friedman treats Renee like a sister and appears to be afraid of her.

Renee sat reading a magazine through the first session with her mother, Mr. C., and Allison, pointedly ignoring everyone and refusing to put the magazine down. In the process of family therapy, the social worker assisted Mrs. Friedman to defer the marriage for a short time and begin to work on her relationship with Renee. She needs to work on taking over in issues with Renee that she considers important. There were separate sessions with Renee and her father. Her father eventually was able to encourage Renee to listen to her mother, thus beginning to resolve some of the triangle. Her mother made an agreement with Renee over issues, such as school, hours of bedtime and weekends. Mrs. Friedman agreed to spend time with her, but not involve her in Mrs. Friedman's relationship with Mr. C. The social worker had considerable concern about Allison, since she seemed to have the most to lose from her father's new arrangement. Deferring the wedding gave Mr. C. some time with Allison, and they were encouraged to reconnect. There needed to be some resolution of these triangles before adding another one with the marriage. The Friedman case us a good example of the complex work of the post-divorce family and the role of the social worker in that work.

Blended Families

Blended families are one further structural shift in a family that has already experienced losses. The Friedman family (case study 8.2), with the impending marriage to Mr. C., has the problems of a blended family superimposed on the relational tasks of a divorcing family. The blended family needs to develop new traditions while preserving what may be worthwhile from its older traditions or patterns. It has to find a way to integrate itself without denying the reality of the older family relations. New alliances need to be formed while preserving the old alliances that are still important. This all takes time and cannot be hurried. Perennial issues in blended families are issues of insiders versus outsiders; boundary disputes; power issues; conflicting loyalties; rigid, unproductive relational triangles; and unity versus fragmentation of the new couple relationship (Visher & Visher, 1982). As was implicit in the Friedman family dynamics, the more the blended family organizes itself to deny the loss and to substitute a stepmother or stepfather for the mother or father lost, the less successful it is likely to be. Step-parents have a very difficult time being accepted. Fewer than 20 percent of young adult stepchildren feel close to their stepmothers (Hetherington, 2002). We can see all of these dynamics in the case of Rich and Marcia Jones in the following case study, even though their divorces were somewhat less complicated than the divorce in the Friedman family.

CASE STUDY 8.3

Rich and Marcia, both recovering from alcoholism, met in a treatment group. It is the second marriage for both. Rich, age fifty-six, had been married for twenty years prior to his divorce. He is a successful businessman and has two married daughters, ages twenty-five and thirty-six. While they were growing up, he was drinking heavily, and he regrets that he had so little contact with them. The relations with his first family are strained and full of regrets on his part. Additionally, he had a very strict upbringing and his knowledge of teenage behavior appears to be limited. Marcia was married ten years before her divorce. She was deserted by her husband when her daughter, Julia, now sixteen, was a baby. Marcia and Julia have a very close relationship, "like sisters." Marcia's upbringing was much more relaxed, and she reflects that in her patterns with Julia. Since their marriage a year ago, Rich and Marcia have experienced constant arguments over Julia. This has absorbed most of their energy, so their rela-

tionship remains somewhat undeveloped. Rich, strongly motivated to be the father he never was to his own daughters, tries to take over the parenting of Julia. When Rich gets involved with Julia, Marcia gets protective of her and undercuts his authority. When this happens, Rich becomes more harsh and Marcia becomes more indulgent. Neither seem to have well-developed communication skills, and one extreme seems to bring out the other. Moreover, when Marcia tries to become the mediator between Julia and her husband, it seems to prevent her daughter from developing a real relationship with Rich. Julia never had a relationship with a father and actually would like one with Rich. She has no idea of how to achieve it, especially in view of Rich's extreme behavior and her mother's protectiveness.

The social worker met only with Rich and Marcia in the beginning. She began by normalizing for both of them some of the stepfamily issues they were facing. They couldn't treat the family as if nothing had happened, as if Julia and Marcia did not have a long and deep relationship. Neither one would or should accept that change. Although Julia is growing older and is at a point where she can gradually assume some of her own responsibilities, Marcia ultimately needed to remain as the parent in charge. Rich could at best be second in command with authority delegated from Marcia. With this arrangement Rich could then develop a different relationship with Julia. The social worker worked with Rich and Marcia, guiding them through the steps of a relational shift, and then included Julia in a few family sessions until the relationships became more manageable and stabilized. However, when relations with Julia stabilized, it became clear that Rich and Marcia needed to do the unfinished work on their own relationship that the focus on Julia had absorbed. There was a lot of hurt left over from their previous relationships and from their families of origin that the problems with Julia had covered up. They contracted with the social worker for marital counseling. Working together on the issues with Julia made their marital issues clear and gave them a start on this process.

THE UNDERORGANIZED FAMILY

If the ability of the family to function well depends on the degree to which the family relational structure is well defined, cohesive, and flexible, the underorganized family shows deficiencies in the degree of constancy, differentiation, cohesiveness, and flexibility of its relational structure. Family members have a limited repertoire of relational patterns and structures to manage internal situations (their own dynamics) or external situations with community institutions, resources, and relational structures. Family members have learned rigidity in using the relational patterns they do possess, and they are inconsistent in their use of these patterns and structures. These patterns may be handed down over generations, resulting in considerable isolation of the family and a lack of awareness of these patterns necessarily as problematic. Not all poor families are underorganized by any means. Indeed, it is remarkable how resilient so many families are in the face of what appear to be insuperable obstacles. Harry Aponte (1986) suggests there can be a relation between the situation of poverty, deficits in relationships with community institutions, resources and relational structures related to poverty, and internal deficits or relational patterns and structures as well. To help these families reconstruct their relationships with the inside and the outside is to help them to learn to acquire the resilience that other families somehow have managed to develop, but now they are working under conditions of extreme duress. The long-term job of the social worker is to interrupt the cycle and help the family reconstruct both internal relationships and external relationships with their environment at the same time. Indeed, to reconstruct the outer relationships effectively, the inner relationships also need reconstruction, and vice versa (Aponte, 1986). This takes considerable time and the ability to overcome the inevitable barriers of mistrust. We will discuss relationships for the most part on the inside of these families in this chapter. In the following chapter, we will discuss relationships with outside institutions, resources and relational structures for these as well as other families.

The Hannon Family

Harry Aponte (1986) uses the Hannon family case[1] as an extended illustration of the assessment and intervention processes with underorganized families. We will also use Aponte's record of one session as a way of summarizing our previous discussion of the interaction process with families and applying some of the skills discussed in previous chapters. The interview can be divided into eight phases. The helping process of subsequent interviews is built on this interview.

CASE STUDY 8.4

The Hannon family is a poor, African-American family of nine members from four generations. Mrs. Hannon, forty-seven, is the head of the family. She has five children, ranging in age from twenty-two through eleven, living with her. Her oldest daughter Vera, twenty-two, is fearful of living on her own. She has two children, Rita, three, and Curt, one and a half, also living with them. Mrs. Hannon's senile father also lives with them, but he is not present in this family session. Mrs. Hannon, previously on public assistance, works from 11 P.M. to 7 A.M. cleaning offices. She is exhausted and finds little energy to give to complex issues in the family. She had delegated authority to a parental child, Joan, age seventeen, who appeared to be the only one of her children able to take leadership. Now she is particularly concerned because Joan's leadership has become very uneven, her relationships at her high school seem to have broken down, and she is in danger of dropping out. She makes an appointment at the mental health clinic and the whole family, with

the exception of her father, comes to the session. To clarify assessment and interaction, parts of the interview are summarized. The focus rests mainly on Mrs. Hannon, Vera, and Joan.

1. *Introduction*   In the beginning, the family seated itself in the interview room in a chaotic manner. Mrs. Hannon remained quiet and uninvolved and Joan fruitlessly attempted to organize them. People were talking at once. Vera's two children were somewhat out of control, but the mother did nothing to manage them. The therapist introduced himself without response on the family's part. He initially tested out whether Joan's sister or brothers would be able to quiet things down. When they could not, it became clear that of the older children Joan has leadership. He then tried to engage Mrs. Hannon, who appeared to him to be withdrawn and unhappy. Joan quickly began speaking for her and he was not able to keep her centralized for long.

Therapist: Mrs. Hannon, everybody else looks pretty happy except you.
Joan: She ain't got no sleep, that's why.

---

[1] The Hannon case is used with the permission of Aponte (1986), pp. 531–545.

Vera and Mark: [speak simultaneously, inaudible]

Therapist: Did you just get home from work? [He walks across room and sits next to Mrs. Hannon.]

Mrs. Hannon: Uh huh.

Joan: Tired as a . . . [inaudible because Vera talks simultaneously and Curt yells]

Earl: [brother, age eleven] I bet she is gonna go to sleep as soon as she go home.

Therapist [to Mrs. Hannon]: Where do you work?

Mrs. Hannon: Horsham, Pennsylvania.

Therapist: How far away is that?

Mrs. Hannon: On the other side of Willow Grove. [The youngsters quiet down, except for Curt, who is still fussing.]

Therapist: What do you work at?

Mrs. Hannon: Cleaning offices, eleven to seven.

Therapist: Eleven to seven every night?

Mrs. Hannon: Uh huh.

Therapist: And you have all these children to take care of by yourself? [The children are teasing Curt, who suddenly yells as the noise escalates]

Vera: We all take care of each other.

Therapist: Are you just tired, or are you really as unhappy as you look?

Mrs. Hannon: No, I'm just tired.

Vera: She's not unhappy.

Joan: [Curt yelling persistently as Joan talks] Yes she is unhappy. She just don't want to tell nobody. I'll tell you why she is unhappy. She is sick and tired of us. She wants me to go to school and get graduated,

but I don't like school. She wants her [points to her sister, age eighteen] to stop acting like a fool. She wants him [points to her brother, sixteen] to mind his own business and stop messing around. She wants her [points to Vera] to get an apartment and get her kids and get together. She wants him [points to her brother, eleven] to get straightened out and go to school. . . . And me, I got nerves. Boy I got some nerves on me!

2. **Initial Assessment** The therapist got the picture of the family from the first interactions. Joan speaks for Mrs. Hannon and gives a picture of the dilemmas of everyone in the family, including herself. In the following interaction the therapist continues to try to bring out Mrs. Hannon without Joan talking for her. During this time the children go out of control. When the therapist asks what she does to manage it, Mrs. Hannon responds that she "puts on her gorilla suit. That's all." Curt yells and kicks. The therapist is stymied by Curt and Vera offers no help.

Mrs. Hannon: Just ignore him. [To Curt] Sit down, boy. Hey, sit down. Down.

Joan: [Overlapping] Sit down, man.

Mrs. Hannon [To his brother]: Just ignore him. Hey, sit down. Sit down. I'll bet I'll bash you if you don't sit down. [Children guffaw.]

Brother: Sit your behind down, boy. You better sit down.

Joan: That is why he is so super mean. 'Cause he don't like nobody to tell him what to do. (Mrs. Hannon walks up with a rolled-up newspaper and strikes Curt lightly on the legs.)

Mrs. Hannon: Sit down! [Excited comment and laughter from the children as Mrs. Hannon physically takes Curt off the coffee table and sits him on the chair. Curt whimpers a bit and then sits quietly.]

Mrs. Hannon: You better shut up. [Vera laughs like one of the children.]

Mrs. Hannon: [To everyone] Now leave him alone. It's not funny.

Therapist [to Vera]: Would he listen to you the way he listens to her?

Vera: Nope.

Joan: No, he won't listen to anybody.

Therapist: So you're kind of a mother to everybody.

Mrs. Hannon: I am the mother of them all.

The basic, problematic family patterns came out clearly. While Mrs. Hannon sought refuge for the events in the family through her withdrawal, Joan was the overriding personality. When Curt took over the session with his screaming, Joan is unable to manage it. Eventually, Mrs. Hannon took action by putting on her "gorilla suit." Everyone then settled down, but the burdensome weight of the family was totally on Mrs. Hannon's shoulders. When overwhelmed, she would withdraw and leave the family in chaos. Joan would take over, attempting to pull the family together. In the process, she became the family lightning rod. She paid a price for this role. At this point in the inter-

view, the family had settled down and Joan was able to address her problems with school and the lack of support the family is getting from the school system. Vera was able to talk about her concerns about getting work, getting together with her husband, and getting an apartment. She was afraid to be in a house by herself. The neighborhood was dangerous. Mrs. Hannon was able to protect the youngsters but was unable to instill in them the strength she possessed. The girls were looking to their mother for support and direction. The young men did not see themselves as having any role to play at home. With the family started on its work and a beginning assessment made, the therapist could get started, now with Joan and Mrs. Hannon only, separate from the others.

3. **Beginning** The therapist began with Mrs. Hannon and then shifted to Joan as she identified her part in Mrs. Hannon's concerns. He is reaching for feelings, putting feelings into words, reaching inside of silences, and partializing concerns. What emerges will be a clearer picture of what is going on, at the same time assisting Joan and Mrs. Hannon to differentiate their concerns. The therapist began moving toward middle-stage work with them. He eventually wanted to help mother and daughter to elaborate a focus. For the moment, he drew conversation from each that was pertinent to an emergent dialogue with each other. This eventually can lead to more middle-stage work, that is, to express feelings and thoughts so they can be heard and discussed, and to listen to the other and reflect the other's thoughts and feelings.

We see only a hint of that now, but the direction is clear.

Therapist: Mrs. Hannon, I don't know how you can do it.
Mrs. Hannon: Uh huh.
Therapist: You know, you really have more than one problem at home. You know that?
Mrs. Hannon: The whole batch is a problem. [She speaks with a strong voice for the first time in the interview.]
Therapist: That's right. Why did you pick Joan to ask for some help for her?
Mrs. Hannon: This is suppose to be my sensible one.
Therapist: Yeah?
Mrs. Hannon: And when she starts goofing off, I know the whole house is crazy.
Therapist: She helps hold things together?
Mrs. Hannon: Right, and when she starts blowing her stack and falling apart, it's time to find out what's the problem.
Therapist: Okay. You need her to help you. You can't afford not to have her.
Mrs. Hannon: I can always depend on her, you know.
Therapist: Yeah.
Mrs. Hannon: But when she starts falling apart, well shucks [shaking her head].
Joan: That's why I fell apart.
Therapist: That's why you fall apart. Because she depends on you?
Joan: Nope.
Therapist: Because what?
Joan: Because when she wants me to do something and I can't do it.

[She buries her face in her hands and starts to cry quietly.]
Therapist [to Mrs. Hannon]: She's upset.
Mrs. Hannon [nodding] [long pause]
Joan: I got tears. [She giggles tearfully.]
Therapist: That's all right.
Joan: I don't like to cry. [She moves closer to Mrs. Hannon and gets tissues.]
Therapist: That's all right. That's okay.
Joan: No, no. That's all. No more. I get mad at myself when I cry.
Therapist: You don't have to.
Joan: I do [dabbing eyes quietly and recomposing herself]. Now let's talk.
Therapist: Okay.
Joan: [pause] If I get simple, then I can tell you what's wrong with my mind. If I don't get simple, I cry.

4. Middle-stage Work   With this last statement Joan clarified why her manner has radically changed when the other youngsters in the family left. Now she no longer needed protect her mother with her "simple" behavior. But when she let go of this compelling need, she felt the hopelessness of the situation from her perspective. She was overwhelmed and began to cry. The therapist worked with Joan in front of Mrs. Hannon and Joan clarified her concerns.

Therapist: All right, okay. What's wrong with your mind then?
Joan: Boy I worry too much. She [Mrs. Hannon] going off to work, she have an accident [She laughs

tearfully as she relates her imaginary fears].

Therapist: Go ahead. Go ahead.

Joan: Jack [her brother] gets shot walking down the street. Earl [brother] having a train accident.

Therapist: Yeah?

Joan: Rita and Curt choked to death. Vera gets shot by her husband, and me—I'm going crazy.

Therapist: Yeah, but you haven't always been this upset. Why are you getting upset? Why have you been upset lately?

Joan: 'Cause they don't do what I say. And I know I'm right.

Therapist: How long has it been? How long have you been getting so upset? Since everything's been getting so bad?

Joan: Since June I guess.

Therapist: Since June? What happened? What happened then?

Joan: A whole lot. I can't stand it. Well, not so much, except they just get on my nerves.

Therapist: No, no, something happened. Something has changed at home since June. Why is it worse since then?

Joan: Let's see. They don't listen to what I say.

Therapist [to Mrs. Hannon]: Do you know what happened?

Mrs. Hannon: Think I do.

In this exchange, the therapist assisted Joan to explain her concerns and tracked them concretely. They were *her* concerns, rather than her mother's. Mrs. Hannon was a part of this, although she was silent, and when Joan couldn't recall some of the issues of the previous June, the therapist shifted to

Mrs. Hannon. She filled in that Vera got married. She was going to move out, but she couldn't because of difficulties with her new husband and presumably because she was afraid to become independent. Joan, her confidante, who readily takes others' burdens, seems to have been worrying about it more than Vera.

5. *Focus on Joan I*   In the next phase, the therapist tracked Joan's tendency to worry for others. He paradoxically illustrated her chosen role: "you're supposed to worry about the other people in the family." He continued the paradox by relating this to Mrs. Hannon's concerns.

Therapist: So Vera tells you her problems. Who else do you have to worry about?

Joan: I don't know. I just worry for no reason, I guess.

Therapist: No, but you're supposed to worry about other people in the family.

Therapist [to Mrs. Hannon]: She's really been like a part of you.

Mrs. Hannon: Uh huh.

Therapist: To take care of things and hold them together, because you can't possibly do this by yourself, and she's been the only one you could really depend on to handle things.

Mrs. Hannon: Uh huh. Right.

6. *Focus on Mrs. Hannon*   With Mrs. Hannon's agreement, the therapist now moved to a point of clarification with Mrs. Hannon of her situation and Joan's, and the differences between the two. In the discussion he encouraged

Mrs. Hannon to take the viewpoint of the other, and also implicitly encouraged Joan to identify her situation and differentiate it from her mother's. On this basis, at a later point they could begin to separate personal from relational tasks and solve problems together.

> *Therapist*: You know, when I talk to you, when you first came in here, you looked very tired. You looked out of it. The kids have all left and I can really see you now and your eyes are very clear, and I think they're very clear because you see a lot. And I think maybe your nerves are as bad as they are, because you see too much and there's nothing you can do about it.
>
> *Mrs. Hannon* [softly]: I'll go along with that.
>
> *Therapist*: And she [Joan] is trying to carry this burden with you. [Mrs. Hannon nods.] [Pause] I can understand why she can't worry about school; she's got the worries of any woman, not a seventeen-year-old kid. [Mrs. Hannon nods] She couldn't have more worries if she had ten kids of her own. [Pause]
>
> *Therapist*: You don't really have any help from the outside?
>
> *Mrs. Hannon*: No, they don't even care.

7. **Move to Tasks**   The last exchange between the therapist and Mrs. Hannon shifted the focus from perceptions, thoughts, and feelings to an assessment of her current situation and what could be done. Now there would be a gradual shift into sorting out tasks (per-

sonal and relational) and problem solving. With the focus on Mrs. Hannon, there was some discussion of what might be most important for the family to do. What emerged from the discussion with Mrs. Hannon was, first of all, the need to help Vera to become independent and then find some care for Mrs. Hannon's father. Joan kept wanting to be a part of these concerns. The therapist acknowledged her, but deflected the focus of work to Mrs. Hannon, who is beginning to be able to see herself taking charge. The following exchange reflected a longer process in the interview:

> *Therapist*: Joan, you have so much on your mind that I think you need to forget a few things. You can't keep all these things in your head at once or you'll go crazy.
>
> *Joan*: I know I'm crazy. That makes me mad [laughing] 'cause I can't do nothing about it.
>
> *Therapist*: Yeah, this kind of thing would drive anybody crazy. You're crazy because you have too much to deal with. [Pause] [To Mrs. Hannon]: I guess in a way that what we should really be concentrating on first is Vera and her kids. If we can get something done for her and the kids.
>
> *Mrs. Hannon*: Right, right!

The process continued with the focus on Vera and Mrs. Hannon's father. This discussion didn't need to get too concrete, since that would come in a discussion between Mrs. Hannon and Vera in later interviews. The important thing at this point was to help Mrs. Hannon to take over and to relieve Joan of some of the responsibilities she had assumed. She still feels hopeless about herself.

8. *Focus on Joan II*

In the next phase the focus turns back to Joan. The therapist gives a fairly clear formulation of the problem, and Mrs. Hannon, with the therapist's coaching, addresses Joan's concerns.

Joan: And you know, I think things will never go my way.
Therapist: Why do you say that, Joan?
Joan: I don't know. . . 'Cause they don't.
Therapist: Joan, right now you can't live for yourself. You're living for a lot of other people. At this point in your life, you're not thinking about what you're going to do for yourself or where you want to go tomorrow.
Joan: Nope.
Therapist: You're thinking about what you're going to do for all these other people in your house.
Mrs. Hannon [to Joan]: And that will make you sicker than anything in the drug store. It will, because you can't solve everybody's problems. This you can't do. We just have to make arrangements with them and if they can't solve the problem, I can see if I can help them solve the problem and get them off your back, and maybe you can solve some of your own problems. (This is the crucial move in the interview. Mrs. Hannon spontaneously takes over from Joan, dismissing her from the job of worrying for the rest of the family.)

9. *Support New Structure*

In this phase, the therapist supported this new configuration of the relationship emergent between Joan and her mother. There was problem-solving discussion about finding a new school for Joan where she could begin again. With their jobs sorted out from one another, Joan and Mrs. Hannon were less burdened. The therapist supported this and connected this with the concrete work each would be doing in the future and in future sessions. The foundation was now set for further sessions with this family, assisting them with relational and family tasks. From the systems perspective, issues were related to each other. When the family is helped to resolve one issue, others come closer to resolution. Once the family is able to manage, the therapist may be available but may not need to be so deeply involved. In the further narrative of the Hannon family's story, Vera was reunited with her husband, who joined the Air Force. They moved to the West Coast. Joan did not return to school, but earned her high school diploma by passing the GED examination. Mrs. Hannon's father died at home. It was rumored that, as things developed, Mrs. Hannon eventually entered some form of the ministry.

From Aponte's perspective, the therapist needed to identify specific issues of the family and to assess how the dynamics of the individual, the family, and the social context converge in relation to these issues. The therapist entered the system to shift its configuration in a way that would resolve the problem. At the same time, he worked between the family and the external structures, the community resources and the agencies that have such a powerful effect on them. Resolving the leadership in the family would allow them to use these structures beneficially. Joan could let go and pursue her education. Mrs. Hannon could manage her concerns, and Vera could manage hers. Working between the family and these institutional structures and community resources will be discussed in the following chapter.

SUMMARY

The family experiencing serious relational loss and reconstructing itself adds another level of complexity and profoundly changes what otherwise would be classic family life-cycle stages. The additional stress of the loss brings temporary underorganization and a greater threat of breakdown. Some families remain underorganized over generations, somehow carrying on with the basics of family living but with minimal external and internal adaptations. Families experiencing losses and underorganization, whether over one or more generations, frequently draw in other social institutions to support their functioning. These may be the courts, the schools, child welfare agencies, and health and mental health agencies. Social workers often work for these organizations and work between these families and the social institution. In this sense, the next chapter, which adds the dynamics of social institutions to the internal dynamics of the family, is a natural completion of the discussion begun in this chapter and in the previous one on elaborated families.

REFERENCES

Amato, P., & Booth, A. (1997). *A generation at risk*. Cambridge, MA: Harvard University Press.

Aponte, H. (1986). If I don't get simple, I cry. *Family Process, 25*(3), 533–544.

Aponte, H., & Van Deusen, J. M. (1981). Structural family therapy. In A. S. Gurman & D. Knishkern (Eds.), *Handbook of family therapy* (pp. 310–360). New York: Brunner-Mazel.

Bauserman, R. (2002). Child adjustment in joint custody vs. sole custody arrangements. *Journal of Family Psychology, 16*, 1.

Beal, E. W. (1980). Separation, divorce and single parent families. In E. M. Carter & M. McGoldrick (Eds.), *The family life cycle: A framework for family therapy* (pp. 241–264). New York: Gardner Press.

Beal, E. W. (1980). *Adult children of divorce: Breaking the cycle and family fulfillment in love and marriage*. New York: Delacorte Press.

Bryner, C. L. (2001). Children of divorce. *Journal of the American Board of Family Practice, 14*(3), 178–183.

Glick, P. S. (1979). Children of divorced families in demographic perspective. *Journal of Social Issues, 35*, 170–182.

Goldstein, J. R. (1999). The leveling of divorce in the United States. *Demography*, 36, 409–414.

Herzog, E., & Sudia, C. E. (1973). Children in fatherless families. In B. M. Caldwell & H. N. Ricciuti (Eds.), *Review of child development research* (pp. 141–232). New York: Russell Sage.

Hetherington, M. (2002). *For better or for worse: Divorce reconsidered*. New York: Norton.

Montalvo, B. (1982). Interpersonal arrangements in disrupted families. In F. Walsh (Ed.), *Normal family functioning* (pp. 277–296). New York: Guilford.

Norton, A. J., & Miller, L. F. (1992). *Marriage, divorce and remarriage in the 1990's*. Washington, DC: U.S. Bureau of the Census.

Popenoe, D. (2001). *The top ten myths of divorce*. The National Marriage Project. http://marriage.Rutgers.edu/Publications/pubtoptenmyths.htm.

Visher, E. B., & Visher, J. S. (1982). Stepfamilies and stepparenting. In F. Walsh (Ed.), *Normal family functioning*. New York: Guilford.

Wallerstein, J. S., & Blakeslee, S. (1989). *Second chances: Men, women and children a decade after divorce*. Boston: Houghton-Mifflin.

Wallerstein, J. S., & Kelly, J. (1980). *Surviving the breakup: How children and parents cope with divorce*. New York: Basic Books.

Wallerstein, J. S., Lewis, J., & Blakeslee, S. (2000). *The unexpected legacy of divorce*. New York: Hyperion.

Waite, L., & Gallagher, M. (2000). *The case for marriage*. New York: Doubleday.

CHAPTER 9

Working Between Families and Outside Social Institutions: Schools, Courts, and Health Care

Families, particularly vulnerable families such as those in transition and underorganized families, could not operate without supportive connections with outside social institutions. Social workers in large part work for these institutions and work between the family and the social institution, attempting to help both family and institutional process proceed optimally. This chapter systematically examines this practice in the judicial system, in schools, and in health and mental health systems, all of which comprise the bases of fields of practice in social work.

FAMILIES AND OUTSIDE SOCIAL INSTITUTIONS

In this chapter we take the systems model, inherent to social work, one step further to include the relationships of families with social institutions and community resources. The social worker often works between these institutional structures or community resources and families. Social institutions are established to promote public order, to protect, to provide resources, and sometimes to set appropriate standards for individuals and family members. The institutional missions and tasks, whether of education, health care, or justice, often shape the relational tasks of the family. But the dilemma of the institutions is always how to work with the family: how to assist the family to do its work without distorting, taking over, or colonizing the family.

To say that these institutional structures are outside the family is somewhat paradoxical. They are often outside families in the sense that families are unable to use them in their functioning. However, if they are really outside, that itself becomes the problem. Social institutions such as schools, health care, the judicial system, child welfare agencies, public assistance, and even at times the military service or work organizations have important functions that, if they are used, place them on the inside of families. Families need social institutions to carry out certain functions. In the case of the military or work organizations, the organization needs the assistance of family members. The more complex the situation or the deeper the need of a member, the more the institution or community resource needs to exercise an inside role with family functioning—without, however, disturbing the family's natural exercise of its own appropriate functioning. If family is vulnerable to institutions, the reverse is also true. For the most part, social institutions cannot carry out their missions without the help and participation of families.

Social workers can help the institution and the family carry out their respective functions harmoniously. They can facilitate the complex relationships between vulnerable families and their necessary social institutional environments, through their work on the inside of both the social institution and the family. They can make a connection between the institutional mission, family relational tasks, and the intervention. They have done this for a century in different fields of social work practice, focusing on the needs of vulnerable persons but also related to the work of social institutions dealing with human vulnerability.

Social Work with Vulnerable Persons in Families

Social work practice, first of all, grows out of the needs of vulnerable persons. Persons who most often need care and protection are children, the elderly, or those with disabilities. These persons often live in families who are their first resource for care. Emergent fields of practice comprise:

- *Child welfare—work with children and their parents and/or caregivers.* Child welfare is about helping children and families sustain or reconstruct secure attachments and connections. It creates a context for children to grow appropriately as persons of dignity, worth, and emergent competence. When the family is unable to care for a child appropriately, child welfare workers may work with that family or that kinship unit to rehabilitate itself, or they may connect the child with a unit of substitute care, often another family.
- *Social work with the elderly and their caregivers.* When elderly persons decline in their ability to manage independently, maintenance in their family or placement in an assistive living unit often requires significant assistance for the elderly person and for the family. An example is the O'Connor family (case study 7.9).
- *Social work with adults with disabilities and their caregivers.* As another vulnerable population similar to the aging, social workers often work with adults who have disabilities and their caregivers.

Social Work in Social Institutions: Health and Education

Parallel to work with vulnerable persons is work with families in social institutions such as health care and education.

- *Social work in health care and mental health.* Many of the events in health care: birth, death, a difficult treatment regimen, disability, the need for a more intensive care in a patient's environment, demand more than medical intervention. Often these are family events even more than medical events. In some cases, such as birth and death, medical intervention is secondary to profound human meanings, and the social relational work that must be done. The social worker in the health care setting works with patients and their families, struggling with the relational issues when social functioning is affected by illness or disability. The issues for the patient in mental health are often profoundly connected with the family. Many patients could not survive without the family's ongoing assistance and support.

- *School social work.* The school social worker works to construct a workable relationship between child, family, and school that may assist children to carry out their developmental work of intellectual, social and physical maturation. The family is the first educator of the child, and the school cannot accomplish its purpose without at least the implicit support of the family. When the child may be vulnerable there is need for a more developed relation between family and school.

Other institutions where social workers are involved with families are in the world of work, in trade unions, in corporations, and in military organizations. Social workers also work in the system of justice with the courts, with the police, and in corrections.

Religion as a Social Institution

Social workers often work for religious sponsored agencies serving families and children (Kohs, 1966). Religion, culture, and family become the guidance systems of human action and meaning. Religion, as a social institution, celebrates the spiritual in the social and personal context of each person's essential relationships and obligations. Although religion is very diverse, it defines common meanings and supports and links families with each other.

SOCIAL WORK FIELDS OF PRACTICE

Social workers have a long history of working between families, social institutions, and community resources where people and their environments are in exchange with each other. This relationship in many ways is the underlying paradigm of social work. It is the duality of focus on people and their environments that distinguishes social work from other professions (Joint Task Force, 1979). Social workers work between institutional resource systems and family systems to establish a match between resources, standards and needs, assisting both to develop this match in an optimal way (Gordon, 1969, 1979). Fields of practice in social work grow from the need for mediation between persons and social institutions to meet common human needs. Practice within each field is unique to that field. It is defined by a particular clientele, a point of entry, a social institution with its institutional purposes, and the contribution of social work practice—that is, the contribution of social work knowledge, values, and its appropriateness to the institutional purpose and to common human needs (Bartlett, 1971).

The problem is the relation of a social institution, such as the court or the school, to a family, such as the J. family (case study 4.7), the Hong family (case study 4.5), or the Hannon family (case study 8.4). The social institution should not take over the appropriate functions of family members or attempt to substitute for them, but instead should support family members and their appropriate functions. The dangers are that, without a mediator who can also work on the inside of the family, the family could become paralyzed or the institution fail its mission. In the best sense, the social institution or community resource could become a part of the family for a time, and the social worker could monitor the complex relationship between institutional resources and standards and family functioning. Practice would then take place not simply as a transaction between practitioner and client system, but more broadly, involving social institutional structures and community resources. In this sense, the beginnings, middles, and endings inherent to a helping process are also beginnings, middles, and endings with the social institution or community resource as well as with the social worker (Smalley, 1967, pp. 3, 4). Representing the institution as well as the family, the social worker assists family members to use the institution to carry out relational and personal tasks. In turn, the family assists the institution in fulfilling its societal functions.

When families interact with social institutions, there is a natural and continuing concern that family members will either be controlled by the social institution or lose their functions. Yet if they oppose the institution, they fear losing what the institution can offer the family, or even possible punishment. This is the dilemma for families. Schools, the police and court systems, child welfare, and health care all have different meanings to different families, meanings that are defined by the family culture and the family history. Families develop patterns and complex linkages with institutions, often handed down through generations. Generations of disappointing relationships in one's family history may be difficult to overcome. Nineteenth-century Irish Americans had great difficulty with the schools and child welfare systems, to the point of developing their own alternative, religiously and culturally compatible, systems. When they achieved power in the police and political systems, they had less difficulty. In the wake of reconstruction, African Americans experienced prejudice and discrimination from all systems. They lacked the resources to develop alternate institutions, except for religion and to some extent child welfare. Only in the last decades of the twentieth century has this situation changed. Native Americans have long been in the same position, although sometimes the tribe can act as a mediator.

As in the case of the Hmong family earlier in this book, institutions may be quite insensitive to cultural differences and family needs. They depend on families to meet their objectives, but they need to work hard to acquire sensitivity to families. This means that the family social worker often must advocate strongly to assist the institution to adapt to the needs of its clientele and their families. The social worker does a great deal of work with the institution, developing resources, helping them to fit with family needs and meanings, and removing obstacles that prevent families from using these resources.

Underorganized Families

Underorganized families need particular assistance from the outside to reorganize themselves and to relate effectively with social institutions. With multiple needs, they often have multiple involvements with different social institutions and great difficulties getting what they need. These multiple involvements can be confusing. They can put the family at risk of further loss of functions and eventual collapse. Differing institutions themselves can become like contentious families, at odds with one another over a particular family. In the resulting confusion, nothing gets done and the risk to the family grows. The social worker can bring services together to resolve issues around families with multiple needs and involvements, keeping family members appropriately in charge of their own functions and responsibilities, and keeping agencies in workable relations with each other (Kordesh & Constable, 2002).

The concept of relational justice, previously applied to relationships on the inside of families, can also be applied to transactions between institutions and families. The needs of families are often dependent on institutional processes. The J. family (case study 4.7) could not change without the court. Indeed, the expectations of the court largely set its goals and defined its tasks. Ultimately, with the mediation and family work of the social worker, these expectations assisted the family to make changes they would never make on their own. The social worker works in schools with the multidisciplinary team, in the hospital with the medical team, in the military with the commanding officer, in the justice system with the judge, and in the police system with the police. The aim of the work is to adapt the institution to the needs of the family (and vice versa), so that family members can carry out their tasks and meet appropriate institutional expectations. Family members can then support the institution's work.

Ecomaps

Ecomaps are particularly useful to illustrate the relationships between family members and institutions, for assessment and for intervention. They put the relationship of family members to community agencies in graphic form. They are also useful when there is more than one agency involved, and when the relationships are complex (Hartman & Laird, 1983). In case study 4.7 the J. family had a very complex relationship with the court that was supervising Mr. J. (see figure 4.2).

WORKING BETWEEN INSTITUTIONAL AND FAMILY SYSTEMS

Social Work in Schools

We use the schools as an extended example of the process taking place within the family, with the institution, and with the social worker. Schools and families are the crucial institutions in the socialization of children. Effective education is essential if children are to participate in a globalized economy, as citizens, and ultimately as family members themselves, raising a new generation. School has become the place where children come to participate in a common experience of membership and personal achievement within the broader society. The history of education in modernizing societies is an uneven history of a gradually increasing awareness of individual differences in ability, culture, and class, and increasing inclusiveness of these differences as they affect learning. School has become more than simply learning language arts, social science, or mathematics. The mission and meanings of education have broadened and become intertwined with concerns that each pupil develop as a human being and realize his or her potential contribution to society. Research evidence points out that, particularly with vulnerable children, schools cannot accomplish their mission to educate any child without an implicit partnership with parents (Bailey, Blasco & Simeonson, 1992; Hanson & Carta, 1995; Hanson & Hanline, 1990; Frey, Greenberg & Fewell, 1989; Bristol & Gallagher, 1982). No amount of educational inputs, money for teachers, classrooms, and so on, will be effective without the support and involvement of parents, without the school being a partner to and agent of the parents (Walberg & Lai, 1999).

Social workers in the school are positioned at the central point in the ecosystems of child development, at the meeting point between parents, pupil, and school. They work with children at risk. The school social worker makes education possible for many children who otherwise would have difficulty coping with the educational process. The school social worker works in multiple functions within the most vulnerable parts of the educational process, where the education process can break down in its relations with the child and with the family. The basic unit of attention in school social work is the constellation of teacher, parent, and child. The school social worker may work with teachers, families, and children to address individual situations, or may work as a consultant to help schools to be more effective with children and respond appropriately to them (Constable, McDonald & Flynn, 2002). As of the 1998–1999 school year, there were approximately 15,000 school social workers in U.S. public schools working with children with disabilities alone (U.S. Department of Education, 2002).

The School as a Community of Families   From the origins of public education, schools in the United States have often operated in relative isolation from their constituent families. As long as this isolation of school from the family sphere has been taken for granted, the school social worker's role has been to span the boundaries between schools and families as expeditiously as possible (Litwak & Meyer, 1966). The complexity of the challenges facing schools today has developed the conception that the school is a community of families and teachers in partnership. There have been numerous recent experiments with parent-sponsored schools, and that trend is now becoming very important. The development of this supportive community is even more important when the community is off-balance and in crisis, when children, families, communities and schools have special needs, where the connection between home and school is not easily developed, or where

there is cultural or linguistic diversity. It is a commonplace in education that resilience in children is promoted when the resources in the school, family and community are united and dedicated to the healthy development and educational success of children (Wang, Haertl & Walberg, 1998, p. 55; Christensen & Sheridan,
2001; Kelleghan, Sloane, Alvarez & Bloom, 1993; Webster-Stratten, 1993). This relationship of school, family, and community, central to the work of the school social worker, is becoming recognized as central to effective education, resilient children, and school reform as well.

The Necessary Arrangement of Relations Between Family and School[1]   There
is a necessary order in the relationship between family and schools. Families cannot
educate their children in a complex modern society without the assistance of
schools, and schools cannot educate without the cooperation of families (Walberg,
1984; Walberg & Lai, 1999). Each can prevent the other from accomplishing its
proper function. This is particularly true for vulnerable children and families. Families are the first educators of their children. When the family acts in its capacity to
educate, its educational functions take place in a child's life prior to the school's
function and they remain most important through the child's developing years. The
school's functions exist to help the family accomplish its prior functions in accordance with the needs and standards of society and the rights of members of the family. Children are in a recognized position of vulnerability and require protection
from their environments. They have a right to receive adequate nurture and socialization whenever possible in their own families. The community, often represented
by the school, is obligated to ensure that families have all the assistance—economic,
social, educational, political, and cultural—that they need to face all their responsibilities in a human way. It is not the function of the school to take away from families the child-rearing functions that families can perform on their own or in cooperative associations. Rather, in the spirit of "subsidiarity," the school must support these
functions, when possible, particularly when they are at risk.

The relationship of the family to the school and the community can be encapsulated by three principles:

1. The family has primary functions in the care and socialization of its children. It has rights and responsibilities derived from this function. These responsibilities include the economic, social, educational, and cultural provision for the needs of its members. As such, the family is the basic social
   unit of society.
2. The school's primary functions are helping the family to accomplish its responsibilities and supplying certain cognitive instruction that the family
   cannot take on. The work of the family is always personal. Transactions *en
   famille* are expected to be based on affection and respect for the other person. Particular types of learning would be distorted if they excluded this di-

---

[1]From Constable and Walberg (2002, p. 375). Used with permission.

mension of affection and respect for the person as a person, as worthwhile in his or her own right. In families, this personal dimension is experienced and learned in work, worship, gender roles, respect for others in social relations, and respect for one's developing sexuality. When affection and respect break down, the partnership of home and school can be developed through social work services that assist the family in developing or redeveloping respect and affection among members.

3. A secondary function of the school (and, in a broader sense, of the community) is to monitor potential abridgment of rights of children as pupils and citizens when external conditions of society or internal conditions within the family make it impossible for the family to accomplish its primary function. This must be done, as in the first principle, without inappropriately abridging the family's exercise of those functions it is able to accomplish.

These principles involve a balance between family and school, an order, and a defined relation between their respective functions. The increased awareness of the importance of effective families, the increasing numbers of vulnerable families, and the increasing school responsibility for the education of vulnerable children inevitably lead to the need for more integrated relationships between school and family. The danger is that, in the face of the weakness of the family and the complexity of the child's problems, schools might attempt to substitute for family functions. This never works well. When services take over, rather than empower families to carry out their duties, they limit the effectiveness of the partnership. Schools need to redefine their relationship with families so that true collaboration emerges with all families.

Working Between Pupil, Family and School The quality of a child's interaction with others in school is usually a very accurate barometer of his or her broader developmental issues and the family situation. The school is a stage with opportunities for each child to play out the great developmental issues: separation-individuation, self-esteem, social relationships, language, imagination, emotions, assertiveness, achievement, competition, productive work, and the discovery and use of one's self. If used well, it is a great normalizer. In many respects, the school is the basic (and the best) place for services to be delivered to children in families.

There are many possible approaches to social work practice with pupils and families in school. Intervention, running from consultation and multidisciplinary teamwork through individual, group, or family involvement to assisting in policy and program development can vary with the emergent needs of the child and the situation. These services may continue throughout the school experience at different levels of intensity. In an elementary school, it is possible that the social worker might know and work with a pupil and family for up to nine years.

In Alan's case the social worker carried out a wide range of functions with different units of attention to support Alan's functioning and eventual developmental maturation. It is a good example of school social work practice with children, families, and the school as a system. Alan faced a chaotic family and personal situation in second grade. He had great difficulty. His world, as he knew it, was falling apart.

CASE STUDY 9.1[2]

Alan, age seven, was referred for evaluation by his second-grade classroom teacher about five weeks after the start of school. The social worker found him quite withdrawn with considerable emotional energy tied up with his parents' divorce process. He felt that his parents yelled a lot at each other, and at him, and at his brother. He could also say he felt angry when he didn't get his way. A transfer student from another school, he had difficulty following directions and concentrating on his work. He was easily distracted and he had poor fine motor coordination and poor visual perception. He would often try to copy from his neighbors or just sit, suck his fingers and not attempt to do his work. Testing showed that his support systems were eroding and his self-concept was rapidly deteriorating along with his academic performance. His reading difficulties could be an indicator of possible learning disabilities.

Alan lived with his mother, his ten-year-old brother, and his three-year-old sister in a mobile home park. His mother and father had separated at the end of his kindergarten year and the divorce became final after first grade. At this time the family moved to the mobile home park, where the mother's parents lived. During this time, the father would take the children on weekends. He was most consistent in doing so, and both children and father seemed to enjoy the time very much. There were also contacts with the extended family on both sides.

The social worker met with the parents and recommended that Alan receive outside counseling. They did not agree to this, and so he decided to monitor him on a consultative basis until further direct work could be arranged. He provided consultation to Alan's second-grade teacher. The second-grade teacher was somewhat rigid and unresponsive to Alan, and not particularly receptive to direct suggestions. Consequently the social worker worked closely with the learning disabilities teacher and the reading teacher, who were in different ways involved with Alan's situation. When the second-grade teacher left on maternity leave in February, Alan's new teacher was warm, caring, and creative. She liked Alan and was responsive to suggestions. Alan was also provided with more direct learning disabilities help. Shortly after this, Alan began to respond. On the other hand, he also drew a picture of himself with a noose around his neck and talked with the social worker about his sad feelings. The social worker discussed this with the mother. Although the mother was open and cooperative, she resisted any suggestion of outside help for Alan. The father wanted to get outside counseling. They agreed on a plan that Alan would check in with the social worker every

---

[2]This case is adapted from Wolkow (2002, pp. 364–370), with permission.

day for the remainder of the year. The social worker also saw Alan in a group. He remained in contact with the parents and provided consultation to his teachers. Alan gradually became more outgoing and showed improved social skills, first in the group, and later in the classroom. The social worker encouraged the teachers to support Alan's progress in class, and Alan continued to do better for the remainder of the school year.

At the end of the second-grade year, the social worker met with the parents and again recommended outside counseling help. The mother continued to be reluctant: it would not be something she would ever do. The father was able to follow through with arrangements and bring Alan to his appointments. In third grade, the social worker was able to match Alan with a male teacher who was very warm, accepting, and competent. He provided regular consultation, helping the teacher to institute a behavior modification program for the whole class that was focused on positive social interaction, as a way of keeping a handle

on Alan's real social progress. In fourth grade, Alan continued to show considerable improvement, with the social worker moving toward monthly check-ins, except when Alan had concerns to discuss. At this time the mother remarried. Alan showed his concern about this new development in class discussion. The social worker met with the mother and the stepfather and they agreed to come in throughout the year to talk about issues surrounding their relationship with the children, especially Alan. He began seeing Alan again in a social skills group. Alan made improvements in anger control, remained in contact with his father, and managed to have a good relationship with his stepfather as well. He continued his progress for the next four grades, although he continued to have learning disabilities in the area of reading. He was still shy and a loner, but managed to have friends in his father's neighborhood. In the following grades, the school social worker remained available. Alan continued to maintain his progress academically, socially, and emotionally.

In the beginning, Alan was dealing with the changes in his family, his move from his old neighborhood, and his learning disabilities. When his school situation improved, he was able to express his depression and even suicidal ideation. His family went through profound changes—severe marital upset, separation, divorce, single parenthood with joint custody, and remarriage. While the social worker's focus remained on Alan, he was a resource for both parents and for his stepparent. The school in some ways became a type of "holding system" for the whole family during this time of turmoil. Alan was able to use the support of the school to avert possible deterioration and showed considerable change over the period of seven years. Throughout all this change, he was working steadily on the same problems. Working between the family and school worlds, the social worker helped the teachers, the parents, and Alan in different ways to develop this holding system, to support Alan's strengths, and—as Alan grew and matured—to help him to put things together.

Although Alan's case is not particularly complex, it illustrates well several important points about school social work and about social work practice in the contexts of families and social institutions. In contrast to the cases of community-based work with families that we have discussed up to this point, the relational tasks of the person and the family were related to the work of the social institution. Alan's family situation reflected itself in the massive breakdown of his ability to cope with educational and social tasks, his thoughts of dying, and his chronic sadness. The helping process built itself on Alan's developmental thrust to adapt to school. It centered on the transaction between the pupil and the school, but also included the family. The parents were open to this process at a time when they would have had difficulty using any other resource. The social worker, embedded in the school, worked at different levels of intensity throughout Alan's elementary school experience, attempting to bring all the elements of the situation together in an optimal way. The focus on different units of attention varied according to the particular situation. He would provide consultation to all at different times. He met with Alan individually and in groups, according to Alan's current need. Mostly, he set the conditions for Alan and his family to resolve this complicated situation. To do this he needed to know a good deal about individual development, families, schools as resources for pupils like Alan, and the ways he could use himself with all parties involved to make the process work over time.

Social Work in the Judicial System

A number of fields of social work practice come from the judicial system: child welfare, juvenile corrections, adult corrections, and police social work. For our purposes we will be particularly concerned with the family court, which exercises jurisdiction over families and youngsters under eighteen, and thus with the fields of child welfare and juvenile corrections.

The law and the judicial system set standards of child protection and care for families and for children. When children are endangered by the inability of a family to care for them appropriately, or when minors are in violation of the law, it is the function of this system to assist families and members of families to meet these standards, to deal with the implications of not meeting them, and to assist victims when possible. Social workers or probation officers within these systems work with family members to carry out these institutional purposes. In both systems, clients are mostly involuntary. For any person and for whole families as well, being referred to court is indeed a crisis. The J. family (case study 4.7) is a good example of this. Most of the time they are not explicitly asking for help, but if the process is to succeed, they must come to a point where they want help, and can use help to meet the standards of the law and the court.

For families, this is a delicate and uncertain transition. First, it means that energy directed to resisting the implications of the judicial process needs to be converted into energy available for a sort of self-transformation to meet the expectations of the law. In many cases, particularly when the focus is on one person alone, these transformations never occur. The energy of the court confronts the oppositional energy of the child and the parents. It requires a special type of skill on the social worker's part to keep the court and the family systems appropriately open and separate, in charge of their own concerns and able to transform themselves. Second, when children and adolescents are involved, this transformational process needs to be a family process as well. The J. family (case study 4.7) is a good example of the social worker working between both systems, helping the family keep its own system open so that productive work can be done. As we saw in the example of Alan in the school (case study 9.1), the social worker is not providing some generic therapy, now in a school, child welfare, or probation setting. Rather, the social worker is also helping family members meet the expectations of the institution, in this case, the court. If change does not take place, the court can take custody and, through *parens patriae*, itself takes on the role of parent. In many ways, the helping process in these contexts can be much more complex and fraught with difficulty than family therapy in the community. On the other hand, as with schools, the supervision of the court and the law and its procedures can provide a framework for growth and self-transformation where nothing else may be possible.

Social Work in Child Welfare

The status of child, by its nature, demands parents. For the last several decades, the field of child welfare has been shifting from a strict child protection approach with minimal family involvement to a child-centered, family-focused approach (Leiderman, 1995). Child welfare has to be family welfare as well, whether it means working with a child's family at home or working with substitute caregivers, whether these are foster homes, adoptive families, or residential homes. The first goal of child welfare is to strengthen, support, and preserve families and keep children with their parents whenever possible and when it is in the best interests of the child. Recent studies report that only a small percentage of children reported to child protective services are ever placed in some form of substitute care, whether this takes the form of foster care, residential care or adoption (Pecora, Reed-Ashcraft & Kirk, 2001). In six major states about four in a thousand children ages 0 to 4 will enter foster care, and about two in a thousand children ages 5 to 17 will enter foster care (Pecora et al., 2001). This means that, in most cases, the child welfare worker may work mainly with the family of origin. When there is a foster placement, there is a broader focus: on the family of origin, on the foster home, and on the child. The child has a type of membership in both families.

Family Preservation

Family preservation services have emerged as a more intensive effort to help parents support and care for their children. This is done through 1) family resource, support, and educational services; 2) family-focused casework services that address problems as they arise, and 3) intensive family-centered crisis services that seek to stabilize families when there is an imminent risk of child placement because of abuse or neglect. Sometimes these services are provided by a state child welfare agency, sometimes by a subcontracted agency. However, the process of family re-organization needs to be the same, with the state agency and the court monitoring whether the family intervention is successful. The following case of the Clark family[3] shows the wide range of services necessary, even in an intensive, short-term intervention, to help the family respond to the needs of their children.

CASE STUDY 9.2

The Clark family was referred by a public health nurse when their premature daughter was released from the hospital. Toby, age three, had recently been diagnosed as hyperactive with some brain damage. Children's Protective Services and the nurse were suspicious about Toby's three concussions over the past year. Another child in the same family had died not long ago from sudden infant death syndrome. The nurse wondered if Toby and the baby shouldn't be placed in foster care.

When the social worker arrived, she immediately noted the smell of gas leaking from the furnace. Pam, the mother, twenty-two, appeared very depressed and said she hadn't felt up to going to the public phone to call for help. She had no phone, although with her premature child, the clinic advised her to get one. The social worker immediately assisted the mother to get dressed and call the landlord. Then they talked. She was very thin, pale, and weak, had a chronic cold, and had lost her front teeth. She said she had been very depressed since her baby's birth, and had often felt the child did not belong to her. She was also extremely

upset about her Toby's "wild" behavior and wondered if he didn't have a "bad seed" in him. She had been thinking she would rather kill him now rather than see him grow up to be a murderer like his uncle. She had had three children and four miscarriages in five years of marriage. She was very lonely. Her husband, Ralph, was usually away from the house from mid-morning to late at night, unsuccessfully trying to sell life insurance. He had not sold a policy in five months. She told me that every counselor they had ever seen had told her that her husband was "rotten" and that she should leave him. But she said she loved him and he didn't beat her. They had moved from another state last June so that they could stay married and still be able to get help from the state.

The next day they approached a local organization to secure the $50.00 needed to have a telephone installed. They also got two old bedsheets that could be nailed up as curtains, since she had expressed fears about sitting alone at night with no curtains for privacy. A man had been peering through her window. She had been raped before and was very afraid it might happen again.

On her next visit to the family, the mother and the social worker discussed

---

[3]From Kinney, Haapala, and Booth (1991, pp. 133–135). Adapted with permission.

Toby. Pam said that she did not love him and described a variety of what she described as self-destructive and wild behaviors that he engaged in. She reported incidents such as him throwing himself backward off of furniture, touching the hot stove and laughing, turning on the kitchen burners, banging his head against the wall until unconscious, and biting, scratching, and hitting other people. Although he was three, he was not talking at all. She was concerned that Children's Protective Service would think she was abusing him because he hurt himself so much, or because they locked him in his room at night. They did this because he slept only two or three hours at a stretch. When awake he would go into the kitchen at night and eat until he vomited. She said she thought she should put him in an institution because she couldn't handle him. He would not kiss or show any affection to people. She said that he had been removed from the home by Children's Protective Services when she had a "nervous breakdown" and was hospitalized. Since that time, the parents had already voluntarily placed Toby once because "she couldn't cope" with him. She was also afraid she might harm him because he made her so angry sometimes.

Before leaving they made a list of what Pam could do if she felt her son's behavior was so bad she would want to place him again. The social worker let her know that she felt it was a good idea to put him in his room sometimes, and explained the concept of "time out." If she did it right, she might not have to lock the door. The list also included calling the social worker (their phone was to be installed the next day). They then made an appointment to take the son to a local children's hospital learning center to see about enrolling him in a special school program. Finally they talked about the mother getting some free time for herself. The social worker would like to meet Toby and could stay with him for several hours later that week. Pam accepted her offer.

During the social worker's time with Toby, she got to know him and learned a lot about him. He did try some of the behaviors Pam had described. But he could respond to positive reinforcement and time out. She taught him to play a game where he expressed affection to a cuddly bear. It was proof for both of them that Toby could change. Pam cried the first time they played the game and he kissed her.

During their second week, Pam began to talk more about her discontent in the marriage. She said she knew Ralph wasn't really working all the times he was gone. She expressed resentment over the fact he dressed nicely and she had only one outfit, that he was free to play all day and night while she sat in their apartment, and that he would not get her a driver's license but also would not drive her places. The social worker coached her to respond, but also be appropriately assertive. She also helped her to call the public assistance office and get authorization to get her front teeth replaced.

Ralph began to be curious about what was happening and decided to stay home one day to meet the social worker. He shared his frustrations with having to be on welfare and agreed to attend the next session. In the next sessions, they moved to focus with Pam and Ralph primarily on behavioral child management skills. In the process, the social worker began to help them work on their own communication and come to some agreement on how to handle Toby. Toby had begun attending the school program, and the mother rode the bus with him every day, and later met his teachers and other staff. She began to report having some positive feelings about Toby, and no longer felt she should send him away. With a temporary cap on her teeth, she began to smile more. She was also beginning to gain some weight.

As the end of the intervention period approached, the social worker explored ways the mother could continue counseling. She decided she would go to a counselor at a local mental health center. She had known the counselor from the time right after the baby was born.

A follow-up call from this family several months later revealed that, although there had been many upsetting events that had occurred after the social worker left, they were still together as a family. Pam had been seeing her counselor and was working on some of her depression. Pam and Ralph were also going for marital counseling. Ralph quit selling insurance and was in a job training program. Toby was attending a new school, and his mother was participating in a parent education program required by the school. Toby was starting to talk and did not seem as wild. The infant daughter was doing well.

The Clark family case is a good example of family preservation work. The work is often quite concrete and crisis oriented, but the direction is the gradual restructuring of family relationships and better use of community resources, as relationships inside the family get better. Careful contracting is particularly important, since families may well at first be unwilling clients. Someone has made a complaint to the state department of child welfare about the possibility of child maltreatment by the family. The social worker needs to proceed carefully, not from a one-up position but as a consultant to the client (Baker, 1999). The contract agreement respects the fact that the parents are still in charge and the social worker and the resources of the community are there to help them provide safe and nurturing relationships with their children, and to care for themselves in the process.

The big danger with this type of work is that, when confronted with the difficulties clients have in managing issues, such as calling the landlord about the gas leak, the social worker could become overactive and do it for them. This would confirm and reinforce the previous patterns. Instead, the social worker helps Mrs. Clark to call the landlord, to put up the curtains, to begin to cope with Toby, and to develop communication with her husband. As new patterns develop, she encourages Mr. and Mrs. Clark to own them. The nature of the service: short-term, time-limited, and intensive with an evaluation encourages this ownership. There is an ending with a follow-up. By the follow-up, Mr. and Mrs. Clark are continuing their progress. The child welfare agency has subcontracted this case with an outside agency, focused mainly on the intensive services connected with family preservation. For this reason, the formal court referral process found in many other child welfare cases is missing. When court process is necessary, it becomes a framework for the parents to work on particular goals and to decide whether they have a strong enough unit to refrain from abusing their children and, if the children have been placed outside the family, to get them back, when appropriate.

Substitute Care Arrangements

In 1993, approximately 442,000 children were placed out of their homes in substitute care arrangements. These could be a group residence for children, care by a relative, adoption, or family foster care. Adoption, a permanent placement arrangement, can be a complex process, demanding the highest level professional skills (Triseliotis, Shireman & Hundleby, 1997). Over the previous decade, about 75 percent of all substitute care is family foster care (Everett, 1995). Family foster care, intended to be temporary, is contingent on the natural parents' making improvements in their ability to care for a child. Often this does not happen. The long-term problem with foster care is that children can be left in a "temporary" arrangement that has become permanent (Maas & Engler, 1959). The temporary nature of the placement may also make it difficult for foster parents (or foster children) to invest themselves in the relationship.

Work with foster homes is a process of helping the foster parents to "make room" for the child(ren), to accommodate their special needs and the inherent uncertainties of their attachments, to provide for them and work with the school, to accept the complexities of their relationships with birth parents and with visitation, and to let them come back to their parents in a natural and comfortable way when the time comes. It is remarkable how well foster parents and children often manage these relational acrobatics! It is also not surprising when foster homes do fail to be the homes of permanent attachment that children need. In the last analysis, they are not designed to be such homes. One can only hope that children will use them as well as they can, sorting out their different attachments from each other.

CASE STUDY 9.3

When Alice and Michael Smith decided to become foster parents, their son, James, was nine and daughter, Johanna, was thirteen. Michael is an engineer and Alice teaches part-time in a high school. They live in a comfortable suburban development. As both children grew older, the parents wondered about taking in a younger child whom they could help. The child welfare agency had three siblings, Jane Barclay, age ten, Lisa Barclay, six, and Joey Barclay, five. The agency wanted to place the siblings together, and Alice and Michael agreed to be foster parents to them. Their mother was working to get her children back as soon as her drug problems alleviated. It was understood that the children would stay with Alice and Michael for at least a year. For the Barclay children, Alice and Michael's home and family was a totally strange and different world. Adapting to their routines was difficult. Alice felt the brunt of the placement. She felt overwhelmed by all of the needs she became aware of, and felt caught between getting the children to change patterns or adapting to them. She was particularly concerned about integrating the children into school. Her old problems of depression started to come back and she increased her medication. Michael, normally a busy engineer, wanted to support Alice, but found himself becoming authoritarian, particularly with Joey. Jane Barclay, a parental child with severe learning disabilities in school, had been accustomed to her own control of Lisa and Joey Barclay. Lisa was highly disorganized and Joey was defiant, both at home and at school. James Smith felt that Jane, older by a year, had displaced him and was "bossing" him. Johanna Smith remained aloof from the turmoil in the home, but profoundly missed the time and attention she was accustomed to having from her mother. The judge was ambivalent about whether Mrs. Barclay was ready to take her children back. A decision about the Barclays was delayed from one hearing to another, and three years elapsed before they returned home.

The social worker worked closely with Alice and Michael and, despite initial chaos, the two older children did settle in the Smith home. Jane took over some responsibilities in her accustomed way but also developed a relationship with Alice. When Alice secured help in school for Jane's learning disabilities, she eventually found herself making progress. Lisa followed Jane closely and began to organize herself. Joey was in constant difficulty. It became manageable when Michael learned quietly to support the good things Joey was able to do rather than to overreact.

With their mother's improvement, the court ordered the children to return to their home. It was a difficult adjustment in reverse, with Jane feeling much of the conflict now. Their mother had been clean of drugs for six months. She had worked things out with her boyfriend in order to accommodate her children. He was not their father and, except for their visitations, he had hardly known the children. Visitation time was gradually increased so the change would not be so abrupt for them. However, both mother and children felt the loss of three years of their relationship. They needed a lot of help to readjust. Michael and Alice miss the children but are ready to move on with their lives. They have no regrets about being available to them and have learned a great deal from the experience. James and Johanna, now three years older, also feel they learned something from the experience, painful as it was for them.

Social Work in Juvenile Corrections

The juvenile court is meant to be a court that acknowledges the special status and special needs of youngsters who have violated the law in some way. Approximately one in every twenty youngsters come to the attention of the juvenile court in any one year (Barton, 1995). Somewhat more than half of all youngsters adjudicated delinquent are placed on probation. The probation arrangement usually consists of a set of conditions for the youngster mandated by the court: regular attendance at school or work, compliance at home, and perhaps community service work or restitution. If the youngster fails to meet these conditions, he or she may be placed in a more restrictive setting. The probation officer's responsibilities in each case are to monitor the youngster's compliance with these conditions through regular (perhaps monthly) meetings, and to act as a sort of counselor and case manager to the youngster. Since the officer has other responsibilities, such as making preadjudication reports and recommendations, there is a very limited amount of time available for work on any one case. On the other hand, many courts have recognized that some cases will inherently take more time, and that, contrary to the traditional focus on the youngster alone, there is often a need for family involvement. The Moorhead case, presented in the next case study, involves a protracted struggle by parents with the juvenile court over the issue of the court's involvement in the family and its effect on parenting.

CASE STUDY 9.4

Billy Moorhead, a very bright youngster of thirteen, never previously in trouble, had constructed a small bomb-making laboratory in his garage. After a series of incidents, he was caught attaching a bomb to the ignition system of an auto in his wealthy suburban enclave. Fortunately, only one of the previous bombs he had attached to cars had caught fire, and the fire had been doused before it went to the gas tank. As part of the preadjudication report, the judge had asked for a psychiatric evaluation, which the parents would have to initiate. Both Mr. and Mrs. Moorhead came in as if it were they who were the subjects of the hearing. Both were indignant that they would have to be involved, refused permission for the psychiatric evaluation, and vowed to fight legal action with every resource they had. Although he wasn't really aware of much of Billy's life, Mr. Moorhead had an evident and deep identification with

Billy. In many ways he was afraid the court would take over his parental role. This prevented him from coming to terms with the implications of Billy's behavior and seeing Billy's need. It was as if he were on trial. Mrs. Moorhead supported her husband's resistance to the court process. With considerable empathy the social worker listened carefully, reflected and clarified what they were saying, gently pointed out the danger for others, and gradually over several sessions helped them to deal with the inevitable realities of Billy's situation, and correspondingly with theirs. Eventually they began to see Billy's needs separate from their own and began to work with the court, giving permission for an evaluation with their own psychiatrist. When the results pointed out a deep and serious disturbance, they again went into crisis. The social worker was gradually, over time and with much struggle, able to help them to work in partnership with the court to deal with Billy's needs.

Approximately one-third of juvenile courts have initiated intensive supervision programs (Barton, 1995; Krisberg, Rodriguez, Bakke, Neuenfeldt & Steele, 1989, in Barton). These programs may be used for youngsters with more complex needs, or, in some serious cases, as an alternative to residential correctional placement. Intensive supervision might mean as much as daily, rather than monthly, meetings. Furthermore, many juvenile correctional settings are now developing a mix of residential placement and home placement with community supervision. The court, through the probation officer, then becomes a type of case manager, using a variety of approaches such as community-based residential programs, training schools, "boot camps," and so on. Since the family is often involved in different ways with the situation, many of these approaches work with the family. Often one part of the problem is the confused parental subsystem after the loss of a parent.

CASE STUDY 9.5

His mother found Julio Chavez, fourteen, impossible to control after her boyfriend, Allen Bell, moved in. When Julio got into trouble, Mrs. Chavez asked Mr. Bell to take over Julio. Julio has never accepted Mr. Bell. The trou-

bles only escalated the more Mr. Bell got involved. When the police called on suspicion that Julio stole and sold some merchandise, Julio had cursed Mr. Bell and refused to talk about it to him. Mr. Bell punched Julio repeatedly when he wouldn't respond to him or respect his authority.

A program that is often effective with early-stage offenders is parent training (Patterson, 1982; Bank, Marlow, Reid, Patterson, & Weinrott, 1991). In a series of group-oriented classes, parents practice and learn techniques of making consistent rules, enforcing them consistently, establishing positive and negative consequences, and effective communication. These techniques are generally effective with adolescents. Even more than learning effective techniques of responding to their adolescent, the very fact of taking a class together can assist parents to clarify an appropriate family structure, and to respond to and communicate with their youngster. Similar to the Friedman example (case study 8.2) in Julio's situation, Mrs. Chavez cannot simply put Mr. Bell in charge and withdraw. She needs to take a more active role and use the support of the court to help Julio deal with its expectations and hers as well. Together they could stabilize the situation.

In the Pollack/Rush situation, a combined approach involving parent training, family sessions, and a community-based institutional program was used.

CASE STUDY 9.6

Daniel and Kevin Pollack, age ten and twelve, had a history of numerous station adjustments for delinquent behavior and running away. In school

there were behavior problems in the classroom and poor academic performance. Most recently, the boys burned down a garage in their neighborhood. The home is "chaotic." Mrs. Rush admitted that she had not provided the structure and limit setting the boys needed while growing up. She attributed this to the confusion in the family surrounding the divorce five years ago from their father, George Pollack. She never was able to take over with the boys. The father has always undercut Mrs. Rush. Now he is mostly intoxicated when he visits at all. Mrs. Rush has felt increasingly overwhelmed and powerless. She and the stepfather needed help, as well as Daniel and Kevin.

The boys were placed in a residence for ninety days, for an initial study. The residence recommended to the court that long-term placement be considered. The court, the child welfare agency, and the father decided to try family treatment with the goal of family reunification. They developed a service contract with the parents and Daniel and Kevin. Parent and stepparent would go for intensive parent training. There would be visitation and weekly family sessions. The family sessions reinforced the parenting classes and encouraged Mrs. Rush to take charge with the support of Mr. Rush. The focus on Daniel and Kevin's issues helped her gradually to let go of some of the issues left over from the divorce. Now with the boys at home, the parents have been more consistent in setting limits and providing structure. Daniel and Kevin's running away has ceased. The school reports have been more positive. So far there has been no delinquent behavior, although the boys do test limits, disobey, and "talk back." The entire situation will be reviewed at the next court hearing.

Social Work in Health Care

Social work has nearly a century of history in health care. In 1905, Dr. Richard Cabot introduced medical social workers at Massachusetts General Hospital to help patients deal with personal and social factors that affect disease onset and recovery (Poole, 1995). Cabot believed that medicine and social work were branches split off the same trunk—the care of people in trouble (Carlton, 1984). With the stress of disease in both chronic and acute health conditions, there is often a corresponding loss of social functioning. On the other hand, problems in social functioning often result in health problems. Thus the purpose of direct social work practice in health care is to enhance, promote, maintain, and restore the best possible social functioning of individuals, families, or small groups when their social functioning is affected by actual or potential stress caused by illness, disability, or injury (Poole, 1995).

Birthing, dying, struggling with loss of one's family role brought on by illness or disability, caring for an elderly parent—these are all family issues as well as issues in health care. Similarly, one person's serious illness or special need can affect the entire family. Social functioning is intertwined with the stresses related to illness, disability, injury, or medical processes themselves. Social functioning is also related to family functioning, and thus the social worker in health care often works with families. We saw some of the personal and family issues surrounding the increasing disability of parents in the O'Conner family in case study 7.9. The stress of illness in the grandparents' generation affected the entire family. In the Jimenez family in the following case study, the needs for relational work early in the marriage were combined with the stresses of poverty, of being undocumented immigrants, of inability to speak the language of the country where they resided, and finally of the special needs and risks of their child, Teresa.

CASE STUDY 9.7

Teresa Jimenez is a four-year-old child with a deficiency of the enzyme PKU. When this deficiency is discovered at infancy, the child will normally need to go on a very specialized and expensive diet. The diet will prevent the otherwise inevitable retardation that accompanies the lack of this enzyme. Teresa's levels have been very low, an indication that she is not following her diet. Her parents, Manuel and Victoria, can apply for a state stipend to pay the cost of this special diet, but they are undocumented and they speak very little English. They are fearful that, if they applied for the stipend, they would be reported to the Immigration and Naturalization Service (INS) and deported.

Laura, a bilingual social worker and herself from a Latin American country, worked with the Jimenez family. As she got to know the family, more complexities unraveled. Mrs. Jimenez is so overwhelmed by the dilemmas they are facing, together with unresolved marital stress, that her first thought is to run away, to return home to her parents without Teresa. This would be effectively abandoning Teresa, since it is unlikely that Mrs. Jimenez would be able to return. She feels like a failure because she cannot feed her daughter well. They are afraid of the INS. She married in haste in Guatemala and left her family there, but never got to know

Manuel very well. She is young, close to her family, and she misses them. Manuel promised that things would be better, but he is always working. Even when he is free, he is moody and they do not communicate well. He can't understand why Teresa needs a special diet.

Laura started the helping process in the hospital with Victoria, but quickly moved to involve Manuel. This was not easy, since he was constantly working and seemed fearful and reluctant to get involved. In a joint interview, it became clear that their communication was very poor and full of confusion around Teresa's situation. The family's difficult economic conditions and the precariousness of the marriage made Teresa's needs even more difficult to face. Laura perceived that, in focusing with them on Teresa's situation, she was also focusing on Victoria's loneliness and lack of self-esteem, Manuel's issues with Victoria, the fears connected with being undocumented, and their problems in communication. She worked concretely on helping them to make the application for the stipend to pay for Teresa's special diet. They checked into the implications of receiving the grant with an advocacy foundation. When they learned it would not be reported to the INS, they did apply. However, Laura realized that much more was involved. When Victoria blurted out that she might go home to her parents,

Laura gently pointed out that it would be like ending the marriage and losing Teresa. Victoria herself knew she wouldn't be able to return from Guatemala. Did she really want to do that? Victoria started to cry and said she really didn't know what she wanted to do, but it all seemed so hopeless. Talking directly to Manuel, she encouraged him to reflect exactly what he had heard Victoria say. For the moment he shouldn't add his own feelings. He did reflect what Victoria was saying and his eyes filled with tears. Victoria had never seen him cry before. He had always been so strong and distant. Then Laura helped him to respond without anger or defensiveness, and Victoria reflected what he was saying. Their communication got a little better. Victoria agreed to wait on any decision. They met a number of times. After they received the grant, Teresa's condition started to improve. Laura referred them for marital counseling to a Spanish-speaking worker at Catholic Charities who specialized in work with Hispanic immigrants. They are continuing to work with Catholic Charities, and they check in from time to time with Laura when they visit the clinic. They still have difficulties, but things are better, and Teresa is better. She is looking forward to kindergarten next month.

As in the O'Conner family in case study 7.9, serious health problems faced by a family member have serious effects on the total network of family relationships. There are often major role shifts needed. In the face of poor communication, guilt, rigid perspectives on role, or a poorly developed relationship, these shifts may not take place. Accompanying the role shift, often lifestyle changes are needed. Illness and poor communication often shuts down a person's ability to act (agency), together with his or her ability to receive or give support to others (communion). Family members must find meaning in the illness and grieve for the many losses the illness causes. The challenge for the couple is helping the partners accept the changing situation, communicate about it, adjust to it, and balance their needs for agency and communion with the demands of the illness (Ruddy & McDaniel, 2003). In the face of Peter O'Conner's illness and disability and Maura's increasing difficulty with Parkinson's disease, neither the couple nor the broader family were able to manage the tasks. The same can be said of Manual and Victoria, as they faced Teresa's condition and the other stresses having to do with culture, marital history, and their undocumented status. Their human agency and communion in relation to the problem and the situation shut down. They stopped functioning as an effective family.

Social Work in Mental Health

There are few illnesses as stressful for social relationships, particularly within the family, as mental illness. This was recognized early in the history of social work. As social work in health care began, so also did social work in mental health.

Presently, social workers are nearly twice as prevalent in the mental health field as psychiatrists or psychologists (Ginsberg, 1992, p. 140), a ratio that has remained for at least a half century. Using an interdisciplinary approach, social workers provide direct treatment, case management, and family involvement in community mental health centers, hospitals, and residential centers. Although adapted to the particular problem, the service is not entirely different from social work in other areas. The case of Charlotte at the end of this chapter (case study 9.9) is a good example of this process.

A special contribution, often made by social workers, is psychoeducation for family members of patients exhibiting schizophrenia. Living with a schizophrenic family member often brings out anxiety and a sense of vulnerability in other family members. Without assistance and education about schizophrenia, family members would often try to confront the patient in episodes of high expressed emotion, criticism, hostility, or emotional overprotectiveness. These environmental stressers, as the patient would see them, often were related to a subsequent psychotic episode (Zubin & Spring, 1977). During the 1980s and more recently, effective models of psychoeducational interventions have been developed (Anderson, Reiss & Hogarty, 1986; Hogarty, Anderson, Reiss, Kornblith, Greenwald, Javan & Madeira, 1986; Hogarty, Anderson, Reiss, Kornblith, Greenwald, Ulrich & Carter, 1991) that could lower hospitalization rates or at least postpone this outcome. These interventions helped family members to develop coping strategies, lowered tensions, and increased the patient's medication compliance. These findings, initially reported among families of schizophrenic patients, have also been reported among families of patients with bipolar disorder. In any case, educating a couple about what behaviors of the ill partner or child can and cannot be attributed to the disorder, and enhancing their communication and problem-solving behavior in the aftermath of an episode, have the potential to improve their functioning and reduce the seriousness of episodes (Miklowitz & George, 2003, p. 679).

In the case of the Maxwell family in case study 7.7, the social worker helped Mary Maxwell respond to the parts of John's verbalizations that were not psychotic, but to avoid engagement with his talk when it turned psychotic. It became something of a game that John himself recognized and encouraged. He pointed out himself that he didn't want Mary to take him seriously when crazy parts took over. Since most of the time he made a good deal of sense, it wasn't difficult to recognize an abrupt switch in communication and wait for his more in-touch parts to come back. They always did, particularly when Mary didn't involve herself with the other parts.

Although most mental health services are carried out in the community, sometimes a patient requires hospitalization for an extended period. In the case of Jack C. part of the approach to the family was psychoeducational. Another part of the approach was to assist family members, particularly Jack's wife, Barbara, to accommodate Jack in a meaningful role upon his return from the hospital and develop a more workable family structure.

CASE STUDY 9.8

Jack had spent several months in the hospital when he exhibited symptoms of severe schizophrenia. During the years leading up to his hospitalization, his role in the family had gradually become marginalized. His wife, Barbara, herself somewhat depressed, became centralized in the family. Having difficulty taking on a parental role alone, she acted more like an older sister than a parent to their two daughters, Marie and Ann, now twelve and fourteen, respectively. The girls would fight all the time, and Barbara felt helpless to manage the problems. In fact, the fighting seemed to bring on Barbara's helplessness and her sense of hurt and depression, and vice versa. Before Jack returned home from the hospital to day treatment, George, their social worker in the community mental health center, suggested Barbara attend some group sessions for families of patients with schizophrenia that George was running. With coaching from George and help from other relatives of patients, Barbara developed a low-key approach to relations with Jack. George had been particularly concerned that Barbara's deep identity with her daughters, coming out of her own loneliness and depression, was inappropriately empowering the daughters, isolating Jack, and could cause an explosive situation in the future.

Jack was willing and ready to work in a family format regarding some of the shifts needed upon his return to the family. So George set up a family session with Jack, Barbara, and their two daughters Ann and Marie. Initially the session was chaotic. Barbara focused on her personal problems and concerns, and the girls started fighting. At the same time, Barbara tended to unite with the girls in their resentment of Jack and reinforce their rebellion. Jack and Barbara would find themselves in disagreement about the girls, while the girls would ignore both of them. Jack felt disqualified as a father. He would be watching a program on television. One of the girls would simply switch the channel to her preferred program and then complain that "He always wants to watch what he wants on TV." When conflict erupted, Jack and Barbara said the girls were beginning to hit them at home. Both were intimidated by the hitting and unsure what to do.

In the initial family session, rather than focus on Barbara's complaints, or Ann and Marie's fighting, George focused on Jack and Barbara. The family was in chaos. What could they do as parents about it? Barbara's response was to identify her resentment that Jack was away so long. What could she do? George responded by normalizing the stress they were all feeling at the time. Jack was gone. Things got very difficult before his hospitalization. Now Jack is back. We know that when parents work together, things do get a little bit better. He asked Barbara to talk to Jack about how he could help her now. The girls started to giggle as Barbara started to talk to Jack. George calmly intervened, saying that if the girls wanted to stay, they needed to let their mother and dad talk about this. Barbara was hesitant, but for the rest of the session Barbara and Jack did try to communicate and develop a tentative alliance, while the girls periodically interrupted and tried to redirect the interaction to themselves. Barbara and Jack eventually succeeded in keeping them on the sidelines while they made tentative efforts to communicate.

George was very active in supporting both parents in their very tentative communication with each other and their efforts to keep the girls on the sidelines. This family interview set the tone for a family process that went on for several months. Much of the work was done between Jack and Barbara, with the girls coming in for occasional sessions. Barbara needed help to let Jack gently back into the parts of his role that he could handle, and to communicate without high emotion, hostility, or the need to control Jack. As crises alleviated, George continued to educate Barbara and Jack on communication and management skills effective when one person has schizophrenia. Although there were still conflicts, testing of limits, and a tendency for Barbara to align with her girls against Jack, there were also more and more episodes of Barbara and Jack working together on issues. There was a relation between Jack's improvement and the improvement in the family situation. Eventually Jack was able to find a job, but continued his treatment. The family sessions became monthly check-ins. Barbara and Jack joined a couples' group.

The social worker employed two approaches with Barbara and Jack's family. He helped the family make a structural shift. Barbara, chaotically aligned with the girls and hardly able to exert appropriate parental controls, realigned with Jack with the worker's support. Barbara needed Jack's support, but couldn't place too much pressure on him. The worker also took a psychoeducational approach with both. The worker's support, the structural shifts, and the skill training would be crucial in the family managing its crisis.

Outpatient Work in Mental Health

At other times in outpatient situations, the social worker, as a key member of the psychiatric team, takes major responsibility for work with patients who are also working with individual and family issues. Charlotte DesJardins was struggling with issues connected with differentiation and connectedness with her family as she was moving toward independence.

CASE STUDY 9.9

Charlotte DesJardins, age twenty-three, became severely depressed and suicidal in the middle of her college experience. She is the second of three children in a prominent but somewhat emotionally disengaged African-American family in New Orleans. She left college, came home, and got a job in a restaurant. Charlotte's return home with failing grades was met with anger, resentment, and hopelessness by her parents. In response, Charlotte became even more withdrawn and spent most of her time at home in her room and away from her parents. Unable to continue at the restaurant job with her depression, she took a leave of absence and received outpatient treatment from the psychiatric clinic at Samaritan Hospital. Dr. Smith put Charlotte on antidepressants and checked up with her periodically. Charlotte did most of her work with her social worker, Astrid. Astrid encouraged her to talk about her feelings and thoughts about the complex situation she faced at home. She needed to deal with her isolation, develop a support system, and take steps to alleviate her severe depression. Since Charlotte had extreme difficulty with verbal expression, she was encouraged to write down her thoughts and feelings in a daily journal. Therapeutic discussion often focused on these entries. Charlotte recontacted two old friends and began an exercise program at the YMCA.

Faithful about her medication and her individual sessions, after six weeks she was able to return to work. Charlotte was very confused about the direction of her life. She wondered if she should return to college or find a career. She felt like the "failure" in her high-achieving family, particularly in comparison with her younger sister, Eloise, age nineteen, whom she saw as vivacious, intelligent, "successful in everything," and going to college. Charlotte felt emotionally isolated from her family, dependent, and unable to assert herself in both familial and extrafamilial situations. She wanted to become independent and eventually move out and establish a life of her own, but didn't feel she could. She had never told her family about her problems. Only with

considerable help and repeated role plays with Astrid was she able to tell her mother and her sister about some of her concerns and needs. No one had informed her father, and Charlotte was afraid to talk to him. She would feel even more like a failure. Her mother was willing to participate in a family session, but the session was postponed until Charlotte had told her father. He was already peripheral to the family, and it would not be desirable to reinforce this.

Charlotte did tell her father, but only after she told Matthew, her thirty-year-old brother who was living at home after a divorce. Matthew and Charlotte told her father together. Her father, a high-powered lawyer, did something entirely unpredictable. He started to cry and blame himself for what had happened with Charlotte and with Matthew. He should have spent more time with them. He related that there were so many things going on in this family that no one ever talked about. Charlotte was deeply touched by this entirely unexpected response. The family session took place with the mother, the father, Matthew, and Charlotte. Eloise was away at college, but her absence also allowed a clear focus on Matthew's and Charlotte's concerns. The session was difficult, with a lot of underlying tension and blaming, particularly between the mother and father. The family had never talked to each other about these issues before. Astrid needed to be very active in framing out and setting boundaries on their communication. She would normalize feelings and issues that had been latent and undiscussed for so many years. The four sessions they had were almost too much for them. As a result, Charlotte developed a somewhat closer relationship with her father and brother. The mother and father began marital counseling. Charlotte continued to make progress on her depression. She decided to get training as a paralegal, and after two years found an apartment of her own and left home comfortably. Her father and brother helped her move.

WORKING BETWEEN FAMILIES AND COMMUNITY RESOURCE NETWORKS

Recently, human service reforms have sought to break down barriers between categorical programs and make formal service systems more responsive to families, communities, and diverse cultures. The theme of integration of educational, health, and social welfare services now reverberates through local, state, and national dialogues. Certain basic principles run through these discussions and experiments. They are:

1. Services are to be designed and delivered with respect for the diverse cultures of clients, or, to use the term more predominant in reform language, "customers." "Culturally competent" practices are required by policies to ensure that human services help recipients utilize the strengths in their cultural traditions and institutions.
2. Services are to empower families to take active roles in the design, implementation, and evaluation of programs that serve them.
3. Services are to prevent problems from occurring, rather than to respond to problems only after the fact.
4. Services are to be accessible to people in the neighborhoods where they live.
5. Services are to be linked in comprehensive strategies, drawing on multifaceted resources from mental health, health, economic development, delinquency prevention, and other traditionally separate fields.
6. Services are to conduct assessments and provide interventions that address the problems and resources of whole families, rather than of individuals only.
7. Services are to emphasize the strengths, or "assets," of the communities in which they are located, rather than stressing the deviance and deficiencies that might be present.[4]

These shared aspirations have called forth new institutional models for services. Many child welfare services and health and mental health services have positioned themselves in schools, both as individual agencies and as parts of broader, communitywide efforts. Many school reform strategies are also leading to the placement of human services in educational facilities. For example, federal goals for ed-

---

[4]See Kordesh & Constable (2002, p. 87). Adapted with permission.

ucational reform espouse the routine objective of having "every child ready to learn" by the time he or she reaches kindergarten. This objective has been used to justify many new preschool initiatives in schools. The goal of making schools safer has prompted more juvenile delinquency and prevention initiatives to be based in schools. The goal of increasing the job readiness of students has led to more integration of employment training and job counseling into the formal curriculum and in school-to-work programs. Moreover, health clinics and substance abuse prevention programs are increasingly repositioned into schools because they are seen as supportive of a healthy education setting. A vast array of methods for involving families in schools is being tested. More schools are experimenting with programs that keep them open into the evenings, on weekends, and during summers, allowing them to function as community centers for a wide range of populations with a wide range of services, rather than only as sites for classroom-based teaching.

Family centers create places in schools for whole families to receive services, to deliver mutual support to one another, and to deepen the involvement of parents in the school itself. Complex prevention initiatives take advantage of the fact that the school provides the best setting in which to reach the greatest numbers of children who are at risk of failure or have serious health or social problems. Brokered service networks reposition human services into schools in order to keep children in school and to allow teachers to focus on basic education. These are particularly important where there are multiple needs and underorganized families.

The family is central to the process that brings together family and child with school and community resources into an interagency team or "wraparound" ("wrap") team. The following cases illustrate work with the family and agency systems of a ten-year-old boy in school and two young adults in transition out of schools.

CASE STUDY 9.10

Danny is a ten-year-old African-American boy with pervasive developmental disorder. In class he was disruptive, showed poor attention to tasks even with assistance, showed very poor academic performance, was aggressive with other children, and tended to isolate himself from them. Danny seemed strange to other children and they were afraid of him. Having come recently from living in Germany, his father in military service, he spoke a mixture of English and German that wasn't easily understood by others. According to his paternal grandmother, with whom he lived, he had been developing reasonably well in early childhood, and walked and talked normally. Both parents have a history of severe drug and alcohol abuse. When he went to Germany he experienced severe physical abuse by his mother, neglect by his father, and was heavily involved in the military social service program for children. At the time of referral, his mother was in a residential substance abuse program; his father was still in the Army. Danny was being raised by his grandmother. She had given up her twenty-year business to take care of him.

The following agencies and individual services were involved with the case:

- The state child protection agency
- The state department of mental health
- The Adair School
- A big brother program
- A homemaker services agency
- Karate lessons from a community volunteer
- In-home therapy from a contract therapist especially trained in pervasive developmental disorders
- Tutoring twice a week

The state child protection agency sponsored the transagency team through the school and paid for the services provided through its LANS (local area network services) program. The grandmother was overwhelmed with all the services involved. The placement needed to be stabilized, particularly if either parent would return. There were differences within the team about whether Danny should remain in this placement or be hospitalized. The main goal at the moment was that Danny maintain himself at school and that the home continue to provide appropriate parenting, belonging, and security for him. This was beginning to happen, although the situation both at home and at school, was very delicate. The team, including the grandmother, met monthly, to discuss and work out issues.

The major tasks of the team were to support the grandmother's parenting of Danny and to work out agency issues with each other. These were both quite difficult and time consuming. When the grandmother did strengthen her coping, Danny did somewhat better. However, at this time the father came back from Germany and the mother came out of her residential substance abuse program. The grandmother became uncertain of her role again, and Danny regressed. When it was resolved that the grandmother would remain in charge with the father supporting and the mother visiting, the grandmother strengthened her coping again and Danny did better in his long-term process of development.

The following two cases involve the transition out of school of young adults with severe disabilities.[5] They imply a possible continuation of the transagency team, this time for adults with disabilities:

CASE STUDY 9.11

Doris was an eighteen-year-old adolescent with severe psychological disturbance. Her reactivity to a symbiotic conflict with her mother and resultant self-destructive behavior has led to several hospitalizations. Whenever there was a possible separation from mother, she showed increased disturbance. The school had found itself reacting to the behavior and programming for Doris alone, rather than getting the mother and daughter into contact with help. The mother and daughter began with a social worker in private practice. The school brought Doris into a one-hour-per-day class in

---

[5] Adapted from Kordesh and Constable (2002b, pp. 400–401). Used with permission.

ceramics with only the instructor present. When this was eventually established without incident, Doris became involved with a pet zoo run by another agency. Because the situation between the mother and daughter was potentially explosive, a shelter arrangement with a relative to be used in a crisis was worked out. It was used occasionally. This arrangement kept Doris in the community. The social worker worked with Doris and her mother, supporting each as separate persons with separate problem-solving abilities. When the social worker made make further gains with the mother and Doris' school adjustment stabilized, the next step was to develop a program with the state department of vocational rehabilitation. The state agency was involved in the plan and agreed to give special consideration to Doris' needs.

CASE STUDY 9.12

Michael was a twenty-one-year-old severe and barely stabilized diabetic, legally blind, who lived in a nursing home because his single working parent was unable to care for him. He was about to graduate from his special education program because of his age. A plan was developed in the wrap team to make it possible for Michael to return home by using public assistance, Medi-caid, and homemaker and home health care services to support him when his mother was working. Some further medical and vocational assessment was done. The social worker from the school worked with Michael and his mother, coordinating with other agencies. When the two had solidified their own direction and connections with other services, the social worker passed case management responsibilities onto another agency.

Although such cases present complex needs and will take work over a span of years, they are not particularly unusual. A combination of resources could prevent institutionalization or make movement from an institutionalized setting possible. Furthermore, none of the "hard" service provision, no matter how flexible, could have been effective or even possible without the "soft" services to parents and children that helped them deal with the situation and link their processes and needs with programs and resources. To make complex plans for families without their choice, involvement, and participation—indeed, not to make the individual-in-family-unit the center of the decision process is to court disaster and set up an unproductive struggle around power and control. In addition to highly skilled family-oriented work, the social worker is a member of the interagency team, a colleague, and a consultant to others on the team.

SUMMARY

Our discussion of the helping process with families and outside service institutions, such as schools, courts, and health care institutions is necessarily brief. It illustrates the general parameters of practice with families in the context of social institutions. There are other sources that adequately illustrate social work in particular fields of practice (see, for instance, Carlton, 1984; Constable & Walberg, 2002). These sources develop the nature of a particular field of social work practice. The systems concept and the concept of relational justice are extended to the family's relationship with outside social institutions. Without these internal and external connections, families could not maintain themselves.

REFERENCES

Anderson, C. M., Reiss, D. J., & Hogarty, G. E. (1986). *Schizophrenia and the family: A practitioner's guide to psychoeducation and management.* New York: Guilford.

Bailey, D., Blasco, P., & Simeonson, R. (1992). Needs expressed by mothers and fathers of young children with disabilities. *American Journal on Mental Retardation, 97,* 1–10.

Baker, K. A. (1999). The importance of cultural sensitivity and therapist self-awareness in working with involuntary clients. *Family Process, 38*(1), 55–68.

Bank, L., Marlowe, J. H., Reid, J. B., Patterson, G. R., & Weinrott, M. R. (1991). A comparative evaluation of parent-training interventions for families of chronic dropouts. *Journal of Abnormal and Child Psychology, 19,* 15–33.

Barton, W. H. (1995). Juvenile corrections. In R. L. Edwards & J. G. Hopps (Eds.), *Encyclopedia of social work* (19th ed., pp. 1563–77). Washington, DC: National Association of Social Workers.

Bartlett, H. (1971). *The common base of social work practice.* New York: National Association of Social Workers.

Bernier, J. (1990). Parental adjustment to a disabled child: A family system perspective. *Families in Society, 71,* 589–596.

Bristol, M. M., & Gallagher, J. J. (1982). A family focus for intervention. In C. T. Ramey & P. L. Trohanis (Eds.), *Finding and educating high-risk and handicapped infants* (pp. 137–161). Baltimore: University Park Press.

Carlton, T. (1984). *Clinical social work in health settings: A guide to professional practice with exemplars.* New York: Springer.

Christensen, S. L., & Sheridan, S. M. (2001). *Schools and families: Creating essential connections for learning.* New York: Guilford.

Constable, R. T., & Walberg, H. (2002). Working with families. In R. T. Constable, S. McDonald, & J. P. Flynn (Eds.), *School social work: Practice, policy and research perspectives.* Homewood, IL: Dorsey.

Everett, J. E. (1995). Child foster care. In R. L. Edwards & J. G. Hopps (Eds.), *Encyclopedia of Social Work* (19th ed., pp. 375–389). Washington, DC: National Association of Social Workers.

Frey, K., Greenberg, M., & Fewell, R. (1989). Stress and coping among parents of handicapped children: A multidimensional approach. *American Journal on Mental Retardation, 95,* 240–249.

Ginsberg, L. (1992). *Social work almanac.* Washington, DC: National Association of Social Workers.

Gordon, W. E. (1969). Basic concepts for an integrative and generative concept of social work. In G. Hearn (Ed.), *The general systems approach: Contributions toward an holistic conception of social work.* New York: Council on Social Work Education.

Gordon, W. E. (1979). *The working definition of social work practice: The interface between man and environment, 1979.* Paper presented at the Council on Social Work Education Annual Program Meeting, Boston, MA.

Hanson, M. J., & Carta, J. J. (1995). Addressing the challenges of families with multiple risks. *Exceptional Children, 62*(3), 201–212.

Hanson, M. J., & Hanline, M. (1990). Parenting a child with a disability: A longitudinal study of parental stress and adaptation. *Journal of Early Intervention, 14,* 234–248.

Hartman, A., & Laird, J. (1983). Family centered social work practice. New York: Free Press.

Hogarty, G. E., Anderson, C. M., Reiss, D. J., Kornblith, S. J., Greenwald, D. P., Javna, D., & Maderia, J. J. (1986). Family psycho-education, social skills training: One year effects of a controlled maintenance chemotherapy in aftercare study treatment of schizophrenia on relapse and adjustment. *Archives of General Psychiatry, 43,* 633–642.

Hogarty, G. E., Anderson, C. M., Reiss, D. J., Kornblith, S. J., Greenwald, D. P., Ulrich, R. F., & Carter, M. (1991). Family psycho-education, social skills training and maintenance chemotherapy in the aftercare treatment of schizophrenia: Two year effects of a controlled study treatment on relapse and adjustment. *Archives of General Psychiatry, 48,* 340–347.

Joint NASW—CSWE Task Force on Specialization (Joint Task Force). (1979). Specialization in the Social Work Profession (NASW Document no. 79-310-08) Washington, DC: NASW.

Kelleghan, T., Sloane, K., Alvarez, B., & Bloom, B. S. (1993). *The home environment and school learning.* San Francisco: Jossey-Bass.

Kinney, J., Haapala, D., & Booth, C. (1991). *Keeping families together: The homebuilders model.* New York: Aldine de Gruyter.

Kohs, S. C. (1966). *The roots of social work.* New York: Association Press.

Kordesh, R., & Constable, R. (2002a). Policies, programs and mandates for developing social services in the schools. In R. T. Constable, S. McDonald, & J. P. Flynn (Eds.), *School social work: Practice, policy and research perspectives* (pp. 83–100). Chicago: Lyceum.

Kordesh, R., & Constable, R. (2002b). Case management, coordination of services and resource development. In R. T. Constable, S. McDonald, & J. P. Flynn (Eds.), *School social work: Practice, policy and research perspectives* (pp. 385–403). Chicago: Lyceum.

Krisberg, B., Rodriguez, O., Bakke, A., Neuenfeldt, D., & Steele, P. (1989). Demonstration of post adjudication, nonresidential, intensive supervision programs: Assessment report. San Francisco: National Conference on Crime and Delinquency.

Leiderman, D. S. (1995). Child welfare overview. In R. L. Edwards & J. G. Hopps   AU: Page #
    (Eds.), *Encyclopedia of social work* (19th ed., pp. 00–00). Washington, DC:
    National Association of Social Workers.
Litwak E., & Meyer, H. (1966). A balance theory of coordination between bureau-
    cratic organizations and community primary groups. *Administrative Science
    Quarterly, 11* (June) 31–58.
Maas, H., & Engler, R. (1959). *Children in need of parents.* New York: Columbia.
Miklowitz, D. L., & George, E. L. (2003). Couple therapy complicated by a bio-
    logically based psychiatric disorder. In A. S. Gurman & N. S. Jacobson (Eds.),
    Clinical handbook of couple therapy. New York: Guilford.
Patterson, G. (1982). *Coercive family process.* Eugene, OR: Castalia.
Pecora, P., Reed-Ashcraft, K., & Kirk, R. S. (2001). Family centered services. In E.
    Walten, P. Samdau-Beckler, & M. Mannes (Eds.), *Balancing family-centered
    services and child well being.* New York: Columbia.
Poole, L. (1995). Health care: Direct practice. In R. L. Edwards & J. G. Hopps
    (Eds.), *Encyclopedia of social work* (19th ed., pp. 1156–1167). Washington,
    DC: National Association of Social Workers.
Ruddy, N. B., & McDaniel, S. H. (2003). Couple therapy and medical issues:
    Working with couples facing illness. In A. S. Gurman & N. S. Jacobson (Eds.),
    Clinical handbook of couple therapy. New York: Guilford.
Smalley, R. (1967). *Theory for social work practice.* New York: Columbia.
Triseliotis, J., Shireman, J., & Hundleby, M. (1997). *Adoption: Theory, policy &
    practice.* London: Cassell.
U.S. Department of Education. (2002). *23rd Annual Report to Congress on Special
    Education* (Table D. c3, Appendix, part II) Washington, DC: Author.
Walberg, H. J. (1984). Improving the productivity of America's schools. *Educa-
    tional Leadership, 41*(8), 19–27.
Walberg, H. J., & Lai, J. (1999). Meta-analytic effects for policy. In G. J. Cizek
    (Ed.), *Handbook of educational policy* (pp. 418–454). San Diego, CA: Acade-
    mic Press.
Wang, M. C., Haertl, G. D., & Walberg, H. J. (1998). *Building educational re-
    silience.* Bloomington, IN: Phi Delta Kappan Educational Foundation.
Webster-Stratten, C. (1993). Strategies for helping children with oppositional defi-
    ant and conduct disorders: The importance of home-school partnerships.
    School Psychology Review, 22, 437–457.
Wolkow, H. (2002). The dynamics of systems involvement with children in school:
    A case perspective. In R. T. Constable, S. McDonald, & J. P. Flynn (Eds.),
    School social work: Practice, policy and research perspectives (pp. 364–370).
    Chicago: Lyceum.
Zubin, J., & Spring, B. (1977). Vulnerability: A new view of schizophrenia. *Journal
    of Abnormal Psychology, 86,* 103–126.

CHAPTER 10

Ending Processes with Families

The ending process can be understood as the completion of all that has gone before. Endings are made by couples, by families, and by institutions with the assistance of the social worker. This process is outlined as a final review of the content and process of working with families.

SOCIAL WORKERS AND THE ENDING PROCESS

The social worker is like a temporary steersman who for a time helps crews to guide a ship through difficult waters or to a safe harbor, and then moves on as he or she is no longer needed. For the family, an ending is first of all a milestone marking a transition, and then it is an ending with the guide who has helped them steer through the shoals. It is only for the social worker that an ending process is fully an ending. In the best of circumstances, family members begin to invest themselves in coping together with a problem that up to this point has mystified them. They may have felt hopeless about any possibility of change. Perhaps some changes did occur, and now they face different circumstances. It may be that the hoped-for changes did not occur and they have to modify their expectations, even give up on what they hoped would take place. Whether or not they have achieved a change, they face an altered set of possibilities.

A chapter on ending processes is rightfully brief because it presupposes and builds on all that has gone before. The ending processes with a family also are a test of all that has gone before: of whether family members, and the family as a unit, have been able to take charge of their experience and make changes together. This is the relational work of the family. The work of the social worker is mainly to help them do it in a way that reinforces their ability to function relatively independently and recognize the new unit that has emerged in the helping process. In the best possible circumstances, the family has sufficiently accomplished the tasks in the work they started so that they can move on. They have been able to finish their tasks with the social worker. The social worker assists the family to finish a process they have begun and begin a new phase in their lives together. The family holding system, formed out of the communication and the agreements of the sessions, is ready to set sail. The experiences and memories of communication, the agreements, the altered patterns and structures become the maps and the charts, the points of reference to deal with the fog and the inevitable storms without a collision and without sinking. Often endings may be tested out over time. In preparation for an ending, the family may meet every month, then every two months, then as needed. In some cases—such as a family with a member with long-term problems such as schizophrenia or bipolar disorder—there are many endings for a time, but there will be other beginnings also.

Other endings are abrupt and unplanned, and the social worker has to work quickly to help the family system establish closure. In other situations it is not possible to establish closure (Walsh, 2003). In these situations the concept "ending" becomes a relative term, an ending for a time. In any case, the family unit continues in one way or another. Nothing has changed except the social worker's part of it, which is now a memory. Although there is a sense of loss in every ending, there are few total endings. Other tasks quickly emerge in the transition.

In many Western cultures, endings take place in a fairly structured way. With relationships closer to each other than with the social worker, family members are ready to move on and out. In other cultures, such as with the J. family (case study 4.7) discussed in chapter 4 and also later in this chapter, the relationship with the social worker could be expected to stretch out over a longer period. The family had made a tremendous change. The social worker had assisted them to reorganize themselves. They reinforced these relationships, and the changes they had made, through periodic check-ins with the social worker.

Ending with the social worker may take place when family members have achieved "good enough" growth in the areas specified in the initial contract. It is useful to return to table 1.2 to examine the basic human needs that the family can support: safety; belonging; communication; the capacity to choose, to be concerned for self and others; and the capacity to grow, to interact, and to take care of self and others. In a particular sense, these areas become themes of every interview, set and revised by the social worker and the family unit. They are the work of the interview. They are also goals to accomplish through the whole of the social worker's work with a family. They are briefly evaluated every time the social worker asks the family how the previous week has been. They indicate whether things are moving in the right direction, whether a modification of course is called for, and whether it is time to wrap up. In this sense, a certain ending process that establishes closure takes place at the end of each session.

Endings with individual clients are quite different from endings with family groups. For Gloria, the Philippine nurse of case study 2.1, the ending was very difficult.

CASE STUDY 2.1 REVISITED

For Gloria, ending with the social worker meant coming to terms with the impossibility of her obsessions and forging a satisfying life for herself in her circumstances. For a long time, the social worker had been her cognitive steersman, and now she was ready to go on without this relationship. As Gloria developed her own cognitive functioning, the ending took about six months of direct planning to establish closure. Her new realism and her good feelings about her achievements were circumscribed by her feelings that she was losing a good friendship. She questioned whether, if it had to end, it was a real friendship at all. When she came to the understanding that in the heart and mind friendship doesn't end even when people don't see each other, she was able to let go and move on.

Endings with families are different because, if successful, the intensity of the friendship with the social worker has been absorbed by other family members with each other. The focus on relational tasks and family interaction, with the family in charge and the social worker as a mentor/coach, makes it easier for the family to let go and move on. In Gloria's situation, the depth of the relationship demanded a great deal of work to let go and establish closure. In contrast, the social worker who works with families is from the beginning assisting them to test what they can do with each other through between-session tasks. As family members discover the possibility of improved relationships, the ending is placed in the context of their growing affirmation with each other. The social worker is no longer as necessary.

Indications for Ending

There are a variety of indications for ending. The first and most obvious indication for ending is that the changes agreed upon in the first session have been sufficiently accomplished for the family to be able to operate on its own. Family members are ready to try these relationships on their own, and they are both fearful and excited about this prospect. There may be a loss of the relationship with the social worker, but there is a gain in their relationships with each other. As in the J. family (case study 4.7), these changes don't have to result in a total revision of the family's relational structure, only enough to go on effectively and continue the process.

Endings with Couples

Among couples we have already discussed were Brian and Lisa (case study 2.5), Joseph and Paula (case study 6.3), and Ashford and Louise (case study 6.6). These couples, stuck at different family life-cycle stages, moved on to resolve conflicts inherent in the demands of the stage. There was a natural ending when the work could likely be completed on their own.

CASE STUDY 2.5 REVISITED

Brian had made progress sorting out personal issues with a previous life style, an old girlfriend, and patterns of binge drinking. Lisa had made progress with her tendency to depression and to spill the depression over to the relationship, and progress with her to need to control. Both found their own relationship with each other reinforcing and invested themselves in the work they had to do to get married. In the last session, both were excited about planning for an apartment and their common life together.

CASE STUDY 6.3 REVISITED

Joseph and Paula continued to work on personal issues of drinking and depression. Each found energy for their relationship with each other as long as they could work on personal issues and there was a little wall of protection. Their twin daughters, now young adolescents, wondered what was happening with their father and mother now that they seemed to be enjoying each other's company.

CASE STUDY 6.6 REVISITED

Ashford and Louise took a trip West together. This was for them the honeymoon they had never had. They argued at times, but they were able to use what they learned about communication to work out some of their issues. When they returned they had one further session. Louise had gone back to her garden, Ashford to his church work, and both in their own ways were including their adult children in their lives. They were excited about all of this and felt comfortable in what they had achieved.

Endings with Families

When children become one focus of help, a shift and realignment inevitably occurs over two generations and the realignment involves both parents and children. The ending reflects this realignment.

CASE STUDY 10.1

Becky, a sixteen-year-old girl, the oldest of an Orthodox Jewish family of four, is a very talented violinist. Becky resembles her father in many ways, including his love for music and his quiet temperament. The two have always been close without needing to acknowledge this with words. Last year she had moved from a private, religious school to a new public high school to get better music instruction. Her mother and father felt that she changed profoundly that year. She had begun to go with a very different crowd, some of whom were acting out sexually. She began to lie to her father and mother. Her mother, an intense, loving, but somewhat controlling person, had an explosive reaction to Becky's lying. The more explosive and controlling the mother became, the more Becky withdrew. Becky's withdrawal drew out the extreme reaction from her mother, and things went from bad to worse. Becky's father quietly withdrew, but felt disappointed by Becky. He felt helpless since he had been actively excluded from her mother's problem solving. In couple sessions, the mother and father developed better communication and were able to agree on a strategy about Becky. In family sessions, the mother learned to become less intrusive, and the father became more involved with his daughter. Becky learned to be both more candid with her mother and father about her concerns and fears of school. Becky was growing up, but that did not mean their basically strong relationships would be diminished. She also learned to take charge of her own choices of friends and gradually became less fearful of school. Ending took place over the first months of school when Becky, although anticipating she would be afraid, found some friends. Her mother managed her anxiety about Becky and found a better relationship that she could trust. Her father became a close resource for Becky when she had certain things to talk over. Their ending sessions were a "recital" and acknowledgment of what had happened. They were an affirmation by Becky that she could handle high school, although not without difficulty.

In some cultures, the ending needs to be stretched out with some relationships continuing. Nevertheless, the focus of the ending is on ending, on showing the social worker that they have changed and are able to handle new realities. They are grateful for all the social worker has done. In family members' minds, he or she is like a member of the family.

CASE STUDY 4.7 REVISITED

It has been approximately two years since the J. family and the social worker said goodbye to each other and the court released Mr. J. from supervision. Over the span of two years, every member of the J. family individually communicated appreciation of what the social worker had done for them collectively as well as personally. Chen brought the letter of reference forms to the social worker for her applications to several Ivy League schools. Kwak kept the social worker's e-mail address and sent him an additional progress report some time after the ending. Mrs. J. prepared a jar of health food as a token of her appreciation. Finally Mr. J. called the social worker on a Chinese holiday, wishing him the very best.

Difficult and Complex Endings

Some endings and transitions are difficult and complex because the relationship itself is complex and multifaceted, and the worker has had to be very active. The deeper the relationship, the more the ending may need to take place over a longer period. Here the understanding of endings, developed in work with individuals (Walsh, 2003), is most valuable. The ending with difficult situations becomes similar to the ending with Gloria.

CASE STUDY 10.2

Michael and Alyson are an African-American couple who have had a tumultuous first ten years of marriage. There have been numerous separations. Both have been involved in infidelities. There has been near constant conflict. Alyson's oldest child, Trisha, had been born when Alyson was fourteen and about five years before she had married Michael. With the birth of Trisha, Alyson never was really able to differentiate herself well as a person from a tight triangle between her mother, Anna, and Trisha. This triangle dominated her relationships during the early years of her marriage. She remained her mother's daughter, and her mother took care of Trisha. Trisha had always had a claim on Alyson prior to Michael. Alyson had little real relational space for Michael. Indeed, she felt pulled between her relationship with Trisha and with Michael. As Trisha grew older, this got worse, and the marriage was threatened. Alyson clearly could not handle Tricia and attend to her marriage at the same time. Eventually Anna became the caregiver for Trisha. Alyson took care of her three younger children and tried to reconstruct a relationship with Michael. Anna herself had been raised by her grandmother and she did not object to the arrangement, although Trisha gave her lots of problems. On the other hand, Trisha wasn't sure where she belonged. She actively shifted back and forth between her mother and her grandmother, depending on her desires and the level of conflict in the situation. The competition and the constant issues between Alyson and her mother created difficulties with Trisha. Trisha had many of the problems Alyson remembers having had herself as a teenager. There was a deep and conflictual identification between mother and daughter.

Michael had grown up as a foster child. He has no contact with his family of origin and regards his foster parents as his parents. He found Alyson's struggle to differentiate herself from her mother and from Trisha confusing. He never sensed he had a stable relationship with Alyson as a real person, but always as someone reacting to Trisha, or her mother, or at times overusing addictive substances. Very loyal to Alyson, he was never certain what to expect from her. He often became impatient with her difficulties, taking them on as his own. He had a tendency to become overresponsible for Alyson's problems, and this would leave Alyson in a position of a rebellious child.

The social worker worked with Michael and Alyson for two years, assisting the family unit to respond appropriately while Alyson was able to shift and rearrange her complex network of allegiances without losing herself. During this time the social worker did marital counseling, individual counseling with Michael and Alyson when necessary, and worked with Alyson's parents. The sessions with the grandparents took place with Alyson and Michael. In these two-couple sessions, Alyson, with Michael's support, worked out child-care arrangements for Trisha and did family-of-origin work with her parents. She worked closely with Alyson's psychiatrist and with Alyson when Alyson went through a severe depression with some psychotic features. Trisha had a long-term relationship with her own therapist and actually managed reasonably well when not subjected to the push and pull of Alyson's relationship with Anna or her relationship with Michael. The social worker coached Alyson in her relationship with Tricia. In the process, Michael and Alyson showed considerable improvement. Alyson gradually learned to deal with her complex triangulated relationship with Trisha and her mother, and also to invest herself in her relationship with Michael and with their other three children. She became very consistent in taking her medication and became predictable to Michael. Michael felt able to respond to her. Their relationship, now much better, was reinforcing to Alyson, so that they began talking about getting a home. When Trisha had problems, Alyson would no longer get caught in a triangle with Anna. Trisha did better with this. She learned to remain close to her mother and Anna in different ways.

The ending process took several months. The relationship with the social worker had become a holding system for everyone. Alyson was able to take steps to manage the relationship with her mother over Trisha so that joint sessions were no longer necessary. At

first neither Alyson nor Michael, nor Anna, believed they would ever succeed on their own as a couple. The act of settling their chaotic financial affairs and looking for a home became a way of testing out the steadiness of their relationship. They moved to interviews every other week and then monthly. In their final contact it was understood they could return when needed. They had developed communication and problem-solving skills and were able to recognize what they had done together.

In some cases the ending is complex because some of the issues remain and will remain, and the family continues to come to terms with these continuing realities, as with John and Mary Maxwell's situation, discussed in case study 7.7.

CASE STUDY 7.7 REVISITED

John and Mary Maxwell and Stephen's situation had a natural ending over about five months. This took place during the summer after Stephen's graduation, prior to his entry into the Army, and extending several months after he entered. During the summer he got a job and gradually learned to take responsibility with their pickup truck. As he waited for a September induction, there was a reduction of conflict. However, John and Mary were more anxious than Stephen until he was inducted. Their relationship remained quite tense. After Stephen was inducted, their concern and anxiety shifted to Mike, his younger brother. This time, however, their experiences with Stephen and the assistance of the worker helped them to manage their concerns about Mike without provoking a destructive reaction from him.

As the boys' problems became less pressing, John and Mary then had to deal with the natural limitations and possibilities of their relationship and their empty nest issues. Facing gradually the limitations and possibilities of their own relationship, they began to feel they had accomplished all they could in couples counseling. It wasn't heaven, but they would manage with each other. Later John's physical condition became life-threatening. He stayed in occasional touch with the social worker to discuss his marital issues and his personal issues as he faced death, as needed. Mary had saved his life when he was found with a blood clot in his leg, and this began a new relationship with her. He began to see her differently from his grandmother, whom he had feared and hated. His contacts with the social worker became the completion of the life narrative he had begun so long ago.

Often, the closer the relationship of the social worker with particular members of the family, the more difficult the ending. With casework relationships of some depth, it is fairly normal to experience termination reactions; this is well discussed in the literature (Hepworth, Rooney & Larson, 1997, pp. 597–615; Shulman, 1992, pp. 164–169). In the one-to-one relationship of some depth, ending inevitably is experienced as a great loss. In these circumstances, it is not unusual for clients to regress, to display anger at the social worker, to deny that an ending might take place, and to deny that they have accomplished anything. The social worker needs to normalize these feelings, give the persons a chance to express and deal with them, help clients to recount what they have accomplished, and help them to realize that they can take all of what they accomplished with them. Family work is different since their relationship itself becomes the holding system. If this system, although problematic, gets better, a loss of the social worker's relationship may not be so devastating. When strong regressions, anger, or denial are characteristic of family sessions, it may be a signal that they are not yet ready to end or that they need to be more in control of the ending process. It may mean that occasional check-ups should take place. It may also mean that the social worker should continue with one member of the family, as with Mr. Maxwell (case study 7.7). If the family appears ready to end but is blocking on it, sometimes an effective approach is to ask them to review carefully and discuss in detail with each other, in session, what each of them would need to do if they were to bring the problem back (Tomm & Wright, 1979).

ENDINGS AND TRANSITIONS INVOLVING SOCIAL INSTITUTIONS

Other endings are built into the structure of the social institution. A school term ends in the summer. The beginnings and endings of school terms set a certain rhythm, and the availability of the social worker when needed during the school year makes a difference for pupils and parents. The respite of the summer is often an opportunity for children and parents to make further progress, built on what had been begun during the school year. In Alan's case (case study 9.1), from second grade through the elementary years and eighth grade graduation there was an ending each June, but then a new beginning of gradually diminishing intensity the following September. Finally all that was needed was for the social worker to continue to be available and interested in a relationship that had continued seven years from their first meeting.

TIME AS THE MEDIUM OF THE HELPING PROCESS: INSTITUTIONAL TIME

In schools, and also in other institutions, time, when attended to by the social worker and the family, can become the medium of the helping process. This phrase of Jessie Taft (1949) means that, in many respects, the work of the helping process, if used well and within reasonable limitations, can fit itself into the time available.

School is perhaps the easiest example of this. School is an institution with expected ebbs and flows of work. Time extends itself through eight years of elementary school and four years of secondary school. The rhythm of the school year is in many ways the rhythm of families, and the two institutions have accommodated themselves to each other over many years. Families, even very difficult and troubled families, readily work with social workers in schools, and accommodate goals of the school as developmental goals for the child. Families often will accept assistance from the school when they will accept it from no other agency.

Other agencies, such as child welfare and juvenile justice institutions, have shorter and more intense time lines. There is only so much time before the hearing. The probation officer with the Moorhead family (case study 9.4) used the time before the hearing together with preparing the family for the hearing and preparing a report as a means of helping the family to clarify their perspectives and realign themselves in relation to Billy's problems. They would have never been able to do this clarification and realignment work on their own and without the deadline of the court hearing.

The Clark family (case study 9.2) had ninety days with their social worker to recompose themselves in order to take care of their children. This time frame served as a stimulus both for the family and for the worker. Family preservation work, detailed in chapter 9, was limited to three months. During this time, the social worker was very active in helping the Clarks recompose almost all aspects of their relationship. As with Alyson and Michael in case study 10.2, the danger of such an active relationship on the social worker's part is that, if it took place over a longer time, the social worker would become like a member of the family. She would become essential to continuing to stabilize the situation and the family could not function without her. She could become "overadequate" in relation to the Clark's progress, and the Clarks could become "underadequate." Paradoxically, with the three-month limit of the relationship, the enforced ending could operate as an external safety valve to motivate the Clarks and the social worker. A ninety-day relationship with an external evaluation sets boundaries. The family can enjoy the temporary infusion of the social worker's energy, but will have to take over their own situation and relationships fully in three months. When they consent to an agreement with the worker for ninety days, the ending is inherent in the beginning. The ending gives them hope that they can eventually manage by themselves. It can motivate them to make the changes necessary to preserve their family unit. As it did with the Moorheads, the institutional boundary helps social worker and family to do what otherwise would be most difficult under other circumstances.

INCOMPLETE OR PREMATURE ENDINGS

Another possibility is that members of the family have not accomplished what they had hoped to achieve and have decided not to continue with the work. These are often very difficult endings because the initial agreement has not been accomplished. There are unfulfilled expectations and feelings of frustration; a different outcome, a different social unit had been hoped for. The social worker, particularly the new social worker, who has also an investment in their goals, may feel a personal sense of loss and personal failure, and may draw in that feeling from family members also. A sense of loss and personal failure can really impede the work that must be done in ending. However, there are fewer illusions. The hoped-for direction will not be possible. What was uncertain, confusing, and challenging may now be less so, or at least it may be different.

CASE STUDY 10.3

Roberta and Sam Piotrowski had sought marital counseling at Evangelical Family Services (EFS) over Roberta's suspicion that Sam was having an affair with a mutual friend. Sam denied all this in the beginning. Roberta accepted Sam's denial. However, their relational work in session seemed flat and ritualistic. Increasingly under pressure from the communication tasks themselves, Sam admitted to the ongoing affair. Although he adored their three-year-old son, Jake, Sam came to some clarity with himself: that he had no intentions of continuing with the marriage or with marriage counsel-

ing. The couple worked out an understanding over Jake's custody and the house in-session. Given the circumstances, they ended couples work as amicably as possible. Sam did not want to do any further work individually. Roberta continued individually for several months, sorting out her concerns and issues over her next steps, the concrete goals in her life situation, and some of the loneliness, depression, and anger with which she was struggling. When she felt clearer and more able to deal with the emergent tasks in her life situation, she ended the individual sessions. She continues to be a major source of referral of others for help at EFS.

In Sam and Roberta's situation, the social worker was able to help them deal with a potentially explosive situation, and individually help Roberta with her disappointment, anger, and depression, as well as the challenges facing her. The social worker, who had dealt with similar situations before, was not taken aback nor drawn into the conflict personally. He was able to help them to manage the situation as well as possible. Similar to the situation with the Maxwells, he switched comfortably to individual work when it was necessary to complete some of the personal tasks generated by the couples work.

EVALUATION

With endings and transitions comes evaluation. In a particular sense, the process of evaluation takes place in every interview and is a formative evaluation. This continual process governs the direction chosen and the feasibility and speed with which certain goals may be attained. In a cumulative sense, evaluation takes place in the ending and is summative. In fact, together with the energy and hope of family members, it becomes a major stimulus for ending. What have been their goals? Have they achieved them? What has changed about each person's understanding of family relationships since they have begun? What can they live with now? Are they ready to end the process of helping? Are they able to use the social worker as a resource in the future? The discussion is tailored to the understandings and agreements arrived at in the beginning and in each formative evaluation. The evaluation process should suit the situation. Not every question is asked in the same way. In some settings and in some approaches to practice, there is a formal instrument to measure movement from a baseline established in the beginning (Corcoran, 2000). In others, the measurement is less formal, more individualized, and more geared to the family's understandings and control. In every case the process is the same.

CONCLUSION AND IMPLICATIONS

The river flows on into the sea. In some seasons it may overflow its borders. There may be floods. Nevertheless, the energy of the river can be partially diverted and directed to the common good.

Social workers help family members to restructure their relationships through communication and interaction. There are many worlds of families: families at different life stages and families in different cultures. Family exists in a multicultural world. This world, however, is not static. It is in constant motion as families form themselves out of differences and as cultures themselves are in dynamic movement in the postmodern world. Living in a larger cultural complex, family creates its own culture of relationships. Applying an essential social work orientation to practice with families, we have drawn from a rich variety of theoretical approaches. Studying actual practice with families, we have made connections between theory, family development, emergent family structure, multicultural realities, institutional and environmental realities, and the work of the social worker. This is only the beginning of the connections that social workers can make in even more complex situations, with many different types of family structure, when the basic social work model with families is well understood.

The content and process of social work with families builds on persons who construct family units. These units are constructed to satisfy needs that only a unit of persons, a relational structure, can provide. Family members act together to secure certain basic needs proper to persons. Among these needs, which make us human, are the needs for interpersonal safety, belonging, the capacity to communicate, to choose what is good, to grow, and to interact and take care of self and others. Persons can grow in this interactional climate. Indeed, they require it. Rooted in a greater complex of cultural meanings and institutions, the family develops its own culture.

Family should be one place where one can be accepted as a human being and as a person. Despite severe contradictions inherent in postmodern life, the expectation that family culture should accommodate the needs of persons moves forward as inexorably as a river toward the sea. Even as they are violated, there are expectations based on trust and permanence of commitment. Relationships are expected to be based less on a utilitarian calculus of contribution, as in a workplace, and more on status, membership, and person bonds. Fractured norms and relationships can be reconstructed, although not easily or surely. Persons interact to form families to construct relationships, seeking in their own way basic human values of respect, belonging, acceptance, communication, choice and care. The family interacts with a social institutional world that can support or undermine this delicate complex of patterns and relationships, what could otherwise be called structure.

Social workers work with families in the process of reconstructing themselves. They work with the needed outside community and institutional world so that families and individual persons are able to survive and flourish in a world of risks, uncertainties, and external stresses with their accompanying felt effects on family life. Social work is value-based activity based on an understanding of the constant worth and needs of human beings. This understanding provides an ethical basis for family intervention, even if a particular family member or social institution may not recognize these facts and values. Social workers assist persons in families and family units where these possible relationships are at risk. They deal with the family as a whole, with its members, and with its environment. They can draw from theories of family functioning and from intervention theory corresponding to these levels of functioning to assist family members to carry out their tasks of securing human need.

Understanding this logic, it is possible to assist family members (and the family itself as a collective unit) to alter patterns and to recompose meanings, and thus in a qualified way to become agents of their own development. Events themselves, happening outside of the family, also may alter these structures and meanings. So, although there can be greater prediction and control when we deal with this complexity, ultimately the outcomes of the work of family and its members remain somewhat unpredictable and uncontrollable.

There are a number of implications of this organizing framework for social work with families.

First of all, the normal relational work of persons with each other and with institutions provides the natural basis for social work. There is a constant reality that persons normally interact with each other. They establish family structures to satisfy profound human needs: to solve problems, to support each other, and to enjoy relationships. The meanings and the relational structures emerge from social interaction. This constant reality provides a rationale to find the best way to understand these complex interactions and the most effective way to intervene in them. Social institutions assist family members in this endeavor. A variety of methods become possible, including working with individual family members, with subsets of the family, with social institutions, and with community networks of services according to the problem and need. Effective methods evolve from an understanding of their functions, of what they are supposed to do to assist family members.

So neither theory nor practice is an imposition on the natural order of people forming families and living in them. It is a natural order because persons need families, seek certain values in family life, and act to form their families. It is complex because there are always differences. Family can never be one dimensional or reduced to one member's process. Family units are formed out of multiple differences. Different relational structures necessarily appear at different phases of the family's developmental process. Among these differences in postmodern society are cultural differences, often experienced in relation to a host culture, often experienced within the family itself. Social work practice with families is built upon values that persons seek from them, such as an affirmation beyond calculus of one's (and reciprocally the other's) worth and dignity as a person. Social work practice assists these processes to take place in an optimal way. Building on differences in a multicultural world, it must by definition become transcultural.

The second implication of this framework is that the variety of cultural and situational meanings make social work practice both a science and an art. Family may compose itself in a variety of ways in different cultures according to external and internal circumstances. Within different situations and consistent with cultural meanings and patterns, there are many different approaches to doing relatively similar things. Some forms of family can be more vulnerable to dissolution or dysfunction than others. The members' understanding of the structure may differ by culture and by internal and external circumstances, and so approaches to intervention may vary. Within some cultures, there may be only a limited ability to communicate and connect a person's internal state with family interaction. In any case, the focus for intervention rests on interaction itself, on assisting family members to create a workable structure rather than extensively talking about it. In other cultures and circumstances, a good deal of talk is a prerequisite to action. These families need to establish meanings clearly before they interact. Social workers need to make that distinction, among others, in their assessment and planning for intervention, but what needs accomplishment is often quite similar.

The third implication is that, it follows necessarily that there is a gap between present theory, which can explain and direct the social worker's actions, and actual and concrete relational realities. Ultimately, the family writes their story. Despite enormous progress, theory itself is still a somewhat limited help to the social worker in assisting families to recompose their realities. Although family therapy has made enormous progress in developing techniques of working with families, it is composed of a variety of competing schools all dealing with the same reality. Social work with families demands an organizing framework. Even with such a framework, there is no accurate prediction, only a recognition of what is happening and an approximation of what may happen. In the same way in the far more developed science of weather, a forecast and an understanding of certain principles may help a navigator deal with a storm, but even this does not pretend to predict the outcome.

The theories about work with families in general are translated into practice through the case. The case is an individual narrative or story of interactive help provided to the family. Story is the particular outcome of a complex of realities, of which only a few are predictable or well understood. This book has been filled with stories, the purpose of which is to teach—to accustom the social worker to the content and process of helping families. These stories are linked to theory with, further links suggested in the footnotes. They are meant for reflection and discussion, and some of their interpretations are open-ended.

Finally, principles of effective practice are also values placed in action. The work of the social worker cannot simply be reduced to techniques. Social workers are part of a living, recursive, and responsive interaction with family members. The social worker is a coach for what family members need to do if they are to satisfy any of their needs through family structure and interaction. In this sense, practice principles are not abstract techniques, but eventually become human qualities of the practitioner responding to family realities. The practitioner develops the ability to respond to the infinite variations of the same themes. Identifying these themes is important as a beginning step.

There are deep roots to social work practice theory. Many different rivers flow into more than a century of practice of social workers and social institutions with families, the ongoing source of meaning and support in a complex society. One purpose of these chapters has been to rediscover what has always been inherent, implicit, and somehow inchoate in social work practice and in its theoretical base. At the same time, a framework for practice needed to be connected with other approaches and to actual social work practice with families. Our hope is that the rediscovery of who we are as social work practitioners will help us to become more fully what we are.

REFERENCES

Hepworth, D. H., Rooney, R. H., & Larson, J. A. (1997). *Direct social work practice: Theory and skills* (5th ed.). Pacific Grove, CA: Brooks-Cole.

Shulman, L. (1992). *The skills of helping: Individuals, families and groups* (3rd ed.). Itaska, IL: Peacock.

Taft, J. (1949). Time as the medium of the helping process. *Jewish Social Service Quarterly, 24,* 2.

Tomm, K., & Wright, L. M. (1979). Training in family therapy: Perceptual, cognitive and executive skills. *Family Process,* 18(3).

Walsh, J. (2003). *Endings in clinical practice.* Chicago: Lyceum.

Index